新航道 NEW CHANNEL 北京新航道

MW01688404

说文解字背单词系列

雅思词汇真经

刘洪波 编著

中国广播电视出版社

图书在版编目(CIP)数据

雅思词汇真经 / 刘洪波编著. －北京：中国广播电视出版社 2005.5

ISBN 7-5043-4637-3

Ⅰ. 雅… Ⅱ. 刘… III. 英语－词汇－高等学校－入学考试，国外－自学参考资料 Ⅳ. H313

中国版本图书馆 CIP 数据核字（2005）第 031768 号

雅思词汇真经

主　　编	刘洪波
特约编辑	周　壮
责任编辑	常　红
监　　印	赵　宁
监　　制	张曲波
出版发行	中国广播电视出版社
电　　话	86093580 86093583
社　　址	北京市西城区真武庙二条 9 号（邮政编码 100045）
经　　销	各地新华书店和外文书店
印　　刷	保定华泰印刷有限公司
开　　本	880 毫米 × 1230 毫米 1/32
字　　数	350（千）字
印　　张	11
版　　次	2005 年 6 月第 1 版 2005 年 6 月第 1 次印刷
书　　号	ISBN 7-5043-4637-3 / H · 219
定　　价	22.00 元

序

刘洪波将《雅思词汇真经》的稿子放到我的案头时，我当时的心情比自己出书还快乐，不仅仅因为新航道“雅思梦之队”的青年才俊再次发力，也不仅仅因为新航道“雅思真经”系列又添一本力作，而是再次看到了新航道雅思考试培训、国外考试培训的学术研究领域后继有人。新航道“创新、学术、励志、激情”八字方针必然得以光大，雅思第四套教材的全面升级证明了这一点，两本真经的问世更让我对此确信无疑。

“说文解字背单词系列”本身就是“创新＋学术”产生的一个了不起的创意，这种记忆单词的方法，不仅仅让读者最终记住单词，更重要的是由此延伸出一种渊源、一种文化、一种文字的美感和人类文化的沧桑感，从而把学员从原来背单词那种枯燥乏味、痛不欲生的状态下解救出来，使其在细细品味把玩单词的过程中，体会一种“意在诗外”的感觉，把记忆词汇的书写到这种程度，恐怕和刘洪波平时涉猎广博、精研诸家是分不开的。

词汇在英语学习当中的重要性是毋容置疑的，学习英语的万里长征中词汇永远是第一步，这一步走出去才会有今后的成长和成功的希望，这个道理所有人都懂，大家都在做；有针对性地将考试涉及的词汇编辑成册则是对症下药，可以为学生节省许多精力和时间，以便去提升英语学习的其他方面，这个方法许多人都在用，并且编辑了不少图书；以词源学的根基为硬件，以深厚的文化底蕴和丰富的现代元素来诠释词汇的内涵、外沿、背景、典故甚至流行用法等等，则很少有人会想到，想到也不一定有能力做得到，有能力做得到也不一定能够做成功。然而刘波洪想了，做了，也做成了，这其中付出的辛苦，新航道的人有目共睹，这种精神就是新航道一直倡导的“我坚持，我成功！”

我相信这本书的问世一定会给雅思学员带来全新的感觉和实用的效果，这正是刘洪波撰写此书，新航道不断出书的根本宗旨。希望每个学员在合上这本书时，都能够说：“我看到了，我读过了，我收获了。”那么写书人和出书人才是获得了真正的成功。

胡敏

2005年6月

前　言

九转功成。

早在2003年当我策划《雅思阅读真经》一书时就有个想法：如果能把课堂上讲解英语词汇时的各种亮点及记忆方法融入词汇表里边，大家在背记词汇时也就不会觉得枯燥乏味了。背单词最重要的是坚持，而兴趣则是坚持下去的最好的原动力。于是我邀请当时教授雅思词汇的大师曲冰同志参与《雅思阅读真经》的写作，并且每隔几个单词挑选出一个来，从词源、文化、实际应用等各个角度加入趣味的注释，希望大家能对英语单词学习产生一点兴趣。

事实证明这种说文解字背单词的方法是成功的。2004年《雅思阅读真经》在全国各大图书销售网站上高居雅思类图书排行榜榜首，各地的许多英语培训机构把它作为指定教材，一版再版。而我也清楚地认识到，这种独辟蹊径的单词注释方法是该书成功的重要原因之一。

当我和曲冰同志决定再一次合作，照此模式共同创作“说文解字背单词系列”书籍（包括《雅思词汇真经》、《托福词汇真经》、《四级词汇真经》）时，不幸的事情发生了：曲冰同时收到了牛津和剑桥的博士offer。更不幸的是不久后她从剑桥打来电话，说什么正在闭关研究孔夫子和耶稣基督的异同，而且还 thoroughly enjoy，红尘俗事不愿再管。悲伤啊。

万般无奈，只好一个人在深夜里奋笔疾书。我坚信付出总是有回报的。终于有那么一天，英语培训界泰斗人物、北京新航道学校校长胡敏教授被我的黑眼圈所吸引，一番长谈后对本书的创作兴趣颇浓，提出了许多宝贵的写作建议。之后更不时的从家里搜出一本本泛黄的英语书籍拿来供我参考。对这些书我从来都是小心翼翼的，不敢用力翻动，怕损毁文物。

得到英语培训界奇才李传伟教授的详细指导也是本书之大幸。李老时常在百忙之中抽空指点词汇的注释亮点，他在词汇学上的功力让人叹服。李老本人精通七国语言，对拉丁文、希腊语、西班牙语、法语的领悟使他对英语词汇的把握进入了极高的一种境界。据说李老在新航道学校考研英语的课堂上偶尔会把各种语言讲审，同学们大跌眼镜之余纷纷高山仰止。

此外，新航道白勇老师、中国雅思梦之队成员雅思词汇主讲牟志龙老师、雅思听力主讲张宏老师等对本书的写作也毫无保留地贡献智慧。新航道学校副校长王渊源（John A Gordon）在最后阶段对本书进行了全面审订，确保了该书的质量。而新航道图书部蔡箐老师、郭遐老师、发行部总监张曲波先生的大力支持使本书和广大的英语学习者终于见面。

衷心致谢。

本书特点

一、精选雅思核心词汇 3000 个

在这3000个核心词汇中，本书首次收录了雅思真实考试中屡次出现的特色单词。例如：cobra 眼镜蛇（阅读）、venom 毒液（阅读）、falcon 猎鹰（听力）、acupuncture 针灸（《剑桥雅思 4》）、hinge 铰链（阅读）等。本书甚至还收录了诸如crocodile（鳄鱼）、raincoat（雨衣）这样简单的单词，那是因为在雅思真实的听力考试中，考生被要求在听到之后把这几个单词正确地拼写出来。在将来的考试中，你有可能还会碰到这套题，需要你正确地拼写 crocodile。所以《雅思词汇真经》收录的所有核心词汇请认真背记。

二、扩展实用词汇 4000 个

每个单词后[同义词]、[反义词]、[记]所扩展的常见词汇和短语搭配，加上贯穿本书始终的词根词缀等构词法知识，使本书的实际词汇容量已达到 7000 以上。足已确立雅思高分基础。

三、例句简练有效

本书例句写作方法选取中庸之道：每个单词给出一个经典例句。既能使读者通过例句完全理解词义，又保证了背单词的效率。

四、分类词汇功能强大

建议考前认真复习本书后面部分的雅思考试分类词汇，它们对短期冲刺雅思考试有很大的帮助。

五、说文解字背单词

这是一本能让你从A读到Z的单词书。

但要完全理解注释中的知识点，请先了解下面的英语词汇学常识：

- 英语词汇中约80%是外来词汇，来自120多种语言；
- 其中古希腊语和拉丁语占了很大的比例，为英语词汇贡献了许多词根词缀；
- 罗马神话借鉴了希腊神话体系，同一位神祇在罗马神话和希腊神话中有不同的名字。比如：爱神在希腊神话中叫Eros（厄洛斯），罗马神话中叫Cupid（丘比特）。它们分别衍生出单词erotic（色情的）和cupidity（贪心，贪婪）。

刘洪波

2005年6月

目　录

Unit 1

abandon [ə'bændən] v.放弃，抛弃；n.放肆，放纵

[例] The pretty woman abandoned her husband and went away with all their money. 那个漂亮女人抛弃了她的丈夫并卷走了两人所有的钱。

[记] abandon yourself to sth. 沉溺于 …

abbreviation [əˌbriːvi'eiʃən] n.缩写，节略

[例] BBC is an abbreviation for British Broadcasting Corporation. BBC 是英国广播公司的缩写。

[记] abbreviation该词本身经常被缩写为“abbr”/abbreviatev v.缩写，简化

abdomen ['æbdəmən] n.腹，腹部

[例] Black widow venom affects his muscles, and may cause severe cramping in the abdomen and other parts of the body. 黑寡妇蜘蛛的毒液侵袭到了他的肌肉，他的腹部和其他部位会因疼痛而扭曲。

> abdominal muscles，腹肌，可简化为 abs, 或 six pack。six pack 是国外常见的啤酒包装：六听。你的腹肌练得像六听啤酒的排列，就是 You have great abs (six pack). 你的腹肌真棒！口语中说的“肚子”则是 stomach。“我肚子不舒服”最地道的英语表达是：My stomach doesn't feel so hot.

abnormal [æb'nɔːməl] a.不正常的，反常的，变态的

[例] El Nino will result in the abnormal weather. 厄尔尼诺现象将会导致气候反常。

aboriginal [ˌæbə'ridʒənəl] a.土著的，土著居民的；n.土著居民

[例] As far as we could determine, there is only one aboriginal culture left here. 我们确定这里只流传下来了一种土著文化。

[记] aboriginal forest 原始森林 /aboriginal inhabitants 土著居民

abortion [ə'bɔːʃən] n.失败；流产

[例] His attempt proved an abortion. 他的企图完全失败了。

[记] have an abortion 流产

absenteeism [æbsən'tiːiz(ə)m] n.旷课，旷工

[例] There was virtually no absenteeism or turnover. 其实就没有旷工和人员流动。

absorb [əb'sɔːb] v.吸收，吸引

[例] A new baby has an enormous capacity for absorbing new information. 新生儿有极强的接受新知识的能力。

[记] be absorbed in 专心于

absolute ['æbsəluːt] a.完全的，绝对的

[例] There is no absolute standard for beauty. 美是没有绝对标准的。
[记] absolutely ad.完全地，绝对地

> 瑞典名酒 Absolute Vodka 绝对伏特加，近年来在《福布斯》*Forbes* 所评选的奢侈品牌排行榜上高居榜首。其经典广告口号 Absolute Perfection 绝对完美，已沿用二十余年，在欧美等国家喻户晓。

abstract [əb'strækt] v.摘要，提炼，抽象化；['æbstrækt] n.摘要；a.抽象的
[例] Irons are abstracted from ore. 铁是从矿石中提取的。
[记] abstracted a.心不在焉的 /abstraction n.抽象 /abstract sb.'s attention from 从…上转移开某人的注意

abuse [ə'bju:z] v.滥用，虐待；[ə'bju:s] n.滥用；辱骂
[例] Some officials abuse their power. 一些官员滥用权力。

academic [ˌækə'demik] a.学术的，学院的，理论的
[例] She loved the city, with its academic atmosphere. 她喜欢这座城市，喜欢其学术氛围。
[记] academic year 学年 /academy n. 研究院,学院

> Academy 最初是一个地理专有名词，指雅典城外西北角的一片小树林。哲学之王柏拉图 Plato 四海云游归来在那里办学授课。学校的大门口刻着一句话：不懂几何者不得入内。后来这个单词进一步用来表示教授文科。

accelerate [æk'seləreit] v.加速，促进
[例] Good economic policies can accelerate the development of a society. 好的经济政策能加速社会的发展。
[记] decelerate v.减速

accept [ək'sept] v.接受，认可，承认
[例] People have come to accept that they will probably have several different jobs over the course of their career. 人们已渐渐地接受了一生换几次工作的现实。

access ['ækses] n.通路，访问，入门
[例] Citizens may have free access to the library. 市民可以自由使用图书馆。
[记] have /gain/get access to 得接近；得会见；得进入；得使用

> 小灵通手机的英文是 PAS：Personal Access Phone System。

accessible [ək'sesəbl] a.易接近的，可到达的，易受影响的，可理解的
[例] Because of the heavy snow, many parts of the countryside are only accessible by helicopter. 由于大雪，农村许多地方只有直升飞机可以到达。

accessory [æk'sesəri] n. 附件，配件

[例] Car accessories include the roof rack and radio. 汽车配件包括车顶架和收音机。

accident ['æksidənt] n. 意外事件，事故

[例] As usual, the fog and icy roads have led to several very nasty accidents. 跟往常一样，大雾和雪天的路上已导致了好几起严重事故。

[记] by accident 偶然 / have an accident 出事故

acclaim [ə'kleim] n. 喝彩，欢呼；v. 欢呼，称赞

[例] He deserves the acclaim he has received. 他得到的称赞是受之无愧的。

[同义词] applaud

accent ['æksənt] n. 重音，口音，重音符

[例] He speaks with a strong southern accent. 他说话带有很浓的南方口音。

> ac-cent— 加强意义＋歌唱，从希腊语借译而来，指古希腊诗篇中的音高安排，进而得来“起强调或着重突出作用的东西”，引申得来“重音、口音”的含义。

accommodate [ə'kɔmədeit] v. 供应，供给；使适应

[例] He worked hard to accomodate her needs. 他努力工作以满足她的需要。

accommodation [əˌkɔmə'deiʃən] n. 住处

[例] Accommodation is expensive in this city. 这个城市住房昂贵。

accompany [ə'kɔmədeit] v. 陪伴，伴随，和…一起发生

[例] She accompanied me to the doctor's. 她陪我去看了医生。

> pan- 表示“面包”，那么 ac-com-pany 表示“加强意义＋共同、一起＋面包”→和某人一起吃面包、进餐。引申为“陪同、陪伴、伴随”；同样道理，单词 companion 可以理解为 com-pan-ion →共同、一起＋面包＋名词字尾，表示“一起吃面包的人”，即“伙伴、同伴、伴侣”。

accomplish [ə'kɔmpliʃ] v. 完成；达到；实现

[例] Whatever he wills he may accomplish. 他决心做的事情都能完成。

[记] accomplishment n.成就，完成

account [ə'kaunt] n. 账目，理由；v. 说明，认为

[例] All the accounts of the firm were certified as correct. 公司所有账目被证明为正确无误。

[记] take... into account 考虑到、顾及 / on account of 由于 / accounting 会计学 / accountant 会计师

> 很多人积极参加的注册会计师考试 CPA 为：Certified Public Accountant。

accredit [ə'kredit] v. 信任，授权，归于

[例] We accredit the invention of the electric light to Edison. 我们把电灯的发明归功于爱迪生。

accumulate [ə'kju:mjuleit] v. 积聚，积累

[例] Huge snowdrifts had accumulated on the airport's runways. 大片的雪堆在机场的跑道上堆积起来了。

accuracy ['ækjurəsi] n. 精确性，正确度

[例] Additional information can often be used to increase correction accuracy and speed. 补充说明通常用来增加校正的准确性和速度。

[记] accurate a. 正确的，精确的 / inaccurate a. 错误的，不准确的

accuse [ə'kju:z] v. 控告，谴责

[例] The police accused him of murder. 警方指控他犯了谋杀罪。

[记] accuse sb. of sth. 指控某人犯…罪 / 错

accustom [ə'kʌstəm] v. 使习惯于

[例] They had to accustom themselves to the hot weather. 他们不得不使自己习惯于炎热的天气。

[记] get / be accustomed to 习惯于

acid ['æsid] n. 酸；a. 酸的，讽刺的，尖刻的

[例] When she spoke, her tone was acid. 她讲话时的语调很尖刻。

[记] acid rain 酸雨

> 在国外的club里听到该词，小心了！Club Drugs俱乐部毒品中有ecstasy（摇头丸），ice（冰毒）等，而最常见的一种迷幻药是acid (LSD)。著名的甲壳虫乐队 The Beatles 唱过一首歌：*Lucy in the Sky with Diamonds*，看看歌名里的大写字母！

acknowledge [ək'nɔlidʒ] v. 承认（…的权威）；对…表示感谢

[例] It is universally acknowledged that dogs have an acute sense of smell. 大家都认为狗的嗅觉敏锐。

> acknowledgement n. 很多英语国家出版的图书目录之前或书末都会看到单独的一部分叫做 Acknowledgements— 致谢、鸣谢。作者在此向为该书写作提供支持的人表示感谢。

acquaintance [ə'kweintəns] n. 相识的人，泛泛之交；所知，了解

[例] I have some acquaintance with English, but I do not know it well. 我稍懂些英语，但并不精通。

> 苏格兰歌曲《友谊地久天长》*Auld Lang Syne* 中第一句：Should old acquaintance be forgotten and never brought to mind? 怎能忘记旧日朋友，心中能不怀想？

acquire [ə'kwaiə] v. 获得，学到

[例] She acquired a knowledge of the English by careful study. 她靠认真学习而精通英语。

[记] acquisition n. 获得

activate ['æktiveit] v. 刺激，使活动，有活力

[例] The yeast's growth is activated by sugar and warmth. 酵母的生长被糖分和温暖激活。

acupuncture ['ækjupʌŋktʃə(r)] n. 针灸，中医针灸疗法

[例] Do you believe in Chinese acupuncture? 你相信中国针灸吗?

[记] puncture v. 刺破，刺穿

acute [ə'kju:t] a. 敏锐的，深刻的；（疾病）急性的

[例] He has given an acute analysis of the situation. 他对形势做了深刻的分析。

> 非典 SARS：Severe Acute Respiratory Syndrome，严重急性呼吸道综合症。acute disease 急性病；chronic disease 慢性病。

adapt [ə'dæpt] v. 使适应；改编

[例] He adapted himself to the cold weather. 他适应了寒冷的天气。

adaptable [ə'dæptəbl] a. 能适应的，可修改的

[例] In this job you need to be adaptable and able to cope with unexpected situations. 做这种工作，需要你有适应和应付各种预想不到的局面的能力。

adaptation [ˌædæp'teiʃən] n. 适应，改编，改写本

[例] The film adaptation was a big hit and won five Oscars. 这部影片的改编获得了巨大的成功，并获得五项奥斯卡奖。

addict [ə'dikt] n./v. 沉溺，上瘾

[例] The children are addicted to computer games. 孩子们对计算机游戏上了瘾。

[记] addiction n. 沉溺，上瘾

addition [ə'diʃən] n. 加，增加；加法

[例] Our baby brother is an addition to our family. 新出生的弟弟使我们家多了一口人。

[记] in addition 另外 /in addition to 除…之外

[反义词] subtraction n. 减法

address [ə'dres] n. 地址，演讲；v.演说

[例] She gave an address to the Royal Academy. 她对皇家学会作了演讲。

ad hoc ['æd'hɔk] adv./a. 特别地（的）

[例] An ad hoc committee has been set up to deal with the problem. 成立了一个特别委员会来处理这个问题。

拉丁词汇 ad hoc 直接进入英语。这种现象很常见，比如：bona fide 真诚的；de facto 事实上的；per se 自身；pro rata 按比例等。

adequate [ˈædikwit] a. 适当的；足够的
[例] We took adequate food for the holiday. 我们为假期带足了食品。
[反义词] inadequate

adhere [ədˈhiə] v. 粘附，胶着，坚持
[例] I will adhere to this opinion until contrary facts appear. 如果没有相反的事实，我将坚持我的意见。
[记] adhere to 粘附，坚持

adjacent [əˈdʒeisənt] a. 邻近的，毗连的
[例] We stayed in adjacent rooms. 我们俩的房间挨着。

adjust [əˈdʒʌst] v. 调节，改变…以适应
[例] He soon adjusted to army life. 他很快就适应了军中生活。
[记] adjustment n.调整，调节 / adjust to 适应，调节

administration [ədˌminisˈtreiʃən] n. 管理，经营
[例] You will need some experience in administration before you can run the department. 你需要有一些行政管理经验才能掌管这个部门。

minister 原意为“小人物，仆人”，字根 min 指“小的”。古代大臣们对君主自称“小人”，老百姓却称他们为“部长大人、大臣”。administer v. 理解为 ad-minister，表示“加强意义+仆人、服务”，为相对大的事业服务，表示“管理”要高于 manage 的意义。MBA 学位就是 Master of Business Administration 的缩写，意为“工商管理硕士”。

admire [ədˈmaiə] v. 赞美，钦佩，羡慕
[例] Everybody admires him for his fine sense of humour. 人人都钦佩他那绝妙的幽默感。

字根 mir 指“惊讶，惊奇”。如：mirage，海市蜃楼；mir（惊奇的）+ age（名词词尾），令人惊奇的景色。mirror，镜子；古人看到镜子里的自己很惊讶。miracle，奇迹。admire，ad（加强）+ mir，总是让你惊讶的人，你就只有佩服了。

admit [ədˈmit] v. 容许，承认，接纳
[例] John has admitted breaking the window. 约翰已承认打碎了窗子。
[记] admission n. 承认；入场费，入场券 / Admission to the concert costs ￡5. 音乐会的入场券是五镑一张。

adolescent [ˌædəuˈlesnt] a. 青春期的，青春的；n. 青少年
[例] It is reported that over 40% of adolescents are smokers in China. 据报道，中国有 40% 多的青少年吸烟。
[记] adolescence n. 青春期

adopt [ə'dɔpt] v. 采取；采用；收养

[例] They adopted our effective methods. 他们采用了我们有效的办法。

[记] adoption n. 采用, 收养

adore [ə'dɔː] v. 崇拜，爱慕

[例] She adores going to the volleyball matches. 她非常喜欢看排球比赛。

> 来源于拉丁文*adorare*。原意是"不断(ad)想和某人说话(orare)"。当你的心中有那样一个人，快乐时、伤心时、或梦中幻影，你总想找机会跟她说话，这就是adore。字根ora是"口头"的意思。如：oral English，口语。

advance [əd'vaːns] n./v. 发展，改进，前进，推进

[例] We have advanced greatly in our knowledge of the universe. 我们对宇宙的认识已经前进了很多。

[记] in advance预先，提前 / He arrived half an hour in advance. 他提前半小时到达。

adventure [əd'ventʃə] n./v. 冒险

[例] All the children listened to his adventures with eager attention. 孩子们全神贯注地听他讲他的冒险经历。

[记] venture n./v. 冒险

adverse ['ædvəːs] a. 敌对的，不友好的

[例] He is adverse to violence. 他反对暴力。

[记] adversary n. 敌手，对手

advertise ['ædvətaiz] v. 做广告，登广告

[例] We advertised through the press. 我们通过报纸宣传。

[记] advertisement = ad n. 广告 / advertising a. 广告的

advocate ['ædvəkit] n. 拥护者，提倡者；['ædvəkeit] v. 拥护，提倡，主张

[例] Extremists were openly advocating violence. 极端主义者公开主张暴力。

aerobic [ˌeiə'rəubik] a. 需氧的，有氧气的；有氧健身的

[例] The aerobic activity can help people to increase their metabolic rate. 有氧活动能帮助人们增强新陈代谢。

[记] aerobic exercise 有氧健身运动

aesthetic [iːs'θetik] a. 美学的，审美的，有审美感的

[例] The chair may be aesthetic but it's not very comfortable. 这把椅子也许很美观，但并不是很舒适。

> 源自希腊文，原意为"可感知的"，后逐渐用于对事物美丑的感知能力或评价，即审美。该词原意在其他单词中仍有体现，如：anaesthesia，an（否定）+ aesthesia（感觉），没有感觉，即"麻醉"。

affect [ə'fekt] v. 影响；感动

[例] The disease affects the central nervous system. 这种疾病侵害的是中枢神经系统。

affection [ə'fekʃən] n. 友爱，爱情，慈爱

[例] I cannot believe that you were quite unaware of my growing affection for you. 我不相信你一点儿都没察觉到我渐渐地爱上了你。

affiliate [ə'filieit] v. （使）加入，接受为会员

[例] She affiliated herself with the impressionist school of painting. 她把自己归为印象画派。

affirm [ə'fəːm] v. 断言，坚决声称

[例] The suspect affirmed that he had been at home all evening. 嫌疑犯声称自己整晚都在家里。

[记] affirmative, positive a. 肯定的，积极的 / negative a. 否定的，消极的

affluent ['æfluənt] a. 富裕的，丰富的，富饶的

[例] We live in an affluent society. 我们生活在一个富裕的社会中。

> 词根flu指“流”。fluid 液体；fluent 流动的；fluency 流利。affluent，a- 加强；原意为“源源不断的流入”，财源不断滚滚流入，引申即为“富裕”。

afford [ə'fɔːd] v. 提供，给予，供应得起

[例] I couldn't afford the rent on my own. 我自己负担不起房租。

[记] affordable a. 买得起的

agency ['eidʒənsi] n. 代理处，代理，中介；力量

[例] The agency is responsible for helping refugees. 这个机构负责救助难民。

[记] sole agency独家代理 / agency general总代理 / agent n.代理人

agenda [ə'dʒendə] n. 议事日程

[例] The government set an agenda for constitutional reform. 政府就改革宪法制定了议事日程。

aggravate ['ægrəveit] v. 加重，加剧，使恶化

[例] Grief aggravated her illness. 痛苦加重了她的疾病。

[区别] aggregate v./n. 合计，总计

agitate ['ædʒiteit] v. 搅动；鼓动，煽动

[例] She was much agitated by the bad news. 坏消息使她的心绪很乱。

agreeable [ə'griəbl] a. 使人愉快的，惬意的

[例] My parents are quite agreeable to my studying abroad. 我父母欣然同意我出国学习。

aid [eid] n. 帮助，援助，救助

[例] An English-Chinese Dictionary is an important aid in learning English. 一本英汉词典是学习英语的重要工具。

[记] first aid 急救 / seek military and economic aid 寻求军事和经济援助 / live on government aid 靠政府救济生活

airborne ['ɛəbɔːn] a. 空运的；空中的；空气传播的

[例] Smoking is forbidden until the plane is airborne.飞机升空时禁止吸烟。

airtight ['eətait] a. 密封的，不透气的

[例] The whole room is airtight. 整个房间是密封的。

[记] an airtight excuse 无懈可击的借口

> tight作形容词指"紧密的"。注意区别airproof和airtight, waterproof和watertight。后缀-proof指"防～的"，所以waterproof（防水的）和watertight（不漏水的）有区别。周润发演过一部电影《防弹武僧》，*Bulletproof Monk*。

aisle [ail] n. 走廊，过道

[例] Don't stand in the aisle. 不要站在通道上。

[记] corridor n. 走廊

alarm [ə'lɑːm] n. 惊恐，惊慌；警报器

[例] They heard the fire alarm. 他们听到了火警警报。

albeit [ɔːl'biːit] conj. 尽管，即使，虽然

[例] He failed the test, albeit by one mark. 他考试没有及格，尽管只差一分。

[同义词] although, though

alchemy ['ælkimi] n. 炼金术

[例] Alchemy is believed to be the beginning of metal smelting. 炼金术被认为是金属冶炼的开端。

> 现代化学脱胎于炼金术，看看单词就知道了。alchemy 的派生词alchemist（炼金术士）在16世纪被缩略为chemist，仍指炼金术士。但这些chemists没有炼出金子，却搞出了许多不知名化合物，创造了许多试验时用的瓶瓶罐罐。chemist 就逐渐被赋予"化学家"的含义了，而chemistry 就是化学了。

alcohol ['ælkəhɔl] n. 酒精，酒

[例] The doctor told me to keep off alcohol. 医生叫我滴酒不要沾。

algae ['ældʒiː] n. 〈alga的复数〉海藻

[例] Most kinds of algae live in water. 绝大多数藻类生活在水中。

algebra ['ældʒibrə] n. 代数学，代数

[例] The young boy is good at learning algebra. 这个男孩擅长学习代数。

> 源于阿拉伯语，古代居然是个医学术语——正骨术(bone-setting)！被古人强行借给了数学的分支来命名！强悍。

alien ['eiljən] a. 外国的，相异的

[例] Their ideas are alien to our way of thinking. 他们的思想和我们的想法不同。
[记] alienate v. 使疏远，使不友好，离间

> 美国著名电影《异形》就选择了这个单词作为电影的英文名。该片类型为：科幻 (sci-fi)、恐怖 (horror)、惊悚 (thriller)，胆小者不宜观看。

alight [ə'lait] a. 点亮的；点着的；v. 下来
[例] The sky was alight with millions of stars. 成千上万颗星星照亮了天空。

allege [ə'ledʒ] v. 断言，宣称
[例] The defendant alleges temporary insanity. 被告以暂时精神失常作为藉口。
[同义词] declare, affirm, announce, assert

allergy ['ælədʒi] n. 敏感症；过敏
[例] People with allergies and other respiratory and heart ailments may be more seriously affected. 有过敏症或其他呼吸和心脏疾病的人可能会受到严重感染。

allergic [ə'lə:dʒik] a. 对…过敏的；对…反感的
[例] He is allergic to penicillin. 他对青霉素过敏。
[记] be allergic to 对…过敏的

alleviate [ə'li:vieit] v. 减轻（痛苦等），缓解
[例] The doctor gave her an injection to alleviate the pain. 医生给她注射以减轻疼痛。

allocate ['æləukeit] v. 分配，配给
[例] One million dollars was allocated for disaster relief. 分配了一百万美元用于救灾。
[同义词] distribute v. 分配

allot [ə'lɔt] v. （按份额）分配，分派
[例] A part of this urgent task was allotted to us. 这项紧急任务的一部分分给了我们。

allowance [ə'lauəns] n. 津贴，补贴；允许量
[例] My monthly allowance is 50 dollars. 我每月的津贴是 50 元。

all-round a. 多方面的，多才多艺的
[例] He is now an all-round athlete. 他现在是一位全能运动员。

allure [ə'ljuə] v. 吸引，引诱
[例] Promises of quick profits allure the unwary investor. 能很快收得到利润的承诺吸引了心存侥幸的投资。
[记] allure sb. from 诱使（某人）离开… / allure (sb.) into/to 把（某人）诱入，骗进

> 源于古法语，al 指 to 去，lure 诱惑→ allure 引诱。

almond [ˈɑːmənd] n. 杏仁

[例] Almonds are used extensively in confectionery. 杏仁被广泛地用于糖果制造业。

[记] almond juice 杏仁露，杏仁汁

alter [ˈɔːltə] v. 改变，更改

[例] These clothes are too large; they must be altered. 这些衣服太大，得修改。

alternative [ɔːlˈtəːnətiv] n./a. 两者择一；供选择的

[例] There was no other alternative but to fight until victory. 除了战斗直到胜利，别无选择。

altitude [ˈæltitjuːd] n. 海拔，高（度），深（度）

[例] We are currently flying at an altitude of 8,000 meters. 我们目前正在海拔 8000 米的高空飞行。

alumni [əˈlʌmnai] n. 男毕业生，男校友

[例] My alumni and alumna were present at my birthday party. 我的男校友和女校友都出席了我的生日晚会。

amateur [ˈæmətə] n./a. 业余爱好者；业余（爱好）的，非职业的

[例] Only amateur athletes were allowed to compete in the Olympic Games. 过去只有业余运动员才能参加奥运会比赛。

> 借自法语，源于拉丁语 amator，即 lover，爱好者。纯粹为了爱好去做一件事就是业余爱好者，非职业了。网球比赛中 play for love 即是为了爱好打球，没有任何功利心就是 play for nothing，just play，玩玩而已，love 就是 nothing。下次电视转播网球比赛请仔细听裁判报比分：“零分”是 love，不是 none。

amaze [əˈmeiz] v. 使大为惊奇，使惊愕

[例] John amazed his friends by suddenly getting married. 约翰突然间结婚，令朋友们大为吃惊。

[记] maze n. 迷宫

amazing [əˈmeiziŋ] a. 令人惊异的

[例] It’s amazing that you often see drivers using mobile phones. 令人惊讶的是你经常会看到司机在驾车时使用手机。

Unit 2

ambassador [æmˈbæsədə] n. 大使，使节

[例] He was appointed ambassador to Korea. 他奉派为驻韩大使。

[记] embassy n. 大使馆

ambiguous [ˌæmˈbigjuəs] a. 含糊不清的，不明确的

[例] This is an ambiguous answer. 这是一个模棱两可的答复。

[记] ambiguity n. 模棱两可

ambition [æmˈbiʃən] n. 雄心，抱负

[例] Her ambition was to be a famous singer. 她的理想是成为著名的歌唱家。

> 前缀 ambi- 指"到处走动"。古罗马政治家为谋求一官半职，需四处走动演讲争取民众选票，因此 ambition 有"志向、野心"等意义。很有点儿中文里"好男儿志在四方"的感觉。同源单词：ambulance 救护车，原意也是"到处走动"，流动的医院。ambiguous 到处走动的，不能确定的→不明确的，模棱两可的。

ambitious [æmˈbiʃəs] a. 有雄心的，野心勃勃的

[例] Tom was intensely ambitious, obsessed with the idea of becoming rich. 汤姆野心勃勃，一门心思想着发财。

[记] be ambitious to succeed 渴望成功

ameliorate [əˈmiːljəreit] v. 改善，改良，减轻

[例] Volunteers could do little to ameliorate conditions in the refugee camp. 志愿者们对改善难民营的状况几乎做不了任何事情。

amend [əˈmend] v. 修改，修订，改正

[例] The UN charter has been amended since World War Ⅱ and great improvement has been made. 经过二战以来的修订，联合国宪章已经日趋完善。

[记] amendment n. 改善，改正

amenity [əˈmiːniti] n. 宜人；礼仪

[例] Stadiums and gymnasiums are just some of the town's local amenities. 运动场和体育馆只是镇上的部分康乐设施。

amid [əˈmid] prep. 在…中

[例] Amid warm applause, the honoured guests mounted the rostrum. 在热烈的掌声中贵宾们登上了主席台。

amphibian [æmˈfibiən] a./n. 两栖动物（的），水陆两用（的）

[例] Nobody knows why amphibians are disappearing, dolphins are dying or coral is turning white. 没有人知道为什么两栖动物逐渐消失，海豚正在死亡，珊瑚变成白色。

ample ['æmpl] a. 大量的，充裕的，丰富的，足够的

[例] You'll have ample opportunity to ask questions after the talk. 等演讲完了，你们会有充分的机会提问。

[同义词] adequate, abundant

amplify ['æmplifai] v. 详述；增强；扩大

[例] He amplified (on) his new findings with drawings and figures. 他用图表和数字进一步阐明他新近的发现。

amuse [ə'mju:z] v. 使开心，使发笑，给…提供娱乐

[例] I amuse myself with reading. 我以读书自娱。

> Muse，希腊神话中掌管艺术的缪斯女神。Muse 的艺术就是 music，Muse 收藏艺术品的地方就是 museum。在电影 *The Muse* 中，Sharon Stone 莎朗·斯通扮演能给人们带来灵感的 Muse。

anaesthetic [ˌænis'θetik] n. 麻醉剂；a. 麻醉的

[例] Eye surgery is often performed using a local anaesthetic. 眼部手术通常采取局部麻醉。

analogy [ə'nælədʒi] n. 比拟，类比

[例] No analogy exists between them. 他们之间没有相似之处。

[记] have an analogy to 具有与…的相似之处

analyse ['ænəlaiz] v. 分析，细察

[例] Lucent carefully analysed the telecom market and won the biggest share in the bidding for the CDMA network equipment supplier to China Unicom. 朗讯公司仔细地分析了电信市场，在中国联通的 CDMA 网络设备供应商投标中成为最大的赢家。

analysis [ə'nælisis] n. 分析，分解

[例] The analysis of the samples from the scene of the murder gave some valuable clues to the police. 对谋杀现场采样的分析为警察提供了一些有价值的线索。

analyst ['ænəlist] n. 分析家，分解者

[例] We want a stock market analyst. 我们需要一位股票市场分析师。

anatomy [ə'nætəmi] n. 解剖；解剖学

[例] We have to do anatomy next term. 我们下学期得学解剖学了。

[记] anatomical a. 解剖的；解剖学的 / anatomist n. 解剖学家

ancestor ['ænsistə] n. 祖宗，祖先

[例] Lions and house cats evolved from a common ancestor. 狮子和家猫是由同一个祖先进化而来的。

ancient ['einʃənt] a. 古代的；旧的

[例] These paintings show the ancient civilizations of Asia. 这些画展现了亚洲古代文明。

animation [ˌæni'meiʃən] n. 有生气；动画片，卡通

[例] We could see how excited he was by the animation in his face. 我们

从他脸上的神气就能看出他有多么兴奋。
[记] cartoon n. 卡通

> 字根 anim 指“呼吸 breath”。如：animal 有呼吸的东西→动物；animate 使有呼吸→使有生气，活泼；inanimate 使没有呼吸→无生命的；unanimous 呼吸一致，一个鼻孔出气→意见一致的，无异议的。

annihilate [ə'naiəleit] v. 消灭，歼灭
[例] Just one of these bombs could annihilate a city of the size of New York. 仅其中的一个炸弹就可以摧毁纽约那样大小的一个城市。

anniversary [ˌæni'vəːsəri] n. 周年纪念
[例] Jack and Kim celebrated their twentieth wedding anniversary in January. 杰克和凯姆一月份为他们结婚二十周年举行了庆典。

announce [ə'nauns] v. 宣布，通告
[例] The government announced that they would build a new highway to the mountain. 政府宣布他们将修建一条通向山区的新公路。
[记] announce sth. to sb. 对某人宣布某事

announcement [ə'naunsmənt] n. 宣告，一项公告，一项私人告示
[例] He waited for the announcement of the result of the competition with bated breath. 他屏息静气地等待宣布竞赛结果。
[记] make the announcement 通告一件事

anonymous [ə'nɔniməs] a. 匿名的
[例] He received an anonymous letter. 他收到了一封匿名信。

> 字根 onym 指“名字 name”。如：an- 没有 +onym 名字→ anonym 匿名者；ant 反 + onym 名字→antonym 反义词；syn 相同的 +onym 名字→ synonym 同义词。

annoy [ə'nɔi] v. 使烦恼，烦扰，打搅
[例] The mayor's commentrs annoyed voters. 市长的评论让选民们生气。

anthropology [ˌænθrə'pɔlədʒi] n. 人类学

> 字根anthrop指“人类”。如：mis- 否定+anthrope人类→misanthrope 厌世者；phil 爱 +anthrop 人类→philanthrope 慈善家；philanthropy 博爱。

antibiotic [ˌæntibai'ɔtik] n. 抗生素
[例] The factory is specialized in the production of antibiotics. 该厂专门生产抗生素。

anticipate [æn'tisipeit] v. 预期，预料；期望；提前做
[例] Sales are better than anticipated. 销售情况比预想的还要好。
[记] anticipate the opponent's next move 先发制人，制敌机先 / anticipate doing sth. 期盼做某事

anticipation [ˌæntisiˈpeiʃən] n. 预期，预测

[例] The audience was filled with anticipation. 听众们充满着期待。

[记] by anticipation 预先，事先 / in anticipation (of) 预先，预料，期待

antique [ænˈtiːk] n. 古物，古董；a. 古时的，过时的

[例] The antique is a fake. 那古董是一件赝品。

[记] an antique dealer 古董商

anyhow [ˈenihau] adv. 无论如何，总之

[例] It sounds crazy, but I believe it anyhow. 它听起来像疯话，可是我相信。

[同义词] anyway

apathetic [ˌæpəˈθetik] a. 冷淡的；漠不关心的

[例] I cannot understand your apathetic attitude. 我无法理解你无动于衷的态度。

[记] apathetically adv. 漠不关心地 / apathy n. 冷漠；漠不关心

apparatus [ˌæpəˈreitəs] n. 器械，仪器，设备，装置

[例] The new piece of apparatus was used in the experiment. 在实验中使用了那件新设备。

apparent [əˈpærənt] a. 明显的，显而易见的

[例] In spite of her apparent indifference, a woman is usually deeply concerned with others' remarks on her figure. 尽管表面上不在乎，女人通常很在意别人怎样议论自己的身材。

[记] apparently ad.显然地

appeal [əˈpiːl] n. 请求，呼吁，上诉，吸引力；v. 呼吁，上诉，吸引

[例] The government is appealing to everyone to save water. 政府呼吁每个人节约用水。

[记] the right of appeal 上诉权 / appealing a. 吸引人的

appearance [əˈpiərəns] n. 外貌，外表，外观，出现

[例] Don't judge by appearances. 不能以貌取人。

append [əˈpend] v. 附加，增补

[例] I append a list of those institutions where you may get necessary information. 我附上一张你可以获得必要信息的机构的名单。

[记] appendix n. 附录；阑尾

appetite [ˈæpitait] n. 食欲, 胃口, 欲望, 爱好

[例] He has a good appetite. 他的胃口很好。

> 字根pet指“寻求seek”。如：appetite寻求的情绪→欲望，食欲；appetizer开胃的食物，开胃菜；appetizing引起欲望的，开胃的；compete一起寻求一样东西→竞争。

applaud [əˈplɔːd] v. 鼓掌称赞，赞同

[例] Everyone applauded when the play ended. 演出结束时，大家都

热烈鼓掌。

appliance [ə'plaiəns] n. 用具, 器具

[例] The household appliances were just bought for his family. 他家刚买回来几件新家用电器。

[记] kitchen appliance 厨房用具

application [ˌæpli'keiʃən] n. 请求，申请；应用

[例] It can take some time for your visa application to be processed. 处理你的签证申请是需要一段时间的。

[记] fill out an application 填写申请书

apply [ə'plai] v. 申请，应用，适用

[例] I applied to four universities and was accepted by all of them. 我申请了四所大学，并且都被录取了。

[记] be applied to 适用于；应用于 / apply to (for) 申请，请求

appoint [ə'pɔint] v. 委派，任命；约定，指定

[例] We must appoint a new teacher at once to the mountain school. 我们必须立即委派一名新教师到那山村小学去。

appointment [ə'pɔintmənt] n. 约会, 指定

[例] I made an appointment to see the doctor.我和医生约好了时间去看病。

appreciate [ə'priːʃieit] v. 赏识，鉴赏，感激

[例] We appreciate your efforts for the development of the company. 我们感激你对公司发展所作的努力。

apprentice [ə'prentis] n. 学徒，实习生；v. 当学徒

[例] His father apprenticed him to a barber. 他父亲让他学理发。

[记] take apprentice 收徒弟 /an apprentice electrician 一个电工学徒

approach [ə'prəutʃ] n. 方法，方式；v. 接近，靠近

[例] He decided to adopt a different approach and teach the Bible through story-telling. 他决定采用一种不同的方式，通过讲故事的方式教授《圣经》。

appropriate [ə'prəupriit] a. 适合的，恰当的

[例] His casual clothes were not appropriate for such a formal occasion. 他的便服不适宜在这样正式的场合穿。

[反义词] inappropriate

approval [ə'pruːvəl] n. 赞成，承认，正式批准

[例] He showed his approval by smiling. 他用微笑表示赞成。

approve [ə'pruːv] v. 赞成，满意；批准

[例] I don't approve of cosmetic surgery. 我不赞成整形手术。

approximate [ə'prɔksimit] a. 近似的，大约的；v. 近似，接近

[例] His description approximated to the truth but there were a few errors. 他的描述与事实已经接近了，但是有一些错误。

apt [æpt] a. 易于…的，有…倾向的；灵敏的

[例] Food is apt to deteriorate in summer. 食物在夏天容易变质。

aptitude ['æptitju:d] n. 天资，才能，聪明

[例] He had an aptitude for journalism. 他有从事新闻工作的才能。

> 美国 College Entrance Examination 高中生毕业考试 SAT 全称为 Scholastic Aptitude Test，意为“学术倾向性测试”。

aquarium [ə'kwεəriəm] n. 水族馆；鱼缸

[例] An aquarium is a place for the public exhibition of live aquatic animals and plants. 水族馆是公开展出活的水族动植物的场所。

aquatic [ə'kwætik] a. 水的，水上的

[记] aquatic sports 水上运动

> 字根 aqua 指“水”。丹麦著名的 Aqua 乐队，中文翻译为“水叮当”或“阿夸”。冠军单曲 *Barbie Girl*、*Doctor Jones* 都是他们的杰作。他们还出过一张专辑叫 Aquarius。Aquarius n.黄道十二宫之宝瓶座。

arbitrary ['ɑ:bitrəri] a. 武断的，专断的，任意的

[例] My choice was quite arbitrary. 我的选择相当随意。

arch [ɑ:tʃ] n. 拱门，弓形结构；v. （使）弯成弓形

[例] The cat arches its back when it sees the dog.猫看到狗，便把背拱起来。

[记] an arch bridge 拱桥

archaeology [ˌɑ:ki'ɔlədʒi] n. 考古学

[例] Archaeology is the study of ancient civilizations. 考古学研究古代文明。

[记] archaeological a.考古学的 / archaeologist n.考古学家

arduous ['ɑ:djuəs] a. 费力的，辛勤的；险峻的

[例] In those days, long-distance travel was slow and arduous. 那时，长途旅行耗时又艰辛。

[记] an arduous task 艰难的工作 / an arduous worker 勤奋的工人 / arduous paths 陡峭的道路

arena [ə'ri:nə] n. 竞技场，舞台

[例] He withdrew from the political arena. 他从政治舞台上退出了。

> arena 拉丁语原义是“沙、沙地”。古罗马圆形剧场 amphitheater 的中央角斗场上有沙土覆盖，用以吸血。西班牙斗牛 bullfight 表演中，也可看到公牛血染“沙场”的情景。现引申为“竞争的场所、舞台”。

arise [ə'raiz] v. 起来；出现，发生

[例] I arose early in the morning. 我每天早上起得很早。

[记] arise, arose, arisen / arise from 由…而引起，由…而产生

aromatic [ˌærəuˈmætik] a. 芳香的

[例] She had filled the room with sweet-scented jasmine and tall aromatic lilies. 她把整个房间放满了散发甜香味的茉莉花和直挺的、芬芳的百合花。

arouse [əˈrauz] v. 唤起，激起，引起

[例] The young man' s behavior aroused the suspicions of the police. 那个年轻人的行为引起了警方的怀疑。

[记] arouse sb.'s interest / curiosity / enthusiasm / anger 激起某人的兴趣 / 唤起某人好奇心 / 激起某人的热情 / 惹起某人的愤怒

arrange [əˈreindʒ] v. 安排，整理，使有条理

[例] Contact your local branch to arrange an appointment. 联络你们当地的分支机构安排一次约见。

artery [ˈɑːtəri] n. 动脉；干线

[例] The wound severed an antery and he died of blood loss. 伤口割断了动脉，他失血而亡。

[记] vein n. 静脉

arthritis [ɑːˈθraitis] n. 关节炎

[例] The medicine can cure arthritis. 这种药可以治疗关节炎。

artifact [ˈɑːtifækt] n. 人造物品

[例] Software is a cultural artifact of the modern world. 软件是现代社会的一种人造文化物品。

> 字根 fact 指"制作"。如：factory 制作的地方→工厂。art 指"艺术"。artifact 制作出来的艺术，非天然的→人造物品，工艺品；artifical 人造的，做作的，虚伪的。

artificial [ˌɑːtiˈfiʃəl] a. 人造的；假的

[例] This fruit juice contains absolutely no artificial flavouring or colouring. 这种果汁绝不含人造香精和色素。

ascend [əˈsend] v. 上升，攀登

[例] The stairs in the five-star hotel ascend in a graceful curve. 这个五星级酒店的楼梯以优美的曲线上升。

[反义词] descend

ascribe [əsˈkraib] v. 归因于；归咎于

[例] He ascribed his failure to bad luck. 他把失败归咎于运气不好。

[记] ascribe to 归因于

aspect [ˈæspekt] n. （问题、事物等的）方面

[例] We must consider a problem in all its aspects. 我们必须全面的考虑问题。

ash [æʃ] n. 灰，灰烬

[例] Investigators sifted through the ashes to find the cause of the fire.为了找到火灾的原因，调查人员仔细筛查这片废墟。

aspiration [ˌæspəˈreiʃən] n. 渴望；志气

[例] Flying is her aspiration. 飞行是她梦寐以求的事。

> 字根 spir 指"呼吸 to breathe"。spirit 呼吸，生命的根源→精神，灵魂；aspire 对着某物呼吸→渴望；inspiration 里面的呼吸，精神的启示→灵感。

aspire [əsˈpaiə] v. 追求，渴望

[例] These college graduates aspire to careers in finance. 这些大学毕业生渴望从事金融方面的职业。

[记] aspire to do sth 渴望做某事 / aspire to (after) truth 追求真理

assault [əˈsɔːlt] n. 攻击，袭击；v. 袭击

[例] He was accused of sexual assault. 他因性骚扰被指控。

[记] assault on / against 对…袭击

assemble [əˈsembl] v. 集合，聚集

[例] A large crowd had assembled outside the American embassy. 一大队人群聚集在美国使馆外。

assert [əˈsəːt] v. 断言，声称

[谚] Justice will assert itself. 正义必将伸张。

assess [əˈses] v. 估定，评定

[例] Damages were assessed at 1,000 RMB. 损失估计达一千元人民币。

[记] assess sb.'s ability 评估某人的能力 / assessment n. 估价，评价

> 字根 sess 指"坐下 to sit"。assess 使坐下→定下，评定；obsess 无法(ob-=against)坐下→使困扰，迷住；possess 朝某物所在的方向坐下→拥有。

assessment [əˈsesmənt] n. 评估；估价

[例] What is your assessment of Micheal Jackson? 你对迈克 · 杰克逊的看法如何？

asset [ˈæset] n. 资产，财产；宝贵的人或物

[谚] Good health is a great asset. 健康是最大的财富。

[记] tangible assets 有形资产 / intangible assets 无形资产 / assets and liabilities 资产与负债

assign [əˈsain] v. 分配，指派

[例] The monitor was assigned to take notes for the meeting. 班长被指派作会议记录。

[记] assignment n. 课外作业，任务

associate [əˈsəuʃiit] v. 使发生联系，使联合；n. 合作人，同事；a. 副的

[例] We often associate roses with love. 我们经常把玫瑰花和爱情联系在一起。

[记] associate... with… 把…与…联系在一起 / associate professor n.

副教授

assort [ə'sɔːt] v. 把…分类；相配；协调

[例] His actions do not assort with his promises. 他的行动和他的诺言不一致。

assorted [ə'sɔːtid] a. 各种各样的

[例] In the centre of the table was a plate of assorted biscuits. 桌子当中有一盘各种各样的点心。

assume [ə'sjuːm] v. 假定，设想；承担，担任

[例] We assume his innocence before hearing the evidence against it. 在未听到对他不利的证词以前，我们假定他是无罪的。

[记] assume office 掌权

assumption [ə'sʌmpʃən] n. 假设，设想；担任，承当

[例] My calculations were based on the assumption that house prices would remain steady. 我是在房屋价格不变的基础上考虑的。

assurance [ə'ʃuərəns] n. 确信，断言，保证，担保

[例] The manager gave her assurance that the plan would succeed. 经理许诺她计划将会成功。

assure [ə'ʃuə] v. 深信不疑地说，保证，担保

[例] I can assure you of the reliability of the news. 我可以向你保证这个消息是可靠的。

astonish [əs'tɔniʃ] v. 使惊讶

[例] We were astonished to hear that their football team had won the championship. 听说他们的足球队获得了冠军，这真叫人意想不到。

[同义词] surprise, amaze, astonish, astound

> 来看这组表示"吃惊"的单词：surprise"惊讶"程度最低；amaze相当于surprise very much，一般指好事；而astonish和astound同源，来自拉丁文extonare，指被雷击中，惊讶程度非常高。astound指"惊骇"，比astonish更显强烈。但是被雷击中astound后还可能幸存，英语中表示惊讶程度最最最高的一个词，是指人听到消息后完全地石像化了，没有任何思维，连吃惊的表情都没有了。该词后面碰到再讲，继续前进吧！

astound [əs'taund] v. 惊骇，使大吃一惊

[例] He was astounded when he heard his son had taken drugs. 他听说他儿子吸毒，不禁大为惊讶。

astronaut ['æstrənɔːt] n. 宇航员，航天员

[例] The astronauts pilot their craft down to the lunar surface. 宇航员驾驶宇宙飞船在月球表面降落。

> 字根astro指"星星star"。如：astrology研究星星的学科→星相学。字根nau指"船，航行"。如：nausea海上航行→晕船，恶心。那么，astro＋naut，就是在星星之间航行的人，宇航员。中国的

第一个宇航员杨利伟叫 taikonaut（taiko- 太空）。随着神州 5 号的发射，极具中国特色的 taikonaut 一词成功进入现代英语词典。

astronomer [ə'strɔnəmə(r)] n. 天文学家

[例] An astronomer specializes in astronomy. 天文学家专门从事天文学研究。

[记] astronomy n. 天文学

asylum [ə'sailəm] n. 庇护；收容所；救济院

[例] The terrorist tried to seek political asylum in that country. 恐怖分子想在那个国家寻求政治庇护。

[记] asylum seeker 寻求庇护者

asymmetry [æ'simətri] n. 不对称；不匀称

[例] In economics, information asymmetry occurs when one party to a transaction has more or better information than the other party. 在经济学中，信息不对称发生在当交易的一方比另一方掌握更多有用的信息的时候。

[反义词] symmetry

atheism ['eiθiizəm] n. 无神论

[例] He believes in atheism. 他信仰无神论。

athlete ['æθli:t] n. 运动员

[例] The athlete has a powerful physique. 这位运动员体格强壮。

[记] athletics 体育；田径运动

atlas ['ætləs] n. 地图册，图表集

[例] Check where Sydney is in your atlas. 在你的地图册里查一查悉尼在哪里。

Atlas 是希腊神话中泰坦（Titans）巨神之一，因背叛宙斯（Zeus）被罚在世界的西边尽头以双肩扛天。16 世纪地理学家麦卡脱把 Atlas 擎天图作为一本地图册的卷首插图。后人争相效仿，即得此意。另外，大家也猜到 Atlantic（大西洋）一词的来历了吧。

atmosphere ['ætməsfiə] n. 大气，空气，气氛

[例] The approaching examination created a tense atmosphere on the campus. 即将到来的考试在校园里造成了一种紧张气氛。

[记] sphere n. 球体 / hydrosphere n. 水圈 / lithosphere 岩石圈

atom ['ætəm] n. 原子

[例] A molecule of water is made up of two atoms of hydrogen and one atom of oxygen. 一个水分子是由两个氢原子和一个氧原子构成的。

古希腊哲学家德谟克利特认为：原子就是小得不能再分割的物质微粒。a（否定）+ tom（分割），不能分割，就是原子。再回忆一个包含 tom 的单词：anatomy 解剖。

attain [ə'tein] v. 达到，获得，到达

[例] Lee Iacoca attained the position of President of the Ford Motors. 李·雅科卡终于当上了福特汽车公司的总裁。

[记] attain one's goal 达到目的

attempt [ə'tempt] n./v. **努力，尝试，企图**

[例] The boys attempted to leave but were stopped by their parents. 男孩子们想离开但被他们的父母们拦住了。

Unit 3

attend [ə'tend] v. 参加，出席，到场

[例] A large number of people attended the wedding. 婚礼上有很多人出席。

[记] attendance n. （学校上课）出勤率 / a high attendance 高出勤率

attorney [ə'tə:ni] n. <美>律师

> 英联邦国家多用 lawyer，barrister，solicitor。lawyer 是法律工作者的统称，使用范围广泛；barrister 指大律师，能在高等法院出庭办案。bar 作名词有"横木，栅栏"之意，也指法庭上围住法官和律师所坐位置的围栏。那么 solicitor 就是和 bar 没有关系的律师啦——小律师，不能出庭说话，一般是 barrister 的助手。

attract [ə'trækt] v. 吸引，引起

[例] She was attracted by the novel advertisement. 她被这则新颖的广告吸引住了。

[记] attraction n. 吸引力

attribute [ə'tribju:t] v. 把…归因于，把…归咎于，认为…属于；['ætribju:t] n. 属性，特性

[例] David attributed his company's success to(or 'for') the unity of all the staff and their persevering hard work. 大卫说他们公司之所以获得成功是由于全体员工的团结和坚持不懈努力工作的结果。

[记] attribute to 归因于

auction ['ɔ:kʃən] v./n. 拍卖

[例] His property was sold at the auction. 他的财产被拍卖了。

[记] auction price 拍卖价格 / put sth. up to(or for) auction 将（某物）交付拍卖

> 原意为"增加"，与 augment（增加）同源，可以一起记忆。拍卖这一方式由古罗马人首创，竞买者（bidder）争相加价（增加），拍卖人（auctioneer）接受最高价成交。

audience ['ɔ:djəns] n. 听众，观众

[例] An audience of three thousand crowded the concert hall. 三千名听众挤满了音乐大厅。

audit ['ɔ:dit] n. /v. 查账，审计

[例] The company has an audit at the end of each financial year. 这家公司在每个财政年度末进行一次审计。

[记] auditing n. 审计学 / auditor 审计员，旁听者

augment [ɔ:g'ment] v. 扩大，增加，加强，提高

[例] With the birth of his third son, he found it necessary to do something to augment his income. 随着他第三个儿子的出生，他感到有必要想办法增加收入。

authentic [ɔː'θentik] a. 真的，可靠的

[例] Is that an authentic painting by Piccaso, or a modern copy? 那幅油画是毕加索的真迹还是现代仿制品？

authority [ɔː'θɔriti] n. 权威，权威人士，权力

[例] You don't have any authority to enter this house. It's private. 你们没有任何权力进入这所房子，这是私宅。

[记] authorities 当局，官方 / author 作者

authorise ['ɔːθəraiz](=authorize) v. 授权，批准

[例] Only Congress can authorize the President to declare war. 只有国会能授权总统宣战。

automatic [ˌɔːtə'mætik] a. 自动的，机械的

[例] The heating system in the hotel has an automatic temperature control. 旅馆里的取暖系统是自动调温的。

auxiliary [ɔːg'ziljəri] a. 辅助的，协助的，备用的

[例] When there is a power outage, they are counting on the auxiliary power supply. 停电的时候，他们依赖后备供电设施。

avalanche ['ævəˌlɑːnʃ] v./n. 雪崩

[例] Yesterday's avalanche killed a party of skiers and destroyed several trees. 昨天的雪崩造成了一批滑雪者死亡，并毁坏了一些树木。

available [ə'veiləbl] a. 可利用的，现成可使用的，可得到的

[例] The lawyer is not available now. 律师现在没空。

[反义词] unavailable a. 不可得到的

avenue ['ævinjuː] n. 林荫道，大街，途径，方法

[例] One of the world's most beautiful avenues is the Champs Elysées in Paris. 巴黎的香榭丽舍大街是世界上最美的大街之一。

> 字根 ven 指"来 come"。如：con- 共同 +ven 来 +tion → 大家一起来 → convention 会议；event 发生而来的 → 事件。avenue 来来去去的地方 → 大街。世界著名化妆品牌之一Elizabeth Arden最出名的香水—— Fifth Avenue（第五大道）。曾由于伊丽莎白·雅顿女士的要求，只在纽约第五大道销售。我们祖国首都著名的"长安街"英译为 Chang'an Avenue。

average ['ævəridʒ] n./a. 平均（的）；中等（的），普通（的）

[例] His results are average. 他的成绩平平。

[记] on (an) average 通常；按平均

aviation [ˌeivi'eiʃən] n. 航空，航空学，飞行术

[例] They were pilots in the early days of aviation. 他们是航空初期的驾驶员。

字根 avi 指“鸟 bird”。所以，avian 鸟，鸟类的；aviate 鸟的动作→飞行；aviator 鸟人→飞行家；aviary 鸟的地方→鸟笼，动物园鸟舍。

aware [ə'wɛə] a. 知道的，明白的，意识到的

[例] The children are not aware of the danger of taking drugs. 孩子们没有意识到吸毒的危险。

[记] awareness n. 意识

awesome ['ɔːsəm] a. 引起敬畏的，可怕的；卓越的

[例] He was thrust into a position of awesome responsibility. 他被推到了一个责任艰巨的职位上。

awkward ['ɔːkwəd] a. 难使用的，笨拙的

[例] The child is still awkward with his chopsticks. 那孩子还不太会用筷子。

[同义词] clumsy

axis ['æksis] n. 轴；轴线

[例] The earth's axis is the line between the North and South Poles. 地轴是南北极之间的线。

bachelor ['bætʃələ] n. 学士；单身汉

[例] To do the job, you must have at least a bachelor's degree in chemistry. 要做这项工作至少也要先取得化学学士学位。

[记] bachelor's degree 学士学位 / Bachelor of Arts/Science 文/理/学学士

国外青年人常说 bachelor pad，是指单身汉之家，可以为所欲为、大开 party 的地方。随着女性的社会地位的提高和独立性的增强，单身女子日益增多，bachelorette 一词的使用也逐渐频繁。

backbone ['bækbəun] n. 脊柱；骨干，中坚；骨气

[例] The bachelors are the backbone of this community. 这些单身汉是这个团体的中坚力量。

background ['bækgraund] n. 背景，（个人出身、受教育）经历

[例] He is a man with a strong cultural background. 他是受过高等教育的人。

backup ['bækʌp] n. 后援，支持；阻塞；v. 做备份；a. 候补的，支持性的

[例] Make a backup of any work you do on the computer. 你在电脑上做的任何工作都要做一个备份。

bacteria [bæk'tiəriə] n.〈bacterium 的复数〉细菌

[例] Bacteria in drinking water have spread the illness. 饮水中的细菌传染了疾病。

badge [bædʒ] n. 徽章，证章；标记；象征

[谚] Wisdom is the badge of maturity. 智慧是成熟的标志。

[记] school badge 校徽

badminton ['bædmintən] n. 羽毛球

[例] He won the award at an under-18 international badminton tournament in Barcelona. 他在巴塞罗那18岁以下国际羽毛球锦标赛上获奖。

[记] badminton tournament 羽毛球锦标赛

> 英格兰西部一庄园名为Badminton，据说羽毛球发源于此，故得名。其实羽毛球运动是19世纪由印度传入英国的。羽毛球运动中球拍叫racket，而羽毛球叫shuttlecock，该词还指踢毽的"毽子"。

baggage ['bægidʒ] n. 行李；包袱

[例] We may have lost some baggage, so we'd like to make a lost baggage report. 我们可能遗失了几件行李，所以必须填份行李遗失报告。

bait [beit] v. 引诱；n.诱饵，诱惑

[例] He is known for baiting his opponents. 众所周知，他善于诱惑对手。

balcony ['bælkəni] n. 阳台；（剧场二楼）楼座，包厢

[例] All bedrooms are twin with private bathrooms, and some come with a balcony. 所有的卧室都套有独立卫生间，有的卧室还带阳台。

bald [bɔːld] a. 秃头的，秃顶的；无装饰的，单调的

[例] He combed his hair and tried to hide his bald patch. 他梳理头发想要遮盖住头上已经秃顶的那一块。

ballet ['bælei, bæ'lei] n. 芭蕾舞，舞剧；芭蕾舞剧团；芭蕾舞音乐

[例] I wanted to be a ballet dancer when I was a child. 当我还是个孩子时，我想成为芭蕾舞演员。

[记] ice ballet 冰上芭蕾舞 / water ballet 水上芭蕾舞 / Swan Lake 天鹅湖（著名芭蕾舞剧）

ballot ['bælət] n. 选票；v. 投票

[例] The club members held a secret ballot to choose the chairperson. 俱乐部成员用无记名投票选举负责人。

[同义词] vote, poll

> 古希腊和古罗马人选举常采用无记名投票方式，那时候没有纸做的选票，他们投的是ball 小石球，白色是赞成，黑色是反对。lot 表示"分配"，如：allot。所以ballot 其实就是"分球"→投票。

ban [bæn] n./v. 禁令，禁止

[例] This is a call to lift the ban on homosexuals. 这是在呼吁解禁同性恋禁令。

[同义词] forbid, prohibit, bar

band [bænd] v. 联合；结合；用带捆扎；n. 乐队，乐团；波段

[例] The people banded together against the robbers. 人们联合起来反

对强盗。

bankrupt ['bæŋkrʌpt] a. 破产的；v. 使破产，使完全丧失

[例] His wife's extravagance soon bankrupted him. 他妻子的奢侈生活很快就使他破产了。

[记] bankruptcy n.破产

> 来源于拉丁文 *banca* 板凳，*rupta* 拆掉。古埃及银行家通常坐在神殿庭院内的条凳上给来往的人们放债或兑换货币。当他们由于资金短缺而被迫中断时，他们的凳子就会被拆掉。

banquet ['bæŋkwit] n. （通常指正式的）宴会；v. 参加宴会

[例] They banqueted her royally when she became the director of the company. 当她就任这家公司的经理时，他们为她举行了盛大的宴会。

[记] give/hold a banquet 举行宴会 / a state banquet 国宴

baptise [bæp'taiz](=baptize) v.（基督教的）给…洗礼

> baptism n.洗礼，基督教入教仪式。牧师以"I believe in God the Father Almighty（我信我全能的天父）"告白开始，在受洗者头上滴几滴 holy water，或将其身体浸入水中，诵到"I baptise you in the name of the Trinity （我奉圣父、圣子、圣灵之命为你施洗）"结束。洗礼象征着洗清人的罪恶，准备接受上帝的恩典。

bar [bɑː] n. 酒吧间；出售酒的柜台；条，棒，杆

[例] There weren't any free tables, so I sat on a stool at the bar. 没有空桌子了，所以我只好在吧台前坐下。

[记] bar chart 柱状图

barbecue ['bɑːbikjuː] (=BBQ, barbie) n. 烧烤；（吃烤烧的）野餐

[例] We both like eating Brazilian barbecue. 我俩都喜欢吃巴西烧烤。

bare [bɛə] a. 赤裸的，无遮蔽的

[例] Don't walk on that broken glass with bare feet. 不要光着脚走在那些碎玻璃上。

[同义词] naked, bald

bargain ['bɑːgin] n./v. 协定，协议；交易，便宜货；v. 讲价，讨价还价；讲条件，谈判

[例] At that low price the house is a bargain. 按那样低的价钱出售，这房子可真够便宜的。

bark [bɑːk] v. （狗等动物）吠；大声嚷；n. 树皮

[谚] Barking dogs seldom bite. 善吠的狗很少咬人。

barrel ['bærəl] n. 大桶；桶状物，圆筒

[例] The wine is aged in oak barrels. 酒被窖藏在橡木桶里。

[记] sit on a barrel of gun-powder 坐在火药桶上〈比喻提心吊胆，随时可能有危险〉

barren ['bærən] a. 贫瘠的，荒芜的；不孕的；不结果实的

[例] That remote barren land has blossomed into rich granaries. 过去的穷乡僻壤变成了富饶的谷仓。

> "男孩地带" Boyzone 演唱过一首经典歌曲 "No Matter What"，其中一段歌词为：And I will keep you safe and strong，and sheltered from the storm；No matter where it's barren，a dream is being born. 不论多么荒芜的地方，都有梦在生长。

barrier ['bæriə] n. 障碍物；屏障

[例] Lack of confidence is the biggest barrier to the improvement of your English. 缺乏信心是你提高英语水平的最大障碍。

[同义词] handicap, obstacle

basis ['beisis] n. 基础，根据；主要部分

[例] Their claim had no a basis in fact. 他们的声明没有事实根据。

[记] on the basis of = based on 基于…

battery ['bætəri] n. 电池，电池组

[例] He charges the battery for his cellphone every night.他每天晚上给手机电池充电。

battle ['bætl] n. 战斗，战役；v. 战斗，竞争

[谚] Life is a battle from the cradle to the grave. 人生是一场从生到死的战斗。

[同义词] combat, war

bead [bi:d] n. 珠子；水珠；v. 串上珠子

[例] She wore a string of beads round her neck. 她脖子上挂了一串珠子。

> 古义为"祈祷"，后来西方有一阵子盛行祈祷时手拨弄念珠，bead 被用来表示"念珠祈祷"，此义仍被保留在英语短语 count one's beads "祷告"中。最后转义为"珠子"、"水珠"。复数形式 beads 指"珠子项链"。

beard [biəd] n. 胡须

[例] He wears a light beard and never shaves it. 他留着一撮稀疏的胡子，从来不刮。

[记] wear a beard 留着胡须 / a heavy/light beard 浓/稀胡须 / mustache [mə'stɑ:ʃ] n. 小胡子

beam [bi:m] n. 光束，光线；梁，横梁；v.（无线电）播送

[例] The beams of the searchlights fingered the sky over the airport. 一道道探照灯光刺破机场的天空。

bear [bɛə] n. 熊；v. 忍受；记住；承担（责任）；支撑（重量）

[谚] The water that bears the boat is the same that swallows it up. 水能载舟，也能覆舟。

[记] bear in mind 牢记在心

beast [bi:st] n. 野兽，畜生；讨厌的人（东西）

Disney 动画片《美女与野兽》*Beauty and the Beast*。

beforehand [bi'fɔ:hænd] ad. 预先，事先；提前地

[例] Don't be beforehand in making up your mind. 不要过早作决定。

[反义词] afterward

behalf [bi'hɑ:f] n. 利益；作为…的代表

[例] The president of our school signed the document on behalf of the school. 我校校长代表校方签署了这份文件。

[记] on behalf of 代表，为了 / on sb.'s behalf 以某人的名义；代表某人

behaviour [bi'heivjə] n. 举止，行为

[例] The teacher will not tolerate bad behaviour in class. 老师不会容忍班上不规矩的行为。

[记] behave v. 行为举止 / behave yourself 行为规矩些

benchmark ['bentʃma:k] n. 基准，标准

[例] Despite her behaviour off-stage, her performances set a new benchmark for singers throughout the world. 不管她在台下的行为如何，她的表演为全世界歌手树立了新标准。

bench 长凳子，mark 作标记，在长凳子上划一条标记，就像课桌上的三八线一样，这是标准，别超过！

bend [bend] v. 俯身；弯腰；弯曲

[例] He bent his steps toward me. 他转身向我走来。

[记] bend over backward to do sth. 尽最大的力量（做某事）

beneficial [ˌbeni'fiʃəl] a. 有益的，有利的，有用的

[例] Sunshine is beneficial to plants. 阳光对植物有益。

beset [bi'set] v. 困扰；围攻；包围

[例] In the swamp, the army was beset by mosquitoes. 在沼泽地，军队受到蚊子的困扰。

bet [bet] n. 赌，打赌 v. 赌，赌钱

[例] I bet our team will win. 我打赌我们队准能获胜。

[记] you bet 当然；的确

beverage ['bevəridʒ] n. 饮料（如牛奶，茶，咖啡，啤酒等）

[例] He is our regular supplier of beverages. 他是我们饮料的定期供应者。

[记] alcoholic beverage 酒精饮料

bewilder [bi'wildə] v. 使迷惑；使昏乱

[例] A new environment can bewilder and frighten a child. 一个新环境能难住和吓住孩子。

[同义词] baffle, confuse, perplex, puzzle

bias ['baiəs] n./ v.（使有）偏见，偏心

[例] His experiences bias him against businessmen. 他的经历使他对商人抱有偏见。

[记] have a bias against 对…有偏见 / have a bias toward 偏重，偏爱

bibliography [ˌbibli'ɔgrəfi] n. 参考书目

[例] The bibliography is a very important part of a paper. 参考书目是一篇论文的重要组成部分。

> 纸莎草 papyrus 是一种地中海水生芦苇，古人用它制成纸草写字，所以有了 paper 一词。而出口这种纸草的腓尼基港口名叫 Byblos，希腊语 *biblos* 即指用这种纸写成的书籍。*biblos* 进入法语成为 *bible*，英语借来后大写首字母特指《圣经》Bible，而字根 biblio 即指“书”。bibliography 写书的记录→参考书目；phil 爱 +biblio 书→ bibliophile 藏书家。

bid [bid] v./n. 出价，投标

[例] They lost the contract because their bid was too high. 他们因索价太高而失去了那份合同。

[记] bidder n. 投标人

bilateral [bai'lætərəl] a. 双边的

[例] They have signed a bilateral peace treaty. 他们已经签署了双边和平协议。

[记] a bilateral agreement双边协定 / bilateral negotiations双边谈判

billiards ['biljədz] n. 台球

[例] He spent a whole afternoon playing billiards. 他打了整整一个下午的台球。

> 大家都玩比较普及的 pool“撞球”，pool 还有一个常见词义“游泳池”；那种台球桌比较大，先打红球再打彩球的是斯诺克 snooker。snooker 一词有“阻挠”的含义，指打球时故意给对手制造障碍。billiards 泛指 pool 或 snooker。

bind [baind] v. 捆，绑；束紧；

[谚] Love rules without a sword and binds without a cord. 爱的统治不用刀枪，爱的捆绑不用绳索。

[记] bind up 包扎，装订成册

bite [bait] v. 咬，（昆虫）叮；吞饵，上钩

[例] The mosquitoes are biting me. 蚊子在叮我。

[记] bite off more than one can chew贪多嚼不烂 / bite the bullet忍辱负重

bizarre [bi'zɑː] a. 稀奇古怪的；异乎寻常的；怪诞的

[例] The story has a certain bizarre interest. 这个故事听起来别有风

趣。

> 法语词，该词读音本身就很 bizarre（怪怪的）。常见同义词有：weird, quaint, odd, eccentric, 另有一个长相发音相似的词，bazaar n.集市。

blame ['bleim] n./v. 责备，谴责

[谚] Bad workmen often blame their tools. 拙匠常怪工具差。

blank [blæŋk] a. 漠然的；不感兴趣的；空白的

[例] She sometimes occupied her blank days with sewing. 她有时做做针线活来消磨日子。

[记] be a blank（头脑）处于空白状态

blend [blend] n./v. 混合，融合；混合物

[例] His manner was a blend of friendliness and respect. 他的态度是友好中带有尊敬。

[记] blend with 混合，调合 / [同义词]mix

bless [bles] v. 祝福, 保佑

[谚] It is more blessed to give than to receive. 施恩比受惠更有福。

[记] Bless you!(别人打喷嚏时说）长命百岁！

block [blɔk] n. 街段；街区；堵塞物

[例] There was a block in the pipe and the water couldn't flow away. 水管里有块东西塞住了, 水流不出。

bloom [blu:m] n. 花；v.开花；兴旺

[例] The trees burst into bloom. 那些树木突然开花了。

blossom ['blɔsəm] n. 花（尤指结果实者）；v. 开花，兴旺，发展

[例] The peach tree has an excellent blossom this year. 今年这棵桃树花开得很好。

> "Blossom of snow, may you bloom and grow, bloom and grow forever." 这段歌词很熟吧，来自美国电影《音乐之声》*Sound of Music* 的插曲 Edelweiss（借自德语，edel 指高贵的，weiss 指洁白的，高贵而洁白的花朵，中文翻译“雪绒花”）。

blot [blɔt] n. 污斑；污渍

[例] The new power station is a blot on the landscape. 那座新建的电厂是这片风景的污点。

blow [bləu] v.(风）吹；n. 用力的一击，打击

[例] The telephone wires were blown down by the rainstorm. 电话线被暴风雨刮落了。

[记] strike a blow for 为…而奋斗

blueprint ['blu:ˌprint] n./v. 蓝图，行动计划

[例] The construction of a music hall is still in the blueprint stage. 音乐厅的建造还在筹划阶段。

老式的晒图机复印出来的图样是蓝色，因而称为blueprint（蓝图），延伸意义包括任何设计图样以及详细的计划或方案。blue还有其他含义，如：blue-collar worker 蓝领工人；心情很blue（沮丧）；blue Monday（忧郁星期一）；blue blood（贵族血统）；blue movie（黄色电影）。blue表“高贵”和“色情”自古就有，如“青楼”，青楼在梁朝以前原指显贵之家。青就是一种blue，君不闻：青出于蓝而胜于蓝。

blunt [blʌnt] a. 钝的，不锋利的；直言不讳的，耿直的

[例] His isolation has made him blunt about the feelings of others. 他的孤立使他对别人的感情木然无知。

[记] a blunt knife 一把钝刀 / a few blunt words 几句直言不讳的话

blur [blə:] v. 使模糊；使看不清

[例] His eyes were blurred with tears. 泪水使他的眼睛一片模糊。

boast [bəust] v./n. 自夸，夸耀

[例] Nobody should boast of his learning. 谁也不应当夸耀自己的学识。

[记] without boasting 不是自夸(用于插入语) / [同义词]brag

boil [bɔil] v. 煮沸，沸腾；n. 沸点

[谚] A watched pot never boils.（被看着的水壶永远烧不开）性急烧水水不沸。

[记] boil down to 归根结底是 / be on the boil 煮着，正在沸腾

bold [bəuld] a. 无畏的；鲁莽的；显眼的

[例] Their bold strategy paid off. 他们大胆的战略获得了回报。

bombard ['bɔmbɑ:d] v. 炮击，轰炸；不断攻击

[例] The speaker was bombarded with questions. 那位发言者遭到了连珠炮般的追问。

bonanza [bəu'nænzə] n. 富矿脉；发财，鸿运

[例] The large jump in profits has resulted in a bonanza for Intel employees. 利润上的飞跃为英特尔的员工带来了厚利。

bond [bɔnd] v. 结合；n. 结合（物）；债券

[例] These two different materials won't bond together. 这两种不同的材料粘合不起来。

bonus ['bəunəs] n. 奖金，红利，红包

[例] The workers got a Christmas bonus. 工人们得到了一份圣诞节红包。

[记] year-end bonus / December bonus 年终奖金

记忆：bon 棒 +us 我们→我们棒！应该给奖金红包bonus吧！其实bon在法语里还真是“棒，好”的意思，如：bonjour=good day；bon voyage 一路平安。bonus为拉丁语，进入西班牙语后成为bonanza，表示“好天气”，后英语中又引入bonanza一词，指“财运”。

boom [buːm] n./v. 繁荣，景气；隆隆声

[例] Canada enjoyed a real economic boom in the postwar years. 战后加拿大经历了真正的经济繁荣。

[记] baby boom 生育高峰

boost [buːst] v./n. 推动，推进

[例] Greater consumer access to the Internet has boosted electronic retailing. 大量的消费者上网推动了电子零售业。

[同义词] raise, increase, promote

booth [buːθ] n. 售货亭，货摊；公用电话间

[例] Our company's booth at the exhibition was right next to our main competitor. 展览会上本公司的展室就在我们主要竞争对手的隔壁。

[记] telephone booth 电话亭 / camera booth 摄影棚

border ['bɔːdə] n./v. 边，边缘，界限

[例] The border incident lead to war between the two countries. 这一边境事件导致了两国交战。

bore [bɔː] v.钻孔；烦扰；n. 讨厌的人；麻烦事

[例] Don't bore me with these kinds of jokes! 别再说这种无聊的笑话来烦我！

原意指钻孔机钻孔。钻孔时发出的声音单调，没有韵律，使人厌烦。引申为令人讨厌的。

botany ['bɔtəni] n.植物学

[例] He was involved in structural botany. 他潜心于植物构造学。

[记] botanic garden 植物园

bother ['bɔðə] v. 费心，尽力（做某事）；（使）苦恼;.打扰

[例] We had a lot of bother finding our way to his house. 我们费了很大的劲才找到他的家。

[同义词] worry, annoy

boundary ['baundəri] n. 分界线，边界，界限

[例] The river is the boundary between the two countries. 这条河是两国的界河。

[同义词] border

Unit 4

bow [bau] v. 鞠躬，躬身行礼

[例] I can’t agree with you but I bow to your greater experience and knowledge. 虽然我不同意你的意见，但我佩服你经验和知识比我丰富。

[记] take a bow 谢幕 / bow out 退休，告老

boycott [ˈbɔikət] n./v. 联合抵制

[例] We boycott all products tested on animals. 我们抵制所有拿动物做实验的产品。

> 从前，在爱尔兰有一个地主管家，姓Boycott。有一年天灾，农作物欠收，农民们生活艰难，但Boycott先生没有一点同情心，变本加厉地收租，激起了大家的愤怒。后来大家采取了一次联合行动，与Boycott先生断绝一切往来：不给他干活，不和他说话，商店不卖给他东西。他最后不得不逃出了村庄，但boycott一词却臭名远扬了。

brainstorm [ˈbreinˌstɔːm] v./n. 集体讨论，头脑风暴，诸葛亮会

[例] Managers get together and brainstorm a more permanent solution to a problem. 经理们聚在一起，群策群力设法找到一个长期有效的解决办法。

[记] brainstorming n. 头脑风暴，自由讨论

brag [bræg] v. 自夸，吹嘘

[例] He constantly brags about how well he plays football. 他老是吹嘘自己足球踢得多么好。

> bag是口袋，中间加入一个字母r，成为brag，感觉是向一个袋子里吹气，吹嘘、夸大的含义。同义词为boast。

branch [brɑːntʃ] n. 树枝；分店；分支机构；分科

[例] The company’s head office is in the city, but it has branches all over the country. 公司的总部在这个城市，但它的分公司遍布全国各地。

[记] extend the olive branch 伸出橄榄枝（表示准备讲和）

brand [brænd] n./v. 商标，牌子

[例] What brand of soap do you like? 你喜欢什么牌子的肥皂？

> brand new 崭新的。brand 古义为“火炬、火”。给某种东西打上火印，就是原始的商标了。brand new 原来指刚出炉的金属品，还带着火光，崭新的。从前有一位荷兰船主将葡萄酒进行浓缩以便运输，打算到了目的地再重新兑水。但浓缩后的酒竟意外地受到欢迎。这就是brandy，字面理解为“烧过的酒，蒸馏浓

缩后的酒”，中文翻译为“白兰地”。

breach [briːtʃ] v./n. 违背，破坏，破裂

[例] A trivial misunderstanding caused a breach between them.小小的误会引起了他们之间的不和。

[记] breach of promise 违背诺言

breakthrough ['breik'θruː] n. 突破

[例] Surgeons have made a great breakthrough in kidney transplantation. 外科医生们在肾移植方面取得了重大突破。

breed [briːd] v. [动物] 繁殖；n. 品种

[例] The blackbird, like most birds, breeds in the spring. 画眉同大多数鸟一样在春天繁殖。

bribe [braib] n./v. 贿赂，行贿

[例] The criminal bribed the policeman to let him go free. 罪犯贿赂那个警察让他逃走。

[记] bribery n.贿赂 / bribee 受贿者 / briber 行贿者 / buy off 收买 / [区别] bride n. 新娘

brief [briːf] n. 摘要，大纲；a.简短的

[例] To be brief (with you), we can't accept such harsh terms. 简单地（对你）说，我们不能接受这样苛刻的条件。

[记] in brief / in short 简而言之

brochure [brəu'ʃuə] n. 小册子

[例] I'll send you the company brochure right away. 我会把公司简介即刻给您寄去。

bruise [bruːz] n. 伤痕，擦伤;(水果的) 擦痕

[谚] Who remove stone, bruise their finger. 搬起石头砸自己的脚。

bubble ['bʌbl] n. 泡沫，幻想的计划；v. 起泡，沸腾

[例] The water was bubbling gently in the pan. 水在锅里轻轻地冒着气泡。

[记] blow soap bubbles 吹肥皂泡

bucket ['bʌkit] n. 桶，水桶

[例] One bucket of paint will be enough for the ceiling. 刷天花板一桶油漆足够用了。

[记] drop a bucket into an empty well 空井打水 / a drop in the bucket沧海一粟

budget ['bʌdʒit] n. 预算；v. 做预算

[例] A new car will not be part of our budget this year. 买一辆新车不在我们今年的预算之内。

单词 budget（预算）和 bulge（膨胀，凸出）都源于拉丁语 *bulga*（皮包，钱袋）。古时店主把收到的钱都放在钱袋里。要作预算（budget）了，看看下个月能挣多少钱，就要打开鼓鼓（bulge）的

钱包（*bulga*），数一数，算一算。

bud

[bʌd] n. 芽；苞；蓓蕾

[例] The plant's first buds will open soon. 这植物的第一批蓓蕾即将开放。

[记] in the bud 萌芽状态

bulge

[bʌldʒ] n./v. 膨胀；凸出

[例] The baby boom created a bulge in school enrollment. 生育高峰造成学校入学人数的暴涨。

[区别] bugle n. 号角

bulk

[bʌlk] n. 大量

[例] The bulk of the work has been done. 工作大部份已经完成。

[记] in bulk / unpackaged 散装的

bully

['buli] v. 威吓；以强凌弱；n.欺凌弱小者

[例] He's always bullying smaller boys.他总是欺侮比他小的男孩子。

源自荷兰语boel情人。后来英语里出现该词，意思是“男朋友”。到了17世纪，bully成了someone who controls a prostitute拉皮条的。词义逐渐贬降。

bump

[bʌmp] v. 猛碰，撞；（车辆）颠簸而行

[例] The cart bumped along the rough road. 马车在不平的道路上颠簸前进。

[记] bump into 偶然遇到

bunch

[bʌntʃ] n. 一束（花），一串（钥匙）

[例] I bought a bunch of lilac. 我买了一束紫丁香花。

buoyant

['bɔiənt] a. 有浮力的, 轻快的

[例] She was taking buoyant steps to go to dance. 她迈着轻快的步伐去参加舞会。

bureaucracy

[bjuə'rɔkrəsi] n. 官僚；官僚主义

[例] The government promised to reorganize the bureaucracy. 政府许诺整顿官僚作风。

burgeon

['bɜːdʒ(ə)n] n. 嫩芽；v. 萌芽

[例] This firm aims at the burgeoning market for digital cameras. 这家公司瞄准了新兴的数码相机市场。

[记] a burgeoning city 一个发展中的城市

burrow

['bʌrəu] n./v. 地洞，地道；住处，藏身处；v. 掘地洞，钻进某处

[例] Prairie dogs store food in their burrows. 土拨鼠把食物贮藏在他们的地洞里。

burst

['bə:st] n./v. 爆炸；胀破

[例] The river has burst its banks. 河水冲破了堤。

[记] burst on 突然来到

bushfire

['buʃfiə(r)] n. 林区大火

[例] The friendly fallow deer were trapped by a bushfire. 这些温顺的小鹿被林区大火困住了。

bustle [ˈbʌsl] v. 匆匆忙忙

[例] Mother was bustling about the kitchen. 母亲在厨房里忙来忙去。

> 一对同义词组成押尾韵的词组，如：hustle and bustle 熙熙攘攘；wear and tear 磨损。

buzz [bʌz] n. 嗡嗡声；v. 嗡嗡作响

[例] The crowd buzzed with excitement. 群众很兴奋，喊喊喳喳交头接耳。

bypass [ˈbaipɑːs] n. 旁路；v. 迂回，回避

[例] Let's bypass the town.我们绕过这座小镇子吧!

byproduct [ˈbaiˌprɔdəkt] n. 副产品

[例] Happiness is not a goal; it is a byproduct. 幸福不是一种目标，而是一种副产品。

[记] bypass n. 旁路，小道 / bypath n.小路 / bywork n. 副业，业余活计 / byname n. 绰号

cafeteria [ˌkæfiˈtiəriə] n. 自助食堂，自助餐馆

[例] This cafeteria serves good honest food. 这家自助食堂供应很好的普通饭菜。

> cafe 咖啡馆；Cyber cafe / Internet cafe / Net bar 网吧；snack bar 小吃店、快餐亭；pub 酒馆、酒吧（Public House 的缩写，英联邦国家常见的饮酒场所）。pub 中一般都有两种酒吧间 bar：大酒吧 public bar 和沙龙酒吧 saloon bar。

calamity [kəˈlæmiti] n. 灾难，不幸的事

[例] A hurricane would be a calamity for this low-lying coastal region. 对于这个地势很低的海滨地区，飓风将是一场灾难。

calculate [ˈkælkjuleit] v. 计算；考虑，打算

[例] Our price has already been closely calculated; there is no room for reduction. 我们的价格是经过精密计算的，无让步余地。

calculation [ˌkælkjuˈleiʃ ən] n. 计算，考虑

[例] After much calculation they decided to give him the position of manager.经过深思熟虑之后，他们决定把经理的职位给他。

[记] calculator n.计算器

calculus [ˈkælkjuləs] n. 微积分；【医】结石

[例] Calculus is a difficult course for most of the college students. 微积分对大部分大学生来说都是一门很难的课程。

> 拉丁文，指小圆石。古代商人用小圆石头来计算得失损益，古罗马的算盘也是用calculus作为算珠。calculate“计算”一词即源于此。所以calculus既有“计算→微积分”的含义，又有“小圆

石→结石”的含义。

calendar ['kælində] n. 日历，历法

[例] The Islamic calendar has fewer days than the Gregorian calendar. 伊斯兰日历比公历少几天。

camp [kæmp] n. 露营地；v. 露营，扎营

[例] They camped by a river. 他们在一条河边扎了营。

camp 一词源于拉丁文，相当于 field（旷野，场地）。campaign，campus，decamp（撤营）等词都出自该词源。

campaign [kæm'pein] n. 战役；运动；竞选活动；v. 参加（或发起）运动；参加竞选

[例] Jean is campaigning for equal rights for women. 琼在参加争取妇女平等权利的运动。

camouflage ['kæmuflɑ:ʒ] v./n. 伪装

[例] Many animals have a natural camouflage which hides them from their enemies. 很多动物都有迷惑其敌人的天然伪装。

[记] disguise v./n. 伪装，假装

campus ['kæmpəs] n. （大学）校园

[例] Campus life is to be treasured. （大学）校园生活值得珍惜。

[记] on campus 在校内 / off campus 在校外

can [kæn] v. 装进罐中；罐装；n. 罐头，听装

[例] She was carrying an armful of cat-food cans and talking to herself. 她抱着几听猫食罐头自言自语。

cancel ['kænsəl] v. 取消，删去

[例] She cancelled her order. 她取消了定货。

candidate ['kændidit] n. 候选人；申请求职者；应试者

[例] They are interviewing candidates for the job of sales manager. 他们在面试应聘销售经理的求职者。

字根 cand 指“白”。如：candle 最初指“白色蜡烛”；candid →坦白的。而 candidate 的来历要说到古罗马，当时凡是要参加竞选公职的人要穿白色的长袍，代表无论此人在性格还是名誉上都毫无瑕疵、洁白如玉。

canteen [kæn'ti:n] n. 临时流动餐馆；小卖部；饭盒；（军用）水壶

[例] He lifted a canteen to his lips. 他把水壶举到嘴边。

汉语拼音记忆：can 餐 +teen 厅→ canteen

capable ['keipəbl] a. 有能力的，有才能的，有技能的

[例] I'm perfectly capable of looking after myself, thank you! 我完全有能力照顾自己，谢谢！

[记] be capable of 有…的能力；有…的倾向 / capability n. 能力；容量

capacity [kə'pæsiti] n. 容量，容积；生产量，生产力；能力

[例] The theater was filled to capacity. 戏院内座无虚席。

[记] breathing capacity 肺活量 / work at full capacity 满负荷工作 / capacious a. 容量大的

capital ['kæpitəl] n. 首都，首府，省会；资本，资金；大写字母；a.重要的

[例] Paris is the world's fashion capital. 巴黎是领导全世界时装的都市。

> 来源于拉丁语*caput*，意思是"头"。大写字母，在一词之"头"，因此叫capital。一个国家首都，可以说是一个国家的"头脑所在"，也是capital。capital作"资本"讲，同样源于"头"，与cattle（家畜、牛群）同出一源。在最初的时候，人们的财富资本，是以他家牛的头数来计算的，即有多少"头"。

capsule ['kæpsju:l] n. 胶囊；太空舱

[例] He was advised to take five capsules a day by the doctor. 医生建议他每天吃五颗胶囊。

[记] syrup 糖浆 / cough syrup 咳嗽糖浆 / tablet 药片 / pills 药丸 / capsule 胶囊 / ointment 药膏

captive ['kæptiv] n. 俘虏；a. 被俘的；被迷住的

[例] Armed gunmen broke into the church and took the priest captive. 持枪歹徒闯入了教堂，俘虏了牧师。

[记] captivate v. 迷住，迷惑

capture ['kæptʃə] v. 捕获，夺得；n. 战利品

[例] The criminal was captured when trying to escape from the city. 罪犯在企图逃离这座城市时被捕获。

career [kə'riə] n. 职业，事业；生涯，经历

[例] He realized that his acting career was over. 他意识到自己的演艺事业结束了。

cargo ['kɑ:gəu] n. （车、船、飞机等运输的）货物

[例] We sailed from Perth with a cargo of iron ore. 我们装了一船生铁从珀斯启航。

[同义词] freight / shipment

carnivore ['kɑ:nivɔ:] n. 食肉动物

> carn这个怪怪的字根指"肉"。carnal 肉欲的，好色的；carnalism 寻欢作乐的纵欲主义，是贪图肉体的享受；甚至连carnation 康乃馨，大多也是粉红色，肉色的。字根vore指"吃"。herbivore 草食动物；folivore 食叶动物。至于大家熟悉的carnival 嘉年华、狂欢节，过去是指在天主教为期40天的大斋戒来临前，人们聚在一起狂啃肉的情景。从字面上理解，拉丁文carne vale相当于英语flesh, farewell，相当于中文"别了，肉（所以现在让我赶紧吃几口）"。

carve [kɑːv] v. 雕刻，切开

[例] The talented artist carved an interesting decoration from this piece of tree root. 天才的艺术家把这块树根雕成一件有趣的装饰品。

cashier [kəˈʃiə] n. 出纳员，收支员

[例] A cashier takes and gives out money in a bank or shop. 出纳员在银行或者商店里收付钱款。

[记] cash n.现金

casino [kəˈsiːnəu] n.(=casino）赌场；娱乐场

[例] Doesn't that club have a casino upstairs? 那个俱乐部楼上没有赌场吗？

casualty [ˈkæʒjuəlti] n. 伤亡，伤亡人员

[例] In the Iran-Iraq War, both sides incurred heavy casualties. 在两伊战争中，双方均伤亡惨重。

catalogue [ˈkætəlɔg] v. (=catalog）编目录；登记，记载 n. 目录

[例] Many plants become extinct before they have ever been catalogued. 许多植物还没被归类就已经灭绝了。

catastrophe [kəˈtæstrəfi] n. 灾难，大祸；彻底失败

[例] Their party turned out to be a catastrophe. 他们的晚会结局糟透了。

[同义词] disaster, calamity, misfortune, tragedy

catalyst [ˈkætəlist] n. 催化剂；刺激（或促进）因素

[例] They hope the election will act as a catalyst for reform. 他们希望选举将会促进改革。

[记] catalyse v. 催化，促成

catching [ˈkætʃiŋ] a. 有传染性的；有感染力的，迷人的

[例] Julia's enthusiasm was catching. 朱莉娅的激情是很有魅力的。

[记] catch v. 捕捉；赶上；感染 / catch on 流行 / catch one's breath 喘气，吓一跳

category [ˈkætigəri] n. 种类，类别，范畴

[例] There are different categories of books in a library. 图书馆里有各种不同种类的书籍。

cater [ˈkeitə] v. 供应饮食及服务，提供娱乐节目；迎合

[例] Most perfume ads cater to male fantasies. 大多数香水广告迎合男性的幻想。

[记] cater to / for 供应饮食；迎合

cathedral [kəˈθiːdrəl] n. 大教堂

caution [ˈkɔːʃən] n. 小心，告诫，警告；v. 警告

[谚] In prosperity caution, in adversity patience. 处顺境时要小心，处逆境时要耐心。

[记] for caution's sake 为慎重起见 / with caution 小心翼翼地

cease [siːs] v. 中止，停止，结束

[例] At last they ceased working for lack of capital. 他们终于由于缺乏资金而停工了。

> 辨析 stop / pause / quit / halt / cease / terminate： stop 停止（最常用）；pause 暂停（to stop for a short time）；halt 中断（to cause to stop）；cease （to stop moving or acting），如：Cease fire! 停火！quit 停止，放弃（to stop doing something and leave）；terminate 终止。

celebrate ['selibreit] v. **庆祝（节日、事件等），参加节庆活动**

[例] They celebrated passing their exams with a party. 他们举行了一个晚会庆祝通过考试。

[记] celebration n. 庆祝，庆典 / celebrated a. 著名的

celebrity [si'lebriti] n. **名人；名声**

[例] This is a celebrity fundraising dinner. 这是一次社会名流筹措资金的晚宴。

cellular ['seljulə] a. **细胞的**

[记] cellular tissue 细胞组织 / cellular phone 手机 / cell n. 细胞

census ['sensəs] n. **人口普查（调查）**

[例] In March 2001 the Chinese government announced the results of the fifth census. 2001 年 3 月中国政府公布了第五次人口普查的结果。

ceramic [si'ræmik] a. **陶器的；n. 陶瓷制品**

[例] The ceramic industry dates from ancient times. 陶瓷业可以追溯到古代。

cereal ['siəriəl] n. **谷类食品，谷类**

[例] It is good for the health to eat food prepared from cereals. 吃谷类调制的食物有利于健康。

> 古罗马遭受大旱，教士们求助女巫占卜，占卜的结果是要立一位新的女神 Ceres，向她供奉，这样她就会给大地带来雨水。此后，Ceres 就变成了庄稼的保护神。cereal 是从拉丁语变化而来。意即“of Ceres”属于谷物女神的。cereals 早餐麦片。

ceremony ['seriməni] n. **典礼，仪式；礼节**

[例] What the old headmaster said at the graduation ceremony dwells in my mind. 老校长在毕业典礼上讲的话一直留在我的脑海里。

[记] the opening (closing) ceremony 开幕（闭幕）仪式 / graduation ceremony 毕业典礼

certainty ['sə:tənti] n. **确定，确实的事情**

[谚] Never quit certainty for hope. 把握现实，胜过寄希望于未来。

[记] certain a. 确定的 / for certain adv. 肯定地 / uncertainty n. 不确定，拿不准

certificate [sə'tifikit] n. **证（明）书；执照**

[例] Can you get a college graduation certificate without an examination certificate of the CET Band-4? 没有大学英语四级考试及格证书，你能拿到大学毕业证书吗？

[记] graduation certificate 毕业证书 / a marriage certificate 结婚证 / certification n.证明，合格证

certify ['sə:tifai] v. 证明，保证；授予证书

[例] I certify on my honour that she is innocent. 我用人格担保她是清白无辜的。

[同义词] affirm, confirm, guarantee, testify, vouch

chain [tʃein] n. 链条，链子；一系列的事件；连锁店

[谚] A chain is no stronger than its weakest link. 一环薄弱，全局必垮。

[记] a chain of restaurants 连锁餐馆 / chain reaction 连锁反应 / chain smoker 连续抽烟的人

challenge ['tʃælindʒ] n. 挑战；v. 向…挑战

[例] He challenged me to (play) another tennis game. 他向我挑战要我跟他再打一场网球。

[记] face the challenge 遇到挑战 / accept/take a challenge 应战 / beyond challenge 无与伦比，无可非议 / challenging a.有挑战性的，有吸引力的

chamber ['tʃeimbə] n. （人体内或机器中的）室，腔；议院；

[例] In Britain the upper chamber of parliament is the House of Lords, the lower the House of Commons. 英国的上议院或国会是贵族议院，下议院是众议院。

[记] chamber music 室内音乐

champagne [ʃæm'pein] n. 香槟酒；香槟色

[例]France produces the best champagne in the world. 法国生产世界上最好的香槟酒。

> 地名，法国东北部Champagne香巴尼省。起泡沫的白葡萄酒——香槟酒于1700年首次在这里酿造。

champion ['tʃæmpjən] n. 冠军，第一名；v. 拥护，支持

[例] As defending champion, he is expected to reach the final. 作为卫冕冠军，他预计会进入决赛。

[记] championship n. 冠军（头衔）；锦标赛

chancellor ['tʃɑ:nsələ] n. 长官，大臣

[例] In Britain the Chancellor of the Exchequer deals with taxes and government spending. 英国的财政大臣负责税务和政府的开支。

> cancel（删除）→ chancel（高坛）→ chancellor（长官）。来自同一拉丁词源cancelli，指“一组斜线”即“////”。人们抄写文字出现笔误时在错误处划上几笔斜线表示注销cancel；教堂内供牧师

用的圣坛chancel，通常围有斜条状的木栅栏，与听众席隔开；站在圣坛上的人，高高在上，chancellor。

channel ['tʃænl] n. 海峡；水道，航道

[例] The English Channel is between France and England. 英吉利海峡在英国和法国之间。

chaos ['keiɔs] n. 混乱，紊乱

[例] The desk was a chaos of papers and unopened letters. 桌上杂乱地堆放着一些纸张和未拆的信。

[记] chaotic a. 混乱的 / [同义词] mess, disorder

汉语拼音记忆：chao 吵 +s 死→ chaos 混乱，吵死啦！

chapter ['tʃæptə] n.（书等的）章，回，篇；（人生或历史的）重要时期

[例] Steamboat travel opened a new chapter in America's exploration of the West. 汽船旅行为开发美国西部翻开了新篇章。

character ['kæriktə] n. 性质，特征；人物，角色

[例] The new buildings have changed the character of the village. 新建筑改变了这个村庄的特点。

characteristic [ˌkæriktə'ristik] a. 特有的，典型；n. 特性，特征，特点

[例] A characteristic of the camel is its ability to live for a long time without drinking water. 骆驼的特点是不喝水也能活很长时间。

charcoal ['tʃɑːkəul] n. 木炭

[例] Prepare a fire in a charcoal grill. 给烤架上准备一盆木炭火。

charge [tʃɑːdʒ] v. 收费；控告；n. 费用；掌管；指控；电荷

[例] That seaside hotel charges exorbitant prices during the summer holidays. 那家海滨旅馆在夏天休假期间漫天要价。

[记] in charge of 负责

charity ['tʃæriti] n. 慈善，施舍，慈善团体

[例] The Red Cross is an international charity. 红十字会是个国际性的慈善机构。

[反义词] cruelty ['kruːəlti] n. 残忍，残酷

charm [tʃɑːm] n. 魅力，魔力，迷人之处

[例] She was a woman of great charm and she knew how to use it. 她是个很有魅力的女人，而且她知道如何运用这种魅力。

[记] charming a. 迷人的

chart [tʃɑːt] n. 图表，曲线；v. 制图

[例] He is looking at the chart showing last year's sales targets. 他正在看有关去年销售额的图表。

英语中 c /k/ 和 ch /tʃ/ 发音相互变化是常见现象。同一字根，依发音不同而拼写和意义不同的词，叫 doublet 骈词。如：arc 弧－arch 拱门；card 卡片－chart 航海图；canal 运河－channel 海峡；

cavalry 骑兵队 – chivalry 骑士精神；catch 捕捉 – chase 追求；cord 绳索 – chord 弦；等。这些成对的词来源于同一词根，所以含义有相同之处。

charter ['tʃɑːtə] v. 租，包（船、车等）；n. 宪章

[例] Charter transportation is mainly used for shipping large consignments. 租船运输主要用于运输大宗货物。

[记] a chartered plane 包机 / the charter of the United Nations 联合国宪章

chase [tʃeis] v./n. 追逐，追求

[例] Police chased the speeding car. 警察追赶那辆超速行驶的轿车。

[记] chase after 追赶，追逐 / [同义词] pursue

cheat [tʃiːt] n. 欺骗, 骗子；v. 欺骗

[例] George cheated me but I'll get even with him one day! 乔治欺骗了我，总有一天我要跟他算账。

[记] cheat on 对…不忠 /cheater n. 骗子 /cheating 欺骗的

checklist ['tʃeklist] n. 清单；选举人名单

[例] The guide contains a useful checklist of points to look for when buying a car. 这本指南含有有用的购车目录。

[记] blacklist n. 黑名单

chef [ʃef] n. 厨师

[例] There is only one chef in that grand hotel. 那个大酒店里只有一个厨师。

[记] chief [tFi:f] n. 首领，主要部分；a. 主要的

cherish ['tʃeriʃ] v. 珍爱；怀有（感情），怀抱（希望）

[例] He cherished the memory of his departed youth. 他缅怀他那一去不复返的青春年华。

源自法语。法语中 cher 指 "dear 亲爱的"。如：mon cher 就是 "my dear 我亲爱的"；cher Papa, ch e Maman 就是 "亲爱的爸妈"。你亲爱的人，当然要 cherish（珍爱，爱惜）啦！

chill [tʃil] v. （使）冷却，（使）变冷；使（某人）感到很冷

[例] The bad news cast a chill over the whole family. 这个坏消息使全家人感到沮丧。

[记] chilly a. 寒冷的

cholesterol [kə'lestərəul] n. 胆固醇

[例] Doctor believe that high cholesterol may cause heart disease. 医生认为高胆固醇会导致心脏病。

Unit 5

chop [tʃɔp] v. 切碎（食物）；劈开（木头）

[例] Onions must be chopped up to make a salad. 要做凉拌菜得把洋葱剁碎。

chore [tʃɔː] n.（=chare）家庭杂务；烦琐之事

[例] It's such a chore to do the shopping every day! 每天上街买东西真烦人！

chronic ['krɔnik] a. 慢性的；长期的

[例] He is good at treating chronic diseases. 他擅长医治慢性病患者。

[记] a chronic disease 慢性病 / a chronic war持久战 / chronicle play 历史剧

> 字根 chron 指"时间 time"。来自希腊神话中宙斯（Zeus）他爸的名字：Cronos。该神害怕自己的子女反抗自己，曾吞食了自己的后代，就像时间的无情，吞噬一切。chronic 耗费时间的，慢性的；chronology 年代学，年表。

chronological [ˌkrɔnə'lɔdʒikəl] a. 按年代顺序排列的

[例]We've found it less difficult to learn the chronological table of the Chinese dynasties in chronological order. 我们发现按时间先后顺序来记中国各朝代的年表就不那么难了。

circulate ['səːkjuleit] v.（使）循环；（使）流通；（使）传播

[例]Rumors circulated rapidly. 谣言迅速散布开来。

circulation [ˌsəːkju'leiʃən] n. 流通，循环；传播；（书报杂志的）发行量，销售量

[例] This magazine has a circulation of over 1,000,000. 这份杂志的销售量超过了一百万份。

[记] put in/into circulation 传播，使流通；发行

circumstance ['səːkəmstəns] n. 环境，条件，情况

[谚] Circumstances are the rulers of the weak, and the instruments of the wise. 弱者困于环境，智者利用环境。

[记] under no circumstances = in no circumstances 决不

circus ['səːkəs] n. 马戏团，杂技团；马戏；（英国城镇十字路口的）圆形广场

[例] Last Christmas, the circus owner, Jimmy Gates, decided to take some presents to a children's hospital. 去年圣诞节，马戏团老板吉米·盖茨决定给一家儿童医院送些礼物。

[记] Oxford Circus 牛津广场 / a circus clown 马戏团小丑

> 字根 circ 指"圆环"。如：circle 圆圈；周期；circulate 循环；

circumstance 周围一圈的，周遭的→环境。

cite

[sait] v. 引用，引证

[例] It's no use citing the Bible to a non-Christian. 对非基督徒引用《圣经》是没用的。

[记] citation n. 引用 / [同义词] quote v. 引用 / quotation n. 引用，语录

civil

['sivl] a. 公民的；国内的，民间的；文明的

[例] Until now, *Gone with the Wind*, a film about the American Civil War, has still been regarded as the best Hollywood make. 直到现在，《乱世佳人》（《飘》）这部关于美国内战的影片仍被认为是好莱坞的扛鼎之作。

[记] civil rights 公民权 / civil war 内战

civilisation

[ˌsivilai'zeiʃən] n.(= civilization) 文明；文化；文明社会

[例] It is generally accepted that the Chinese civilization is one of the oldest in the world. 中国文化被普遍认为是世界上最古老的文化之一。

claim

[kleim] n./v. 要求得到；声称，主张

[例] Every citizen may claim the protection of the law. 每一个公民均可要求法律的保护。

[记] make a claim for 对（赔偿等）提出要求

clan

[klæn] n. 宗族，家族，党派

[例] The whole clan will be here over Christmas. 整个家族将在这里过圣诞节。

[记] KKK（三 K 党）：Ku Klux Klan

clarify

['klærifai] v. 澄清，阐明

[例] The government has clarified its position on equal pay for women. 政府阐明了对男女同工同酬的立场。

classic

['klæsik] a. 第一流的；古典的；典型的；n. 经典作品，经典作家

[例] Her daughter particularly likes reading the classics of Chinese literature. 她女儿特别喜欢读中国古典文学名著。

Four classic Chinese novels 中国四大古典名著，它们被西方翻译为：*Journey to the West*；*Outlaws of the Marsh*（沼泽里的逃犯们）；*Three Kingdoms*；*Dream of the Red Mansions*。有老外是如此理解西游记的：一个中国和尚去西方旅游，骑着一匹白色的马，带着一位名叫 Sandy 的仆人。为了打发旅途的寂寞，他还带了一只宠物猴和一头宠物猪上路了…

classify

['klæsifai] v. 分类，分（等）级

[例] In the post office, mail is classified according to the places where it is to go. 在邮局，邮件会根据其目的地进行分类。

[记] classification n. 分类，分级

clause [klɔːz] n. 分句，从句；条款

[例] A confidentiality clause was added to the contract. 合同附加了一条保密性条款。

clay [klei] n. 粘土，泥土

clearance [ˈkliərəns] n. 清理，清除，出空

[例] A clearance is a sale, generally at reduced prices, to dispose of old merchandise. 出清存货就是以低廉价格处理旧货的销售。

[记] clearance sale 清仓大甩卖

cliche [ˈkliːʃei] n. 老生常谈，陈词滥调

[例] This kind of opera has a cliche in it. 这种歌剧有点陈腐老套。

client [ˈklaiənt] n. 顾客，客户；委托人

[例] He proves a successful lawyer with lots of clients. 他是一个拥有很多客户的成功律师。

climate [ˈklaimit] n. 气候；风气，（社会）思潮

[例] The current political climate of our country is favorable for foreign investments. 我国目前的政治气候有利于外国投资。

[记] in the present economic climate 在当前的经济形势下

climax [ˈklaimæks] n. 顶点，（电影戏剧等的）高潮

[例] It's time to bring matters to a climax now. 是把事情推向高潮的时候了。

[记] come to / reach a climax 达到高潮，达到顶点

> climb 向上爬，攀登 max 最大；向上爬到最高点 climax 高潮。

cling [kliŋ] v. 紧紧抱住（抓住）；坚持，忠实于

[例] They clung together when the time came to part. 分离的时候到了，他们紧抱着不肯分开。

[记] cling to 依附，依靠，坚持

clinic [ˈklinik] n. 诊所；门诊部

[例] The psychological clinic is located near the newly-built railway station. 心理诊疗所位于新建的火车站附近。

[记] school clinic 学校医务所

clinical [ˈklinikəl] a. 临床的，病房用的

[例] The drug has undergone a number of clinical trials. 这种药品已经经过多次临床试验。

[记] clinical medicine 临床医学

clone [kləun] v./n. 无性繁殖，克隆

[例] He was opposed to using this unusual animal husbandry technique to clone humans. 他反对利用这种非同一般的畜牧业技术来克隆人类。

clue [kluː] n. 线索，提示

[例] The police found a clue which will help them catch the robber. 警察

发现了能帮助他们抓住强盗的线索。

> 原意为 clew 线团。传说中希腊英雄 Theseus 自告奋勇去克里特岛除妖，牛头怪位于一座迷宫深处。为避免迷路，他在美女的帮助下带了一个线团闯入迷宫，标记走过的道路，最后杀死了牛头怪，并沿着线团原路返回。因此clew 线团就有线索的含义了。

clumsy ['klʌmzi] a. 笨拙的

[例] You are so clumsy! You've knocked over my cup of coffee! 你真笨手笨脚！把我的这杯咖啡撞翻了。

[同义词] awkward, cumbersome

coach [kəutʃ] n. 教练；长途汽车；v. 训练，指导

[例] He is our head football coach. 他是我们的足球主教练。

[区别] couch [kautʃ] n. 沙发，睡椅

> 过去指“四轮马车”，后马车被汽车取代。古代马车是最快的交通工具，能帮助人们快速到达目的地。同样，有了私人教师或教练的辅导，学生则可较快地进步，取得理想的成绩。根据这个比喻联想，coach 延伸出“教练”，“指导”等义。

coarse [kɔːs] a. 粗的，粗糙的

[例] He is an old man with coarse skin. 他是一个皮肤布满皱纹的老人。

[记] coarse language 粗话 / [同义词] crude, rough

coax [kəuks] v. 诱哄

[例] She coaxed the child to take the medicine. 她哄孩子吃药。

coax sb. to do sth. 诱哄某人去干某事 / coax sth. out of sb. 哄骗某人东西

cobra ['kəubrə] n. 眼镜蛇

[例] The cobra is so poisonous that its bite can have deadly consequences. 眼镜蛇毒性很大，被咬伤后有致命的后果。

cockroach ['kɔkrəutʃ] n. 蟑螂

crocodile ['krɔkədail] n. 鳄鱼，鳄鱼皮

[例] The crocodile is a kind of river reptile. 鳄鱼是一种生活在河里的爬行动物。

[记] crocodile tears 鳄鱼眼泪，假慈悲

code [kəud] n. 代码，密码，电码

[例] The letter was written in code and I could not understand it. 信是用密码写的，我看不懂。

> 2003 年美国最受欢迎的小说为 Dan Brown 的 The *Da Vinci Code*《达芬奇密码》，书中有一段趣闻，说蒙娜丽莎是男女和谐的象征，因为埃及传说中代表男性生殖的神叫 Amon，代表女性生殖的神叫 Isis，古代将其读做 L'ISA。两者合起来就是 AMON L'ISA，即 Mona Lisa 蒙娜丽莎。

coed ['kəu'ed] a. (=coeducational) 男女同校的；n. 男女合校大学中的女生

[例] He lived in a coed dorm. 他住在男女同校的学校宿舍里。

coffee ['kɔfi] n. 咖啡

[例] Would you like some coffee? 你要喝一点咖啡吗？

[记] coffee break（上班时间）喝咖啡间休

cognitive ['kɔgnitiv] a. 认知的，认识的

[例] He is learning cognitive psychology. 他正在学习认知心理学。

[记] cognise v. 认知，认识 / recognise v. 识别；承认，认可

> 市场营销学 Marketing 中有一个重要概念：消费者接受一个商品或品牌的过程分为三个阶段：Cognitive Stage 认识感知该商品；Affective Stage 产生好的情感；Behavior Stage 最终购买。

coherence [kəu'hiərəns] n. 黏合性；连贯性；一致性；黏着

[例] An overall theme will help to give your essay coherence. 完整的主题有助于你论文的连贯性。

coherent [kəu'hiərənt] a. 一致的，连贯的，前后一致的

[例] The government lacks a coherent economic policy. 政府缺乏协调一致的经济政策。

cohesive [kəu'hi:siv] a. 粘合的，聚合在一起的，团结的

[例] Historically, sport has been a cohesive force in international relations. 历史上，体育运动在国际关系中一直是一种凝聚力。

[记] cohesive force 凝聚力，内聚力

coincide [ˌkəuin'said] v. 一致，恰巧相合

[例] If our vacations coincided, we go on holiday together. 如果我们假期时间一致，我们可以一起度假。

[记] coincide with 与…相符

coincidence [kəuin'sidəns] n. 巧合；巧合的事；一致；符合

[例] What a coincidence that I was in Paris at the same time as you! 我在巴黎时你也在那里，多凑巧啊！

collaborate [kə'læbəreit] v.协作，合作

[例] I collaborated with him in writing a play. 我与他合写一个剧本。

> 前缀 col- 等于 com-，表示"一起 together"。col+laborate 工作→一起工作→合作；col+lapse 滑落→一起滑落→崩溃。

collapse [kə'læps] n./v. 倒塌，崩溃

[例] He lost all his money in the collapse of the stock market. 股票市场崩溃了，他失去了所有的钱。

colleague ['kɔli:g] n. 同事，同僚

[例] He is getting along well with his colleagues. 他与同事的关系处得

很好。
[同义词] associate, buddy, companion, partner

collect [kə'lekt] v. 收集，搜集，采集
[例] Before you begin to make a speech, you should collect your thoughts and ideas. 在你开始讲话之前，你应当集中你的思想和观点。
[同义词] accumulate, assemble, gather

collective [kə'lektiv] a. 集体的；共同的；n. 集体
[例] Collective effort and cooperation are extremely important in winning a ball game. 要赢得球赛，集体的力量与配合是极其重要的。
[记] collective efforts 共同努力 / collective action 集体行动

collide [kə'laid] v. 碰撞；抵触
[例] In running round the corner, he collided with another man. 在跑过拐角时，他撞上了另一个人。
[记] collide with 与…相撞；冲突

collision [kə'liʒ(ə)n] n. 碰撞；冲突；互撞事件
[例] The rear-end collision was his fault. 这起追尾撞车事件是他的错。

colony ['kɔləni] n. 殖民地；移民群体
[例] It is a former French colony in Africa. 这是法国过去在非洲的一块殖民地。
[记] colonial [kə'ləunjəl] a. 殖民的，殖民地的；n. 殖民地居民

colossal [kə'lɔsl] a. 巨大的，庞大的
[例] There was a colossal explosion nearby. 附近响起一声巨大的爆炸声。

> 源自拉丁文*Colossus*，指世界七大奇迹之一的地中海罗得岛的太阳神巨像。罗得岛人曾把在战争中缴获的兵器熔化，制成一个巨大的青铜太阳神像。据说Colossus高32米，竖立在港口。巨像的两腿跨在海港入口的两边，船只由其胯下通过，宏伟霸气。后巨像在公元前一次地震中倒塌。

combine [kəm'bain] v.（使）联合，（使）结合
[例] The two small shops combined to make a large one. 这两个小店合并起来成为一个大商店。

comedy ['kɔmidi] n. 喜剧，喜剧性的事情
[反义词] tragedy n. 悲剧，惨案

comet ['kɔmit] n. 【天】彗星

> 汉语俗称"扫把星"。可记忆为：come来+tail尾巴→来了一个有尾巴的东西→comet彗星。历史上最著名的彗星当属哈雷彗星Halley's comet，回归周期76年。而最近一次经过我们是在公元1985年。

comic ['kɔmik] a. 有趣的；滑稽的；n. 喜剧演员；连环画

[例] She is one of the most gifted comic actresses on television. 她是电视上最有天赋的喜剧女演员之一。
[反义词] tragic a.悲惨的，悲剧的

comfort ['kʌmfət] n. 安慰，舒适；v. 安慰，慰问
[谚] A father is a treasure; a brother is a comfort; but a friend is both. 父亲是财富，兄弟是安慰，朋友兼而有之。

command [kə'mɑːnd] n./v. 命令；指挥；统率
[例] The army is under the king's command. 军队由国王直接统率。
[记] have a good command of 能自由应用 / commander n.司令官，指挥官

commemorate [kə'meməreit] v. 纪念
[例] This monument commemorates our victory. 这座碑是为纪念我们的胜利而建的。

commence [kə'mens] v. 开始，着手
[例] I commenced a round of visits. 我开始着手一系列访问。
[同义词] begin, start, take off

comment ['kɔment] n./v. 注释, 评论
[例] (I have) no comment. （新闻采访场景）无可奉告。

commentary ['kɔməntəri] n. 评论；批评；评注；实况报导
[例] The conclusion of the commentary really hit the bull's-eye; it was exactly right. 评论最后的结论十分中肯，说得一点不错。
[记] commentary on current affairs 时事评论

commentator ['kɔmenteitə] n. 注释者；时事评论员，实况广播报道员
[例] I enjoy the sports commentator a great deal. 我非常欣赏这位体育评论员。

commerce ['kɔməːs] n. 商业，贸易
[例] Our country has been trying to broaden its commerce with other nations. 我国一直在努力扩大与其他国家的贸易往来。

> 字根merc指“贸易trade”。如：merchant 商人；merchandize 商品；commerce 大家一起做贸易→商业。

commercial [kə'məːʃəl] a. 商业的，贸易的；n.（广播、电视的）广告
[例] The film was a huge commercial success. 这部电影在商业上是一个巨大的成功。

commission [kə'miʃən] n. 佣金，回扣，委托；v. 委托
[例] She gets 10% commission on her sales. 她卖出东西可得 10% 的佣金。

commit [kə'mit] v. 犯（罪），做（坏事）
[谚]He who commits a fault thinks everyone speaks of it. 做贼心虚。
[记] commit an error 做错事 / commit a crime 犯罪 / commit suicide 自杀

commitment [kə'mitmənt] n. 承诺，保证；承担义务

[例] He doesn't want to get married because he is afraid of any commitments. 他不想结婚，因为他害怕承担任何责任。

> 一生中最大的承诺莫过于婚誓 wedding vow。西方教堂婚礼的常见段子："I, Harvey, take you, Echo, to be my wedded wife, to have and to hold, from this day forward, for better, for worse, for richer, for poorer, in sickness and in health, to love and to cherish, till death do us part." 我愿遵上帝圣仪，娶汝为妻。从今起，无论境遇顺遂或乖逆，富贵或赤贫，康泰或罹疾，当与汝长相厮守，相爱相惜，至死不渝。

committee [kə'miti] n. 委员会；全体委员

[例] They have set up a committee to examine the question of park facilities. 他们成立了一个委员会来审查公园设施问题.

[记] committee meeting 委员会会议 /be on the committee 成为委员会委员

commodity [kə'mɔditi] n. 商品，货物

[例] Air conditioners are one of the many commodities that Haier sells abroad. 空调是海尔许多种出口商品中的一种.

commonplace ['kɔmənpleis] a. 平常的，平凡的，不足为奇的；n.平常的事

[例] Car thefts are commonplace in this part of town. 在城镇的这个地段偷车现象很平常。

communicate [kə'mju:nikeit] v. 沟通，通信，传达

[例] We communicated mostly by e-mail. 我们主要通过电子邮件来传递信息。

[记] communication n. 通讯； 交流

community [kə'mju:niti] n. 社区；团体；生物群落

[例] To host the Olympic games, Beijing needs to expand its English speaking community. 为承办奥运，北京需要扩大说英语的社会团体。

[记] community center 社区活动中心

commuter [kə'mju:tə] n. 经常往返者；乘公交车辆上下班者

[例] The train was packed with sweaty complaining commuters. 火车里挤满了浑身大汗不停抱怨的上下班乘客。

[记] commuter time 上下班时间

compact ['kɔmpækt] a. 紧凑的；简洁的；v. 压紧，压实

[例] The dormitory room is very compact.宿舍里安排得很紧凑。

[记] Compact Disc 压缩光盘 CD / Video Compact Disc 视频压缩光盘 VCD

companion [kəm'pænjən] n. 同伴；同行者

[例] His brother is not much of a companion for him. 他兄弟与他情趣

不甚相投。
[记] companion in adversity 患难之交

comparable ['kɔmpərəbl] a. 可比较的，比得上的
[例] A comparable car would cost far more in Europe. 像这样好的一辆汽车在欧洲可要贵得多。
[记] comparable with 可相比 / comparable to 比得上 / incomparable a. 无与伦比的，不能比较的

compare [kəm'pεə] v. 把…比作
[例] A teacher's work is often compared to a candle. 教师的工作常被比作蜡烛。
[记] compare to 把...比作；比喻 /compare with 与…比较；比得上

comparison [kəm'pærisn] n. 比较，对照；相似
[例] My shoes are small in comparison with my sister's. 我的鞋子比我妹妹的要小。
[记] in comparison with 和...比较起来 / by comparison 比较起来

compatible [kəm'pætəbl] a. 谐调的，一致的，兼容的
[例] The new software is IBM compatible. 新的软件和IBM电脑兼容。
[记] be compatible with 与...相适应，一致 / incompatible a. 不相容的

> 字根 pati 指“忍受 suffer”。patient 忍受（痛苦）的人→病人，耐心的；impatient 无法忍受的→不耐烦的，不耐心的；compatible 能一起容忍容纳的→兼容的。

compel [kəm'pel] v. 强迫，迫使
[例] A body at rest will never move unless a force compels it. 一个静止的物体永远不会运动，除非有一个力强迫它。
[记] compel sb. to do sth. 强迫某人做某事

compelling [kəm'peliŋ] a. 强制的，强迫的；引人注目的
[例] There still exist a host of compelling socioeconomic problems. 仍然存在着许多令人不得不接受的社会经济问题。

compensate ['kɔmpənseit] v. 补偿，赔偿，弥补
[例] Nothing can compensate for the loss of time. 虚度光阴是无法补偿的。
[记] compensate sb. for sth. 为…向某人赔偿 / make up for 补偿

compensation [kɔmpen'seiʃ(ə)n] n. 补偿，赔偿；补偿物，赔偿费
[例] This is the loss compensation for the victims of the air crash. 这是空难受害者的损失补偿。

competent ['kɔmpitənt] a. 有能力的，能胜任的
[例] He is the only party leader competent enough to govern this country. 他是唯一位有足够能力治理这个国家的政党领导人。
[同义词] able, capable, qualified

competence ['kɔmpətəns] n. 能力；胜任；（法院）权限，权能

[例] Doctors have to constantly update their knowledge in order to maintain their professional competence. 医生得不断地更新知识以保持自己的专业能力。

competition [ˌkɔmpiˈtiʃən] n. 竞争，比赛，竞赛

[例] Because there is so much unemployment, the competition for jobs is very fierce. 由于失业（人数）众多，求职的竞争十分激烈。

[记] compete [kəmˈpiːt] v. 竞争 / competitor [kəmˈpetitə] n. 竞争者，对手

compile [kəmˈpail] v. 汇编，编辑

[例] Harvey is compiling an English dictionary for students. 哈维正在编一本供学生使用的英语词典。

com 一起 +pile 堆→汇集在一起，汇编。

complacency [kəmˈpleisənsi] n.满足，安心；n. 自满；满足；安心

[例] Complacency is a drawback to progress. 自满是进步的障碍。

[记] complacent a. 自满的；自鸣得意的 / [同义词] self-satisfied

complement [ˈkɔmplimənt] n. 补充，补足物；v. 补充，补足

[例] Love is the complement of the law. 爱的精神是法律的补充物。

[记] complementary a. 补充的，补足的

complex [ˈkɔmpleks] a. 复杂的，综合的；n. 综合体，综合性建筑

[例] The new sports complex has everything needed for many different activities. 新建的综合体育馆能为多种活动提供所需要的设施。

[记] complexity n.复杂性

Oedipus Complex 俄狄浦斯情结，也叫恋母情节。Oedipus 是希腊神话中的一个王子，成人后杀了他的父亲而娶了自己的母亲。弗洛伊德在《梦的解析》*The Interpretation of Dreams* 中提出小男孩潜意识上对父亲有敌意，与父亲一起争夺母爱。

compliance [kəmˈplaiəns] n. 依从，顺从

[例] Compliance with the law is expected in the state. 该州要求人人守法。

[记] compliant a. 顺从的

complicated [ˈkɔmplikeitid] a. 复杂的，难解的

[例] The situation was complicated. 形势非常复杂。

[记] complication n. 复杂，纷乱 / [同义词] complex

compliment [ˈkɔmplimənt] n./v. 赞美，恭维

[例] They paid him a great compliment. 他们非常恭维他。

[记] give my compliments to sb. 请向…致意 / compliment sb. on 夸奖某人的…

comply [kəmˈplai] v. 照做；遵守；依从；应允

[例]The patient complied with the physician ' s orders. 病人遵从医生的

嘱咐。

[记] comply with 遵守，服从

component [kəm'pəunənt] n. 成分，组成部分

[例] Exercise is one of the key components of a healthy lifestyle. 运动是健康生活方式的重要组成部分之一。

[同义词] element

compose [kəm'pəuz] v. 组成，构成；创作，为…谱曲

[例] Water is composed of hydrogen and oxygen. 水是由氢和氧组成的。

[记] be composed of 由…组成 / composer n.作曲家

> 字根 pos 指"放置"。如：pose 放置的状态→姿势；compose 放在一起→作曲，写作，组成；composition 作文；composer 放在一起的人→作曲家； composite 合成物；decompose 分解。

compound ['kɔmpaund] n. 混合物，化合物；v. 混合

[例] We have compounded a new plan from parts of several former plans. 我们把从前几个计划中的一些部分混合起来，组成了一个新的计划。

comprehensive [ˌkɔmpri'hensiv] a. 全面的，内容广泛的；能充分理解的

[例] The state government gave a very comprehensive explanation of its plans for the development of electronic industry. 州政府对电子工业发展的规划作了详尽的解释。

[记] a comprehensive knowledge 渊博的知识 / a comprehensive mind 宽大的心胸 / comprehend v. 领会，理解；包含 / comprehension n. 理解，领悟

Unit 6

comprise [kəm'praiz] v. 包含, 由…组成包含，包括，构成
[例] The United Kingdom actually comprises (= is actually comprised of) England, Wales, Scotland and Northern Ireland. 英国实际上是由英格兰、威尔士、苏格兰和北爱尔兰构成。
[同义词] consist of, contain, include, involve

compromise ['kɔmprəmaiz] n./v. 妥协，折中
[例] We can not compromise on such terms. 我们不能根据这样的条件和解。
[记] compromise with sb. on sth. 在某方面同某人妥协 / I would rather die than compromise. 我宁死不妥协。

compulsory [kəm'pʌlsəri] a. 必须做的, 义务的, 强制的
[例] Which subjects are compulsory in your school? 在你们学校里哪些课程是必修的?
[记] compulsory education 义务教育 / compulsion n.强迫，强制 / [同义词] compelled, necessary, required

compute [kəm'pju:t] v. 计算，估计
[例] I compute my loss at 500 dollars. 我估计我的损失有 500 美元.
[记] beyond compute 不可计算，无法估计 / computer n. 计算机 / [同义词] calculate, count, estimate

concave ['kɔn'keiv] a. 凹的；n. 凹面
[例] I made a concave mirror all by myself. 我亲手做了一个凹面镜.

> 字根 cav 指“中空的 hollow”。如：cave 洞穴；excavate 向外挖空，挖掘；excavator 挖土机；concave 凹的。反义词：convex 凸的。

conceal [kən'si:l] v. 隐藏，隐瞒
[例] He concealed the sweets in his pocket. 他把糖果藏在口袋里。
[记] conceal sth. from sb. 对某人隐瞒某事 / [同义词] camouflage, cover, hide, veil

concede [kən'si:d] v. （勉强）承认；让与，容许；放弃
[例]After the First World War, Germany conceded much valuable land to its neighbours. 第一次世界大战后，德国让与邻国许多宝贵的土地。
[记] concede to sb. 对某人让步

conceit [kən'si:t] n. 自负；骄傲自大
[例] No one admires a man who is full of conceit. 没有人喜欢一个十分自负的人。

conceivable [kən'si:vəbl] a. 可想象的，可想到的，可能的

[例] We tried it in every conceivable combination. 我们把能想到的各种组合都试了一遍。

conceive [kən'siːv] v. 构想出，设想；怀孕

[例] A century ago it was difficult to conceive of travelling to the moon. 半个世纪前去月球旅行是难以想象的。

concentrate ['kɔnsentreit] v. 集中，浓缩

[例] I can't concentrate on my work when I am tired. 我累了就无法集中精力工作。

[记] concentrate on (doing) sth. 全神贯注做某事 / concentration n. 专心，集中，浓缩

concept ['kɔnsept] n. 概念，观念

[例] I understand some of the concepts of the theory but I'm not sure about its details. 我懂得这个理论的一些概念，但对详细内容可不大清楚。

conception [kən'sepʃ(ə)n] n. 构思，构想；概念，观念；怀孕

[例]Strangely enough, the conception of the book took five minutes, but writing it took a whole year. 说来也怪，构思这本书只用了五分钟，但写这本书却花去了整整一年的时间。

concern [kən'səːn] n. 关心，关注；v. 涉及，关心

[例] As far as I am concerned, I'm not against your plan. 就我而言，我并不反对你的计划。

[记] be concerned about 关心 / everyday concerns 日常事务

concert ['kɔnsət] n. 音乐会；一致

[例] Various performers will present a concert of Broadway music to benefit AIDS charities. 各种艺术表演者将会出席百老汇音乐会为爱滋病捐款。

[记] in concert with 和…相呼应（合作）

> *musicale / concert* 音乐会; *concertmaster* 首席小提琴手; concertgoer 常参加音乐会者；concerto 协奏曲；conductor 乐队指挥；melody 旋律；rhythm 节奏；lyrics 歌词；score 乐谱。

concise [kən'sais] a. 简洁的，简明的

[例] Make your answers clear and concise. 回答要清楚简明。

[反义词] redundant

conclusion [kən'kluːʒən] n. 结论，结尾，结束

[例] I found the conclusion of her story very exciting. 我觉得她那故事的结尾很激动人心。

[记] in conclusion 最后，总之 / conclude v. 结束，终止

concrete ['kɔnkriːt] a. 具体的；n. 混凝土

[例] Have you any concrete suggestions on how to deal with these difficulties? 对怎样解决这些困难，你有没有什么具体建议？

[反义词] abstract

concurrent [kən'kʌrənt] a. 同时发生的，并存的

[例] The exhibition reflected concurrent developments abroad. 展览回顾了同期国外的发展情况。

condemn [kən'dem] v. 判刑；声讨，谴责

[例] Most people are willing to condemn violence of any sort as evil. 大多数人都愿意把任何暴力行为视作恶行加以谴责。

condense [kən'dens] v.（使）浓缩，精简；（气体）凝结，冷凝

[例] A long story may be condensed into a few sentences. 一个长篇故事可缩写成几句话。

condolence [kən'dəuləns] n. 吊唁，哀悼，慰问

[例] On behalf of my family I would like to express our condolences to you for the tragedy that struck yesterday. 我代表我的家庭对昨日发生的悲剧向您表示慰问。

condom ['kɔndəm] n. 避孕套

> 在十七世纪英国控制印度的时期，一位叫Condom的上校用印度产的胶皮发明了预防性病用的套子，得名condom。French letter也指这种东西，French法国和爱神很有渊源，如：French kiss就不是普通那种只碰一下嘴唇的高雅行为，而是使舌尖纠缠在一起的deep kiss；French postcard很可能不是指法国风景明信片，而指“春宫图”。

conducive [kən'dju:siv] a. 有益的，有助的

[例] Fresh air is conducive to health. 新鲜空气有助于健康。

conduct ['kɔndʌkt] n. 举止，行为，品行；v. 处理，经营，实施

[例] His conduct doesn't match up with with his words. 他言行不一。

[记] conductive a.有传导性的；能导（热、电）的 / conductive body 导体

cone [kəun] n. 圆锥体；锥形物

> 最常见的圆锥体是我们在吃冰激凌时蛋卷做成的cone，用来盛冰激凌球。ice cream cone 蛋卷冰激凌，圆筒冰激凌。

confer [kən'fə:] v. 商谈，商议；授予，赋予

[例] The engineers and technicians are still conferring on the unexpected accident. 工程师和技术员们还在讨论此次意外事故。

[记] confer an honorary degree on sb. 授予某人荣誉学位 / confer with sb. 与某人协商

conference ['kɔnfərəns] n. 会议，讨论会

[例] The UN Human Rights Conference should be a place where the common problems of mankind are discussed and the cause of human rights is advanced. 联合国人权会议是一个讨论人类共同面临的问题、

促进人权发展的场所。

confess [kən'fes] v. 供认，坦白；忏悔

[例] The suspect confessed to the crime. 嫌疑犯供认了罪行。

[记] confession n. 招供，认错，交待

confidence ['kɔnfidəns] n. 信心

[例] We have full confidence that we shall succeed. 我们完全有信心取得成功。

[记] confidant 男知己 / confidante 红颜知己

> 字根fid指“信任trust”。翻译界有一个著名的比喻，法语为Belles infideles。Belle指美女（名牌女鞋百丽）；infideles中的fid就是信任，前面的in表否定，infideles即为不值得信任，不忠诚。说翻译作品就是美丽而不忠实的女人：如果她美丽，她就不忠实；如果她忠实，那她就不美丽。

confident ['kɔnfidənt] a. 确信的；自信的

[例] Peter is confident of winning the post of assistant to the managing director. 彼得确信他能获得总经理助理的职位。

confidential [kɔnfi'denʃəl] a. 机密的

[例] Doctors are required to keep patients' records completely confidential. 医生被要求对病人的病历记录绝对保密。

[同义词] secret

configuration [kən,figju'reiʃən] n. 构造，结构，配置

[例] She is into the spatial configuration. 她对立体构型感兴趣。

[记] configure v. 配置

confine [kən'fain] n. 边界，界限，范围；v. 限制，局限

[例] This is outside the confines of human knowledge. 这超出了人类的知识范畴。

[记] be confined to 局限于 / within the confines of 在…（范围）之内

> 字根fin指“结束end”。如果你超速驾车或在禁烟区吸烟，交了fine，就一切结束。final 决赛；finish 结束；confine 共同结束的地方→边界；define 定下界限→下定义；refine 再次完成、再次结束→精炼。

confirm [kən'fəːm] v. 确认，确定，进一步证实

[例] We had better confirm our hotel reservation by telephone. 我们最好打电话确认一下我们预定的旅馆房间。

conflict ['kɔnflikt] n. 斗争，冲突；v. 冲突

[例] Many people feel that religion conflicts with science. 很多人认为宗教与科学相矛盾。

[记] conflict of interest 利益冲突 / armed conflict 武装冲突

conform [kən'fɔːm] v.（使）一致，（使）遵守，（使）顺从

[例] A coat must conform to the figure of the wearer. 衣服必须与穿者的身材相配。

[记] conform to/with 遵守，符合

confront [kən'frʌnt] v. 迎面遇到；（勇敢的）面对，正视

[例] A soldier has to confront danger and death. 军人必须勇敢冷静地面对危险和死亡。

[记] be confronted with 面临，面对

> front 指“正面”。如：frontier 边疆，边境；confront 一起面对；affront 使面对面→公开侮辱，冒犯。

confuse [kən'fju:z] v. 使困惑；把（某人）弄糊涂；混淆

[例] Don't confuse Austria with Australia. 不要把奥地利与澳大利亚弄混淆了。

[记] confuse A with/and B 混淆 A 和 B

congested [kən'dʒestid] a. 拥挤的

[例] He is late for the meeting because of the congested traffic. 因为交通阻塞所以这次会议他迟到了。

congratulate [kən'grætju:leit] v. 祝贺，向…道喜

[例] We must congratulate you on your engagement. 我们一定要庆贺你订婚。

[记] Congratulations! 恭喜！恭喜！

congress ['kɔŋgres] n. 代表大会；国会，议会

[例] The appointment was confirmed by Congress. 那项任命在会议上获得确认。

> Con-gress 表示“一起＋行走”，一群人走到一起去开会、去吵架，这样构成了国会。progress 表示“往前＋走”→进步。还有几个典型的表示国会的单词，Parliament（英国等国），Knesset（以色列等），Diet（日本、瑞士等）。

connect [kə'nekt] v. 连接，联合；接通电话

[例] Has the phone been connected yet? 电话接通了吗？

[记] connect to/with 连接；结合

conquer ['kɔŋkə] v. 征服，战胜

[谚] To conquer or to die. 不成功便成仁。

> 公元前47年，恺撒大帝Caesar率军进入小亚细亚，只用了5天的时间，就平定了庞培部下的叛乱。胜利后的Caesar将所有的喜悦和骄傲都浓缩在三个拉丁词里：Veni, Vedi, Vici 意为：I came, I saw, I conquered. 到，见，胜。这就是历史上著名的“三V文书”。

conscience ['kɔnʃəns] n. 良心，道德心

[例] His conscience troubled him after he took the money. 他拿走钱以

后，良心使他不安。

[记] conscienceless a. 没良心的

conscious ['kɔŋʃəs] a. 有意识的，有知觉的，故意的

[例] The greatest of faults is to be conscious of none. 最大的错误就是没有意识到错误。

[记] be conscious of 意识到 / consciousness n.意识，知觉，自觉

consecutive [kən'sekjutiv] a. 连续的，连贯的

[例] The numbers 4, 5, 6 are consecutive. 数字四、五、六是一组连续数字。

[记] two consecutive weeks 连续两周

consensus [kən'sensəs] n. 一致意见，舆论

[例] Could we reach a consensus on this matter? Let's take a vote. 我们能在该问题上达成一致吗？让我们来表决。

consent [kən'sent] n./v. 同意，准许，赞同

[例] I had to get my mother's consent before I went. 我走之前须征得母亲同意。

consequence ['kɔnsikwəns] n. 后果

[例] Your behavior is of no great consequence. 你的行为没有造成严重的后果。

[记] in consequence 因此，结果 / consequent a. 作为结果的，跟着发生的

conservative [kən'sə:vətiv] a. 保守的，守旧的；n. 保守党，保守者

[例] The researchers made a conservative guess at the population of Tokyo. 研究人员对东京的人口作了一项保守的估计。

[记] conservative 保守的 / moderate 温和的 / radical 激进的

> conservative，英国两大执政党之一保守党即为Conservative Party；很多人用conservative和reticent两个词语来形容英国人的个性。reticent表示其很矜持，轻易不开口讲话。不像很多北美人给人留下的印象IBM – International Big Mouth，从早到晚都在blah。

considerable [kən'sidərəbl] a. 相当大的，相当多的，可观的

[例] The TV play received considerable acclaim. 这部电视剧获得了很高的评价。

consist [kən'sist] v. 由…组成；在于；一致

[例] The beauty of the plan consists in its simplicity. 这个计划妙就妙在简明扼要。

[记] consist of 由…组成 / consist in 存在于 / consist with 与…一致

consistent [kən'sistənt] a. 一致的，符合的，坚持的

[例] What you say is not consistent with what you do. 你言行不一。

consortium [kən'sɔ:tjəm] n. 社团，协会，联盟，（国际）财团

[例] Several big companies have formed a consortium. 几个大公司组成

了一个国际财团。

conspiracy [kən'spirəsi] n. 共谋，阴谋

[例] The conspiracy of the assassination of the president was brought to light in time. 一个刺杀总统的阴谋被及时揭露了。

constant ['kɔnstənt] a. 不变的；持续的；坚决的；n. 常数；衡量

[例] He has become a constant customer of the bookshop. 他成了书店的常客。

[反义词] inconstant a. 变化无常的

constellation [kɔnstə'leiʃən] n. 星座；星群荟萃

[例] A constellation of famous artists attended the party tonight. 一群著名的艺术家出席了今晚的晚会。

> con一起+stell星星→很多星星在一起→constellation星座、星群。stellar a.星星的；zodiac 黄道十二宫。

constitute ['kɔnstitju:t] v. 组成，构成；建立，设立

[例] The federation was constituted in 2004. 这一联盟建立于2004年。

[记] constitution n. 宪法；构造；设立

constrain [kən'strein] v. 克制，抑制

[例] Cold weather constrained the plant's growth. 寒冷的天气抑制了植物的生长。

construct [kən'strʌkt] v. 建造，构造；创立

[例] It is a complex process to construct a bridge. 建桥是一个非常复杂的过程。

[记] construction n. 建筑物 / constructive a. 建设性的

consult [kən'sʌlt] v. 向（专业人士）咨询，请教；参考

[例] I need to consult my lawyer. 我需要咨询我的律师。

[记] consult sb. about sth. /consult with sb. 与某人协商，商量

consultant [kən'sʌltənt] n. 顾问，咨询者；会诊医生

[例] The consultant committee met at the call of the chairman. 顾问委员会应主席的召集而开会。

consume [kən'sju:m] v. 消耗，花费

[例] His old car consumed much gasoline. 他的旧汽车耗油很多。

[记] consumer n. 消费者，顾客，用户 / consumption n. 消耗量，消费量；消耗

contact ['kɔntækt] n./v. 接触，联系

[例] This remote tribe had little contact with the outside world. 这个边远的部落和外界几乎没有什么联系。

[记] be in contact with 和…接触，有联系 / lose contact with 和…失去联系

contain [kən'tein] v. 包含，容纳，容忍

[例] The speech contained some interesting ideas. 这个讲演包括一些有

趣的思想。

contaminant [kən'tæminənt] n. 污染物

[例] We need to warn them of aerial contaminants. 我们有必要提醒他们防止空气污染物。

contaminate [kən'tæmineit] v. 污染

[例] The river was contaminated with waste. 这河水被垃圾污染了。

[记] contamination n. 污染 / air contamination 空气污染 / chemical contamination 化学污染 / [同义词] pollute

contemplate ['kɔntempleit] v. 注视；沉思；期望

[例] The young surgeon contemplated the difficult kidney transplant. 年轻的外科医生为肾移植这一棘手的手术苦思冥想。

contemporary [kən'tempərəri] n. 同代人，当代人；a. 同时代的

[例] He and I were contemporaries at school. 他和我是同期同学。

> 字根 tempor 指"时间 time"。如：tempo 音乐速度、拍子（音符延长的时间）；temporise（为争取时间）应付，拖延；又可指见风驶舵，顺应时势；con 一起 +tempor 时间 +ary 名词词尾→contemporary 同时代的人。

contempt [kən'tempt] n. 轻视；藐视

[例] A liar is held in contempt. 说谎者为人轻视。

[记] in contempt of 不顾，不把…放在眼里；藐视

contend [kən'tend] v. 斗争，竞争，主张

[例] The man contended that it was not his fault. 那人争辩说这不是他的过错。

[记] It is contended that... 人们坚持认为… / contend for 争取

content ['kɔntent] n. 内容，容纳的东西；[kən'tent] a. 满足的，满意的；v. 使满足

[例] We should never content ourselves with a little book knowledge only. 我们切不可满足于仅有的一点点书本知识。

[区别] consent n./v. 同意，赞成

contention [kən'tenʃən] n. 争论，争辩，论点

[例] My contention is that the scheme will never work. 我认为这个方案行不通。

contest ['kɔntest] v. 竞争，比赛；争论；n. 竞争

[例] If the election is one-sided, it is really no contest. 如果选举呈一边倒的局面，那么实际上毫无竞争可言。

[记] contest with 与…争论 / contestant n. 参加比赛的人，争论者

context ['kɔntekst] n. 上下文，语境；前后关系，来龙去脉

[例] We should judge the past in its historic context. 我们应当根据时代背景来看待过去。

continental [ˌkɔnti'nentl] a. 大陆的，大陆性的

[例] The cafe serves continental style cuisine.这家咖啡馆供应欧陆式菜肴。

> 当 Continental 首字母大写时，通常指“欧洲大陆的”。Continental breakfast 欧陆式早餐：面包、咖啡或红茶为主。而 English breakfast 英式早餐以谷类食物 cereal、熏肉 bacon 为主。

contingency [kən'tindʒənsi] n. 偶然，可能性；意外事故
[例] We must always be prepared for every contingency. 我们必须始终做好各种应急准备。

continuous [kən'tinjuəs] a. 连续的，持续的
[例] The brain needs a continuous supply of blood. 大脑需要连续供血。
[记] continuously adv. 不断地，连续地

contract ['kɔntrækt] n. 合同，契约；[kən'trækt] v. 收缩；感染（疾病）
[例] Metal contracts as it cools. 金属随着冷却体积缩小。
[记] sign a contract 签订合同

contradict [kɔntrə'dikt] v. 反驳；同…矛盾
[例] Your actions contradict your principles. 你的行为与你的道义相矛盾。
[记] contradiction n. 反驳，矛盾 / in contradiction to 反之，与…相反

contrary ['kɔntrəri] n. 相反（事物）；a. 相反的
[例] He passed the examination, contrary to what I hed expected. 他考试及格了，和我预料的情况相反。
[记] on the contrary 相反

contrast ['kɔntræst] n. 对比，对照；[kən'træst] v. 使与…对比，和…成对照
[例] Her out-going character is in sharp contrast with her sister's shyness. 她外向的性格和她的妹妹害羞的性格形成鲜明对比。
[记] by/in contrast 对比之下

contribute [kən'tribju:t] v. 捐献，贡献，投稿
[例] She seldom contributes to the discussion. 她在讨论中很少发言。
[记] contribute to 捐献

contribution [ˌkɔntri'bju:ʃən] n. 捐献，贡献；投稿
[例] He is suspected of appropriating the contributions to the relief fund. 他有挪用救济基金捐款的嫌疑。

controversy ['kɔntrəvə:si] n. 争议，争论，辩论
[例] The new traffic regulations caused much controversy among drivers. 新的交通规则在司机中引起了很大争议。
[记] controversial a. 有争议的

convenience [kən'vi:njəns] n. 方便，便利；便利设施
[例] Please come at your convenience. 请在你方便的时候前来。

[记] convenient a. 方便的，适宜的 / inconvenient a. 不便的

> 国外常见的 24/7 convenience store，指 24 hours a day, 7 days a week，随时营业的便利店。

conventional [kən'venʃənl] a. 惯例的，常规的；符合传统的
[例] The chairman made a few conventional remarks. 主席说了几句客套话。
[记] convention n. 大会；习俗，惯例

converse ['kɔnvə:s] a. 相反的，逆的，颠倒的；v. 交谈，谈话
[例] I hold the converse opinion. 我持反对意见。
[记] conversation n. 谈话，交谈 / [区别] conservation n. 保守

convert ['kɔnvə:t] v. 使转变，使…改变信仰（态度、观点等）；n. 皈依者
[例] Coal can be converted to gas. 煤可以转化为煤气。
[记] convert defeat into victory 转败为胜

convict ['kɔnvikt] v. 证明…有罪，宣告...有罪；n. 罪犯
[例] He was convicted of murder. 他被判犯有谋杀罪。

> 字根 vict/vinc 指"征服 conquer"。如：victor 胜利者；victory 胜利；convict 一起征服→宣告有罪。我们一起去征服别人之前，应该先宣告对方有罪。就像美国攻打伊拉克之前一样。convince 完全地征服了对方，引申为"说服，使信服"。

convey [kən'vei] v. 运送，输送；表达，传递
[例] I can't convey my feelings in words. 我的情感难以言表。

convince [kən'vins] v. 使确信，使信服，说服
[例] He finally convinced us of his innocence. 他终于使我们相信他是清白的。
[记] convince sb. of sth. 使某人相信某事 / convincing a. 令人信服的

cooperate [kəu'ɔpəreit] v. 合作，协作，配合
[例] Leopards cooperate with each other in hunting game. 美洲豹在猎食时相互协作。
[记] cooperation n. 合作，协作 / [同义词] collaborate

coordinate [kəu'ɔ:dinit] v. 调整，协调
[例] Our efforts need to be further coordinated for higher efficiency. 为了获得更高的效率我们的工作需要进一步协调。
[记] coordinates n. 坐标 / coordinator n. 协调人；调度员

cope [kəup] v. 应付，处理
[例] I'm afraid I can't cope with those troubles. 恐怕我应付不了这些麻烦。
[记] cope with 应付，对付

copyright ['kɔpirait] n. 版权
[例] He retained the copyright of his book. 他保留此书的著作权。

cord [kɔːd] n. 绳索, 弦
[例] Our voices depend on the vocal cords. 我们的声音取决于声带。

> 字根 cord 指"心"。它的变体为 chord 琴弦，和音，情绪。strike a chord / touch the right chord 就是"打动对方心弦"的意思。cordial 强心剂，兴奋剂；discord 不一致；concord / accord 心在一起→和谐，一致。本田雅阁 Accord。

core [kɔː] n. 中心，核心；果核
[例] He is the core of the working staff. 他是这个工作小组的核心。

corporate [ˈkɔːpərit] a. 团体的；公司的；共同的
[例] Corporate executives usually have high salaries. 公司管理人员一般享有高薪。

corporation [ˌkɔːpəˈreiʃən] n. 大型公司；大企业；企业集团
[例] John works for a large American chemical corporation. 约翰为一家美国大的化学公司工作。
[区别] cooperation [kəuˌɔpəˈreiʃən] n. 合作，协作

corpus [ˈkɔːpəs] n. 尸体；文集；本金
[例] He asked his children to have his corpus burnt after his death. 他叫后人在他死后把他的尸体火化。
[同义词] corpse

> 字根 corp 指"身体"，与 cord 相对。corps 很多身体→军队，团体；古人认为人由 cord 和 corp 组成。灵魂（心）驻在心脏。没有 cord 的身体是 corpse/corpus，从而产生"尸体"之意。corpus 一词"文集、本金"之意就是 a collection or body of knowledge or money 知识体，资金体。而公司 corporation 其字面意思为"无心的组织"，可见公司建立自己的企业文化是多么重要。

Unit 7

correspond [ˌkɔriˈspɔnd] v. （to, with）相符合，成一致；（with）通信
[例] These goods don't correspond with my order. 这些货物与我的订货单不符。
[记] correspond with sb. 与某人通信

corridor [ˈkɔridɔː] n. 走廊
[例] Go down the corridor, to the second room on the right. 沿着走廊，右边第二个房间。

corrupt [kəˈrʌpt] a. 腐败的，贪污的；v. 腐烂，堕落
[例] Excessive campaign spending is corrupting the American political system. 过多的竞选花销正在使美国的政治体制堕落。

cosmetic [kɔzˈmetik] n. 化妆品；a. 化妆用的；美容的
[例] Are you on the diet for health or cosmetic reasons? 你节食是由于健康还是美容的原因呢？
[记] cosmetic surgery 美容手术 / cosmetics box 化妆盒

cosmopolitan [ˌkɔzməˈpɔlitən] a. 来自世界各地的，国际的
[例] London is a very cosmopolitan city. 伦敦完全是个国际大都市。
[记] metropolitan a. 大城市的，大都会的

costume [ˈkɔstjuːm] n. 服装；化装服，戏服
[例] Her national costume showed which country she came from. 她的民族服装显示了她来自于哪个国家。
[记] academic costume 学位服 / costume ball 化装舞会

> 当下流行的Cosplay，即Costume Play，翻译为“角色扮演”、“服饰装扮”或“白日梦服饰”。主要指动漫爱好者将自己装扮成所喜爱的动漫及游戏角色的表演活动。如果你小时候曾经拿条毛巾当披风，用鸡毛掸子作宝剑扮过大侠的话，这个单词的含义就能完全理解了。

cottage [ˈkɔtidʒ] n. 村舍，小别墅
[例] He lives in a thatched cottage which far away from the town. 他住在离镇子很远的小村舍里.

counsellor [ˈkaunsələ] n.（=counselor）顾问；律师；辅导员
[例] I'd like to talk to my counsellor before I answer any of your questions. 在见到我的律师之前,我不会回答你提出的任何问题。

counter [ˈkauntə] adv./prep. 相反地；n. 柜台；工作台；v.还击
[例] He countered my proposal with one of his own. 他以他自己的一个建议来反对我的建议。

> 很多人喜欢玩名为CS的游戏，Counter Strike! 中文将这个游戏的名字翻译为“反恐精英”，这样就容易理解它作为前缀counter-表示的含义：“相反、相对”，CS基本含义指的是“有人打了我，我就回手反击”。counter+feit 做，反着做→伪造。

counterfeit ['kauntəfit] n. 赝品，伪造品；a. 伪造的；v. 伪造，假冒
[例] This gold necklace is a counterfeit. 这条金项链是假的。
[记] counterfeit currency/money 假钞 / [同义词] fake

counterpart ['kauntəpaːt] n. 互为补充的人（或物）；对应的人（或物）
[例] The Prime Minister is to meet his European counterparts to discuss the war against drugs. 首相将会见其他欧洲国家的总理或首相讨论反毒品战。

counterproductive ['kauntəprəˌdʌktiv] a. 反生产的，使达不到预期目标的
[例] Violation of the court order would be counterproductive. 对法庭秩序破坏将无益于达到胜诉的目的。

couple ['kʌpl] n. 夫妻，情侣；两三个，几个
[例] I waited a couple of hours. 我等了几个小时。
[记] a newly married couple 一对新婚夫妇 / go in couples 总是成双成对

coupon ['kuːpɔn] n.（附在商品上的）赠券，（连在广告上的）优惠券
[例] I've kept the special coupon from the box of washing powder, so that I can get my next box cheaper. 我留下了洗衣粉盒子上的优惠券，这样我下次买时可以便宜些。

courteous ['kəːtjəs] a. 有礼貌的，谦恭的
[例] It is courteous of you to write a letter of thanks to me. 你实在太客气了，还写一封感谢信给我。

> court一词除了指“法庭，球场”等，还指“宫廷”。其实courteous的古义就是指“有宫廷气派的”。宫廷气派的一大特点不就是礼仪繁多吗？反义词discourteous。有英国民谣——绿袖子Greensleevs如是吟唱：Alas my love, you do me wrong; To cast me off discourteously. 我思断肠，伊人不臧；弃我远去，抑郁难当。

cover ['kʌvə] v. 覆盖；保护；包括 n. 盖子，封面
[例] The town covers 5 square miles. 小镇占地5平方英里。

> 玩CS游戏最熟悉的句子：“Go,go,go, cover me.” 前进，前进，前进，掩护我。

coverage ['kʌvəridʒ] n. 覆盖；新闻报道
[例]The test includes coverage of all of the 10 units. 考试的范围包括这10课的所有内容。

crack [kræk] v. 破裂；发出爆裂声；n. 裂缝
[例] The door opened just a crack. 这门只打开一条缝。

cradle ['kreidl] n. 摇篮；发源地

[例] Greece was the cradle of western civilization. 希腊是西方文明的发源地。

[记] from the cradle to the grave 从摇篮到坟墓；从生到死；一生 / cradlesong 摇篮曲

craft [krɑ:ft] n.工艺，手艺

[例] He knew the craft of making furniture. 他有做家具的手艺。

[记] handicraft n. 手工艺，手工艺品 / aircraft n. 飞行器，飞机

craftsman ['krɑ:ftsmən] n. 工匠；艺术家

[例] The original designs were made by highly skilled craftsmen. 原始的图案是由技艺高超的工匠绘制的。

crash [kræʃ] v./n.坠落，坠毁；（汽车）撞坏；（公司等）倒闭

[例] The plane crashed within seconds of taking off. 飞机在起飞后几秒钟之内便坠毁了。

crater ['kreitə] n. 弹坑；火山口；（月亮上的）环形山

[例] The battlefield was full of craters made by exploding shells. 战场上布满了炸弹留下的弹坑。

crawl [krɔ:l] v./n. 爬行，蠕动，徐徐行进

[例] The baby crawled towards his mother. 婴孩向他妈妈爬去。

creature ['kri:tʃə] n. 生物

[例] The crocodile is a strange-looking creature. 鳄鱼是一种模样古怪的动物。

> 东西方古代神话中各种生物都是神造出来的，《圣经》中上帝花了五日时间创造了大地万物，到了第六日他说：Let us make man in our image, like us. 所以各种动植物包括人类都是creature，是被神 create 出来的。

credit ['kredit] n. 信任，相信；学分；v. 信任；（to）把…归于

[例] I don't have enough credits to graduate. 我的学分不够毕业。

[记] credit ... to... 把…归功于 / academic credit 学分

creep [kri:p] v. 爬行；蹑手蹑脚悄声行进；蔓延

[例] We crept upstairs so as not to wake the baby. 为了不吵醒婴儿，我们蹑手蹑脚地上了楼梯。

crew [kru:] n. 全体工作人员；全体船员；全体乘务员

[例] I'd like to thank you on behalf of the crew. 我谨代表全体工作人员向你表示感谢。

> 男孩子国外剪头须知：crew cut 船员发型，平头；buzz cut 板儿寸（来源于理这种发型时推子所发出的声音）；如果想表现放荡不羁的个性，可考虑 mop top，拖把头；当然如果你想省钱，可以理 Harvey 的这种 shaved head 光头。

crime [kraim] n. 犯罪（总称）

[例] The latest crime statistics show a worrying rise in violent crime. 最近的犯罪统计数字表明暴力犯罪数量有所增加,这一情况令人担忧。

[记] commit a crime 犯下罪行

criminal ['kriminl] n. 罪犯，犯罪者；a. 犯罪的

[例] Police have described the man as a violent and dangerous criminal. 警察把那个男子描述为一个暴力的危险的罪犯。

cripple ['kripl] n. 跛子

[例] She was crippled in the car accident. 在一次车祸中她的腿伤成了残废。

crisis ['kraisis] n. 危机;紧要关头

[例] The sudden rise in oil prices led to an economic crisis. 石油价格骤升引发了经济危机.

[记] political/ economic/ military crisis政治/经济/军事危机 / at a crisis 在紧急关头

criteria [krai'tiəriə] n.（criterion 的复数）（批评、判断等的）标准，准则，尺度

[例] To quality for a grant, students must satisfy certain criteria. 学生必须达到一定的标准才有资格得到奖学金。

criticism ['kritisiz(ə)m] n. 批评，批判

[例] The film *Crouching Tiger*, *Hidden Dragon* still met with sharp domestic criticism although it had won several international prizes. 尽管电影《卧虎藏龙》获得了一些国际奖项，在国内它仍受到尖锐的批评。

[记] criticise/criticize v. 批评 /critic n. 批评家，评论家 / critical a. 评论的，批评的

> 字根 crit 指“判断 judge”。上面的几个单词都含此意；crisis 古义为决定，是一个医学术语，指“危象”。古代医生要病人的病情到了 crisis 的时候才能判断病情的好坏走向。后引申为“危机，转折点”。

crucial ['kru:ʃəl] a. 至关紧要的，关键性的

[例] This is a crucial match for the two teams. 对两个队而言,这都是关键的一场比赛。

[记] a crucial moment 决定性时刻；紧要关头 / be crucial to/ for…对…是决定性的

crude [kru:d] a. 天然未加工的；粗糙的；粗俗的，粗鲁的

[例] The crude oil needs processing further to be made into fuel. 原油须经过进一步加工才能成为燃料。

cruise [kru:z] v./n. 巡游，巡航

[例] We cruised along the highway at 100 kph. 我们以100公里的时速在高速公路上兜风。

crush [krʌʃ] v. 压碎，压坏，压扁

[例] There was such a crush on the train that I could hardly breathe. 列车上这么拥挤我几乎透不过气来。

> 该词的经典用法是在表达爱情的场景中，指“暗恋”或“暗恋对象”。如 David has a crush on her. 大卫暗恋她。身体和心灵时刻都被你的 crush（暗恋对象）给 crush（挤压）得透不过气，那就是 crush（暗恋）。

crystal [ˈkristl] n. 水晶，水晶饰品；a. 水晶般的；结晶状的

[例] Few have got a pair of crystal eyes like his. 很少有人像他那样生着一副水晶般的眼睛。

> 有种预言家叫crystal-gazer，通过看水晶球crystal ball来占卜；结婚十五年叫crystal wedding 晶婚；液晶显示屏叫LCD（Liquid Crystal Display）；商场里具有天鹅水晶标志的奥地利名牌Swarovski（施华洛世奇）专卖crystal；当被人问道“Is that clear?”时，我们回答“Clear as crystal.”。

cube [kjuːb] n. 立方体，立方

[例] She dropped a cube of sugar into her tea and stirred it with a spoon. 她将一方糖放入茶水中后用勺子搅了搅。

[记] ice cube冰块 / cubic a.立方体的，立方的 / a cubic meter 立方米

cultivate [ˈkʌltiveit] v. 耕作；培养

[例] Many people are attending the evening class in order to cultivate a love of art. 很多人正通过参加夜校学习来培养对艺术的爱好。

[记] cultivate the habit of... 养成…的习惯 / cultivate one's mind 陶冶思想、情操

> 字根 cult 指“耕种”。culture 文化；古时最早的文化当然是农耕文化了。怎样播种、如何灌溉、何时收获，就是人类最早的文化culture。

curative [ˈkjuərətiv] a. 医疗的；n.药品

[例] This herb was once thought to be curative. 这种草本植物过去被认为有治疗作用。

curb [kəːb] n. 路缘，路边；约束；v. 控制，约束

[例] High interest rates put a curb on spending. 高利率抑制了消费。

cure [kjuə] v. 治疗，治愈；n. 疗法，药，对策

[谚] What can't be cured must be endured. 没办法解决的事就得忍耐。

curious ['kjuəriəs] a. 好奇的，好求知的；奇特的
[例] It is good to be curious about the world around you. 对你周围的世界感到新奇是件好事。
[记] curiosity n. 好奇心

curl [kə:l] n. 卷发；v. 使卷曲
[例] Mary had her hair in curls. 玛丽把头发弄成卷曲状。

currency ['kʌrənsi] n. 流通，货币
[例] The electronic currency is becoming popular now. 电子货币已慢慢流行起来。
[记] gain currency 开始广泛传播

> 字根 cur 指"跑"。如：cursor 跑来跑去的东东→鼠标；current 跑动的，引申为"气流、水流、电流"；currency 在市场上流通的货币；occur 跑出来→发生；cursive 草书，草体的；curriculum 各种课程都跑一遍→全部课程。

current ['kʌrənt] a. 当前的，现行的；n. 潮流；电流，水流，气流
[例] Newspapers influence the current of thought. 报纸影响当前的思想潮流。

curriculum [kə'rikjuləm] n.（学校等的）全部课程
[例]The curriculum is scientifically arranged in the school. 那个学校的课程设置很科学。
[记] curriculum schedule 课程表 / curriculum vitae 简历

curse [kə:s] v./n. 诅咒，咒骂
[谚] A light purse is a heavy curse. 无钱万事难。
[记] be under a curse 被诅咒，遭天灾

curve [kə:v] n. 曲线，弯曲；v.（使）弯曲
[例] The path curves around the lake. 这条道路绕着湖延伸。

cushion ['kuʃən] n. 垫子；缓冲物
[例] The air cushion can be used in a chair to make it more comfortable. 气垫用在椅子上可以使椅子更舒服。

custody ['kʌstədi] n. 监护权；保管
[例] The father was given custody of the children. 父亲获得了对孩子的监护权。

custom ['kʌstəm] n. 风俗，习惯
[例] It is the custom of the local people to do so. 这种作法是当地人的习惯。
[记] customs 海关

cute [kju:t] a. 聪明伶俐的；逗人喜爱的
[例] She looks cute in those clothes. 她穿那件衣服很可爱。
[记] cutie/cutey 美人儿

cycle ['saikl] n. 周期，循环；自行车；v. 骑自行车

[例] In many universities, students cycle from their dorm to the classroom or library. 在许多大学里，学生骑自行车从寝室去教室或图书馆。
[记] occur in cycles 周期性的发生 / cyclic a. 循环的，周期的

> 字根 cyc 指"圆环 ring"。如：cyclist 骑自行车的人；bicycle 两个圆环→自行车；cyclone 旋风；recycle 再循环，再生。

cylinder ['silində] n. 圆筒，圆柱体；汽缸
[例] The car is equipped with a six-cylinder engine. 这辆汽车配有一个六汽缸的引擎。

dairy ['dɛəri] n. 奶制品；奶品店
[例] We bought milk at the dairy. 我们在乳品店买了牛奶。
[区别] diary ['daiəri] n. 日记

dam [dæm] n.水坝；障碍；v.控制
[例] A new dam is now being built in the valley. 河谷里正在建一座新水坝。

damage ['dæmidʒ] n./v. 损害，伤害
[例] An earthquake sometimes causes great damage. 地震有时造成重大损失。

damp [dæmp] a.潮湿的，湿气重的
[例] The damp match won't strike. 这潮湿的火柴擦不着。

dash [dæʃ] v. 猛冲，猛击，撞击
[例] He dashed the bowl to bits on the ground. 他把碗猛扔到地上，摔得粉碎。

data ['deitə] n. (datum 的复数) 数据，资料
[例] The data we have collected is not enough to be convincing. 我们所收集的资料还不足以令人信服。

dawn [dɔːn] n. 黎明，破晓
[例] I woke up at dawn. 我在黎明时醒了。
[记] from dawn till dusk 从早到晚

deadline ['dedlain] n. 最后期限
[例] All postal votes must be posted before the deadline. 所有邮寄的选票必须在截止日期以前寄出。

> 源自美国南北战争期间战俘营铁丝围栏附近的界线，谁逾此线格杀勿论。此后监狱周围的死线也叫 deadline。再转义成为如今的"截止期限"。

deadly ['dedli] a. 致命的，致死的；adv. 非常
[例] I am deadly serious about it. 对这事我绝对是认真的。
[记] deadly enemies 不共戴天的死敌 / [同义词] lethal, deathful, fatal, mortal, vital

dealer ['diːlə] n. 商人；贩子

[例] Tribal wars stirred up by the slave-traders never stopped. 由奴隶贩卖商掀起的部落战争从未停止过。

dean [diːn] n. 系主任；（大学的）学院院长

[例] She is the dean of the Faculty of Social Sciences. 她是社会科学院院长。

> 由表“十”的拉丁文decem派生而来。原指古罗马时的一种官职，所管人员为十人。在军队中指“十个士兵之首”，教会中指“十个教士的头儿”等。现在dean指“系主任”、“学院院长”，所管人员远不止十人了。on the dean's list，系主任的名单上的人，指学校里的“优等生”。

debate [di'beit] v. /n. 辩论，争论

[例] The government is debating the education laws. 政府正在就教育法进行辩论。

[记] debate about/on/upon sth. 就某事进行辩论 / have/hold a debate with sb.与某人进行辩论

debris ['debriː] n. 碎片；残骸

[例] We are searching for his corpse among the debris after the explosion. 我们在爆炸后的碎片中寻找他的尸体。

decade ['dekeid] n. 十年

[例] In that decade, New York City's overall cost of living rose by 88%. 在那十年间纽约市总的生活费用上升了88%。

decay [di'kei] v. 腐朽，腐烂，衰退

[例]What made the Roman Empire decay? 什么导致了罗马帝国的衰亡?

deceive [di'siːv] v. 欺骗

[例] He has deliberately deceived us. 他有意欺骗我们。

[记] deceive sb. into doing sth. 骗某人做某事

decent ['diːsnt] a. 得体的，体面的，像样的

[例] He made a decent record. 他成绩尚佳。

[反义词] indecent a. 下流的

decimal ['desiməl] a. 十进制的；小数的

[例] The decimal system is widely used. 十进制被广泛地运用。

[记] decimal point 小数点

> 前缀deci- 表示“十分之一”。如：decimation 古罗马对待叛军的惩罚为每十人中抽杀一人→大批杀害；decimeter 十分之一米→分米。厘米当然就是百分之一米：centimeter；毫米是千分之一米：millimeter。

decimation [ˌdesi'meiʃən] n. 大批杀害，屠杀

decipher [di'saifə] v. 破译（密码等）；解释

[例] Anthropologist is still trying to decipher the writing found on the

grave. 人类学家们仍然在尽力破译在这个坟墓里发现的神秘文字。
[记] cipher n. 密码，零 / encrypt v.加密 / decode v. 解密

declare [di'klɛə] v. 宣布，宣告；声明
[例] She declared that she didn't want to see him again. 她宣称她再也不愿见到他。

decline [di'klain] n. /v. 下降，减少；衰落；v. 拒绝
[例] The birthrate in China has been declining for several years. 中国人口的出生率几年来一直下降。
[记] declination n. 倾斜 / declining a. 倾斜的；衰退的

decompose [ˌdi:kəm'pəuz] v. (使) 分解；(使) 腐烂
[例] You can apply heat to decompose organic compounds. 你可以加热来分解有机化合物。
[同义词] disintegrate

decorate ['dekəreit] v. 装饰，装潢，修饰
[例] Using extremely different decorating schemes in adjoining rooms may result in lack of unity in style. 相邻的房间用悬殊太大的装修方案会破坏统一的风格。
[同义词] adorn, beautify, ornament

decoration [ˌdekə'reiʃən] n. 装饰；装饰品
[例] His major is interior decoration. 他的专业是室内装潢。

decorative ['dekərətiv] a. 装饰的，装潢的
[例] The poem had been embroidered on a pretty decorative pillow. 那首诗被绣在精致的装饰品枕头上了。
[记] decorative art 装饰美术 / decorative surgery 整容外科

decrease [di:'kri:s] n./v. 减少，减小
[例] His interest in this subject has gradually decreased. 他对这个科目的兴趣逐渐在减退。

dedicate ['dedikeit] v. 献身，致力于
[例] He felt that the cause to which he could dedicate himself was the most important cause in the world. 他感到他所献身的事业是世界上最重要的事业。
[记] be dedicated to... 献身于… /dedicate oneself to... 献身于… / [同义词] devote

deduce [di'dju:s] v. 推断，演绎
[例] What can you deduce from what he said? 从他的话中你可以推断出什么结论?

> 字根duc指“引导lead”。deduce往下引导→推论，推导；deductive推论的；induce往里引导→归纳，引诱；inductive归纳的；an inductive method归纳法；educe向外（e-=ex-）引导→引出，唤起；education教育。所以education不是给予，而是引导出学习的兴趣和天性，引导正确的学习方法。

deem [diːm] v. 认为；相信

[例] The board deemed it urgent that these files be printed right away. 董事会认为务必马上印出这些文件。

default [diˈfɔːlt] n. 默认值，缺省；缺席；v. 疏怠职责；缺席

[例] He won the case by default. 他因对方缺席而胜诉。

defeat [diˈfiːt] v. 战胜，击败；n. 失败

[例] They were defeated in the football match. 他们在足球赛中输了。

> 如果你读过海明威Hemingway的*The Old Man and the Sea*，那么一定记得这段话："Man is not made for defeat. A man can be destroyed but not defeated."（你可以毁灭我，但不能打败我！）这是全书的主题，也是海明威一生的写照。

defect [diˈfekt] n. 缺点，过失

[例] There exist in our educational system many defects. 我们的教育制度还存在着不少缺陷.

[同义词] fault, flaw, shortcoming, weakness, demerit

defend [diˈfend] v. 保卫，捍卫；为…辩护

[例] She demonstrated how best to defend oneself. 她示范了最有效的自卫方法。

[记] defend against 保卫，抵抗

defensive [diˈfensiv] a. 防御性的

[例]We took a defensive attitude in the negotiation. 我们在谈判时取守势。

[记] defensive weapons 防御性武器 / [反义词] aggressive, offensive

defer [diˈfəː] v. 推迟，延期

[例] We have to defer our departure because of the heavy rain. 因为大雨，我们不得不推迟行程。

[记] defer payment 延期付款 / [同义词] delay, postpone, put off

deficiency [diˈfiʃənsi] n. 缺乏，不足

[例] Vitamin deficiency can lead to very severe illness. 缺乏维生素会引起严重的疾病。

[记] deficient a. 缺少的，不足的

define [diˈfain] v. 给…下定义，阐述

[例]It is perhaps best to define it more precisely for scientific purposes. 为了科学研究，最好能给它下一个更准确的定义。

[记] definition n. 定义；清晰度

definite [ˈdefinit] a. 明确的，确切的

[例]There are definite restrictions on the sales of alcoholic beverages. 关于酒类的销售是有明确限制的。

[记] definitely adv. 明确地；肯定地

deflect [diˈflekt] v.（使）偏斜；（使）偏离；（使）转向

[例] The bullet struck a wall and was deflected from its course. 那子弹因击中了墙壁而偏离方向。
[记] deflection n. 偏斜，偏转，偏差

deforest [diː'fɔrist] v. 滥伐森林
[例] The land is severely eroded as a result of widespread deforesting and intensive farming. 土地因大面积乱砍滥伐和过度耕种而受到严重破坏。

degrade [di'greid] v.（使）降级，（使）堕落，（使）退化
[例] You degrade yourself when you tell a lie. 说谎会贬低自己的身分。
[反义词] upgrade

degree [di'griː] n. 度（数）；程度；学位
[例] The students show various degrees of skill in doing the experiments. 学生们做实验时，表现出各种不同程度的技能。

delay [di'lei] n./v. 耽搁，延迟，拖延
[例] We decided to delay our holiday until next month. 我们决定将休假延至下个月。

Unit 8

delegate ['deligeit] n. 代表；v.委派…为代表

[例] The boss delegated me to approach the local press. 老板派我去和当地新闻界打交道。

[记] Chinese delegation 中国代表团

> 字根leg表示“指定，派送”，de离开+leg指定+ate动词→被指定离开→委派为代表。legacy指定给人的东西→遗产。

delete [di'li:t] v. 删除，删掉

[例] References to places of battle were deleted from soldiers' letters during the war. 在战争中，士兵们的信件中提到作战地点的地方均被删掉。

deliberate [di'libəreit] a. 深思熟虑的；故意的；从容的；v. 深思熟虑

[例] He deliberated the question before he made an answer. 答复以前，他仔细地考虑了这个问题。

delicate ['delikit] a. 精致的；微妙的；脆弱的

[例] Delicate plants must be protected from cold wind and frost. 娇弱的植物必须妥为保护以避免风霜的侵袭。

[同义词] fine, exquisite, subtle

delicious [di'liʃəs] a. 美味的，可口的

[例] The soup is delicious. 汤的味道美极了。

[同义词] tasty, yummy

delight [di'lait] v.（使）高兴，（使）欣喜；n. 乐趣

[例] She delights in cooking lovely meals. 她以烹饪美食为乐。

[记] delight in 因…高兴

deliver [di'livə] v. 传送；投递

[例] You don't have to go out into the rain since the store delivers free of charge. 你不需要下雨时外出，因为商店可以免费送货上门。

[记] delivery n. 递送，交付

delta ['deltə] n. 三角洲

[例] The Nile Delta used to be a fertile land. 尼罗河三角洲过去是一片肥沃的土地。

> 希腊语第四个字母Δ，因为状似三角，被用来表示“(河流的)三角洲”或“三角形物”。

demand [di'mɑ:nd] n./v. 要求；需求

[例] This work demands your patience. 这项工作需要你的耐心。

demanding [di'mɑ:ndiŋ] a. 过分要求的，苛求的

[例] Emily is a very demanding child. 埃米莉要大人花很多的精力照看。

demerit [di'merit] n. 缺点，过失

[例] You get demerits if you miss a meeting. 如果你缺席会议会被记过的。

[反义词] merit

demise [di'maiz] n. 死亡；君权的转移或授与，禅让；v. 遗赠，转让

[例] The land demised to a charitable institution. 土地被遗赠给慈善机构了。

democracy [di'mɔkrəsi] n. 民主，民主制，民主国家

[例] The military government promised to restore democracy within one year. 军政府答应在一年之内重新建立民主政治。

[记] democratic a. 民主的 / democratise/democratize v. 使民主 / democrat n. 民主主义者

> 字根 dem 指“民众 people”。cracy 为法语 kratia，指“rule 统治”。democracy 人民统治→民主。

demographic [demə'græfik] a. 人口的；人口统计学的

[例] I have no knowledge of demographic theory. 我对人口统计学理论一无所知。

demolish [di'mɔliʃ] v. 毁坏，破坏，拆除，推翻

[例] The fire demolished the town. 大火烧毁了这座城镇。

demonstrate ['demənstreit] v. 示范，演示；证明

[例] He demonstrated how to use the new machine. 他演示了怎样使用这台新机器。

[记] demonstration n. 示范；示威 / demonstrative a. 感情外露的；喜怒形于色的 / demonstrator n. 示范者；游行示威者

> 字根 monstr 指“表示 show”。所以 monster 就是“表示出来的，醒目的东西”，与众不同，跟大家不一样，一眼就能分辨→妖怪！ monstrous a.奇形怪状的；demonstrate 中 de- 表示 fully，该词就是“充分表示→示范，证明”。我们常说的某歌星出了新唱片的 demo（演示）版，demo 即是 demonstration。

denote [di'nəut] v. 指示，表明，是…的标志

[例] The mark “∧” denotes a place of omission. “∧”记号指示有脱漏的地方。

dense [dens] a. 密集的；稠密的

[例] There will be dense fog in northern parts of the country tomorrow. 本国北部地区明天将有浓雾。

[反义词] dilute, sparse, thin

density ['densiti] n. 密度；浓度

[例] The population density of big cities is larger and larger. 大城市的人

口密度越来越大了。

dental ['dent(ə)l] a. 牙的；牙科的

[例] Some hospitals in Ireland provide free dental treatment to certain citizens. 爱尔兰的一些医院为某些公民提供免费的牙科治疗。

[记] dentist n. 牙医

deny [di'nai] v. 否认，拒绝

[例] The accused man denied that he had been there. 被告否认他曾到过那里。

[记] deny sb. nothing 对某人百依百顺 / denial n. 否认，拒绝

depart [di'pɑːt] v. 离开，启程，上路

[例]When does the next train depart? 下一次列车什么时候开？

[记] depart from 离开，从…出发

departure [di'pɑːtʃə(r)] n. 离去；离开

[例] The departure of the train was delayed. 火车开出的时间推迟了。

[反义词] arrival

department [di'pɑːtmənt] n.（行政、企业等机构的）部门；（学校，学术机构等的）系，研究所

[例] At that time, Robert Kennedy was head of the Justice Department. 那时，罗伯特 · 肯尼迪是司法部部长。

depend [di'pend] v. 依靠，依赖；取决于

[例] You can depend on this dictionary. 你可以信赖这本辞典。

[记] That/It depends. 要看情况而定。/ dependent a. 依靠的，依赖的 /be dependent on 依靠 / independent a. 独立的

depict [di'pikt] v. 描述，描绘，描写

[例] In this new biography, she is depicted as a lonely and unhappy woman. 在这本新的传记中，她被描写为孤独、不幸的女人。

> 字根 pict 指“画 paint”。pictograph 用画画来写字（-graph）→象形文字；picture 画，照片；depict 画下来→描绘，描写。

deplete [di'pliːt] v. 耗尽，大大减少

[例] Mankind must take care not to deplete the earth of its natural resources. 人类必须注意，切莫耗尽地球上的自然资源。

[记] depletion n. 损耗，耗尽

deploy [di'plɔi] v. 展开，散开；配置，部署

[例] Air bags are only deployed when the car is struck from the front. 只有当汽车受到前方的撞击时，安全气囊才会张开。

deposit [di'pɔzit] n. 存款；押金，保证金；堆积物；v. 存放，堆积

[例] The interest of the current account is lower than that of the deposit account. 活期存款的利息比定期存款的低。

[记] bank deposit 银行存款

depress [di'pres] v. 压抑；使沮丧；压下

[例] The rainy days always depress me. 雨天总是使我沮丧。
[记] depressed a. 沮丧的，消沉的 / depressive a. 压抑的，不景气的

depression [di'preʃ(ə)n] n. 沮丧，消沉；萧条，不景气
[例] A holiday will help his depression. 度假会帮助他改善抑郁情绪。

> Great Depression 大萧条：美国历史上一次空前严重的经济危机。1929 年 10 月股票价格开始猛跌 40%以上。1929 年至 1932 年美国众多银行公司倒闭。据 1932 年 9 月《幸福》杂志估计，美国全国总人口的 28%无法维持生计，200 万人到处流浪。在这次大萧条中，工业、农业、信用危机同时并发，并波及整个资本主义世界，使世界工业生产总产值下降 36%，世界贸易缩减 2/3。

deprive [di'praiv] v. 剥夺
[例] Sickness deprived me of the pleasure of meeting you. 疾病使得我未能和你经常欢聚。
[记] deprive sb. of... 剥夺某人的… / deprivation n.剥夺，丧失

deputy ['depjuti] n. 代理人；副手
[例] John will be my deputy while I am away. 我不在时，约翰将是我的代理人。

derive [di'raiv] v. 得到，源自
[例] I derived a lot of pleasure from meeting new people in college. 在大学里,我从结识新朋友中得到了许多乐趣。
[记] derive from 得自，由来

descend [di'send] v. 下来，下降，遗传
[例] Men are descended from ape-men. 人是由类人猿转变而来的。
[反义词] ascend

descent [di'sent] n. 降下，降落；血统，遗传
[例] He traces his descent from an old Norman family. 他追溯到他的祖先是属于一个古诺曼底家族。
[反义词] ascent n. 上升

describe [dis'kraib] v. 描述，叙述，形容
[例] Words cannot describe the beauty of the scene. 语言难以描述出这景色的优美。

desert [di'zə:t] v. 放弃，遗弃，逃跑；['dezət] n. 沙漠
[例] The fort had been hurriedly deserted. 这堡垒被仓促地放弃了。
[区别] dissert v. 论述；写论文 / dessert n. 餐后甜点

deserve [di'zə:v] v. 应受，值得
[例] If you do wrong, you deserve punishment. 你如做错事，应当受罚。

design [di'zain] v. 设计，规划；n. 设计；图样
[例] He had already designed a good excuse for not attending the conference. 他已经编造了一个好的借口，不参加这次会议。

designate ['dezigneit] v. 指明，任命，指派
[例] He designated Smith as his successor. 他指定史密斯为他的继承人。
[同义词] appoint, indicate, nominate

desire [di'zaiə] n./v. 愿望，欲望；请求
[例] He desired a college education. 他想受大学教育。

despair [dis'pɛə] v./n. 绝望
[例] This boy is his mother's despair. 这个男孩使他妈妈绝望了。

desperate ['despərit] a. 绝望的；孤注一掷的，不顾一切的
[例] The man lost in the desert was desperate for water. 在沙漠中迷失方向的人极度渴望得到水。

> 字根 sper 指"希望 hope"。如：pro- 前面 +sper 有希望→ prosper 使繁荣，成功；prosperity 繁荣；desperate 没有希望的→绝望的；desperation 绝望；desperado 绝望的人（-ado）→亡命徒。

despite [dis'pait] prep. 尽管，不管
[例] Despite the bad weather, we enjoyed our holiday. 尽管天气不好，我们的假期仍过得很愉快。
[记] despite of... 不顾，尽管，不论

destine ['destin] v. 注定；预定
[例] They were destined never to meet again. 命运注定他们永不重逢。
[记] destination n. 目的地；终点 / final destination 终点

destiny ['destini] n.命运，定数
[例] Destiny brought them together.命运把他们连在一起。
[同义词] fate

destitute ['destitju:t] a. 困穷的，缺乏的
[例] The floods left many people destitute. 水灾使许多人一无所有。

destroy [dis'trɔi] v. 破坏，毁坏，消灭
[例] The heavy rain destroyed all hope of a picnic. 大雨粉碎了野餐的一切希望。

detach [di'tætʃ] v. 分开，分离，派遣
[例] He had to detach himself from social activities for the time being in order to concentrate on his studies. 为了专心致志于学业，他只好暂时撇开社交活动。

detail ['di:teil] n. 细节，详情 v. 详述
[例] Give me all the details of the accident—tell me what happened in detail. 给我说说事故发生的详情，详细告诉我发生了什么事。
[记] in detail 详细地 / go into detail(s)详细叙述

detect [di'tekt] v. 察觉，发觉；侦察
[例] He is responsible for detecting weak signals of some kind. 他负责探测某种微弱的信号。

detective [di'tektiv] n. 侦探 a. 侦探的

[例] She hired a detective to find out if her husband was having an affair. 她雇侦探调查她丈夫是否有风流韵事。

> 字根tect指“遮住to cover”。如：pro-在前面+tect遮住→protect保护；detect 拿走遮掩物→发现，探察；detector探测器，metal detector 金属探测器；lie detector 测谎仪；detective 侦探；private detective 私人侦探。世界上最著名的detective 当属于Sir Arthur Conan Doyle 柯南·道尔爵士笔下的Sherlock Holmes福尔摩斯。

deter [di'təː] v. 阻止

[例] The security camera was installed to deter people from stealing. 安装摄像头是为了防止有人偷盗。

[同义词] discourage, hinder, prevent, prohibit

detergent [di'təːdʒənt] n. 清洁剂，去垢剂

[例] Scum is formed when soaps and detergents react with hard water. 肥皂，洗涤剂与硬水反应时形成泡沫。

deteriorate [di'tiəriəreit] v. 使恶化，变糟

[例] Relations between the two countries has deteriorated sharply in recent weeks. 最近几周那两个国家间的关系严重恶化了。

[反义词] ameliorate, improve

determine [di'təːmin] v. 决定，下定决心；查明

[例] I am determined to do better than Mike.我决心比迈克做得更好。

> be determined to do sth.决心做某事 /determine on 决定

detriment ['detrimənt] n. 损害，损害物

[例] Smoking is now considered a detriment to good health. 现在人们认为吸烟对健康有害。

detrimental [ˌdetri'mentl] a.有害的，不利的

[例] Lack of sleep is detrimental to one's health. 缺乏睡眠是有害于健康的。

devastate ['devəsteit] v. 毁灭，摧毁，使荒废

[例] They intended to devastate the town at one stroke. 他们企图一举摧毁全城。

> 形容词形式devastating；所谓devastating beauty，其字面意思是“具有毁灭性的美丽”，其实说的就是某人的美貌“倾国倾城”。

deviate ['diːvieit] v. 偏离，背离

[例] His statement deviates from the truth. 他的陈述偏离了事实。

[记] deviation n. 偏离，偏差

device [di'vais] n. 装置，设备；手段，策略

[例] These newly-designed devices will appear at the exhibition next

month. 这些新近设计的装置将在下月的展览会上展出。
[同义词] apparatus, implement, instrument

devil ['devl] n. 魔鬼，恶棍
[例] That enemy officer is a devil incarnate. 那个敌军军官简直是魔鬼的化身。
[同义词] demon, Satan ['seitən] n. 撒旦，魔鬼

devise [di'vaiz] v. 设计，发明
[例] The team is trying to devise a new system for handling mail orders. 这个小组正设法设计一个新的信件处理系统。

devote [di'vəut] v. 投入于；献身于，专心致力于
[例] After she graduated she continued to devote herself to research. 毕业后她继续致力于研究工作。
[记] devote to 把…献给 / [同义词] dedicate

devour [di'vauə(r)] v. 吞食；贪婪地吃
[例] The lion devoured the deer. 狮子狼吞虎咽地把鹿吃了下去。

diagnose ['daiəgnəuz] v. 诊断；判断
[例] The teacher diagnosed the boy's reading difficulties. 老师找出了那孩子阅读上困难的原因。

> 字根 gno 和 cogni 都有"认识，知道"的含义。如：recognize 承认；ignore 忽视；dia 通过 + gnose 认识，在医学上通过各种手段了解病情→诊断。咱们传统中医理论不也是要求通过（dia）望闻问切各种方式来认识（gnose）病情吗。

diagonal [dai'ægənl] a. 斜的，斜纹的，对角线的 n. 对角线，斜纹织物
[例] The two diagonals of a square cross in the centre. 正方形两条对角线交于正方形的中心。

diagram ['daiəgræm] n. 图表，示意图，图解
[例] The teacher drew a diagram showing how the blood flows through the heart. 老师画了张示意图,显示血液如何流过心脏。

dialect ['daiəlekt] n. 方言，地方话，土语
[例] The local dialect is sometimes hard to understand. 当地的方言有时很难理解。

diameter [dai'æmitə] n. 直径
[例] The earth is slightly flat at the poles, so that the polar diameter is slightly less than the equatorial diameter. 地球在两极扁平一点，所以其直径略小于赤道直径。
[记] radius n. 半径；半径范围

dictate [dik'teit] v. 口授，让（某人）听写；命令，指令
[例] The French teacher dictates to the class every other week. 法语教师每隔一周给这班学生做一次听写。
[记] dictate to 口述，使听写 / follow the dictates of 听从…的命令 / dictation n. 听写，口述

> 字根 dict 指“说”。如：dictation 就是说出来的东西→听写，笔录；diction 说的方式→措辞；dictionary 说话方式集合的地方（-ary）→字典；pre- 提前 +dict 说→ predict 预言；contra- 反着 +dict 说→ contradict，就是反驳，顶嘴啦。

diction ['dikʃən] n. 措辞，用语

[例] His diction is noted for its freshness and vividness. 他以用字遣词清新生动见长。

diet ['daiət] n. 饮食，食物；节食

[例] A sugar-free diet is recommended for diabetics.（医生）建议糖尿病患者使用无糖食谱。

[记] on a diet 节食

differ ['difə] v. 不一致，不同于

[例] We differ on many things. 我们在很多事情上意见都不一致。

[记] differ from和…不同 / differ in在…方面不同 / different a. 不同的

differentiate [ˌdifə'renʃieit] v. 区分，区别

[例] This company does not differentiate between men and women — they employ and pay both equally. 这家公司对男女职工一视同仁——男女职工他们都雇用而且同工同酬。

diffuse [di'fju:z] v. 扩散，散播；[di'fju:s] a. 弥漫的，扩散的

[例] Television is a powerful means of diffusing knowledge. 电视是传播知识的强有力手段。

digest [di'dʒest] v. 消化，理解领悟；n. 摘要,文摘

[例] Mary can't digest fat. 玛丽吃肥肉不消化。

[记] digestion n. 消化力，领悟

dignity ['digniti] n. 尊严，尊贵

[谚] It is but a few short years from diapers to dignity and from dignity to decomposition. 从尿布到尊严、又从尊严到解体，只不过是短短的一段岁月而已。

dilate [dai'leit] v.（使）扩大，（使）膨胀；详述

[例] The pupils of your eyes dilate when you enter a dark room. 当你进入暗室时，你眼睛的瞳孔就会扩大。

dilemma [di'lemə] n. 窘境，困境，进退两难

[例] The bad weather put us into a dilemma. 糟糕的天气使我们进退两难。

> dilemma 可分为 di 两个 + lemma 论点，在两个选择之间，进退两难。常见同义词 plight，predicament。其中 plight 除了作“困境”讲，还表示“婚约，订婚”。如果你已经和一个女孩子订婚，她现在还不能和你住在一起照顾你，你也不能够去找其他女孩，那可真是进退两难，plight!

diligent ['dilidʒənt] a. 勤奋的，勤勉的

[例] A diligent detective investigates all clues. 勤奋的侦探会调查所有

的线索。
[记] diligent in勤勉于…

dilute [dai'lju:t] v. 冲淡，稀释；a. 淡的；微弱的
[例] The nurse diluted the drug with saline water. 护士用生理盐水把药加以稀释。

> 名词形式dilution。美国前总统尼克松Richard M. Nixon在*In the Arena*一书中曾评论一次会晤或谈话的质量与参与谈话人的数量之间的关系：Every person you add to a meeting dilutes the quality of the conversation. 意为：参加谈话的人越多，谈话质量越低。

dim [dim] a. 暗淡的，隐约的，不乐观的
[例] The lights in the theatre began to dim. 戏院里的灯光开始暗下来。

dimension [di'menʃən] n. 尺寸，尺度，维（数）
[例] Time is sometimes called the fourth dimension. 时间有时被称为第四度空间。

> 我们经常说的3D动画，3D就是three dimensions，有X轴、Y轴、Z轴。1D是线性，比如时间time；2D是平面plane，3D即三维立体。爱因斯坦Einstein在相对论中提出宇宙是4D，空间三维加时间维，又称四度空间，四次元。

diminish [di'miniʃ] v.（使）减少，（使）缩减
[例] His income diminished as he retired. 他退休后收入减少了。
[同义词] curtail, decrease, lessen, reduce

dip [dip] v. 蘸，浸
[例] She dipped her hand in the sea to find out how cold it was. 她把手放入海水中看看水有多凉。

diploma [di'pləumə] n. 毕业文凭，学位证书
[例] The secretary had diplomas in both education and linguistics. 这个秘书取得了教育学和语言学两个方向的毕业文凭。

diplomat ['dipləmæt] n. 外交官，有外交手腕的人，有权谋的人
[例] As a natural diplomat, Baxter found it easy to get the two sides to agree. 作为一位天才的外交官，他觉得很容易使双方达成一致。

diplomatic [ˌdiplə'mætik] a. 外交的；世故的，圆滑的
[例] Julia joined the diplomatic service after her graduation from the university. 朱丽娅大学毕业后就到外交部门工作了。

disable [dis'eibl] v. 使丧失能力，使残废
[例] An accident disabled him from playing football. 一场意外事故使他不能踢球了。

disadvantage [ˌdisəd'vɑ:ntidʒ] n. 不利条件，劣势
[谚] Every advantage has its disadvantage. 凡事有利也有弊。

disaster [di'zɑ:stə] n. 灾难；灾祸；天灾

[例] There was a great flood disaster in East China. 华东发生了严重的水灾.
[记] disaster film/movie 灾难片 / disastrous a. 灾难性的

> 古罗马人爱夜观星相。某一天晚上突然发现，咦，有颗星辰的星位不正，那可不是好兆头！dis 否定+aster 星星→星星不见了，星位不正→disaster 不吉祥，有灾难。另外，asterisk 指“*”号；asteroid 指“小行星”。

discard [dis'kɑːd] v. 丢弃，抛弃
[例] Outdated theory should be discarded. 过时的理论应该抛弃。

> 来自扑克牌戏，dis-+card→将这张牌扔掉、不要，引申得来“放弃”之意。一副扑克牌有四种花色 four suits：spade 黑桃、heart 红桃、clubs 梅花、diamonds 方块，如果一位牌友出了一张spade，通常要求其他人跟着出同样花色的牌，即都要出黑桃，这种作法叫做“follow suit”；但如果你手中没有 spade，随便跟了一张其他花色，如扔了一张club，那么这个时候这张梅花就被你 discard 啦。

discern [di'səːn] v. 看出，觉察出；认识，了解
[例] The child finds it hard to discern between blue and green. 那孩子对于分辨蓝绿二色感到有困难。
[记] discernible a. 可辨别的 / discerning a. 有辨别力的，有眼光的

discipline ['disiplin] n. 纪律；学科；v.训练
[例] Martial arts teach respect, discipline, and cooperation. 武术教人要互相尊重、严于律己、相互合作。

disclose [dis'kləuz] v. 透露，揭露，泄露；公开
[例] The president disclosed the fact that he was put into prison wrongly twenty years before. 董事长透露说他自己在二十年前曾被冤枉地送进监牢。

discount ['diskaunt] n. 折扣；v. 忽视，低估；打折扣
[例] They give a 10% discount for cash payment. 现金付款，他们给以九折优待。

discourage [dis'kʌridʒ] v. 使灰心，使气馁；劝阻
[例] Try to discourage him from driving too fast. 设法劝他开车不要开得太快。
[反义词] encourage

discreet [di'skriːt] a. 言行谨慎的；小心的；有智谋的
[例] My secretary is very discreet. She never tells anyone unconcerned anything about the company's business. 我的秘书很谨慎，她对公司的业务从不对任何无关的人谈起。
[同义词] careful, cautious, considerate, prudent

discrete [dis'kri:t] a. 分离的，互不连接的，不相关联的

[例]The change happens in a series of discrete steps. 变化分一系列互不相关联的几个步骤产生。

> 拼写时注意discrete中的两个e被字母t分离，那么discrete指“分离的”；区别单词discreet adv.谨慎地。discreet 中两个e没有分开，小心地拼写，谨慎地。

Unit 9

discrepancy [dis'krepənsi] n. 差异，矛盾

[例] This discrepancy will prevent me from obtaining a visa. 因为这一差错，我将得不到签证。

discriminate [dis'krimineit] v. 歧视；区别，区别对待

[例] This new law discriminates against lower-paid colored workers. 这项新法律歧视低工资的有色人种工人。

[记] discriminate against 歧视 / discriminate between 区别对待

discrimination [dis,krimi'neiʃən] n. 歧视;区分

[例] It's necessary to eliminate all forms of sexual discrimination. 有必要消除任何形式的性别歧视。

discussion [dis'kʌʃən] n. 讨论，谈论

[例] After much discussion among the directors the matter was settled in the end. 董事们经过大量的讨论后问题终于得到了解决。

disguise [dis'gaiz] n./v. 假装，伪装

[例] Mulan disguised herself as a man and became a soldier. 木兰女扮男装从军。

[记] a blessing in disguise 因祸得福之事

disgust [dis'gʌst] v. 令人厌恶;使作呕 n. 厌恶，嫌恶

[例] The smell filled me with disgust.这股气味使我作呕。

disillusion [,disilju:ʒən] n. 幻灭，觉醒；v. 使觉醒，使幻灭

[例] He disillusioned his fans with his awkward play. 他笨拙的表演使他的崇拜者们大失所望。

dismay [dis'mei] v./n. 忧虑，失望，沮丧；惊慌

[例] She was dismayed to learn that her favorite dancer used drugs. 获悉她喜爱的舞蹈演员吸毒，她感到很失望。

dismiss [dis'mis] v. 解散，解雇；拒绝考虑

[例] He was dismissed from school. 他被开除学籍了。

> 字根miss指“送，投掷”。所以被投掷出的玩意儿叫missile导弹；送给你的任务叫mission，完不成的任务就叫*Mission Impossible*（碟中碟）；dis-分离+miss送→零零散散地送走→dismiss下课，解散。

disorder [dis'ɔ:də] n. 无秩序，混乱，杂乱；（身体机能的）失调

[例] The bandits fled in disorder when they heard that a regiment of soldiers were marching to their den. 土匪们听说有一个团的士兵正向他们的巢穴进军就四处溃逃。

disparity [dis'pæriti] n. 不同，不一致，悬殊

[例] There was such disparity in the standards of living between rich and poor. 贫富生活的水平相差如此悬殊。
[记] disparity in position 地位悬殊 / disparity in age 年龄的不同

dispatch [dis'pætʃ] v. 分派，派遣；迅速处理
[例] He dispatched his breakfast and left. 他匆匆吃完早饭就离开了。

> 国外报纸上有一个版面叫做 Hatch, Match and Dispatch；登载五花八门的个人广告，比如恭喜谁家生了小孩啦 hatch，找工作、征婚啦 match，哀悼某人去世啦 dispatch（被派遣到上帝身边了）。

displace [dis'pleis] v. 位移；取代，替代
[例] He displaced a bone in his knee in the crash with another player. 他在与另一名运动员相撞时膝部有一块骨头移位了。
[记] displacement n. 位移，替代

display [di'splei] n./v. 陈列，展览，显示
[例]All the parents were looking at the display of children's work. 所有的父母都在看孩子们的作品展览。

dispose [dis'pəuz] v. 处理，布置，安排
[例] We have to dispose of this pile of old papers and magazines. 我们得把这堆旧报纸和杂志处理掉。
[记] dispose of sth. 处理，安排

> 字根pos指"放、置"。如：pose就是放置的状态→姿势；position位置；compose 放在一起→写作、作曲；deposit 往下放→沉淀、存钱；propose 放在前面→提议、计划；dispose 分开放→安置，处理。俗语有云：Man proposes, god disposes. 即：谋事在人，成事在天。

disposal [dis'pəuzəl] n. 处理，布置，安排
[例] His disposal of the difficulty pleased everybody. 他对困难的处理使大家都感到满意。

dispute [dis'pju:t] v./n. 争论，辩论
[例] They disputed how to bring into full play the potential of the staff. 他们争论如何才能充分发挥全体员工的潜力。
[同义词] argue, contest, debate

disregard [ˌdisri'gɑ:d] v. /n. 忽视，忽略
[例] Disregarding all difficulties, we succeeded in bringing them around in the end. 尽管困难重重，我们最终说服了他们。
[记] in disregard of 不顾，无视

disseminate [di'semineit] v. 散布；传播
[例] Good news is disseminated quickly. 好消息传播迅速。

dissolve [di'zɔlv] v. 溶解，分解，解散

[例] Sugar dissolves in water. 糖溶于水。

dissertation [ˌdisə(:)'teiʃən] n.（学位）论文

[例] I will finish my master's dissertation in a week. 我一周后就可以完成我的硕士论文了。

> 一起来区别一些恐怖的词：essay 短论文；thesis 学士或硕士毕业论文；dissertation 硕士或博士专题论文；paper 则泛指各种论文；assignment 作业。

distil [di'stil] v.(=distill) 蒸馏，提取…的精华

[例] The notes I had brought back were waiting to be distilled into a book. 我带回的笔记准备提炼整理成一本书。

distinct [dis'tiŋkt] a. 截然不同的，明显的，独特的

[例] Those two suggestions are quite distinct from each other. 这两个建议截然不同。

[记] distinctive a. 与众不同的，独特的

distinction [dis'tiŋkʃən] n. 区别，差别；特征，个性

[例] There is no appreciable distinction between the twins. 在这对孪生子之间看不出有什么明显的差别。

distinguish [dis'tiŋgwiʃ] v. 区别，辨别；使杰出，使著名

[例] People who cannot distinguish between colours are said to be colour-blind. 不能分辨颜色的人被称为色盲。

[记] distinguished a. 卓著的，著名的 / distinguished guest 贵宾

distort [dis'tɔ:t] v. 扭曲，歪曲

[例] Stop distorting what I've said. 不要再歪曲我所说的话。

[记] distortion n. 扭曲，曲解 / distorted a. 被扭曲的

distract [dis'trækt] v. 分散注意力；使（某人）分心

[例] The royal scandal has distracted media attention from the economic crisis. 王室丑闻转移了媒介对经济危机的注意力。

> 字根tract指"拉拽draw"。唱片上被唱机指针拉出的音轨叫track；拖拉机tractor；拉到一起→contract 合同；往回拉→retract 撤消，收回；去拉一拉→attract 吸引；拉出来→abstract 抽象，摘要（一个事物的实质内容被拉走了）；拉着离开→distract 分心。

distraction [dis'trækʃən] n. 娱乐，分心，分心的事物

[例] There are too many distractions in the hotel for me to work properly. 旅馆里使人分心的事物太多，使我难于集中精力工作。

distress [dis'tres] n. 悲痛，穷困，不幸；v. 使伤心，使忧虑

> 俗语 Two in distress makes sorrow less.指的是如果两个人都很痛苦，那么相互倾诉一下，或者不用倾诉，一方只要看到另一方的苦痛，就都不会觉得自己是世界上最痛苦的人了。

distribute [di'stribju:t] v. 分发，分配

[例] His part-time job on Sunday was to distribute leaflets on the street. 他在星期天的兼职是要到街上去派发传单。

[记] distribution n. 分发，分布 / distributor n. 分发者；批发商

district ['distrikt] n. 地区，区域，行政区

[例] Each residential district in the city is fenced in with elms. 城内每个住宅区的四周用榆树修了篱笆。

disturb [dis'tə:b] v. 打扰，扰乱

[例] Please don't disturb him. 请别打扰他。

diverse [dai'və:s] a. 不同的，多种多样的

[例] There are diverse dialects in the Chinese language. 汉语里有各种不同的方言。

> 字根 vers/vert 指"转向 to turn"。如：di- 个别 +verse 转向→diverse 不同的；diversify 使不同；divert 离开向着其他方向→转移注意力，娱乐。

diversify [dai'və:sifai] v. 使不同，使多样化

[例] A factory must try to diversify for further development. 一个工厂要获得进一步发展就要努力使产品多样化。

diversity [dai'və:siti] n. 多样性，差异

[例] Charles Darwin saw in the diversity of species the principles of evolution that operated to generate the species: variation, competition and selection. 查尔斯 · 达尔文在物种的多样性中发现了致使物种进化的原则：变异、竞争和选择。

[记] a great diversity of methods 各种不同的方法

divert [di'və:t] v. 转移，转向；娱乐

[例] A loud noise from the street diverted my attention. 街上的一阵喧闹声转移了我的注意力。

dividend ['dividend] n. 股息，红利；【数】被除数

[例] I don't know when my dividend will be paid. 我不知道什么时候能被付给股息。

divine [di'vain] a. 神的；上帝的；天赐的；极好的

[例]Here is another divine performance of the concerto. 又是一次美妙的协奏曲演奏。

divorce [di'vɔ:s] n./v. 离婚，脱离

[例] Never be divorced from real life. 千万不要脱离现实生活。

[记] be divorced from 与…离婚，与…脱离

dizzy ['dizi] a. 头晕目眩的，眩晕

[例] The old woman was dizzied by the strong wind. 那位老太太被风吹得头昏眼花。

doctorate ['dɔktərit] n.（大学授予的）博士学位

[例] She received her doctorate in history in 2004. 2004 年她拿到了历史学博士学位。

> 字根 doc 指“教导 to teach”。doctor 教导者→博士，医生；doctrine 教导的事情→教条，学说；document 文件，公文。

document ['dɔkjumənt] v. 用文件记载；n. 文件，文献，文档

[例] The book is highly documented.这本书记录了大量的史实。

documentary [ˌdɔkju'mentəri] n. 记录片

[例] This is a documentary about coal miners. 这是反映煤矿工人的纪录片。

documentation [ˌdɔkjumen'teiʃən] n. 文件

[例] Applicants must provide supporting documentation. 申请者必须提供支持性文件。

domain [dəu'mein] n.（活动、学问等的）领域；领土，领地；

[例] This is out of my domain. 这不属于我的范围。

dome [dəum] n. 圆屋顶

[例] There were several lesser towers, the corner ones with domes. 有几个较小的塔楼，其中的偏角塔有圆顶。

> 字根 dom 既指“房屋 house”又指“统治 to rule”。指“房屋”如：dome，domestic 房屋的→家庭的，国内的；指“统治”如：domain 所有地，领土；king 国王 +dom 统治→ kindom 王国；dominate 统治，支配。

domestic [də'mestik] a. 国内的；家庭的；驯服的

[例] Foreign-made cars and textile were sweeping into the domestic market. 外国车和纺织品正涌进国内市场。

[记] domestic and foreign news 国内外新闻 / domestic goods/products 国货

dominate ['dɔmineit] v. 支配，统治；占优势

[例] A great man can dominate others by force of character. 伟人能以人格的力量支配他人。

dominant ['dɔminənt] a. 有统治权的，占优势的，支配的

[例] The right hand is dominant in most people. 大多数人右手比左手有力。

donate [dəu'neit] v. 捐，赠

[例] Local people lined up to donate blood for the brave girl. 当地群众排队给这位勇敢的姑娘献血。

[记] donation n. 捐赠，捐款 / donator n. 捐赠者 / blood donator 献血者

doom [du:m] n. 命运；厄运，毁灭；死亡；v. 注定；判决

[例] Dissonance among the three partners doomed the project. 三个股东间的不调和注定了那个计划的失败。

dormant ['dɔːmənt] a. 睡着的，休眠的，暂停活动（或作用）的

[例] The dormant volcano has recently shown signs of life. 那座休眠的火山最近显现了活动的迹象。

> 字根 dorm 指"睡眠 sleep"。如：dormitory 睡觉的地方→宿舍。dormitory 一词常被简写为 dorm；如果你把 dormitory 一词的字母打乱重新组合，可拼写出 dirty room! 这种游戏叫 Anagrams，再比如：eleven plus two = twelve plus one；Mother-in-law = Woman Hitler!

dormitory ['dɔːmitri] n. 宿舍

[例] Children sleep in dormitories when they live at school. 孩子们住在学校时，在宿舍睡觉。

dose [dəus] n. 剂量；v.（给…）服药

[例] Here is your medicine — the dose is two spoonfuls every four hours. 这是你的药，剂量是每四小时服两匙。

dot [dɔt] n. 点，圆点；v. 在…上打点

[例] On the map, towns were marked by a red dot. 在地图上，城镇是用小红点标出的。

> 很多现代人认为比较舒服的朋友间关系是在交往过程中很有默契，双方都不必"dot every i and cross every t"，字面含义是"不用给每个字母 i 都加点，也不用在每个字母 t 上都写下它的最后一笔"。即便一方没有把自己的意思百分之百地表达出来，对方也充分明白了他或她的意图。心有灵犀一点 dot 通。

double ['dʌbl] n./v./a. 两倍（的）

[例] Many things now cost double what they did a few years ago. 许多东西比数年前贵了一倍。

downpour ['daunpɔː(r)] n. 倾盆大雨

[例] For the past six hours the downpour had been continuous. 过去的 6 个小时里倾盆大雨持续不断。

[同义词] downfall, rainstorm /rainfall n. 降雨，降雨量

downsize ['daunˌsaiz] v. 裁员；缩小尺寸

[例] American manufacturing organizations have been downsizing their factories. 美国的制造商们一直在缩小它们的工厂规模。

> 同义表达 lay off 解雇。西方公司裁员 corporate downsizing 常用减肥术语来类比，如：trimming the fat 抽脂，getting lean and mean 瘦身，shedding weight 抛重，掉膘。公司这么做一般是为了 restructuring 重组，rightsizing 合理精简，reallocating resources 资源重新配置等。

doze [dəuz] v. 小睡，打瞌睡，打盹儿

[例] He dozed away the afternoon. 他瞌睡了一下午。
[同义词] drowse, nap

draft [drɑːft] v./n. 草稿；起草
[例] I have just finished the draft for the speech tomorrow. 我刚刚写完明天演讲的草稿。

drainage ['dreinidʒ] n. 排水（法）；排水装置
[例] The drainage of the city is not good, as some of the pipes are broken. 这个城市的排水系统不好，有些排水管都破裂了。

drama ['drɑːmə] n. 戏剧
[例] The witness' unexpected disclosure was filled with drama. 证人出人意料的揭发充满了戏剧性。
music and drama 音乐和戏剧 / TV drama 电视剧

dramatic [drə'mætik] a. 戏剧性的，令人激动的
[例] She made a dramatic speech at the meeting. 她在会上发表了激动人心的演说。

drawback ['drɔːˌbæk] n. 缺点，欠缺；退款
[例] The only drawback to her plan is that it costs too much. 她那个计划的唯一缺点就是花费太大。
[记] duty drawback 关税退税

dredge [dredʒ] n. 挖泥机，挖掘机 v. 挖掘；撒在食物上
[例] She dredged a little sugar over the cake. 她在点心上撒了点糖。

drift [drift] v. 飘移，漂流，漂泊
[例] The currents drifted the dead body ashore. 水流把尸体冲到岸边来了。

drill [dril] n. 钻孔机；（反复）练习；军事训练；v. 训练，钻孔
[例] The Saudi government has announced plans to drill for water in the desert. 沙特政府已经宣布在沙漠钻井探水的计划。
[记] an electric drill 电钻

drip [drip] v. 滴水，漏水
[例] Be careful—your paintbrush is dripping. 小心——你的漆刷在往下滴漆。

> drip 和 drop 都是象声词，仔细听一听雨滴掉在地上的声音。东西方历史上都有一种水刑 water tortures：犯人头低脚高地被固定在刑凳上，嘴和鼻塞满了亚麻布，刑吏将水不断地滴 drip 在布上以窒息犯人。

drought [draut] n. 干旱，缺乏
[例] Many areas of Africa have suffered severe drought this year. 今年非洲的很多地区遭受了严重的干旱。

drown [draun] v. 淹死；把（某物）浸泡在（液体）中
[例] She attempted to drown herself in the river. 她企图投河自尽。

dual ['djuəl] a. 双的，双重的
[例] He has dual nationality. 他具有双重国籍。

due [dju:] a. 应支付的，应得到的，预定应到的，期满的
[例] I am due for a rise in pay. 我应该提工资了。
[记] due to 由于，因为 / become due 到期，满期 / overdue a. 迟到的

dull [dʌl] a. 无趣的，沉闷的；迟钝的；愚笨的
[例] I thought the book dull and unoriginal. 我认为这本书既沉闷又无新意。

dumb [dʌm] a. 哑的，说不出话的
[例] They remained dumb at the meeting. 他们在会上保持沉默。
[记] dumb bell 哑铃 / mute n. 哑巴

dump [dʌmp] v. 倾倒；丢弃；乱扔
[例] There are special places where you can dump things you don't want. 有一些指定的地方，你可以把不需要的东西倒在那里。

duplicate ['dju:plikeit] a. 复制的；完全一样的；n. 复制品，副本；v. 复制，复印
[例] He duplicated his former mistakes. 他又犯了和以前一样的错误。

> 字根pli指"折叠 fold"。如：replicate 向回叠→折转，反复；complicate 重叠在一起→使复杂；explicit 向外叠开→外在的，明白的；duplicate 折叠成两份(du-)→复制，加倍。duplication n.复制品。

durable ['djuərəbl] a. 耐用的，持久的
[例] The parts of the machine that experience a lot of fiction have to be made from durable materials. 机器里要承受很多摩擦的部分要由耐用材料制成。
[记] durable goods 耐用品 / durable cloth 耐用的布

duration [djuə'reiʃən] n. 持续，持久；持续期间
[例] We hope the war will be of short duration.我们希望战争是短期的。

dusk [dʌsk] n. 黄昏，傍晚
[例] The street lights go on at dusk. 街灯在黄昏时亮起来。

duty ['dju:ti] n. 义务，责任；（购物缴纳的）税
[例] He felt a sense of duty towards his parents. 他对他的父母有一种责任感。
[记] do one's duty 尽职，尽本分 / on duty 值班，上班 / off duty 下班 / duty free 免税店；免税的 / [同义词] obligation, responsibility

dwarf [dwɔ:f] n. 小矮人，侏儒

> 童话fairy tale 中的著名人物：Snow White and the Seven Dwarfs / Dwarves 白雪公主和七个小矮人；Cinderella 灰姑娘；mermaid 美人鱼。

dwell [dwel] v. 居住

[例] He duelt in a cabin by the sea alone after he retired. 他退休后独自居住在一间海滨小屋里。

[记] dweller n. 居住着 / dwelling n. 住处

dwindle ['dwindl] v. 缩小，减少

[例] The number of people going to the cinema seems to dwindle steadily. 上电影院看电影的人数似乎在持续下降。

dye [dai] n. 染料，染色；v. 染

[例] She's dyed her hair red — it looks so unnatural. 她把头发染成了红色，看起来很不自然。

[记] pigment n. 颜料

dynamic [dai'næmik] n. 动力的；有活力的，精力充沛的

[例] If you are young, attractive and dynamic, you don't need to worry about finding a date. 如果你年轻、动人、活力四射，不必担心找不到约会的人。

dynasty ['dinəsti] n. 王朝，朝代

[例] The Habsburg dynasty ruled in Austria from 1278 to 1918. 哈普斯堡王朝从 1278 年至 1918 年统治奥地利。

[记] change a dynasty 改朝换代

dysfunction [dis'fʌŋkʃən] n. 【医】功能紊乱，官能障碍

[例] The neurological dysfunction disabled him. 神经机能障碍致使他残疾。

> dys- 表示"困难的,有病的"之义，如：dysaesthesia 感觉迟钝；dystrophy 营养失调；dysfunction 功能紊乱。

eccentric [ik'sentrik] a. 古怪的；离心的

[例] The old lady has some eccentric habits. 这位老妇人有一些古怪的习惯。

echo ['ekəu] n. 回声；v. 发回声；随声附和；v. 摹仿；反射

[例] The cathedral roof is echoing joyous hymns. 教堂的天顶回响着欢乐的赞美诗。

> 希腊神话中 Echo 是居于山林水泽的仙女，但她丧失了独立说话的能力，只能重复别人说话的尾音。之后她爱上了一位美少年，但遭到拒绝。从此终日抑郁，山林间只剩叹息。现在当我们在山间高喊时，仔细听一听，有 Echo 的叹息在回应。

eclipse [i'klips] n./v. 日蚀；月蚀；衰落，使黯然失色

[例] A solar eclipse occurs when the moon passes between the sun and the earth. 当月球运行到太阳和地球的中间时便今出现日食。

ecology [i(:)'kɔlədʒi] n. 生态学

[例] I am interested in the ecology of the desert. 我对沙漠生态学很感

兴趣。
[记] ecological a. 生态学的 / ecologist n. 生态学者

economy [i'kɔnəmi] n. 经济；节约
[例] His views on the knowledge economy have been accepted with unanimity. 他关于知识经济的观点得到了一致公认。
[记] economics n. 经济学/ economic a. 经济上的，经济学的 / economical a. 节约的，经济的 / economise v. 节省；有效地利用 / economist n. 经济学家

edge [edʒ] n. 刀口，刃；边缘；优势；v. 使锋利
[例] That knife has a sharp edge. 那把刀的刃口很锋利。
[记] gain the edge 取得优势 / lose the edge失掉优势

edible ['edibl] a. 可以吃的，可以食用的
[例] Are these berries edible, or are they poisonous? 这些草莓是可以吃，还是有毒?
[反义词] inedible

> 形容词尾 -ible = -able 指“有能力的”。如：audible 听得见的；inaudible 听不见的；visible 可见的。可饮用的是 drinkable。

edit ['edit] v. 编辑，校订；剪辑
[例] The newspaper edits letters before printing them. 报纸先将来信进行编辑，然后印出。
[记] editor n. 编辑 / chief editor 主编，总编

edition [i'diʃən] n. 版本，版
[例] The new edition of the encyclopaedia will appear in the bookstores next week. 新版百科全书下周就会在书店摆出来。

effect [i'fekt] n. 结果，效果，作用，影响
[例] Punishment had very little effect on him. 惩罚对他没有什么效果。
[记] have an effect on 对…有影响；对…起作用

effective [i'fektiv] a. 有效的，能产生（预期）效果的
[例] The medicine is an effective cure for a headache. 这种药治头痛有很好的疗效。
[记] take effective measures 采取有效措施 / effectively adv. 有效地 / ineffective a. 无效的

efficient [i'fiʃənt] a. 有效率的，高效率的；能胜任的
[例] The new secretary is a quick, efficient worker, and the boss is quite satisfied with her. 新来的秘书是个敏捷的、效率高的工作人员，老板对她很满意。
[记] efficiency n. 功效，效率 / efficiently adv. 有效地

egalitarian [igæli'teəriən] a. 平等主义的；n. 平等主义
[例] Clearly the egalitarian society remains a dream. 显然平等主义社会仍然是一个梦。

ego ['iːgəu] n. 自我，利己主义；自负

[例] That promotion really boosted her ego. 那次提升真的使她更加自负了。

> 拉丁文，指“我，I”。egocentric 自我为中心的；egoism 自我主义，利己主义；egoist 利己主义者。

elaborate [i'læbərət] a. 精心制作的，周详的；v. 详细说明，精心制作

[例] The chairman just wanted the facts; You don't need to elaborate on them. 主席只想了解事实，你不必作详细说明。

elapse [i'læps] v.（时间）过去，流逝

[例] Five months have elapsed since he joined the army. 他参军已经五个月了。

Unit 10

elastic [i'læstik] a. 有弹性的

[例] The swimming costume is made of elastic material. 这件泳衣是用弹性材料制成的。

elasticity [ilæs'tisiti] n. 弹力，弹性

[例] Don't destroy the skin's natural elasticity. 别破坏皮肤的自然弹性。

elective [i'lektiv] a. 选任的，由选举产生的；（课程）选修的，可以选择的

[例] Forbes, 48, a multimillionaire funding his presidential campaign with his own money, has never held elective office. 四十八岁的福布斯，一个用自己的钱资助自己竞选总统的百万富翁，从来没有组建过选举办公室。

elegant ['eligənt] a. 优雅的，精致的

[例] The table was covered with an elegant lace cloth. 桌上铺着一块精致的花边布。

element ['elimənt] n. 元素；基本组成部分

[例] Both hydrogen and oxygen are elements. 氢和氧都是化学元素。

elevate ['eliveit] v. 提升，提高

[例] Reading good books can elevate one's mind. 阅读好书可提高人的心灵修养。

> 字根 lev 指“升、举 to raise”。如：lever 轻易举起的东西→杠杆；leverage 杠杆作用→方法，手段；elevate 举起来→提升；elevator【美】电梯；lift【英】电梯。

elicit [i'lisit] v. 引出，得出，发出

[例] After much questioning among the people concerned, the headmaster at last elicited the truth about the incident. 经在有关人员中反复询问，校长终于问出了那件事的真相。

eligible ['elidʒəbl] a. 有资格的，符合条件的

[例] Are you eligible to join this club? 你有资格加入这俱乐部吗？

[同义词] fit, qualified

eliminate [i'limineit] v. 除去，消除；淘汰

[例] She has been eliminated from the swimming race because she did not win any of the practice races. 她已被取消了游泳比赛，因为她在训练中没有得到名次。

elite [ei'li:t] n. 精英；精华；中坚

[例] The army was controlled by a small elite group of officers. 军队由军官中的少数精英控制。

elusive [i'lju:siv] a. 难懂的，难捉摸的，易忘的

[例] She managed to get an interview with that elusive man. 她设法采访了那位难以捉摸的人。

embark [im'ba:k] v. 上船（或飞机、汽车等）；从事，着手

[例] We embarked at Liverpool for New York. 我们在利物浦上船前往纽约。

> bark 一词前面已学过，指“狗叫”和“树皮”。在这里，bark 由树皮引申为木头。当古人从岸边跳上水中的一块木头时，就是 em (in)+bark，上船。相当于 aboard (prep./ adv.) 的含义。board，木板，aboard（在船上）就是在一块木板上。

embarrass [im'bærəs] v. 使尴尬，使窘迫，使局促不安

[例] I was embarrassed by their compliment. 对他们的称赞我感到很不安。

[记] embarrassment n. 窘迫；经济困难 / financial embarrassment 财政拮据

embed [im'bed] v. 使插入；使嵌入；埋入

[例] That terrible day will be embedded in the children's memory. 那可怕的一天将深深印在孩子们的记忆中。

embellish [im'beliʃ] v. 修饰

[例] The door of the old church was embellished with decorations. 老教堂的门是用雕饰美化的。

embody [im'bɔdi] v. 具体表现，体现

[例] Words embody thoughts and feelings. 言语具体表现各种思想和感情。

embrace [im'breis] v. 拥抱，怀抱；包含；采取

[例] He held her to him in a warm embrace. 他热列地拥抱她。

> “brace”来自古法语，表示“手臂”，那么“embrace”的基本含义表示“放在手臂里”，指“拥抱”这个动作；什么又是“brace<u>let</u>”呢？“let”放在一些名词的后边表示“小、在…上佩带的小饰物”，所以 bracelet 表示“手镯”，piglet 是“小猪”。anklet 不就是“脚链、脚镯”吗。

embroider [im'brɔidə] v. 刺绣；装饰；给…添油加醋

[例] Her shirt is embroidered with roses. 他的衬衣上绣着玫瑰花。

embryo ['embriəu] n. 胚胎；胎儿；a. 胚胎的；初期的

[例] The plans are still in embryo. 计划仍在酝酿中。

emerge [i'mə:dʒ] v. 浮现，出现

[例] The sun emerged from behind the clouds. 太阳从云层后面露出来。

emigrate ['emigreit] v.（使）移民

[例] He did not receive permission to emigrate to the United States. 他没

有获准移民美国。
[记] emigrate自本国移出 / immigrate ['imigreit] 自他国迁入 / immigration n. 移民；移居 / the immigration law 移民法

eminent ['eminənt] a. 著名的，有名望的
[例] The students are expecting the arrival of an eminent scientist. 同学们正期待一位著名科学家的来访。

emit [i'mit] v. 散发（热光，气等）；发出（声响）
[例] The exhaust pipe of the motor vehicle emitted poisonous fumes. 机动车的尾部排气管排出了有毒的浓烟。

emission [i'miʃən] n.（光、热等的）散发，发射，喷射
[例] Britain has agreed to cut emissions of nitrogen oxide from power stations. 英国同意减少电厂氧化氮的排放。

emotion [i'məuʃən] n. 情绪，情感，感情
[例] She was good at hiding her emotions. 她善于隐藏自己的感情。

> 字根 mot 指"移动 to move"。如：motion 运动，动作；motive 动机；motor 马达；motivate 激发；promote 向上移动→晋升；remote 向后移动→遥远的；emotion 移动到了外面（e-=ex-）→感情，情绪。

emphasize ['emfəsaiz] v. 强调
[例] He emphasized the need for hard work. 他强调了苦干的必要。
[记] emphasis n. 强调，重点

empirical [im'pirikəl] a. 凭经验（或观察）的，经验主义的
[例] His theory is inconsistent with the empirical evidence. 他的理论和经验证据不一致。
[反义词] theoretical a. 理论的

employ [im'plɔi] v. 雇用；使用，运用
[例] She employs her time wisely. 她善于运用时间。
[记] employer 雇主，老板 / employee 雇员，职工 / employment n. 雇用，工作 / unemployment n. 失业

emulate ['emjuleit] v. 努力赶上（或超过）
[例] You must work hard to emulate your brother's success. 你必须努力工作，赶上你哥哥的成就。

enable [i'neibl] v. 使能够
[例] This dictionary enables you to understand English words. 这本词典能使你理解英语词汇。
[记] enable sb.to do sth. 使某人能够做某事

enact [i'nækt] v. 制定（法律）；颁布；扮演，担任…角色
[例] They enact the role of hero and heroine in the play. 他们在这出戏中担任男、女主角。

enclose [in'kləuz] v. 围住，围起来；放入封套，随信寄上

[例] The football field is enclosed by a wall. 足球场被一道墙围了起来。

encompass [in'kʌmpəs] v. 环绕，包围；包含，包括

[例] The general art course at the university encompasses wide range of subjects. 大学文科包括的科目范围很广。

> compass 指南针，罗盘；compasses 圆规；encompass 在（en-）罗盘，圆面的范围之中→环绕，包围。

encounter [in'kauntə] v./n. 偶然碰到，相遇，邂逅

[例] The more dangers we encounter, the harder should we push forward. 越是艰险越向前。

[同义词] come across

encyclopedia [en,saikləu'pi:diə] n. 百科全书

[例] A dictionary explains words and an encyclopedia explains facts. 词典解释词义，百科全书解释事物。

> 源于希腊词*enkyklios paideia*：en即"in"; kykilos, "circle" paideia, "education"，合起来即"包罗整个教育以及知识领域的事物"。

endanger [in'deindʒə] v. 使处于险境，危及

[例] If you work hard without rest, you will endanger your health. 你若辛勤工作而不休息，会把身体弄坏的。

endeavour [in'devə] (=endeavor)v. 努力，尽力；n. 尝试；努力

[例] We must always endeavour to improve our work. 我们总要努力改进自己的工作。

endorse [in'dɔ:s] v. 在（票据）背面签名；签注（文件）；认可，签署

[例] The Prime Minister is unlikely to endorse this view. 总理不可能认同这种观点。

endow [in'dau] v. 捐赠，赋予

[例] She is endowed with great writing ability. 她具有杰出的写作天赋。

[记] endowment n. 捐赠，捐赠的基金（或财产）；天赋

endure [in'djuə] v. 忍耐，忍受；耐久

[例] I can' t endure her endless complaint noise a moment longer. 我一刻也忍受不了她那没完没了的抱怨。

[记] endurable a. 可忍受的

energetic [,enə'dʒetik] a. 充满活力的，精力充沛的

[例] He is an energetic tennis player. 他是一个精力充沛的网球运动员。

[记] energy n. 精力，活力；能量

enforce [in'fɔ:s] v. 实施，执行，使生效；迫使

[例] The police are there to enforce the law. 警察在那里执法。

engage [in'geidʒ] v. 使忙碌，使从事于；雇用，聘请；参与

[例] His good nature engages everyone. 他善良的性情吸引着每个人。
[记] be engaged in 从事于 / be engaged to同…订婚

engagement [in'geidʒmənt] n. 婚约；保证；雇拥
[例] My brother has just told me about his engagement to Anne. 我弟弟刚告诉我他和安妮订婚了。

enhance [in'haːns] v. 提高；增强
[例] A good score in IELTS will enhance my chance of getting the post. 一个好的雅思考试成绩将会增加我获得这个职位的机会。

enlighten [in'laitn] v. 启发，教导，启迪
[例] For all my effort to enlighten her, she is still all adrift. 尽管我设法使她开窍，她却仍然莫名其妙。

> en(in)+light+ en(动词词尾)，将一个人由黑暗带到有光线（光明）的地方，就是enlighten，启蒙，启发。

enormous [i'nɔːməs] a. 巨大的，庞大的
[例] The banquet was held in an enormous hall. 宴会在一个大厅里举行。
[记]enormously adv. 非常地；巨大地

enquiry [in'kwaiəri] (=inquiry) n. 询问，打听，查问
[例] Many thanks for your reply to our enquiry of March 1. 非常感谢贵方对我们3月1日询问信件的答复。

enrich [in'ritʃ] v. 使富足，使充实
[谚] Give much to the poor, do enrich a man's store. 多施舍，财富多。

enrol [in'rəul] (=enroll) v. （入学、参军）登记，注册
[例] I like your institute but I do not want to enrol. 我喜欢你们学院但我不想报名去读。
[记] enroll sb. as... 招收某人为… / enroll sb. in... 使某人加入… / enrollment n. 入学；注册，登记

ensue [in'sjuː] v. 跟着发生，继起
[例] A hand grenade exploded by accident and I got lost in the ensuing confusion.一枚手榴弹意外地发生了爆炸，接着是一片混乱，使我不知所措。

ensure [in'ʃuə] v. 确保，保证
[例] We can ensure that the work shall be done in the right way. 我们可以保证把工作做好。
[记] ensure sb. sth. / ensure sth. to sb. 保证某人一定得到某物

entail [in'teil] v. 使人承担；使必需
[例] Producing a series of TV plays entails a lot of work. 拍摄一部电视连续剧需要做大量的工作。

enterprise ['entəpraiz] n.企业，事业；进取心，冒险精神
[例] He works in a state-owned enterprise. 他在一家国有企业工作。

enterprise 和 organisation 都可指盈利性和非盈利性企业、组织。如: public service enterprise 公用事业企业; non-profit organisation 非盈利性企业。而 company, firm, cooperation 专指盈利公司。

enterprising ['entəpraiziŋ] a. 有事业心的，有进取心的，有魄力的
[例] Some enterprising students are designing management software for the university. 一些有进取心的学生正在为学校设计管理软件。

entertain [,entə'tein] v. 娱乐，招待，款待
[例] The Smiths entertain a great deal. 史密斯一家常款待客人。

enthusiasm [in'θju:ziæzəm] n. 热情，热心
[例] Anthropology is his enthusiasm. 人类学是他热心研究的学科。

enthusiastic [in,θju:zi'æstik] a. 热心的, 热情的
[例] The retired worker is very enthusiastic about neighbourhood affairs. 这个退休工人对社区工作非常热心。

entire [in'taiə] a. 整个的，全部的
[例] Due to bad cold, she spent the entire day in bed. 她因重感冒在床上躺了一整天。

entitle [in'taitl] v. 给…权利（或资格）；给…题名；给…称号
[例] The token entitles you to free admissions to the museum. 凭此券你可以得到两张参观博物馆的免费入场券。
[记] be entitled to sth. 对…享有权利 / be entitled to do sth.有(做某事)的权利 / be entitled A 题目是 A；称为 A

entity ['entiti] n. 实体
[例] Each creature is a separate entity. 每一个人都是一个独立的整体。

environment [in'vaiərənmənt] n. 环境，自然环境
[例] The rural environment lent itself to the restoration of his health. 农村环境有助于他恢复健康。

envisage [in'vizidʒ] v. 想象，设想
[例] When do you envisage being able to finish the experiment? 你设想什么时候能做完这个实验?

envy ['envi] v./n. 羡慕, 嫉妒
[例] The boy’s new electronic toy train was the envy of his friends. 这男孩的新电动玩具火车使他的朋友们很羡慕。
[记] envy sb. (for) sth. 因某事羡慕某人

epic ['epik] n. 史诗；叙事长诗
[例] The Odyssey is an epic of ancient Greece. 《奥德塞》是古希腊的一首史诗。

著名的荷马史诗 Homer’s Epic Poems 有两部:《伊利亚特》*Iliad* 和《奥德塞》*Odyssey*。而由于 *Odyssey* 是描述希腊英雄奥得修斯 Odysseus 在特洛伊 Troy 战争后回转故乡时所经历的种种磨

难，长达十年；odyssey一词便在英语中引申为“漫长的冒险旅程”。

epidemic [epi'demik] n. 流行病；a. 流行性的

[例] Violence is reaching epidemic levels in some films and TV plays. 在一些电影和电视剧中暴力已经快到泛滥程度了。

episode ['episəud] n. 插曲；一个事件；（电视剧）一集

[例] The rest of the episodes of this TV play will be broadcast next week. 这部电视剧的最后几集将于下周播出。

equate [i'kweit] v. 等同，使相等

[例] Nowadays, many people equate passing examinations with being educated. 当今很多人把考试及格与受过教育等同起来。

equation [i'kweiʃən] n. 相等，平衡；方程式，等式

[例] If you're trying to get healthy by losing weight, exercise should be part of the equation. 假如你要通过减肥来保持健康，锻炼应当是必不可少的。

equilibrium [ˌi:kwi'libriəm] n. 平衡，均衡；沉着，安静

[例] This kind of ear disease can affect people's equilibrium. 这种耳疾能影响人们的平衡感。

[记] the equilibrium of demand and supply 供求均衡

equip [i'kwip] v. 配备，装备

[例] He equipped himself for a long journey. 他为长途旅行准备行装。

[记] be equipped for 准备好，对…有准备 / be equipped with…装备；安装

equity ['ekwiti] n. 公平,公正；资产净值

[例] All human beings want to be treated with equity and respect. 所有的人都想得到公平和尊重。

equivalent [i'kwələnt] n. 相等物，等价物；a. 相等的，相当的

[例] He changed his pounds for the equivalent amount of dollars. 他把英镑换成了等值的美元。

[记] be equivalent to... 相当于…

era ['iərə] n. 时代，历史时期，纪元

[例] Our era produces a host of heroes and heroines. 我们的时代英雄辈出。

eradicate [i'rædikeit] v. 根除，消灭，杜绝

[例] Scientists are working to find a serum to eradicate the disease. 科学家试图发现一种血清来根除这种疾病。

字根radi指“根，root”。如：radical指从根儿上就变了，彻底的→激进的，激进分子。我们吃萝卜是吃它的根，所以萝卜叫radish。

erase [i'reiz] v. 删除；抹去

[例] Jim tried to erase the idea from his mind. 吉姆努力忘掉这一念头。

erect [i'rekt] v. 竖立，建立；a. 竖直的

[例] This monument was erected in honour of the martyrs during the civil war. 这座纪念碑是为内战中牺牲的烈士们而建立的。

erode [i'rəud] v. 侵蚀，腐蚀

[例] The running water from the mountain top eroded a gulley along the slope. 从山顶上流下的水在山坡上冲蚀出一条沟渠。

[记] erosion n. 腐蚀，侵蚀

error ['erə] n. 错误，过失

[例] The accident was caused by human error. 这次事故是由人为过错造成的。

[记] trial and error 反复实验

eruption [i'rʌpʃən] n. 喷发，爆发；喷出物

[例] The eruption of the volcano caused great loss. 火山喷发造成了巨大损失。

escalate ['eskəleit] v. 逐步上升，逐步升级

[例] The cost of living is escalating in the country. 这个国家的生活费用在上涨。

> 拉丁文中 scala 指"梯子 ladder"。escalate 沿着梯子往上（e-）爬→逐步上升；escalator（商场里的）自动扶梯。

escalator ['eskəleitə(r)] n. 自动扶梯；滚梯

[例] I could never find the escalators, or the door I came in. 我根本找不着自动扶梯以及进来时走的那个门。

essay ['esei] n. 论说文；散文

[例] The other day I came across an interesting essay on the Napoleonic Wars. 前几天我偶然地读到一篇关于同拿破仑作战的有趣文章。

essence ['esns] n. 本质，实质；精髓

[例] The essence of his religious teaching is love for all men. 他宣扬的宗教教义要旨是爱天下人。

[记] in essence 本质上；大体上

> 各种护肤洗发用品的什么"精华素"、"天然草本精华"，"精华"就是 essence。如果要表示"精华中的精华，最精华"一义，考虑单词 quintessence。它的构成可以理解为"quint-essence"—"第五精华"。它的理念来自中世纪哲学，认为除空气、水、火、土之外的构成天体的第五要素是精华中的精华。

essential [i'senʃəl] a. 本质的，实质的，必不可少的

[例] It is essential for us to try to decide whether television is a blessing or a curse. 我们有必要来评断电视到底是福还是祸。

[记] be essential to/ for 对…来说很重要，不可缺少 / essentially adv. 本质上，基本上

establish [is'tæbliʃ] v. 建立，设立（机构或组织）

[例] The Minister established a commission to suggest improvements in the educational system.部长组织了一个研究组，为改进教育制度提供建议。

[记] established a. 已确立的；已被确认的

establishment [i'stæbliʃmənt] n. 建立，成立；商业机构

[例] These two hotels are both excellent establishments. 这两家旅馆都是出色的商业机构。

estate [i'steit] n. 房地产，财产

[例] When he died, his estate was valued at over a million dollars. 当他去世后，他的财产价位超过了一百万美元。

[记] real estate 不动产；房地产

esteem [is'tiːm] n./v. 尊重，尊敬

[例] He is held in high esteem by his peers. 他倍受同伴们的尊敬。

estimate ['estimeit] v./n. 估计，估价，评估

[例] Now I've realized that my estimate of her character was one-sided. 现在我认识到我对她品格的评价是片面的。

eternal [i'təːnəl] a. 永恒的

[例] Rome has been called the Eternal City. 罗马被称为永恒之城。

[记] eternity n. 永恒，不朽

> 20世纪80年代美国四人乐队Bangles成为女子乐坛No.1。其经典单曲《永恒的火焰》*Eternal Flame*横扫英美排行榜，一时无两。Close your eyes, give me your hand, darling. Do you feel my heart beating, ...

ethic ['eθik] n. 道德规范，伦理

[例] Marketers must observe their code of ethics. 市场营销人员需遵守他们的道德规范。

[记] ethical a. 伦理的，道德的 / ethics n. 伦理学

ethnic ['eθnik] a. 民族的；种族的，人种的

[例] She is keen on ethnic dance. 她热衷于民族舞蹈。

etiquette ['etiket] n. 礼仪，礼节

[例] He felt very sorry for his breach of etiquette.他为他的失礼行为而深感抱歉。

> 法语借词，原指“标签，签条”。法国宫廷礼节曾极为繁琐，举办盛宴前要发给参加的宾客一张纸片签条，上面写着这次宴会的特殊礼节和穿着打扮要求等。这张写满礼仪要求的签条就是etiquette。英语中ticket（票，入场券）一词也来源于它，读音近似。

evade [i'veid] v. 逃避，躲避

[例] You needn't evade the question. 你不必回避这个问题。

[同义词] avoid, bypass, escape

evacuate [i'vækjueit] v. 疏散，撤出；排泄

[例] The village was evacuated because of the danger of a flood. 由于洪水的威胁，村里人都撤走了。

[记] evacuation n. 疏散，撤离

evaluate [i'væljueit] v. 评价，估价

[例] The research project has only been under way for three months, so it's too early to evaluate its success. 这个研究项目进行了不过三个月，所以要对它的成绩作出评价为时尚早。

[记] evaluate sb. as sth. 把某人作为…进行评价 / evaluate sb. by sth. 以某事物来评价某人

> 字根 val 指"价值"。如：value 价值；invaluable 无价的，非常贵重的；devaluation 贬值；evaluate 评估出（e-）价值；invalid 没有价值的→无效的。

evaluation [iˌvælju'eiʃən] n. 估算，评价

[例] Students frequently do have good grounds for mistrusting their teacher's methods of evaluation. 学生们常常确实有理由质疑老师的评估方法。

evaporate [i'væpəreit] v.（使）蒸发，消失

[例] The pool of water on the playground evaporated in the sun. 操场上水坑里的水在阳光下蒸发了。

Unit 11

even ['iːvən] a. 平的；一致的；平均的；【数】偶数的；v. 使平坦；使相等

[例] He won the first game and I won the second, so we're even.他赢了第一局的比赛，我赢了第二局，因此我们打平了。

event [i'vent] n. 事件，大事；比赛项目

[例] National Day and International Labour Day are great events in China. 国庆节和国际劳动节在中国是重大的节日。

eventual [i'ventjuəl] a. 最终的，最后的

[例] Being a top student demonstrates the eventual success of his efforts. 成为尖子学生是他努力的最后成果。

[记] eventually a. 最后，终于

everlasting [ˌevə'lɑːstiŋ] a. 永恒的;持久的

[例] Mona Lisa is known for her everlasting smile. 蒙娜丽莎以其永恒的微笑蜚声世界。

[同义词] eternal

> 包含ever的合成词：evergreen 常绿的，常绿植物；Everest珠穆朗玛峰。

evidence ['evidəns] n. 证据，根据，迹象

[例] Can you show me any evidence for your statement? 你能给我看你供词的证据吗？

[记] in evidence 明显的，显而易见的 / [同义词] indication, proof, sign

evident ['evidənt] a. 明显的，明白的

[例] It's evident that you are tired. 显然你累了。

[记] evidently a.明显地，显然

evoke [i'vəuk] v. 唤起，引起；博得

[例] The newly published review on the book has evoked much controversy. 这篇新发表的书评引起了很多争论。

evolve [i'vɔlv] v.（使）进化；（使）发展，逐步形成

[例] The developmental history of animals tells us that man has evolved from the ape. 动物发展史告诉我们人是从类人猿进化而来的。

[记] evolve from... 从…进化而来

> 拉丁文*volvere*是"滚，转"的意思，过去分词为*volutus*。所以英语单词中包含volve和volut的字母组合即有to roll的含义。evolve滚动着向上→发展，进化；evolution进化，演变；involve滚在里边→包含，牵涉；revolve重新滚动→旋转，考虑；revolution革命。

exact [ig'zækt] a. 准确的；精确的；v. 强求，索取

[例] This work exacts the closest attention and care. 这项工作要求高度的专心和细心。

[记] exactly adv. 确实如此；准确的

exaggerate [ig'zædʒəreit] v. 夸大，夸张

[例] The significance of their scheme has been exaggerated. 他们计划的意义被夸大了。

[记] exaggeration n. 夸张；夸大之词

example [ig'zɑːmpl] n. 例子，榜样

[例] This palace is an example of ancient Chinese architecture. 这座宫殿建筑代表着中国古代的建筑式样。

[记] for example/instance 比如说，例如

excavate ['ekskəveit] v. 挖掘，开凿

[例] The workmen excavated a hole in the wall to let the sewage pipe pass through. 工人们在墙上掘了个洞让污水管通过。

exceed [ik'siːd] v. 超越，胜过

[例] The results of the competition exceeded our expectations. 比赛的结果比我们预料的好。

[记] exceed sb./sth. in... 在…方面超过某人 / 某事 / exceedingly adv. 极其，非常

excel [ik'sel] v. 擅长，优于，胜过他人

[例] Francis excels as a long-distance runner. 弗朗西斯是个出色的长跑选手。

> Office 软件包中的 Excel，表格处理软件。

exception [ik'sepʃən] n. 例外，除外；例外的事物

[谚] No rule without an exception. 凡是规则，总有例外。

excess [ik'ses] n. 过量，过多，（饮食烟酒）无节制；a. 过量的；额外的

[例] You have to pay for excess luggage on a plane. 在飞机上你得付超重的行李费。

[记] excessive a. 过多的，过分的

exclude [iks'kluːd] v. 把…排除在外，拒绝接纳

[例] They excluded people under 18 from joining the club. 他们拒绝接纳十八岁以下的人加入俱乐部。

[记] exclusive a. 排外的，独占的；n. 独家新闻

excursion [iks'kəːʃən] n. 远足，游览，短程旅行

[例] We went on an excursion to the city. 我们到这个城市去旅行。

> 该词的字面意思为：跑（cur）到外（ex）面去了→excursion 远足。

execute ['eksikjuːt] v. 执行，实行；将…处死

[例] He asked his nephew to execute his will. 他请自己的侄子执行遗嘱。

[记] execution n. 实行，执行；死刑

> 某公司的CEO即指Chief Executive Officer首席执行官。CFO：Chief Financial Officer财政总监；CIO：Chief Information Officer咨询总管；COO：Chief Operation Officer运营总监。当然，CEO也可能指Chief Entertainment Officer首席娱乐官；那么CGO呢？Chief Gate Officer看大门总监。

exemplify [ig'zemplifai] v. 举例说明，作为…的例证（或榜样、典型等）
[例] He exemplifies the new liberalism. 他反映了新自由主义的观点。

exempt [ig'zempt] v. 免除，豁免；a. 被免除
[例] Perfume is not exempt from import duty. 香水是不免税的。
[记] exemption n. 免课；免税；免除

exert [ig'zəːt] v. 运用，行使，发挥
[例] For college students, doing a part-time job will exert a profound influence on their personality and life. 打工对大学生的个性培养和今后生活都具有深远的影响。

> 字根sert指“结合，join”。如：desert指脱离(de)结合(sert)→荒凉的，沙漠；insert指在内部（in）结合→插入；ex-外部+sert结合→自己的能力、技巧等与外部结合→exert发挥、运用。

exhale [eks'heil, eg'zeil] v. 呼气；发出，发散
[例] Take a deep breath, then exhale slowly. 深吸一口气，然后慢慢呼出。
[反义词] inhale

exhaust [ig'zɔːst] v. 使精疲力竭，用完，耗尽
[例] The enemy troops were exhausted and demoralized. 敌军疲劳不堪，士气低落。
[记] exhausted a. 精疲力竭的

exhibit [ig'zibit] n. 展览品，陈列品；展览会；v. 展览，展现
[例] Most of the state leaders viewed the exhibits en masse and gave high praise to them. 大多数国家领导人看了全部展览品,给予了高度赞扬。

exhilarate [ig'zilәreit] v. 使高兴，使愉快
[例] His bold designs exhilarate the viewer's imagination. 他大胆的设计激起了观众的想像力。

exotic [ig'zɔtik] a. 异国情调的，外来的，奇异的
[例] He was fascinated by the exotic buildings. 异国情调的建筑使他着迷。

> 注意和erotic区分开。exotic来源于希腊语*exo*外面的；而erotic则源自希腊神话中爱神Eros厄洛斯，是一位带有双翼的美少年，相当于罗马神话中的Cupid丘比特。不管是Eros还是Cupid，都成天不爱学习，在天上飞来飞去练习射箭，搞得大家心慌慌。所

以他们派生出的单词都含贬义：erotic 色情的；cupidity 贪心，贪婪。

expand [iks'pænd] v. 扩张，扩展

[例] The business has expanded from having one office to having twelve. 这个公司已从一个分公司发展到拥有 12 个分公司了。

expedition [ekspi'diʃ(ə)n] n. 远征

[例] This is an expedition to find the source of the Changjiang River.这是一次寻找长江源头的探险。

expel [iks'pel] v. 驱逐，开除，排出，发射

[例] The pupil was expelled for stealing. 那学生因偷窃被开除。

expert ['ekspəːt] n. 专家，高手，权威

[例] Rex soon became an expert at opening the gate. 雷克斯很快就成了开门能手。

expertise [ˌekspə'tiːz] n. 专门知识（技能），专长

[例] We are amazed at his expertise on the ski slope. 他斜坡滑雪的技能使我们赞叹不已。

expire [iks'paiə] v. 期满；呼气

[例] My passport is due to expire. 我的护照要到期了。

[记] expiration 终止，截止，期满

explicit [iks'plisit] a. 坦率的；外在的，清楚的

[例] They were explicit in their criticism. 他们直截了当地表达了他们的批评意见。

[记] be explicit about sth.对某事态度鲜明 / [反义词] implicit

explode [iks'pləud] v.（使）爆炸；急剧扩大，激增

[例] The boiler exploded and a big fire ensued. 锅炉爆炸了，随着而来的就是一场大火。

古罗马人看演出时，如不满意会发嘘声喝倒彩，把演员轰下台去。explode 的古义就是拍手（applaud）把演员赶出去（ex-）。

exploit [iks'plɔit] v. 开发，开采，开拓

[例] They plan to exploit oil under the sea. 他们计划开发海底石油。

[记] exploitable a. 可利用的，可开发的 / exploitation n. 开发，利用

exploration [ˌeksplɔː'reiʃən] n. 勘探；探测；探险

[例] He took part in the Arctic exploration. 他参加了那次北极探险。

explore [iks'plɔː] v. 勘查，考察；探讨

[例] We must explore all the possibilities for the solution of the problem. 我们必须探讨解决这个问题的所有可能性。

explosion [iks'pləuʒən] n. 爆发，发出；爆炸

[例] The explosion was caused by a burst gas pipe. 这次爆炸是由于一个爆裂的煤气管引起的。

exponent [eks'pəunənt] n. 解说者；倡导者，示范者

[例] He is an exponent of the opinions of Einstein. 他是爱因斯坦理论的拥护者。

export ['ekspɔːt] n. 出口（物），输出品；[ik'spɔːt] v. 出口；输出

[例] China exports to many other countries and regions. 中国向许多其他国家和地区出口货物。

expose [iks'pəuz] v. 使暴露，使曝光

[例] The crime of the corrupt officials must be exposed without any reserve. 对贪官污吏的罪行一定要毫无保留地予以揭发。

[记] exposure n. 暴露，揭露，曝光

exquisite ['ekskwizit] a. 精致的；优美的，高雅的

[例] He has exquisite tastes and manners. 他有高尚的情趣和举止。

> 字根 quisit 指"追求 to seek"。如：acquisition 获得；exquisite 追求到的，选拔出来的→精妙的，高尚的；requisite 再次追求→必须的；prerequisite 追求之前的，事先必备的→先决条件，前提，（大学）必修课。

extend [iks'tend] v. 延伸；延长；使延期；提供，给予

[例] His power extends to other lands. 他的权力扩张到别国。

[记] extensive a. 广大的，广阔的，广泛的 / extension n. 延伸，延长

extent [iks'tent] n. 长度，宽度，广度；程度；

[例] No one knows the extent of his debts. 没有人知道他负债多少。

exterior [eks'tiəriə] a. 外部的，外表的；n. 外表，外部

[例] He needs to have the exterior walls of his house painted. 他想找人把房子的外墙刷一下。

[反义词] interior

exterminate [iks'təːmineit] v. 灭绝，根除

[例] We've made great efforts to exterminate mosquitoes and flies. 我们作了很大努力来消灭蚊蝇。

[同义词] eliminate, eradicate, wipe out

external [eks'təːnl] a. 外部的；外国的

[例] This local newspaper doesn't pay much attention to external affairs. 这家地方报纸不太注重国外新闻。

extinct [iks'tiŋkt] a. 绝种的，灭绝的

[例] Many animals and birds are now extinct. 许多鸟兽现已绝种。

[记] extinction n. 灭绝，消失

> 字根 stinct 和 sting 指"刺，刺激物"。ex- 指 out，extinct 就是刺激没有了，灭种了；instinct，内在的刺激→本能。distinct 和 distinguish 中的 dis- 指"分开的"，想想它们的意思，再区别 extinct 和 extinguish。

extinguish [iks'tiŋgwiʃ] v. 灭火；使（想法、感情）破灭

[例] They tried every means to extinguish the fire. 他们想尽各种办法试图扑灭大火

[记] extinguisher n. 灭火器

extra ['ekstrə] a. 额外的

[例] We do not ask for extra pay. 我们不要求额外报酬。

extract ['ekstrækt] n. 摘录；提出物；[iks'trækt] v. 拔出；提炼出

[例] She read me a few extracts from her new novel. 她把她自己的新小说念了几段给我听。

[记] extract... from... 从…中提取 / to extract a tooth 拔牙

extracurricular [ˌekstrəkə'rikjulə] a. 课外的

[例] Most families lacked the money to get their children involved in extracurricular activities. 大多数家庭都缺钱资助孩子参加课外活动。

extraordinary [iks'trɔːdinəri] a. 不平常的，特别的，非凡的

[例] Her strength of will is extraordinary. 她意志的力量是不平常的。

extravagant [iks'trævəgənt] a. 奢侈的，浪费的，过度的

[例] She's very extravagant — she spends all her money on clothes. 她很奢侈，花掉了所有的钱来买衣服。

extreme [iks'triːm] n. 极端；a. 极端的，极度的

[例] Sometimes he eats too much and sometimes nothing. He goes from one extreme to the other. 他有时吃得太多，有时不吃，从一个极端走到另一极端。

[记] extremely adv. 极端地，非常地

> extreme sports 极限运动。如：蹦极 bungee jumping；街头雪橇 street lugging；空中滑板 sky surfing 等。sky surfing 是滑板运动 skateboarding 和跳伞运动 skydiving 的结合，从飞机上向下跳，在降落伞未打开之前表演滑板冲浪，被视为 Ex-sports 中最危险、也最刺激的一种。

fable ['feibl] n. 寓言；神话

[例] We may take the story of Job as a fable. 我们可以把关于约伯的故事当作历史或者神话。

fabric ['fæbrik] n. 织物；构造，结构

[例] The usual fabric was timber. 通常的建筑材料是木材。

fabricate ['fæbrikeit] v. 捏造，伪造；制造

[例] They fabricated evidence and threatened witnesses. 他们伪造证据并威胁目击者。

fabulous ['fæbjuləs] a. 极好的；绝妙的；巨大的；传说中的

[例] We had a fabulous holiday. 我们过了一个非常愉快的假期。

> 口语表达“好”，“真棒”常用：good, great, wonderful, terrific, fabulous, awesome, excellent。表达“好得难以置信”用 incredible；一个人或一个事物比 beautiful 和 pretty 还美，美到极点，用 gorgeous。

facet ['fæsit] n.（多面体的）面；（问题等的）一个方面

[例] No single theory can embrace and explain every facet of human behavior. 没有一种理论能包括并阐释人类行为的每个方面。

[同义词] aspect, phase, side, view

facilitate [fə'siliteit] v. 使便利，促进

[例] It would facilitate matters if you were more co-operative. 要是你再合作些，事情就会变得更容易。

facility [fə'siliti] n. 熟练；设施；方便，便利

[例] He showed great facility in performing the task. 他工作很熟练。

factor ['fæktə] n. 因素，要素

[例] Her friendly manner is an important factor in her rapid success. 待人友好是她迅速获得成功的重要因素。

faculty ['fækəlti] n.（大学的）系；全体教员；才能，能力

[例] She has the faculty to learn languages easily. 她有轻而易举学会语言的才能。

fade [feid] v. 逐渐消失；褪色

[谚] Beauty fades like a flower. 红颜易逝。

[记] fade away 消失；逐渐减弱；褪色

Fahrenheit ['færənhait, 'fɑːr-] n. 华氏温度

[例]Water freezes at 32 degrees Fahrenheit. 水在 32 华氏度结冰。

> G.D. Fahrenheit 德国物理学家，华氏温度计 Fahrenheit thermometer 的发明者。摄氏温度 Centigrade，32 华氏度 = 0 摄氏度，212 华氏度 = 100 摄氏度。

faint [feint] a. 模糊的，微弱的；v. 晕倒，昏厥

[例] He felt faint for lack of food. 他因饥饿而晕倒了。

fair [fɛə] a.（肤色）白皙的；干净的，公平的；（天气）晴朗的；adv. 公平地；清楚地；n. 展览会，市集

[例] English people usually have fair skin. 英国人通常是白皮肤。

faith [feiθ] n. 信念；信仰；信任

[例] I have faith in you; I am sure you will do well. 我相信你，我肯定你会做好的。

fake [feik] n. 赝品，假货

[例] The antique is a fake. 那古董是一件赝品。

falcon ['fælkən] n. 隼，猎鹰

[例] His falcon flew through a window of the empty castle and did not return.他的猎鹰飞进了那座空城堡的窗内就未回返。

fame [feim] n. 名声，名望；v.使闻名

[例] Let me introduce the concert violinist of international fame.我来介绍一下这位国际闻名的小提琴演奏家。

[记] famous a. 著名的，出名的

familiar [fə'miljə] a. 熟悉的
[例] This song sounds familiar. 这首歌听起来很熟悉。
[记] be familiar with 熟悉

famine ['fæmin] n. 饥荒
[例] Many people die of famine every year. 每年有很多人死于饥荒。

fang [fæŋ] n. 尖牙；犬齿；（毒蛇的）毒牙
The deadly weapons of the king cobra are its fangs. 眼镜蛇的致命武器是它的毒牙。

> 美国著名作家杰克·伦敦 Jack London 于 1906 年创作的名著《白牙》*White Fang* 描写了一只名叫“白牙”的野狼从野蛮到驯服的故事。

fantastic [fæn'tæstik] a. 幻想的，想象的；极好的，极出色的
[例] Li Yundi's piano performance is really fantastic. 李云迪的钢琴表演实在是太出色了。
[记] fantasy n. 想象；幻想

fascinate ['fæsineit] v. 迷住，吸引；使…着迷
[例] The city fascinates him. 这座城市强烈地吸引着他。
[记] be fascinated with... 迷上了…

fascinating ['fæsineitiŋ] a. 迷人的，有极大吸引力的
[例] Walking in the rain is really most fascinating. 雨中漫步的确非常令人陶醉。

fashion ['fæʃən] n. 时髦，时尚；样子，方式；v. 制作，使成形
[例] Loose trousers are the latest fashion. 宽大的裤子是最新的时髦服装。
[记] come into fashion 流行起来，开始风行 / out of fashion 过时

fasten ['fɑːsn] v. 扣牢，系牢，缚紧
[例] Please fasten your seat belts while the plane is taking off. 飞机起飞时请系好安全带。

fatal ['feitl] a. 致命的，毁灭性的
[例] The fatal hour has come. 该来的时刻终于来了。

> 听过 the fatal sisters（命运三女神）吧。一看她们的大理石雕塑，不就三位纺织女工么。别小瞧啦，她们正纺织的是我们的生命线！小妹编织生命线；二姐测量生命线；大姐选择时间切断每个人的生命线。

fatigue [fə'tiːg] n. 疲劳；v. 使疲劳
[例] The patient fatigues easily. 病人容易疲劳。
[记] metal fatigue 金属疲劳

fault [fɔːlt] n. 过错，缺点；故障，毛病
[例] Your only fault is carelessness. 你唯一的缺点是粗心大意。

favourite ['feivərit] (=favorite)a. 最喜欢的；n. 最喜爱的东西

[例] What's your favourite music? 你最喜欢的音乐是什么？

feasible ['fi:zəbl] a. 可行的，切实可行的

[例] Your plan sounds quite feasible. 你的计划听起来很可行。

feat [fi:t] n. 技艺；功绩，壮举

[例] Everybody was surprised at the small boy's feats of horsemanship. 每个人对那个小男孩的马术都感到吃惊。

feature ['fi:tʃə] n. 特征，特点；面貌，相貌；v. 以…为特色

[例] Her eyes were her best feature. 她的眼睛是她容貌最漂亮的部分。

[记] feature films 故事片 / features 特别报导

federal ['fedərəl] a. 联邦的，联合的

[例] Switzerland is a federal republic. 瑞士是联邦制的共和国。

[记] federation 联邦政府；联盟

> FBI 美国联邦调查局 Federal Bureau of Investigation；CIA 美国中央情报局 Central Intelligence Agency。

fee [fi:] n. 费（如会费、入场费、手续费等）

[例] Park entrance fees have gone up to $15. 公园的门票已经涨到了15美元。

feeble ['fi:bl] a. 虚弱的，无力的，微弱的

[例] Grandmother has been getting feebler lately. 近来祖母愈益衰弱了。

feedback ['fi:dbæk] n. 反馈，反馈的信息

[例] The teacher asked the students for feedback on the new curriculum. 老师征求学生对新课程设置的反馈。

female ['fi:meil] n. 女子；a. 女的，雌性的

[例] We've got three cats — two females and a male. 我们有三只猫，两只母的和一只公的。

ferment ['fə:mənt] v. (使) 发酵；(使) 激动；(使) 动乱；n. 酵素；发酵；动乱

[例] The whole country was in a state of ferment. 全国处于骚乱状态。

[记] yeast n. 酵母，发酵粉

ferry ['feri] v. 渡运，摆渡；n. 渡船，渡口

[例] A ferry crosses the river every hour. 渡船每小时过河一次。

fertile ['fə:tail] a. 富饶的，肥沃的；能生育的

[例] A large area of desert was reclaimed to turn to fertile soil in the northwest region. 在西北地区有一大片沙漠经过改良变成了肥沃的土地。

[反义词] infertile

> 字根 fer 指"运载"，构词能力很强。如：ferry 古时运载东西的地方→渡口；conference 各自带来（物品、思想）凑到一起→开会；refer 运回原处→参考，提到；fertile 能承载的→肥沃的；我们表达"多产作家"，可以是 productive writer，更高级表达就是 fertile writer 了。

fertilizer ['fəːtiˌlaizə] n. 化肥；【动】受精媒介物
[例] Studies show that most golf courses use large amounts of chemical poison and fertilizer. 研究表明大多数高尔夫球场使用大量的化学毒药和化肥。

festival ['festəvəl] n. 节日；a. 节日的；快乐的
[例] Christmas is one of the Christian festivals. 圣诞节是基督教的节日之一。

flip [flip] v. 空翻；轻弹
[例] We flipped a coin to see who would go first. 我们抛硬币决定谁先来。

fiber ['faibə]（=fibre）n. 纤维；构造
[例] My sock unraveled when I pulled a loose fiber hanging from it. 我把袜子上的一根松纤维线抽出，袜子开了线。

fiction ['fikʃən] n. 小说，虚构的事
[例] Happy marriages may be more common in fiction than in real life. 美满幸福的婚姻也许更常见于小说而不是现实生活。
[记] sci-fi (science fiction) 科幻小说

field [fiːld] n. 原野；场地；（研究、活动的）领域，范围
[例] His is a recognised expert in the field of cloning. 他是一位在克隆领域公认的专家。

Unit 12

fierce [fiəs] a. 凶猛的；激烈的，狂暴的

[例] The famous boxer killed a fierce wolf with his bare hands. 那位著名的拳击师赤手空拳打死了一头凶猛的恶狼。

figure ['figə] n. 数字，符号；人物；身材；v. 考虑

[例] I could see a tall figure near the door. 我可以看见门附近有一个高大的人影。

> 看看各种身材的表达：a slender/slim figure 苗条；a curvy figure 曲线玲珑；a hot figure 惹火身材；a round figure 浑圆（注意 round figure 在数学中指整数）；an hourglass figure 沙漏身材 —— 不许笑！这可是夸奖女子身材玲珑有致，魔鬼身材！

file [fail] n. 文件夹；v. 把（文件等）归档；提出（申请等）

[例] Here's our file on the results of the business over the past five years. 这是我们过去五年来经营成绩的案卷。

[记] on file 存档 / file for（通过法律）正式申请 / filing n. 文件归档

filter ['filtə] v. 过滤；渗透；n. 过滤器；筛选

[例] Sunlight filtered through the chinks of the shutters. 阳光从百叶窗的缝隙中透过来。

[记] filter out/through 渗透；泄露（消息等）

final ['fainəl] a. 最后的，最终的；n. 决赛

[例] The final thing she did before she left the house was to lock the door. 她离开房子前做的最后一件事是锁门。

[记] semifinal n. 半决赛

finance ['fainæns] / [fai'næns] n. 财政，金融，金融学；v. 供给…经费

[例] Unless we get more finance, we'll have to close the branch offices. 如果得不到更多的资金，我们就不得不关闭分支办事处。

[记] applied finance 应用金融

financial [fai'nænʃəl] a. 财政的，金融的

[例] Southeast Asia's financial crisis has taught people a profound lesson. 东南亚的金融危机带给人们深刻的教训。

finite ['fainait] a. 有限的，有穷尽的

[例] We must save energy because the natural resources of the earth are finite. 我们必须节约能源，因为地球的自然资源是有限的。

[记] finitely adv. 有限地；限定地 / finiteness n. 有限；限定 / [反义词] infinite

firm [fəːm] a. 坚定的，稳固的；n. 公司

[例] You must always build on firm ground. 你必须始终脚踏实地。

flame [fleim] n. 火焰；光辉，光芒；热情，激情

[例] The sticks burst into flames. 柴烧起来了。

> 字根 flam 指"火焰"。如：flammable 可燃的；in 内部的 +flame 火焰→inflame 红肿，激怒；flamboyant 男孩烧蚂蚁→火焰的，神气的，炫耀的；flamingo 走动的一团火焰，猜猜是什么？

flash [flæʃ] v. 闪光，闪现；飞驰，掠过

[例] The good news was flashed across the country. 好消息闪电般传遍了全国。

flat [flæt] a. 平坦的；无生气的，沉闷的

[例] His fever is allayed, but his appetite is still flatted. 他发烧减轻了，但食欲仍然不振。

flatter ['flætə] v. 奉承，讨好，向…谄媚

[例] He flattered her on her cooking. 他奉承她的厨艺。

flavour ['fleivə] n. (=flavor) 味道，风味；特色，风格

[例] You may choose any one from the six popular flavours of ice cream! 你可以在六种流行味道的冰淇淋中任意挑选一种!

flaw [flɔː] n. 瑕疵，缺点，缺陷

[谚] The absence of flaw in beauty is itself a flaw. 美中无瑕疵，本身是瑕疵。

[同义词] defect, fault, weakness, shortcoming, demerit

flee [fliː] v. 逃，逃走

[谚] Follow love and it will flee, flee love and it will follow thee. 追求爱情它高飞，逃避爱情它跟随。(thee 你，<古>thou 的宾格)

> 来练一段 twister 绕口令: A flea and a fly flew up in a flue. Said the flea, "Let us fly!" Said the fly, "Let us flee!" So they flew through a flaw in the flue.

flexible ['fleksəbl] a. 易弯曲的；灵活的；有伸缩性的

[例] We can visit your company on Monday or Tuesday; our plans are fairly flexible. 我们可以在星期一或星期二到你们公司来，我们的计划是相当灵活的。

[记] flexibility n. 弹性，适应性，机动性 / inflexible a. 执著的，不屈的

float [fləut] v. 漂浮，漂流；浮动

[例] The smell of roses floated around. 玫瑰花的芳香在四周飘荡。

flock [flɔk] n. 兽群，鸟群；v. 聚集

[例] Sheep usually flock together. 羊通常是结群的。

flora ['flɔːrə] n. 植物，植物群

[例] He is studying the flora of the Alps. 他在研究阿尔卑斯山脉的植物群。

[记] fauna 动物群

> 源自古罗马神话中的花神Flora芙洛拉。她嫁给了西风之神Zephyr，丈夫送给她了一座满是奇花异草的园子。春天时，Flora和丈夫Zephyr会手挽手在园子里漫步，他们一路上走过的地方百花齐放。英文单词flower, flour, flourish, floral, florist和美国的Florida州都和她有关系。

flourish ['flʌriʃ] v. 繁荣，兴旺，茂盛
[例] Plants will not flourish without water. 没有水植物就不会长得茂盛。

flu [flu:]（=influenza）n. 流行性感冒
[例] The bird flu can spread quickly. 禽流感传染很快。

fluctuate ['flʌktjueit] v. 波动，涨落，起伏
[例] The price of vegetables and fruits fluctuates according to the season. 蔬菜和水果的价格随季节而波动。
[记] fluctuation n. 波动，起伏

fluid ['fluid] n. 流体；a. 能流动的
[例] When you are sick, you should drink plenty of fluids. 生病时多吃点流食。

focus ['fəukəs] n. 焦点，集中点；v. 集中
[例] Because of his strange clothes, he immediately became the focus of attention when he entered the office. 他由于服装奇特，一走进办公室便成了大家注意的中心。
[记] focus on (doing) sth. 集中做某事

> 拉丁文，这个单词在古代很温馨，指"壁炉边"，相当于hearth。focus一词指古代一家人饭后围坐在温暖的壁炉fireplace旁边，大人们闲话家常，孩子们在周围嬉笑打闹。focus即是家庭生活的中心，焦点。

fold [fəuld] v. 折叠，对折
[例] She folded the letter so that it would fit into her bag. 他把信折起来，以便可以装到袋里。
[记] foldable a.可折叠的

folklore ['fəuklɔ:(r)] n. 民间传说
[例] Many of the fairy tales come from English folklore. 许多神话故事都是由英语民间传说得来的。
[记] folk music 民间音乐

forbid [fə'bid] v. 禁止，阻止，使成为不可能
[例] The storm forbids us to go out. 暴风雨使我们不能外出。
[记] forbid sb. (doing) sth./ forbid sb. to do sth. 禁止某人做某事

forecast ['fɔ:kɑ:st] v. 预测，预报；n. 天气预报

[例] The recent statement by the President forecasts a change in the situation. 总统最近的一次讲话预示着形势将有所变化。

foresee [fɔː'siː] v. 预见，预知

[例] They can not foresee how things will turn out. 他们不可能预知事情的结果。

forgive [fə'giv] v. 原谅，宽恕，饶恕

[例] I'll never forgive you for what you have done wrong to your parents. 你伤害了你的父母,我永远也不会原谅你。

> 前缀 for- 表否定含义。如：forbid 禁止；forget 忘记；forgive 不再给予，就此作罢→原谅；forgo 不去了→放弃。前缀 fore 表示“前面的”。如 foresee 预见；forearm 前臂；forebear 以前生(bear)的人→祖先；forefather 爸爸之前的爸爸→祖先。

forge [fɔːdʒ] v. 铸造；锻造；伪造

[例] In the past, kitchen knives were made in a forge. 过去厨房用刀是在锻造厂打出来的。

[记] a forged passport 伪造的护照

forgo [fɔː'gəu] v. 作罢，放弃

[例] We'll have to forgo our rest hour to gather in the wheat before the storm begins. 为了在风暴来到之前收完小麦,我们就只好放弃休息的时间了。

format ['fɔːmæt] n. 格式，版式；v. 安排…的格局

[例] The format of the book made it easy to read. 书的版式使其易读。

formation [fɔː'meiʃən] n. 构成，形成

[例] Clouds are formations of tiny drops of water in the sky. 云是由空中极细微的水滴构成的。

former ['fɔːmə] a. 从前的，前任的；pron. 前者

[例] Did he go there by air or by train? The former seems more likely. 他是乘飞机还是坐火车去的?前者似乎可能性更大些。

[反义词] latter n. 后者；a. 后者的

formidable ['fɔːmidəbl] a. 令人敬畏的；强大的

[例] The head of the research section was a formidable old professor. 研究室主任是个令人望而生畏的老教授。

formula ['fɔːmjulə] n. 公式，规则；配方

[例] The chemical formula for water is H_2O. 水的化学分子式是 H_2O。

> 国际顶级赛事一级方程式赛车，因为参加比赛的车量都是严格按照标准制造，同时这项运动又有着几乎和公式一样的苛刻的规则，所以叫做 Formula One，简称 F1。看看一些鼎鼎大名的单词：Ferrari 法拉利；Porsche 保时捷；Williams 威廉姆斯；Benetton 贝纳通；Renault 雷诺。

formulate ['fɔːmjuleit] v. 构想；规划；明确地表达

[例] The idea of setting up this corporation was formulated over coffee. 创办这家公司的想法是在喝咖啡时形成的。

[记] formulation n. 构想；阐述 / formulator n. 设计者，阐述者

forthcoming [fɔːθ'kʌmiŋ] a. 乐意帮助的；即将来临的

[例] None of them were very forthcoming. 他们中没人很热心相助。

fortnight ['fɔːtnait] n. 两星期，十四天

[例] The play folded within a fortnight. 那话剧演了两个星期就停演了。

forum ['fɔːrəm] n. 论坛，讨论会

[例] The letters page of this newspaper is a forum for public argument. 这份报纸的读者来信栏是公众意见的论坛。

> 古罗马城镇的广场叫forum，当有大事发生时，民众在广场集会，公开讨论，引申为"论坛"之意。网上论坛BBS，是Bulletin Board System 电子公告牌。

fossil ['fɔsl] n. 化石；a. 化石的

[例] Coal is a fossil fuel. 煤是一种矿物燃料。

foster ['fɔstə] v. 养育，培养，鼓励，抱（希望）

[例] Frequent cultural exchange will certainly help foster friendly relations between our two universities. 经常进行文化交流肯定有助于发展我们两校之间的友好关系。

[记] to foster an interest in music 培养对音乐的兴趣 / [同义词] cultivate

foul [faul] a. 污秽的，恶劣的；v. 弄脏；腐烂；犯规

[例] Murder is a foul deed. 杀人是邪恶的行为。

found [faund] v. 创立；建造

[例] The rich businessman founded a hospital and a school in the town where he was born. 那个有钱的商人在他出生的城镇创办了一家医院和一所学校。

foundation [faun'deiʃən] n. 基础，地基；基金会

[例] He laid the foundations of his success by study and hard work. 他以读书和勤劳奠定了成功的基础。

[记] foundation course 基础课程 / the Ford Foundation 福特基金会 / founder n. 创建人；奠基人

fountain ['fauntin] n. 喷泉，源泉

[例] A group of children are playing in the fountain in the park. 有一群孩子在公园的喷泉中玩耍。

fraction ['frækʃən] n. 一部分，片断；【数】分数

[例] She spends only a fraction of her earnings. 她只花了所赚的钱的一小部分。

fragile ['frædʒail] a. 易碎的，脆的

[例] The fragile boxes arrived intact. 这些易碎的箱子完整无损地运到了。

fragment ['frægmənt] n. 碎片，碎块，片断

[例] He was still in bad condition and could recall only a fragmented account of the accident. 他的情况仍然不好，只能回忆起那次事故的零碎片断。

fragrance ['freigrəns] n. 芬芳，香气

[例] I like the fragrance of roses. 我喜欢玫瑰的芬芳。

> 闻"香"辨单词：odour / scent / perfume / fragrance / aroma。odour=odor 表示气味，可香可臭；scent 一般指较弱的气味或香味，Al Pacino 主演的《闻香识女人》*Scent of a Woman*；perfume 则指较浓的香味，尤指香水。fragrance 意为芬芳，尤指花香，Fragrant Hills 北京香山；而 aroma 除了指气味，芳香以外，还可以表示"风味，气氛"，如 the aroma of success 胜利的气氛。

framework ['freimwə:k] n. 框架，结构；体系

[例] This bridge over the river has a steel framework. 这座跨江大桥是钢骨结构。

franchise ['fræntʃaiz] v.赋予特权；赋予公民权；特许经营；n. 特权；公民权

[例] In Britain, women were given the franchise in 1918. 英国妇女于1918年获得了选举权。

[记] franchiser n. 经销商

fraud [frɔ:d] n. 骗子；欺骗，欺诈行为

[例] People who tell your future by means of a pack of cards are frauds. 用一叠纸牌为你占卜未来的人都是骗子。

freeze [fri:z] v.（使）结冰，（使）冻结

[例] Freeze or I'll shoot! 不许动！否则我开枪了！

freight [freit] n. 货物；货运

[例] This aircraft company deals with freight only; it has no passenger service. 这家航空公司只办理货运业务，没有客运服务。

frequency ['fri:kwənsi] n. 频率，发生次数

[例] This radio signal has a frequency of 800,000 cycles per second. 这个无线电讯号的频率是每秒八百千周。

[记] frequent a. 时常发生的，频繁的

fresher [freʃə] n. 大学一年级新生；高中一年级学生

[例] Only a few months ago university freshers started student life feeling quite flush. 就在几个月前，大一新生开始了他们令人激动的学生生活。

friction ['frikʃən] n. 摩擦，摩擦力；不和，抵触

[例] In designing a machine it is necessary to reduce friction as much as possible. 在设计一种机器时，必须尽可能减低摩擦。

[记] family friction 家庭的不和

fridge [fridʒ]（=refrigerator）n. 电冰箱

[例] They have a better taste if not eaten straight away from the fridge. 如果不是刚从冰箱里拿出来，这些食物的味道更好。

fringe [frindʒ] n. 边缘；刘海；a. 边缘的；额外的；v.在…上加以缘饰

[例] A fringe of trees stood round the pool. 水池的四周耸立着一圈树木。

frustrate [frʌs'treit] v. 挫败，阻挠

[例] He was frustrated by his poverty. 他因贫穷而灰心丧气。

frustrating [frʌs'treitiŋ] a. 产生挫折的，使人沮丧的

[例] After three hours' frustrating delay, the train at last arrived. 经过三个小时令人厌烦的耽搁后,火车终于到达了目的地。

fuel [fjuəl] n. 燃料；v. 加燃料

[例] Aircraft is fueling in the air. 飞机正在空中加油。

[记] add fuel to the fire 火上加油 / fuel up 加燃料

> 来源于刚才提到的单词focus（古义“壁炉边”），是focus的变形。壁炉边上有什么东西呢？当然是柴火啦。

fulfill [ful'fil]（=fulfil）v. 履行，实现，完成；满足

[例] We are determined to fulfil the task. 我们决定完成这项任务。

fume [fju:m] n.（浓烈或难闻的）烟，气体；一阵愤怒（或不安）；v. 烟熏；冒烟

[例] Petrol fumes from car engines poison the atmosphere. 汽车引擎排放的汽油烟气污染大气。

function ['fʌŋkʃən] n. 功能，用途；宴会；v. 起作用

[例] The function of an adjective is to describe or add to the meaning of a noun. 形容词的作用就是修饰名词。

fund [fʌnd] v. 资助；投资；n. 资金；基金

[例] The work is funded by the government. 这项工程由政府提供基金。

[记] a relief fund 救济基金 / alumni fund 校友基金 / to attract funds 吸引资金

fundamental [ˌfʌndə'mentl] a. 基础的，基本的；n. 基本原则

[例] Fresh air is fundamental to good health. 空气新鲜是身体健康之必需。

be fundamental to…对…是必要的

fungus ['fʌŋgəs] n. 菌类，蘑菇

[例] Don't eat that fungus. It might be poisonous. 别吃那种蘑菇,可能有毒。

furious ['fjuəriəs] a. 狂怒的，暴怒的

[例] The furious workers agitated for a strike. 工人们愤怒地鼓动罢工。

[记] fury n. 狂怒,愤怒 / furiously adv. 猛烈地

> 希腊神话中复仇女神三女神。她们是"土地"和"黑暗"的女儿，以清算罪恶为职责，被描绘成庄严、美丽的女郎，Fury 为其中之一。

furnish ['fə:niʃ] v. 装备，配备家具

[例] The house is well furnished. 房屋室内布置得很好。

furniture ['fə:nitʃə] n. 家具；（工厂等的）设备

[例] This old Chinese square table is a very valuable piece of furniture. 这张旧的中国八仙桌是一件很珍贵的家具。

[记] a piece of furniture 一件家具

furthermore ['fə:ðəmɔ:] adv. 而且，此外

[例] The house is too small, and furthermore, it's too far from the office. 这座房子太小，而且离办公地点也太远。

fuse [fju:z] n. 保险丝，熔丝；v.熔合

[例] You'll blow a fuse if you put the electric heater and the microwave oven on at the same time. 如果你同时把电暖气和微波炉开着，保险丝会烧断。

[记] fused a. 装有保险丝的 / fusion n. 联合；核聚变 / refuse v. 拒绝

fuss [fʌs] n. 大惊小怪；无谓纷扰

[例] There's sure to be a fuss when they fi nd the window' s broken. 他们发现窗子打破后一定会有麻烦的。

[记] make a fuss about 大惊小怪，小题大做

futile ['fju:tail] a. 无效的，无用的

[例] All his attempts to unlock the car were futile, because he was using the wrong key. 他多次尝试打开车门，但都不得要领，因为他用错了钥匙。

[区别] fertile a. 肥沃的，多产的

galaxy ['gæləksi] n. 星系；银河系

[例] Scientists are dreaming of sending rockets to distant galaxies. 科学家梦想把火箭送往遥远的星系。

> 源于希腊语 galakt 指"牛奶的"，所以银河也被称为奶路"the Milky Way"。希腊神话中天后 Hera 的奶汁很神奇，有长生不老之功效。而她的老公 Zeus（宙斯这哥们儿在传说中总有外遇）有一私生子 Hercules。Zeus 偷偷地把 Hercules 放在熟睡的 Hera 身旁，让孩子吮吸奶汁，谁知孩子吮吸太猛，惊醒了 Hera，她发现吃奶的不是自己的儿子，便把孩子推开。因用力太猛，奶汁直喷上天，便成了 Milky Way。而 Hercules 因为吃过 Hera 的奶汁，后来成了永生的大力神。看看 Disney 的动画片 *Hercules*，猜猜单词 herculean 的含义。

gale [geil] n. 大风

[例] The gale drove the freighter off course. 大风把货船吹出了航道。

gallery ['gæləri] n. 美术馆，画廊

[例] He owns and operates an art gallery that shows only his own work. 他拥有并经营着展示他自己作品的美术画廊。

gamble ['gæmbl] v./n. 赌博

[例] Don't gamble with your future. 不要拿你的前途去冒险。

[记] take a gamble on sth. 冒险从事(某事) / gambler n. 赌徒

gang [gæŋ] n.（常聚在一起闹事打斗的）一帮年轻人

[例] Have you seen any of the gang lately? 你最近见过这批朋友中的哪一位吗?

> "黑帮，黑社会"就是gang。电影《纽约黑帮》Gangs of New York。Gangster 黑帮成员，歹徒；"斧头帮老大"就是Axe Gang Leader!

gap [gæp] n. 缺口，裂缝；差距

[例] There are wide gaps in my knowledge of history. 我的历史知识很缺乏。generation

[记] gap 代沟

garbage ['gɑːbidʒ] n. 垃圾

[例] No garbage here. 不准在此乱堆垃圾!

[同义词] junk, litter, refuse, rubbish, trash, waste

garment ['gɑːmənt] n.（一件）衣服

[例] This garment should be washed carefully. 这件衣服应该小心地洗涤。

gather ['gæðə] v. 收集，搜集

[例] People gathered round, curious to know what was happening. 人们围聚拢来，很想知道发生了什么事情。

gay [gei] n. 男同性恋；a. 同性恋的；快乐的

[例] The children were all gay at the thought of the coming holidays. 孩子们一想到即将来临的假日，都很高兴。

> gay 源自古法语gai，原是一个极其普通的形容词，指"欢快的，艳丽的"。但现愈来愈多的特指"男同性恋"。女同性恋为lesbian，或缩写为Les。同性恋运动会叫gay game，世界最大规模的同性恋游行是澳大利亚悉尼一年一次的Mardi Gras。

gaze [geiz] v. 凝视；注视

[例] The child gazed at the toys in the shop window. 孩子眼睛盯着商店橱窗里的玩具。

gear [giə] n. 齿轮，传动装置；v. 使适合，换档

[例] Education should be geared to children's needs. 教育应适合学生们的需要。

[记] in high gear 以高速档，高速度地 / gear up 增加速度；促进

gem [dʒem] n. 宝石，珠宝；精品

[例] The capital, Tallin, is an architectural gem. 首都塔林的建筑十分精美.

gender ['dʒendə] n. 性别

[例] Please fill in your name, address, age and gender. 请填上你的姓名、地址、年龄和性别。

gene [dʒiːn] n.（遗传）因子，（遗传）基因

[例] Genes can exert great influences upon person's personality.基因对一个人的性格会产生很大的影响。

[记] genetic a. 遗传的 / genome 基因组，染色体组

generalise ['dʒenərəlaiz]（=generalize） v. 归纳，推广，普及

[例] The polls show that it is difficult to generalise about which issues were most important to voters. 民意测验表明，很难归纳出哪一些问题对选民最重要。

[记] generalize... from... 从…概括或归纳出… /generalization n. 归纳，概括

generate ['dʒenəˌreit] v. 产生，发生

[例] When coal burns, it generates heat. 煤燃烧时，产生热量。

generation [ˌdʒenə'reiʃən] n. 一代（约指 20 至 30 年），一代人

[例] Mother and daughters represent two generations. 母亲和女儿们代表了两代人。

字根 gen 指“生产，产生”。如：gene 人类生育的基本单位→基因；regenerate 再生；genius 生来如此→天才。

genius ['dʒiːnjəs] n. 天才，天赋

[例] He's a genius at mathematics. 他是个数学天才。

[记] prodigy 天才（特指神童）

genuine ['dʒenjuin] a. 真的，真诚的，真心的

[例] All genuine knowledge originates in direct experience. 一切真知都是从直接经验发源的。

geology [dʒi'ɔlədʒi] n. 地质学, 地质概况

[例] He devoted all his life to the research of the agricultural geology.他把一生奉献给了农业地质学的研究事业。

[记] geologic a. 地质（学）的

geometry [dʒi'ɔmitri] n. 几何学

[例] Geometry is a big headache for him. 几何学让他很头疼。

[记] geometric a. 几何（学）的

flamingo n. 火烈鸟

herculean v.力气极大的　a herculean task 艰巨的任务

Unit 13

germ
[dʒəːm] n. 微生物，细菌
[例] Disinfectant is used to kill germs. 消毒剂是用来杀死细菌的。
[同义词] bacteria

gesture
['dʒestʃə] n. 手势，姿势；表示
[例] Gestures can help people communicate with each other.手势可以帮助人们交流。

giant
['dʒaiənt] n. 巨人，巨物；a. 巨人般的
[例]Shakespeare is a giant among writers. 莎士比亚是一位文坛巨匠。

> 最容易被偷的自行车—Giant 捷安特。

gift
[gift] n. 赠品，礼物；天赋，才能；v. 向…赠送；赋予
[例]He has a gift for poetry. 他有做诗的天赋。
[记] gifted a. 有才华的；有天才的

gigantic
[dʒai'gæntik] a. 巨大的，庞大的
[例] He has a gigantic appetite and eats gigantic meals. 他饭量特别大，吃得惊人的多。

> 拉丁文中“巨人”拼写为gigant，英语去掉g简化为giant。所以gigantic就是“巨人的，巨大的”。由gigantic衍生出另一词giga，指10的9次方，非常大的数量单位。我们说电脑硬盘有20G，指的就是Giga Byte（GB，千兆字节）；而如果是256MB，指Mega Byte，兆字节的储存容量。

ginger
['dʒindʒə] n. 姜；活泼
[例] The old man grew ginger for a living. 那个老人靠种姜为生。

gist
[dʒist] n.主旨，要点
[例] He cannot understand the gist of their argument. 他不明白他们争论的要点。

gizmo
['dʒizməu] n. 小发明
[例] The modern world is increasly populated by intelligent gizmos whose universal existence has removed much human labor. 现代社会的智能装置越来越多，它们的广泛存在节约了大量的人力。

glamour
['glæmə] (=glamour) n. 魔力，魅力；v. 迷惑
[例] She was fascinated by the glamour of the model. 她着迷于那模特的魅力。

> glamour是grammar的苏格兰语变体。枯燥繁琐的语法（grammar）怎么会有魅力（glamour）呢？古埃及僧侣为了保住权力，把读写技能当作解读神宙的秘密。平民对这种技能怀有盲目的敬畏。

> 即使在16世纪英国的grammar school里的拉丁文法课，在目不识丁的下层人民眼中仍是神秘学。苏格兰方言中grammar就被赋予了“魅力，不可思议，魔书”的含义。

glance [glɑːns] v./n. 一瞥，迅速看一眼
[例] The man glanced the burglar climbing out of the window. 那人瞥见小偷从窗户爬了出来。
[记] at first glance 乍一看；在最初考虑上

gland [glænd] n. 【解】腺
[例] His internal secretory gland cannot work. 他的内分泌腺出了问题。

glare [glɛə] v. 强光闪耀，怒目而视
[例] The glare of the oncoming headlights temporarily blinded me. 迎面车灯刺眼的光照得我瞬间什么也看不见。

glide [glaid] v. 滑行，滑动
[例] He glided away from the classroom. 他溜出了教室。

glimpse [glimps] n./v. 瞥见；一瞥
[例] I caught a glimpse of our new neighbor. 我只看过一眼我们的新邻居。
[记] get a glimpse of 瞥见，一见 / [同义词] glance

global ['gləubəl] a.全球的，全世界的
[例] In the coming decades, the Pacific Rim will become the main impetus of the global economy. 未来几十年，环太平洋地区将成为全球经济发展的主要动力。
[记] globalization n. 全球化

globe [gləub] n. 地球；球体，地球仪
[例] There are Chinese peopleon almost every habitable part of this globe. 地球上几乎每一个有人居住的地方都有中国人。

glorious ['glɔːriəs] a. 光荣的，荣耀的
[例] Our country has a glorious past. 我们的国家有一段光辉的历史。
[记] glory n. 荣誉，光荣

glossary ['glɔsəri] n. 词汇表
[例] You can find the word in the glossary at the back of the book. 你可以在书后的词汇表中找到这个词。
[记] glossary of terms 术语汇编

glow [gləu] v. 发光；n. 光辉
[例] Maple leaves glowed red in the sunlight. 枫叶在阳光里闪耀着红光。

glue [gluː] v. 粘贴；n. 胶，胶水
[例] He carefully glued each page. 他仔细地把每页涂上胶水。

goal [gəul] n. 目标，目的；球门，得分
[例] His goal is a place at University. 他的目标是在大学任教。

[同义词] aim, destination, object, objective, target

golf [gɔlf] n. 高尔夫球；v. 打高尔夫

[例] Other sporting activities available include: mini golf and bowling. 其他适合的体育活动包括：迷你高尔夫和保龄球。

> 曾见过这样的解释："golf一词由Green、Oxygen、Light、Foot的第一个英文字母组成，取意在明媚的阳光下，踩着绿色的草地，呼吸着清新的空气，进行最休闲写意的健身运动。"虽不是学术界的词源解释，倒也颇为有趣。

gorge [gɔ:dʒ] n. 咽喉；暴食；山峡，峡谷；v. 狼吞虎咽

[例] We live near the Yangtse Gorges. 我们住在长江三峡附近。

gorgeous ['gɔ:dʒəs] a. 华丽的，灿烂的

[例] Since it is such a gorgeous day, let's go swimming. 天气这么好，我们去游泳吧。

gossip ['gɔsip] n. 闲话，闲谈；流言

[例] I read about it in the gossip column. 我在闲话栏曾看过有关这件事的报道。

gourmet ['guəmei] n. 美食家

[例] The gourmet is very particular about food. 这位美食家很挑食。

[记] gourmet powder 味精 / gourmet restaurants 美食馆

govern ['gʌvən] v. 统治，支配，管理

[例] You should govern your temper. 你应该控制你的情绪。

[记] government n. 政府

grab [græb] v. 抓取，夺取，攫取

[例] She grabbed the seat near the fire before I could. 她赶在我的前面抢占了靠近火的座位。

graceful ['greisful] a. 优雅的；体面的

[例] She has a graceful carriage. 她举止优雅。

grade [greid] n. 等级，级别；v. 分等级

[例] This grade of wool can be sold at a fairly low price. 这种等级的羊毛可以以相当低的价格卖出。

gradual ['grædjuəl] a. 逐渐的，逐步的

[例] His health showed gradual improvement. 他的健康逐渐恢复。

graduate ['grædjueit] n.（大学）毕业生，研究生；v. 毕业

[例] The graduate rate is expected to be higher this year than ever. 今年的大学毕业率预期要高于往年。

[记] graduation n. 毕业；毕业典礼

grand [grænd] a. 宏伟的，壮丽的；重要的

[例] We met a lot of grand people when we went to the palace. 我们去王宫时见了许多要人。

[记] grandeur n. 伟大；豪华的排场

granite ['grænit] n. 花岗岩

[例] The wolframite is scattered extremely thinly throughout the granite. 钨锰铁矿在花岗岩上分布极少。

graphic ['græfik] a. 绘画似的，图解的

[例] He is interested in the graphic arts. 他对平面造型艺术很感兴趣。

[记] graphics n. 图表

grasp [grɑːsp] v. 抓牢，握紧；完全理解，全面领会

[谚] A man who grasps at too much may lose everything. 贪得无厌的人，可能毫无所得。

grateful ['greitful] a. 感激的，表示感激的

[例] She was grateful beyond words. 她的感激之情无法用言词表达。

gratitude ['grætitjuːd] n. 感激（之情）

[例] I am full of gratitude to you for helping me. 我非常感激你对我的帮助。

gravity ['græviti] n. 地心引力，重力

[例] Enormous energy is needed to launch a spacecraft against gravity. 发射飞船需要巨大的能量来摆脱地心引力。

[记] Newton's law of gravity 牛顿的万有引力定律

greedy ['griːdi] a. 贪吃的，贪婪的

[谚] The greedy man is always needy. 贪心者从不满足。

> 名词形式 greed，七宗罪（the seven deadly sins）之一：Pride 傲慢，Envy 嫉妒，Wrath 暴怒，Sloth 懒惰，Greed 贪婪，Gluttony 暴食，Lust 淫欲。语出《圣经》，人类的七宗原罪。sin 和 crime 是不一样的，sin 指人无法摆脱的原罪，天生缺陷，和完美的天生距离。世人多少都有。

greenhouse ['griːnhaus] n. 温室，花房

[例] The flowers are grown in the greenhouse. 这些花是在温室里养的。

[记] greenhouse effect 温室效应 / greenhouse gas 温室气体（二氧化碳）

greet [griːt] v. 问候，迎接，招呼

[例] The audience greeted his speech with a loud cheer. 听众对他的演讲报以高声欢呼。

[记] greeting n. 问候；致意

grid [grid] n.格子，格栅

[例] The city's streets form a grid. 城市的街道形成了一个网。

grief [griːf] n. 极度悲伤

[例] She did not show her grief when her son died. 她儿子去世时她没有显露出悲伤。

grind [graind] v. 碾碎，磨成粉末

[谚] We need to grind it into powder and then mix it with water. 我们需

要把它磨成粉末，然后加水混合。
[记] grind the teeth 咬牙切齿

groom [grum] n. 马夫；新郎；v. 喂马；推荐，整饰
[例] Monkeys groom each other. 猴子们相互梳理毛发。
[记] bridegroom 新郎

gross [grəus] n. 总额，总量；a. 总的，毛重的
[例] GDP stands for Gross Domestic Product. GDP 表示国内生产总值。
[记] Gross national product 国民生产总值 GNP

grudge [grʌdʒ] n. 怀恨；怨恨；v. 不给予
[例] I always feel she has a grudge against me. 我总觉得她对我怀恨在心。

guarantee [ˌgærən'tiː] v. 担保，为…作保；n. 保证，保证书
[例] They offer a two-year guarantee on all their electrical goods. 他们为销售的电器提供两年产品保证。
[记] bank guarantee 银行担保 / credit guarantee 信贷担保

guardian ['gɑːdjən] n. 监护人，保卫者；a. 守护的
[例] He became the legal guardian of his brother's daughter. 他成为他侄女的合法继承人。

> 英国很有影响的一份报纸《卫报》*The Guardian*，上面有较权威的英国大学排名。

guideline ['gaidlain] n. 指导方针
[例] The hospital has issued new guidelines on the treatment of mentally ill patients. 医院颁布了对于治疗精神病人的新的指导方针。

guilt [gilt] n. 内疚，自责；罪责
[例]His face showed guilt. 他的脸上流露出内疚的神情。

guilty ['gilti] a. 有罪的，内疚的
[例] Whenever I think of how hard my parents are saving for my education and how little I've learned, I feel guilty. 一想到父母为了我能受教育攒钱那么辛苦，而我学的那么少，我就觉得内疚。
[记] guilty looks 做贼心虚的表情; 内疚的神色

gum [gʌm] n. 橡胶；口香糖
[例] There is gum on the back of a stamp. 邮票的背面有胶水。
[记] chewing gum n. 口香糖

gust [gʌst] n. 一阵狂风；突发的一阵怒气
[例] A gust of wind blew the leaves along. 一阵狂风把树叶刮了起来。

gym [dʒim] n. 健身房，体操馆；体操
[例] We played basketball in the gym. 我们在体育馆内打篮球。

> gymnasium 的缩写。源自希腊语 *gymnazo*，意思是“裸体训练”。古希腊运动员在训练时皆赤身裸体，说是有益健康，不受衣着

束缚，能最大限度地自由发挥。古代奥林匹克没有妇女参加，是男人们玩裸奔的地方。所以从字面上讲：gymnast（体操运动员）是“做裸体运动的人”；gymnastics（体操）是“裸体运动”；gym 当然就是“做裸体运动的地方”啦。

habitat ['hæbitæt] n. （动、植物的）生活环境，栖息地

[例] The polar region is the habitat of the polar bear. 北极地带为北极熊的栖息地。

[记] habitant n. 居民，居住者

habitual [hə'bitjuəl] a. 习惯性的，经常的

[例] Ice and snow are a habitual sight in the north. 冰雪在北方是常见的。

[记] a habitual smile 习惯性的微笑 / a habitual thief 惯偷

hail [heil] n. 雹，冰雹

[例] It hailed during the night. 夜间下了冰雹。

hairdressing ['hɛə,dresiŋ] n. 美发，美容

[例] She spent much money and time on hairdressing. 她在美容上花了不少钱和时间。

halt [hɔːlt] n. 停止，停住；暂停

[例]The cab rolled to a halt. 计程车慢慢地停了下来。

hallmark ['hɔːlmɑːk] n.特点

[例]Clear expression is the hallmark of a good speaker. 清晰的表达能力是一位出色的演说家的特征。

hallowed ['hæləud] a. 神圣的

[例] The ancient Olympics were held on hallowed ground near Mount Olympus, where the Greek gods were said to live. 古代的奥林匹克运动会在据说是希腊众神居住的奥林匹斯山附近的圣地上举行。

[记] hallow v. 使神圣；n. 圣人 /All Hallows' Day 万圣节 / Halloween n. 万圣节前夕

万圣节是 11 月 1 日，Halloween 就是 10 月 31 日夜晚。西方人认为这一天地狱大门会打开，许多小鬼们会到人间来寻找一个 body 栖身。所以这时人们干脆先自己化装，戴上各种鬼面具去参加热闹的万圣节 party，让小鬼们人鬼难辨，最后只有失望而返！

hamper ['hæmpə] v. 阻碍，妨碍；牵制

[例] Prejudice sometimes hampers a person from doing the right thing. 偏见有时候妨碍人做正确的事情。

handicap ['hændikæp] n./v. 障碍，阻碍

[例] Lack of money handicapped him in his business. 缺少资金对他的生意十分不利。

handle ['hændl] v. 处理，应付；n. 柄，把手

[例] She handled a difficult argument skilfully. 她巧妙地应付了一场艰难的辩论。

handout ['hændaut] n. 传单；（免费）散发的印刷品（如讲义、广告、传单等）

[例] Please read the handout carefully. 请仔细看看这份分发的资料。

haphazard ['hæp'hæzəd] n. 偶然，偶然事件；a/adv. 偶然的（地）

[例] He can never forget that haphazard vacation. 他永远忘不了那次未做准备的旅行。

[记] by/at haphazard 偶然地，碰巧地

harass ['hærəs] v. 烦恼

[例] A gang of delinquents harried the storekeeper. 一群街头流氓不断骚扰店主。

[记] Sexual harassment 性骚扰

harbour ['hɑːbə] (=harbor) n. 港口，港湾，海港

[例] Our hotel room overlooked a pretty little fishing harbour. 从我们所在的宾馆房间可以俯视一个美丽的小渔港。

harmony ['hɑːməni] n. 协调，和谐，融洽

[例] They worked in perfect harmony. 他们合作无间。

[记] be in harmony with 与...协调一致 / harmonica n. 口琴 / [反义词] disharmony, discord

> 源自古希腊音乐术语，harmony 指"和声"，cord 指"和弦"。诗经小雅对harmony的原义和引申义都有很好的诠释："伐木丁丁，鸟鸣嘤嘤。"伐木叮叮响和鸟儿的鸣唱声是 hormony，和声；又说："嘤其鸣矣，求其友声。"鸟儿长鸣，是寻找朋友的声音。也是寻求 hormony，是寻找心灵上的和谐共鸣，境界更高，是 hormony 的引申义。

harness ['hɑːnis] v.利用，支配…的力量

[例] Some scientists are working hard at how the tides can be harnessed to produce electricity. 有些科学家正在努力研究怎样利用潮汐发电。

harsh [hɑːʃ] a. 严厉的，苛刻的；刺耳的

[例] You have to face the harsh reality bravely. 你必须勇敢地面对严峻的形势。

[记] harsh terms 苛刻的条件 / a harsh climate 令人难受的气候

hatch [hætʃ] v. 孵化；n. 孵化；舱口盖

[谚] Don't count your chickens before they are hatched. 鸡蛋还未孵，别忙数鸡雏。

haul [hɔːl] v. 拖拉

[例] They hauled the boat up onto the shore. 他们用力把船拖上岸。

haunt [hɔːnt] v. 常去；萦绕；（鬼魂等）常出没于；n. 常去的地方

[例] This is one of the cafes I used to haunt. 这是我以前常去的一家咖

啡馆。

[记] haunted house 鬼屋

hazard ['hæzəd] n. 危险，冒险；v. 冒险

[例] There are many hazards on a journey across Africa. 穿越非洲的旅行有许多危险。

[记] in (at) hazard 冒险，在危险中 / at all hazard 不顾一切危险

> 法语词，指“掷骰子赌博”，就是冒险。由 hazard 这种赌博方式演化出了一个有趣的英语表达：at sixes and sevens （六上七下，相当于汉语中的“七上八下”）。你在赌博时押两个骰子（dice）一个出 6 点，一个出 7 点，肯定是属于大脑缺氧，心绪不宁！听一下麦当娜的*Don't Cry for Me, Argentina*：“You won't believe me / All you will see is a girl you once knew / Although she's dressed up to the nines （打扮漂亮） / At sixes and sevens with you”

heal [hi:l] v. 治愈，医治

[例] The terrible wound took a long time to heal. 这重伤费了很长时间才痊愈。

[记] heal-all n. 万能药

heap [hi:p] n.（大而杂乱的）堆

[例] A heap of old clothes was lying in the corner. 一堆旧衣服堆在角落里。

heatstroke ['hi:tstrəuk] n. 中暑

[例] Mary suffered from heatstroke, so she couldn't come to school. 玛丽中暑了，所以不能来上学了。

hectare ['hektεə] n. 公顷（等于 1 万平方米）

[例] Beijing Zoo covers an 86-hectare area and is home to roughly 6,000 animals. 北京动物园占地 86 公顷，约 6,000 头动物以此为家。

hectic ['hektik] a. 狂热的，兴奋活跃的；忙乱的

[例] The journalist leads a hectic life. 新闻记者过着紧张兴奋的生活。

heed [hi:d] n./v. 注意，留意

[例] He pays much heed to my advice. 他很重视我的劝告。

heighten ['haitn] v. 提高，增加，加强

[例] As she waited,her excitement heightened. 她越等心里就越激动。

heir [εə] n. 继承人，后嗣

[例] Richard was his father's only heir, as he had no brothers or sisters. 理查德是他父亲的唯一继承人，因为他没有兄弟姐妹。

[记] heiress 女继承人

helicopter ['helikɔptə] n. 直升机；v. 用直升飞机载送

[例] The president helicoptered to California yesterday. 总统昨天乘直升飞机赴加州。

helix ['hi:liks] n. 螺旋，螺旋状物，[解剖]耳轮

[例] This is a helix on an Ionic capital. 这是爱奥尼亚柱式的柱头上的螺旋形。

[记] the double helix model of DNA DNA 双螺旋结构

hemisphere ['hemisfiə] n. 半球

[例] In the northern hemisphere, spring is in March and April. 在北半球，春季是三月和四月。

hence [hens] adv. 因此，从此

[例] It is very late; hence you must go to bed. 时间已经很晚了，因此你必须睡觉去。

[记] seven years hence 七年以后

herb [hə:b] n. 药草, 香草

[例] There is a herb garden behind the house. 屋后有一个百草园。

herald ['herəld] n. 使者；先驱；预兆；v. 预报；宣布；传达

[例] Early pale green buds are heralds of spring. 早出的绿色嫩芽预示着春天的到来。

> 英文报纸名称喜欢用这个词，如：《纽约先驱论坛报》*New York Herald*；《悉尼晨锋报》*Sydney Morning Herald*；《国际先驱论坛报》*International Herald Tribune*；《格拉斯哥先驱报》*Glasgow Herald* 等。

herbivore ['hə:bivɔ:] n. 草食动物

[例] If the ground is covered with snow, how does this affect the herbivores? 假如大雪覆盖大地，这会对食草动物有多大的影响呢？

herd [hə:d] n. 兽群

[记] a herd of elephants 一群大象

heritage ['heritidʒ] n. 遗产，继承的财产

[例] We Chinese have a great cultural heritage. 我们中国人有伟大的文化遗产。

[记] cultural heritage 文化遗产 / World Heritage Sites 世界文化遗产

heroin ['herəuin] n. 海洛因, 吗啡

[例] When she was young, she was addicted to heroin. 她年纪轻轻的就染上了海洛因毒瘾。

> 德语借词，这种毒品是由德国教授 Paul Dresser 发现的。因为该毒品有亢奋作用，服用后会使人有飘飘然之感，认为自己就是无所不能的英雄，feel like a hero，故取名 heroin。区别单词 heroine n. 女英雄；女主人公

hesitate ['heziteit] v. 犹豫不决，踌躇

[例] Please don't hesitate to do it. 请别犹豫。

hesitation [ˌhezi'teiʃən] n. 踌躇，犹豫

[例] She decided without hesitation. 她毫不犹豫地做出了决定。

hierarchy ['haiərɑːki] n. 等级，等级制度

[例] The government is a hierarchy. 政府是个官阶分明的统治集团。

highlight ['hailait] v. 以强光照射；使显著；n. 加亮区；精彩场面

[例] Growing social problems were highlighted by these events. 这件事情越发突出了日益激化的社会问题。

[记] highlight the problem of... 着重反映…的问题 / yellow highlighter 黄色荧光笔

hijack ['haidʒæk] v. 抢劫，劫持；劫机

[例] The terrorists hijacked the plane and held all the passengers hostage. 恐怖分子劫持了飞机，把所有乘客劫为人质。

> 也拼作 highjack。歹徒在抢劫时害怕反抗，每每高呼："High, Jack!"（Jack 用来称呼不相识的人）意思是"哥们儿，把手举高点儿！"后词义延伸，指"绑架，劫机"等。hijacker 劫匪；skyjack 专指劫机。

hike [haik] v./n. 徒步旅行，远足

[例] He hiked out to the reservoir. 他步行去水库。

[记] hiking n.徒步旅行 /Take a hike! 哪儿凉快哪儿歇着去吧！

hinder ['hində] v. 阻碍，阻止

[例] The noise hindered me in my writing. 嘈杂声妨碍了我的写作。

Unit 14

hinge [hindʒ] n. 铰链；枢纽；v. 依…而转移

[例] The lid of the suitcase had a broken hinge, so it wouldn't open easily. 小提箱箱盖的铰链坏了，因此不容易打开。

hint [hint] v./n. 暗示，提示

[例] When she said she was tired, it was a hint that she wanted us to go. 当她说她累了时，是暗示她想让我们走。

[记] give a hint 暗示，示意；露口风 / take a hint 领会，明白

hire ['haiə] v. 租用；雇用

[例] We'd better hire a car for the weekend. 我们最好租一辆汽车在周末用。

historic [his'tɔrik] a. 有重大历史意义的，历史性的

[例] July 13, 2001 has become a historic day for China—Beijing succeeded in the 2008 Olympic bid. 2001 年 7 月 13 日成为中国历史上具有重大意义的日子——北京申办 2008 年奥运会获得成功。

hive [haiv] n. 蜂房，闹市；v.（使）入蜂箱；群居

[例] This marketplace was once a hive of activity. 这个市场一度是一个繁华的闹市。

holistic [həu'listik] a. 整体的，全盘的

[例] The holistic approach to health impies that health is a complete state of physical, mental and social well-being. 健康的整体分析意味着健康是一个包含身体、精神、社会福利在内的完整状况。

hockey ['hɔki] n. 曲棍球

[例] I always play hockey on Saturday. 我星期六总是打曲棍球。

hollow ['hɔləu] a. 空（心）的；中空的

[例] The square pillars in the hall look solid, but in fact they're hollow. 大厅里的那些方柱子看上去是实心的，其实是空心的。

holy ['həuli] a. 神圣的

[例] The pursuit of peace is our holiest quest. 对和平的追求是最值得敬仰的。

[记] the Holy Bible 圣经

> holy water 圣水；holy war 圣战；holy day 圣日，宗教节日。holy 和 day 二词合成为 holiday，holiday 原来仅指“宗教节日”，现在也指一般休息日了。

homestay ['həumstei] n. 在当地居民家居住的时期

[例] During my homestay, I fell in love with a kind-hearted girl. 我在当地居民家居住的时期，爱上了一位心地善良的姑娘。

homogeneous [ˌhɔməuˈdʒiːnjəs] a. 类似的，均匀的

[例] Computers check whether each text is stylistically homogeneous. 计算机可以检查出每一篇文章的文体是否相同。

[记] homosexual a. 同性恋的；n. 同性恋

honest [ˈɔnist] a. 诚实的，正直的

[例] I shall be quite honest with you. 我将和你完全坦诚相见。

honesty [ˈɔnisti] n. 诚实，正直；坦诚

[谚] Honesty is the best policy. 诚实就是上策。

honk [hɔŋk] n. 汽车喇叭声；雁叫声；v. 按汽车喇叭

[例] The driver honked the horn of his car hoping to disperse the crowd in the street. 司机把汽车喇叭按得嘟嘟响,想把街上的人群驱散。

honour [ˈɔnə] n. (= honor) 尊敬，敬意；荣誉；v. 尊敬；给以荣誉

[例] He's won an Academy Award and a host of other honors. 他获得了奥斯卡金奖以及其他很多荣誉。

[记] honourable a. 可敬的；光荣的

hook [huk] n. 挂钩，吊钩

[例] This dress hooks at the back, not at the side. 这件衣服是在背后而不是在旁边挂钩的。

> 《小飞侠》*Peter Pan* 中的大坏蛋虎克船长 Captain Hook。Hook 船长最可怕的武器是右手的铁钩 hook，那是在一次被肚子里有闹钟的腭鱼吃掉右手后装上的。

hop [hɔp] v. 跳跃

[例] The robber hopped into his ready car and rushed off. 强盗迅速跳进准备好的汽车匆匆离去。

horizon [həˈraizn] n. 地平（线）；眼界；见识

[例] I could see a ship on the horizon. 我可以看见地平线上有一艘轮船。

horizontal [ˌhɔriˈzɔntl] a. 地平线的，水平的

[例] On a map there are horizontal lines and vertical lines.在地图上有水平的线和垂直的线。

[反义词] vertical a. 垂直的；n. 垂直线

hormone [ˈhɔːməun] n. 荷尔蒙，激素

[例] Hormones can control certain organs within the body. 荷尔蒙能控制身体内的某个器官。

horrible [ˈhɔrəbl] a. 可怕的，恐怖的

[例] There was a horrible accident here yesterday. 昨天在这里发生了一起可怕的事故。

[记] horribly adv. 可怕地；非常

hospitality [ˌhɔspiˈtæliti] n. 好客，殷勤

[例] The people of your village showed me great hospitality. 你们村里

的人非常热诚慷慨地接待了我。

> host 主人, hospital 医院, hostel 招待所, hotel 旅馆, hospitality 都源自“东道主，好客”之意。hospital 原是宗教团体办的招待所，收留香客和其他客人。后指收容年老体弱和穷人的慈善机构，再后来指治疗和护理机构——医院。

hostage [ˈhɔstidʒ] n. 人质，抵押品

[例] A British journalist was held hostage for over four years. 一位英国新闻记者被作为人质扣押了四年以上。

[记] ransom [ˈrænsəm] n. 赎金

hostel [ˈhɔstəl] n. 青年招待所；客栈

[例] We found a happy crew of foreign students in the hostel. 我们在青年招待所看到一群快乐的外国留学生。

hostile [ˈhɔstail] a. 怀有敌意的，敌对的，不友善的

[例] Ever since I got better marks than Parker, he has been hostile to me. 自从我比派克得分高以后，他就对我不友好了。

hourglass [ˈauəglɑːs] n. 沙漏

[例] An hourglass is an old device for of telling the time. 沙漏是过去用来计时的。

hover [ˈhɔvə] v. 盘旋；徘徊；摇摆不定

[例] The helicopter is hovering over the crowd. 直升机在人群上空盘旋。

hug [hʌg] v./n. 拥抱

[例] He hugged his daughter. 他紧紧拥抱他的女儿。

hull [hʌl] n.（果实等的）外壳；船体

[例] Rice is gathered, cleaned and hulled before being sold. 稻子经过收割，筛清和去壳以后才出售。

humanity [hju(ː)ˈmæniti] n. 人类；博爱，仁慈

[例] This new drug will help all humanity. 这种新药将有益于全人类。

> 字根 hum 指“土地, ground”。《圣经》说上帝在地上抓了一把土，按照自己的形象捏了一人儿，吹了口气，泥人活了。《淮南子》说女娲娘娘用黄土和水造人。所以呢，我们都是泥人儿，hum-man，human。

humble [ˈhʌmbl] a. 谦卑的；谦虚的

[例] Humility often gains more than pride. 谦逊往往比骄傲受益更多。

> humble 就是地面的，地位低下的→谦卑的；谦虚的。泥人儿 human 都应 humble 一点。别忘了，天使之所以会飞，不是因为有翅膀，而是因为她们把自己看得很轻。

humidity [hjuːˈmiditi] n. 潮湿，湿气，湿度

[例] The milk powder has lumped because of humidity. 奶粉受潮结块了。

humiliate [hju(:)'milieit] v. 羞辱；使丢脸

[例] The country was humiliated by defeat. 该国因战败而受辱。

hurdle ['hə:dl] n. 篱笆，栏，障碍；跨栏

[例] The final hurdles have been removed. 最后的障碍已被排除了。

> 刘翔在奥运会上拿的就是 110 meter hurdles gold medal。

hurricane ['hʌrikən] n. 飓风，狂风

[例] The hurricane flung their motor boat upon the rocks. 飓风把他们的摩托艇抛到岩石上。

hybrid ['haibrid] n. 杂种；混合物；a. 混合的；杂种的

[例] The hybrid of a donkey and a horse is called a mule. 驴和马交配生出的杂种叫骡子。

hygiene ['haidʒi:n] n. 卫生（学）；保健（学）

[例] Wash regularly to ensure personal hygiene. 要经常洗澡以确保个人卫生。

[记] hygienic a. 卫生的 / personal hygiene 个人保健

> 源自希腊健康女神 Hygeia，她的形象是个年轻女子，身着白色长衣（白大褂），头戴祭司冠，用饭碗喂着一条蛇。她的老爸医神 Aesculapius 则经常拿着有巨蛇盘缠的手杖。[怎么 Harvey 你越说越象欧阳锋啊？]手杖象征知识、权威，蛇象征医学。所以蛇与手杖已成为国际通行的医药卫生标志，不信，看看任何一个医药大学的校徽。

hypothesis [hai'pɔθisis] n. 假说，假设

[例] This is only a sort of scientific hypothesis which has not been proved by experiments. 这仅仅是一个尚未被实验证明的科学假说。

[记] hypothetic a. 假设的，假定的

icon ['aikɔn] n. 图标；肖像；偶像

[例] The pop singer is the icon of many young boys and girls. 这位流行歌手是很多少男少女的偶像。

ideal [ai'diəl] a. 理想的，完美的

[例] This dictionary is ideal — it's exactly what I needed. 这本词典很理想，正是我所需要的。

identical [ai'dentikəl] a. 同一的，同样的

[例] Our views of what should be done are identical. 我们双方对应当怎么办的看法是一致的。

[记] be identical with 和…完全相同

identify [ai'dentifai] v. 识别，鉴别；把…和…看成一样

[例] The markings are so blurred that it is difficult to identify. 标记模糊

不清，难以识别。

[记] identify A with B 认为 A 和 B 是一致的 / identify sb./sth. as... 把某人/某物确认为 / identification n. 身份证明；鉴定

identity [ai'dentiti] n. 身份，个性，特性

[例] The police are still uncertain of the murderer's identity. 警察尚未证实杀人犯的身份。

> 上面三个词来源于同一拉丁语 idem，指“一样，same”。身份证即是 identity card，或 ID card。

ideology [ˌaidi'ɔlədʒi] n. 意识形态

[例] Our idologies differ. 我们的意识形态不同。

[记] ideological a. 意识形态的

idiom ['idiəm] n. 成语；方言；习惯用语

[例] To be “hard up” is an English idiom. “hard up（缺钱）”是英语中的习惯用语。

idiot ['idiət] n. 白痴，傻瓜

[例] You are behaving like a perfect idiot. 你表现得像一个十足的白痴。

[记] idiot box 电视机

idle ['aidl] a. 懒惰的，无所事事的；v. 虚度；游手好闲

[例] Men are left idle when machines break down. 机器坏了时，工人们便无事可做了。

[记] idling away the hours 消磨时光 / idleness n. 懒惰 / idly adv. 闲散的

idol ['aidl] n. 偶像，崇拜物；幻象

[例] The football player is the idol of many young people. 这位足球运动员是许多年轻人崇拜的偶像。

[记] idolize v. 偶像化

ignition [ig'niʃən] n. 点火，点燃

[例] The key had been left in the ignition. 钥匙被放在点火装置上了。

[记] ignite v. 点火，使燃烧

ignorance ['ignərəns] n. 无知，愚昧

[谚] Where ignorance is bliss, it is folly to be wise. 难得糊涂。

[记] be in ignorance of.... 对…全然不知

ignorant ['ignərənt] a. 无知的，没有学识的，愚昧的

[谚] Wise men become wiser as they grow older, ignorant men more ignorant. 智者临老更聪明；蠢人老去更昏庸。

ignore [ig'nɔː] v. 不理睬，忽视

[例] It was not right to ignore the doctor's advice. 不听医生劝告是不对的。

illegal [i'liːgəl] a. 不合法的，非法的

[例] It is illegal to steal things. 偷东西是违法的。

illiteracy [i'litərəsi] n. 文盲

[例] We hope to eradicate illiteracy in our country by 2015. 我们希望在2015年我国消除文盲。

illusion [i'lu:ʒən] n. 幻觉；幻想

[谚] Life is only illusion. 浮生若梦。

illustrate ['iləstreit] v. 举例说明，图解

[例] The book was illustrated with color photographs. 这本书配上了彩色照片。

[记] illustration n. 插图；图解

> 字根 lust/luc 指"明亮的"。il(on)+ lustr(bright)+ ate (v.) 使明亮，使清晰→图解说明；lucent a. 光亮的，透明的；美国朗讯科技以此为名。

image ['imidʒ] n. 图像，映像；v. 想象，反映

[例] He saw the image of his face in the mirror. 他在镜子里看到了他的脸。

imitate ['imiteit] v. 模仿；仿效

[例] Children like to imitate adults. 儿童喜欢模仿成年人。

immature [ˌimə'tjuə] a. 不成熟的，未完全发展的

[例] These kids are brilliant, but often socially immature. 这些孩子很有才气，但社交方面还很幼稚。

immediate [i'mi:djət] a. 立即的；直接的，紧接的

[例] A five-day week has found an immediate welcome and much popularity since it was officially adopted across the country. 五天工作制自从在全国正式实行以来就立即受到了人们的普遍欢迎和拥护。

[记] immediate cause 直接原因 / immediate family 至亲，直系亲属 / immediately adv.立刻

immense [i'mens] a. 巨大的

[例] He made an immense amount of money in business. 他在生意中赚了一大笔钱。

immerse [i'mə:s] v. 沉浸，沉浸于

[例] He immersed himself in work so as to stop thinking about her. 他埋头于工作以便不再思念她。

immigrate ['imigreit] v. 使移居入境

[例] Many colonists immigrated to the New World. 英国把大量殖民者移居到了新大陆。

[记] immigrant n. 移民

imminent ['iminənt] a. 即将发生的，逼近的

[例] The conquest of cancer is imminent. 癌症的征服为期不远。

immoral [i'mɔrəl] a. 不道德的，邪恶的；放荡的

[例] Using other people for one's own profit is immoral. 利用别人来谋取私利是不道德的。

[反义词] moral

immune [i'mju:n] a. 免疫的；不受影响的；免除的

[例] The child is immune to measles. 这个孩子对麻疹有免疫力。

[记] immune to 不受影响的 / immunity n. 免疫力 / immune system 免疫系统

> 字根muni指"服务，service"。municipal 为公众服务的→市政的；communicate 一起服务，相互服务→沟通；communism 服务主义，为人民服务[毛主席早就解释过]→共产主义；immune不用服务→免疫，免除。immune system 免疫系统；immunize v. 使免疫

impair [im'pεə] v. 削弱；损伤

[例] Do not put garlic into the stuffing as it can impair the flavour. 不要往馅里放大蒜，那样会破坏味道的。

[记] impairment n. 损坏

impact ['impækt] n. 冲击，碰撞；影响，效果；[im'pækt] v. 冲击，撞击；影响

[例] The entry into the WTO will have a great impact on China. "入世"将给中国带来巨大的影响。

[记] impact on 对…施加影响

impair [im'pεə] v. 削弱

[例] If a witness is allowed to withhold evidence, it impairs the legal process. 假如允许证人拒绝出示证据,就会影响法律程序。

impart [im'pɑ:t] v. 给予，传授；告知，透露

[例] She imparted the secret to her boyfriend. 她把秘密向她的男朋友透露了。

impede [im'pi:d] v. 妨碍，阻止

[例] Nothing can impede his progress. 没有什么能妨碍他的进步。

> 字根 ped 指 "足 foot"。pedal 脚的→脚踏板；pedestrian 步行者，行人；expedition 使脚向外→远征，探险；impede 脚不行了，双脚被缠住了→妨碍。猜猜这个：pedicab 脚踩的计程车？ Harvey 重要提示：成都人称为 "趴耳朵" 的便是。

impetus ['impitəs] n. 推动力，刺激，促进

[例] The car ran down the hill under its own impetus. 汽车借着本身的冲力滑下山。

implement ['implimənt] v. 实施，执行 n. 工具，器具（常用复数）

[例] The committee's decisions will be implemented immediately. 委员会的决定将立即执行。

[记] implementation n. 执行

implicate ['implikeit] v. 使牵连其中；暗指

[例] The police found a letter which implicated him in the robbery. 警察

发现了一封信,这封信把他牵连到抢劫案中。
[记] implication n. 含义；暗示

implicit [im'plisit] a. 暗示的，含蓄的；(in) 不怀疑的；无保留的
[例] She has implicit trust in her secretary. 她对自己的秘书绝对信任。
[反义词] explicit

imply [im'plai] v. 暗指，意味着
[例] His manner of speaking implied that he was not willing to accept the agreement. 他讲话的态度意味着他不愿意接受这份协议。
[记] imply sth./imply that... 暗示、意味着…

impose [im'pəuz] v. 征税；把…强加于
[例] Don't impose yourself on people who don't want you. 不要勉强和不需要你的人在一起。
[记] impose sth. on sb. 把某事强加于某人 / impose oneself on sb. 强迫某人接纳自己 / impose a tax 征税

impress [im'pres] v. 使（人）印象深刻；使铭记
[例] All those qualifications don't impress me at all. 所有的那些限制条件我根本不在乎。
[记] impression n. 印记；印象

improve [im'pru:v] v. 改善，改进
[例] I am unable to improve on his suggestion. 我提不出比他更好的建议了。
[记] improvement n. 改进，进步

improvise ['imprəvaiz] v. 临时准备；即席创作
[例] If an actor forgets his words, he has to improvise. 如果一个演员忘了台词，他必须临时现编。
[记] improvisation n. 即席创作

> 该词分为 im（否定）+pro（之前）+vise（看见）→事先并没有看见→即兴表演，临时准备。字根 vis 指“看见”。provision 事先看到→供应，预备，条款；previse 预见；supervise 从上往下看→监督，管理。

impulse ['impʌls] n. 冲动，一时的念头；推动
[例] A sudden impulse of anger arose in him. 他突然升起一阵怒火。
[记] a man of impulse 易冲动的人 / act on impulse 凭冲动行事

inadequate [in'ædikwit] a. 不充分的，不适当的
[例] The supply is inadequate to meet the demand. 供不应求。

incentive [in'sentiv] n. 动机；a. 激励的
[例] Money is still a major incentive in most occupations. 在许多职业中，钱仍是主要的鼓励因素。

incessant [in'sesnt] a. 不停的，连续的，持续不断的
[例] He was greatly annoyed by the incessant phone calls. 持续不断的

电话使他非常厌烦。
[同义词] ceaseless, constant, continual

incidence ['insidəns] n. 发生率；程度
[例] It is reported that the incidence of illiteracy of China is noticeably decreasing. 据报道，中国文盲率正在显著下降。

incident ['insidənt] n. 事情，事件，事变
[例] Were there any exciting incidents during your journey? 你们在旅行中有没有什么令人激动的事情?
[区别] accident n. 意外，偶然事故 / a car accident 一起车祸

incite [in'sait] v. 激起；刺激；煽动
[例] His bravery incited the soldiers to fight continuously. 他的勇敢激励士兵们继续战斗下去。

> 字根 cite 指“呼叫 to call”。Cite 召唤，引用；exciting 令人叫喊出来（ex-）的→令人兴奋的，使人激动的；incite 心里的叫喊→激动，鼓动；recite 已经知道了，再（re-）叫喊一遍→背诵；recital 朗诵，背诵，独唱会。

inclination [ˌinkli'neiʃən] n. 趋向，倾向；爱好
[例] The child has an inclination to grow fat. 这孩子有长胖的趋势。

incline ['inklain] v. 倾向于，使倾斜；n. 斜坡；倾斜
What he said inclines me to think that he will agree to our plan. 他的话使我觉得他会同意我们的计划的。

inclusive [in'klu:siv] a. 包括的，包含的
[例] The monthly rent is $20 inclusive of everything. 月房租总共二十美元，包括一切费用在内。
[反义词] exclusive

income ['inkəm] n. 收入，所得，收益
[例] What is your income from your job? 你工作的收入是多少?

incorporate [in'kɔ:pəreit] v. 包含，吸收；把…合并，使并入
[例] We will incorporate your suggestion in the new plan. 我们将把你的建议编到新计划中去。

increase ['inkri:s] n. 增加，增长；[in'kri:s] v. 增加，增长，增强
[例] His employer has increased his wages. 他的雇主增加了他的工资。

incredible [in'kredəbl] a. 不可思议的，惊人的；不可信的
[例] The film star has an incredible car in addition to a large house. 这个电影明星除了一幢很大的住宅外还有一辆极好的汽车。

increment ['inkrimənt] n. 增加，增量
[例] You will receive annual salary increments every September. 每年九月你会得到加薪。

incur [in'kə:] v. 招致，引起
[例] The power shortages incurred in 24 provinces has hit its annual peak.

24个省的电力短缺已经达到了每年的高峰。

indefinite [in'definit] a. 不确定的，不清楚的；无限期的

[例] There's an indefinable air of tension at the meeting. 会议上有种难以描述的紧张气氛。

index ['indeks] n. 标志；索引；指数 v. 编入索引中，做索引

[例] A key word index is an enlargement to the book. 主题词索引是这本书的附录。

> 在拉丁语里，index 意思是"食指"。人们在书籍目录上查询时习惯用食指引导自己的视线，故引申为"索引"。大家都知道手指叫 finger，你能猜猜 John 有多少个 fingers？ 8个！ John = E.T.？John = 洪七公的弟弟？西方人把大拇指叫 thumb，不算 finger。正常人当然有 eight fingers 啦。食指 index finger 或 forefinger；中指 middle finger；无名指 ring finger（戒指别戴错了）；小指 little finger。脚趾叫 toe。

indicate ['indikeit] v. 指示，显示；表明

[例] In this map, the towns are indicated by a red dot. 在这张地图上，城镇是用小红点标的。

indicator ['indikeitə] n. 指示物，指示器

[例] Something has gone wrong with the direction indicator. 航向指示器出了毛病。

indifferent [in'difərənt] a. 不感兴趣的，漠不关心的

[例] He is indifferent to this subject. 他对这个话题不感兴趣。

[同义词] aloof

indigenous [in'didʒinəs] a. 土生土长的，本土的；生来的

[例] Indians were the indigenous inhabitants of America. 印第安人是美洲的土著居民。

[同义词] native, aboriginal

* pedicab n. 人力三轮车

Unit 15

indispensable [ˌindisˈpensəbl] a. 必需的，必不可少的

[例] Health is indispensable to everyone. 健康是人人所必需的。

> 字根 pens 和 pend 都指古代用秤"悬挂称量"。如：expense，ex-=out，指用秤称量一定的金银，并给出→花费；independent 不需称量的→独立的；suspend 悬挂；pension 称量计算并给钱→退休金；compensate 一起悬挂，左右重量相等→补偿；dispensable 可分开称量的→能分配的，可有可无的[金钱就是 dispensable，可以拿杆秤分给大家，自己有没有无所谓的]；indispensable 不可分配的→必需的。那么，猜猜 dispensary 是什么地方？dispense 经常用秤实施分配 +ary 表场所 = ________； dispenser ________

individual [ˌindiˈvidjuəl] n. 个人，个体；a. 个人的，单独的

[例] The rights of the individual are considered to be the most important in a free society. 在自由的社会里个人权利被认为是最重要的。

[记] individual economy 个体经济

induce [inˈdjuːs] v. 引诱，诱导

[例] Nothing shall induce me to join their club. 我怎么都不会去加入他们的俱乐部。

[记] induce sb. to do sth. 劝导某人做某事 / inducement n. 诱引，刺激物 / seduce v. 引诱；勾引

indulge [inˈdʌldʒ] v. 放纵；沉溺于

[例] He indulges his children too much. 他对他的孩子太放任了。

[记] indulge in 沉溺于

industrious [inˈdʌstriəs] a. 勤劳的，勤奋的

[谚] A good head and an industrious hand are worth gold in any land. 头脑聪明手勤劳，走遍天下都需要。

inept [iˈnept] a. 不适当的，无能的

[例] He's quite inept at tennis. 他打网球太笨。

inert [iˈnəːt] a. 无生气的；惰性的，不活泼的

[例] Helium and neon are inert gases. 氦和氖为惰性气体。

inevitable [inˈevitəbl] a. 不可避免的，必然的

[例] Such a difficult operation may not succeed; it's an inevitable gamble. 这样难度很大的手术可能不会成功，但这次冒险不可避免。

[同义词] inescapable, unavoidable

infant [ˈinfənt] n. 婴儿；a. 婴儿的，幼稚的

[例] An infant school is a school for children from about five to seven years of age. 幼儿园是五岁至七岁儿童的学校。

infant（婴儿）和 infantry（步兵）从语义上看差得很远，从单词上看很有联系。你能想到婴儿和步兵的共同点吗？对了，他们都是不怎么说话的人。婴儿自然不会说话，古时的步兵也不需要说话。骑兵要在马上吆喝，军官要大喊指挥，而步兵只需扛着枪向前走就行了。拉丁文 infans 指不会说话的人。

infect [in'fekt] v. 传染（疾病给人），感染；使（人）受影响

[例] Her cheerful spirits and bubble laughter infect the whole class. 她那快乐的情绪和爽朗的笑声感染了全班。

[记] infection n. 感染；传染病 /infectious a. 有传染性的，易传染的

infer [in'fəː] v. 推断，推论

[例] I infer from your letter that you have not made up your mind yet. 我从你信中推想，你还没有下决心。

inferior [in'fiəriə] a. 下级的，差的，次的

[例] No inferior products should be allowed to pass. 绝不允许放过任何次品。

infinite ['infinit] a. 无限的、无穷的

英国著名诗人 William Blake 曾写下一段十分美丽的诗句：To see a World in a Grain of Sand, And a Heaven in a Wild Flower; Hold Infinity in the palm of your hand, And Eternity in an hour. 粗略地理解为"从一粒沙子看到一个世界，从一朵野花看到一个天堂，把握在你手心里的就是无限，永恒也就消融于一个时辰"。由小见大，气势磅礴。国内有中文功底深厚者将其译为"一花一世界，一沙一天国；君掌盛无边，刹那含永劫"。

inflation [in'fleiʃən] n. 通货膨胀，膨胀

[例] Inflation erodes the purchasing power of the families with lower incomes. 通货膨胀使低收入家庭的购买力不断下降。

influence ['influəns] n. 影响，作用；v. 影响

[例] My teacher's influence made me study science at college. 由于我老师的影响，我上大学学了理科。

[记] influential a. 有影响力的，有势力的

influenza [ˌinflu'enzə] (=flu) n. 流行性感冒

[例] Many people caught influenza last month. 上个月许多人都患了感冒。

influx ['inflʌks] n. 流入，注入，涌进

[例] There was a sudden influx of household electric products into the market. 大批家用电气产品突然涌进市场。

inform [in'fɔːm] v. 通知，告知

[例] The headmistress informed us that the school would be closed for one day next week. 女校长告诉我们下星期学校将停一天课。

[记] inform sb. of/about sth. 通知某人某事、检举某人 / be informed of

听说；接到…的通知 / information n. 通知；信息

informative [in'fɔːmətiv] a. 提供丰富资料的；增长见闻的

[例] It will be most interesting and informative to hear Mr. Smith. 届时能聆听到史密斯先生的演讲，定会是极为有趣和增长见识的。

infrastructure ['infrəˌstrʌktʃə] n. 基础设施

[例] The local government is too poor to invest in a social welfare program, new infrastructure or anything else. 当地政府很穷，不能对社会福利、新的基础设施或其他的事情进行投资。

infringe [in'frindʒ] v. 破坏，侵犯，违反

[例] The press infringed a copyright agreement. 这家出版社违反了版权协议。

infringe a contract 违反一项合同 / infringe a patent 侵犯专利权

> 单词fringe指边缘，infringe 从外走到了边界的里面，破坏了边缘fringe →侵犯，违反。

ingenious [in'dʒiːnjəs] a. 灵巧的，制作精巧的，巧妙的

[例] He invented an ingenious excuse for his absence. 他为缺席编造了一个巧妙的借口。

ingredient [in'griːdiənt] n. 成分，构成要素

[例] Salt is a crucial ingredient in cooking. 盐是调味的一种重要材料。

inhabit [in'hæbit] v. 居住于（某地）

[例] Thoughts inhabit his mind. 各种思想占据了他的心灵。

inhabitant [in'hæbitənt] n. 居民

[例] The local inhabitants do not like noisy tourists in summer. 当地居民不喜欢夏季喧闹的游客。

inhale [in'heil] v. 吸入；吸气

[例] Do you inhale when you smoke? 你抽烟时是否把烟吸入肺里？

inherent [in'hiərənt] a. 内在的，固有的，生来就有的

[例] Polarity is inherent in a magnet. 极性是磁铁的固有性质。

[记] be inherent in 为…所固有；生来的

inherit [in'herit] v. 继承，遗传而得

[例] She inherited all her mother's beauty. 她继承了她母亲全部的美。

[记] inheritance n. 继承；继承的财产

inhibit [in'hibit] v. 抑制，约束

[例] Shyness inhibited her from speaking in public. 羞怯抑制了她在众人面前讲话。

initial [i'niʃəl] a. 开始的，最初的；n. 首字母

[例] The initial talks were the base of the later agreement. 最初的会谈是后来达成协议的基础。

[记] initially adv. 最初，开头 / initialize n. 初始化

> initials n. 姓名的首字母。例如，西方人熟知的 J. F. K. 代表 John Fitzgerald Kennedy，美国前总统肯尼迪。

initiate [i'niʃieit] v. 开始，创始，发起

[例] He initiated the theory, but his students developed it. 他创始了这一理论，而他的弟子将其发扬光大。

inject [in'dʒekt] v. 注射，注入

[例] We hope to inject new life into our business. 我们希望我们的业务工作充满朝气。

injury ['indʒəri] n. （对身体的）伤害，损害

[例] I take it as a personal injury. 我认为这是对个人的侮辱。

innate ['ineit] a. 先天的，天生的

[例] Correct ideas are not innate in the mind, but come from social practice. 正确的思想不是头脑中固有的，而是来源于社会实践。

inner ['inə] a. 内部的，内心的

[例] Yet more and more, especially in our large cities and suburbs, these inner restrains are loosening. 尤其在大城市和近郊，这种内在的约束力变得越来越弱。

[记] inner feeling / life / peace 内在的感情/精神生活/内心的平静 /反义 outer

innocent ['inəsnt] a. 清白的，无罪的；天真的

[例] Can you provide any evidence that he was innocent of the crime? 你能提供证据证明他没有犯这罪吗？

> 一人拽住 Harvey 说：“哥们儿，是不是你偷了我的钱！” Harvey 赶紧把身上的口袋给他翻了个遍：“大哥，看到了，里边 in 没有 no 一分钱 cent，I'm innocent!”

innovate ['inəuveit] v. 改革，创新

[例] In this age, a company either innovates or dies. 在这个年代，一家公司不创新就会垮掉。

innovation [,inəu'veiʃən] n. 改革，创新

[例] The mass movement for technical innovation is vigorously forging ahead in the factory. 群众性的技术革新运动正在该厂蓬勃开展。

[记] innovator n. 改革者，创新者

innumerable [i'nju:mərəbl] a. 不可胜数的

[例] History is the essence of innumerable biographies. 历史是无数传记的精华。

input ['input] n. 输入，投入

[例] We must have more output with less labor input. 我们必须投入较少的劳动力，产出较多的产品。

[反义词] output

inquiry [in'kwaiəri] n. 询问，调查

[例] For further inquiry, please consult our website. 如需要进一步咨询，请登陆我们的网站。

insane [in'sein] a. **患精神病的；疯狂的**

[例] He must be insane to drive his car so fast. 他把车开得这么快，一定是疯了。

> 字根 san 指“健康的”。如：sane 健全的；sanatorium 对健康有益的地方→疗养院；sanitary 卫生的；sanitation 公共卫生；insane 精神病的，疯狂的；an insane asylum 疯人院。

insect ['insekt] n. **昆虫**

[例] Insects propagate themselves by means of eggs. 昆虫以产卵的方式繁殖后代。

insert [in'səːt] v. **插入，嵌入**；n. **插入物**

[例] He inserted the key in the lock but could not open the door. 他把钥匙插入锁中但没能打开门。

[记] insert sth. in/into sth. 把…插入…

insight ['insait] n. **洞悉力，见识**

[例] Hemingway's novels show deep insight into human character. 海明威的小说深刻地洞察了人性。

[记] have an insight into... 对…有深刻见解 / give sb. a insight into... 使某人了解…

insist [in'sist] v. **坚持，坚决认为，坚决主张**

[例] We insist on self - reliance. 我们坚决主张自力更生。

[记] insist on/insist that... 坚持；坚决主张…

insomnia [in'sɔmniə] n. **失眠，失眠症**

[例] He suffered from insomnia and was taking sleeping pills each night. 他失眠非常痛苦，每天晚上都在吃安眠药。

> 希腊神话中夜之女神 Nyx 有两个双胞胎 twin 儿子，一个是睡神 Hypnos，罗马神话中称之为 Somnus，另一个是死神 Thanatos。Hypnos 衍生出单词 hypnosis 催眠；hypnotist 催眠师；Somnus 演生出单词 insomnia 失眠；hypersomnia 嗜睡；somnambulist 梦游者；而死神则衍生出 thanatology 死亡学等单词。

inspect [in'spekt] v. **检查，视察**

The government sent sb. to inspect our school. 政府派人来视察我们学校。

[记] inspection n. 检查，视察，检阅 / inspector n. 检查员；视察者

inspire [in'spaiə] v. **鼓舞，激励**

[例] I was inspired to work harder than ever before. 我受到了激励，比以往任何时候都更加努力地工作。

[记] inspiration n. 灵感

install [in'stɔːl] v. 安装（设备）

[例] We're installing a new heating system. 我们正在安装新的取暖装置。

[记] installation n. 装置，设备；安装

installment [in'stɔːlmənt] n. 分期付款，债款的分期摊还数

[例] You can buy a car on instalment purchase. 你可以分期付款购买小轿车。

instance ['instəns] n. 实例；情况，场合

[例] There are many instances of good people and good deeds nowadays. 现在好人好事的例子很多。

instantaneous [ˌinstən'teinjəs] a. 瞬间的，即刻的，即时的

[例] Relief was instantaneous. 痛苦的消除是瞬间的事。

instinct ['instiŋkt] n. 本能，直觉，天性

[例] Birds learn to fly by instinct. 鸟儿学飞是出于本能。

institute ['institjuːt] n. 学会，学院；v. 创立，设立

[例] He works at a foreign language institute. 他在一所外语学院工作。

> 字根 stitut 指“站立 to stand”。如：constitute 站在一起→组成，设立；constitution 构造，宪法；destitute 站都站不稳了，饥寒交迫→贫穷的，赤贫的；institute 从内部站立→创立；prostitute 以站在众人之前来维持生计的人→妓女；restitute 重新站立→复原；substitute 在下面站着的→替代品，候补队员；superstition 在上面站着的→迷信，偶像崇拜。

institution [ˌinsti'tjuːʃən] n. 社会公共机构；学校

[例] Universities are educational institutions. 大学是教育机构。

instruct [in'strʌkt] v. 教导，指导

[例] I've been instructed to wait here until the lecturer arrives. 我得到指示在这儿等到讲课老师到来。

[记] instruct sb. to do sth. 命令某人做某事 / instructor n. 教师 / instruction n. 指示；用法说明 / an instruction book 说明书

instrument ['instrumənt] n. 仪器，器具；乐器

[例] All surgical instruments must be sterilized before use. 每件外科手术器械使用前都必须消毒。

insufficient [ˌinsə'fiʃənt] a. 不足的，不够的；n. 不足

[例] The food and drinks were insufficient for the needs of twenty lads. 食物和饮料不够二十个小伙子吃。

[反义词] sufficient, adequate

insulate ['insjuleit] v. 使绝缘，隔离

[例] Many houses in the north are warm in winter because they are insulated so that the heat is not lost. 北方的许多房子在冬天很暖和,因为它们都作了隔热处理，使热量不致散失。

[记] insulation n. 绝缘 / insulator n. 绝缘体 / insularity n. 岛国性质

insult ['insʌlt] v. /n. 侮辱，凌辱

[例] He insulted her by calling her a stupid fool. 你叫她笨蛋，你侮辱了她。

insure [in'ʃuə] v. 确保,给…保险

[例] It is advisable to insure your life against accident. 最好参加人寿保险，以防意外。

[记] insurance n. 保险；保险费 / an insurance salesman 一位保险推销员

insurmountable [ˌinsə'mauntəbl] a. 不能克服的，不能超越的

[例] The children met with insurmountable difficulties. 孩子们遇到了难以克服的困难。

intact ['intækt] a. 完好无损的，未经触动的

[例] The fragile boxes arrived intact. 这些易碎的箱子完整无损地运到了。

intake ['inteik] n. 吸收，吸入（数）量，纳入（数）量

[例] The company decided to reduce this year's intake of employees. 公司决定减少今年雇员的招收量。

integrate ['intigreit] v. 使完整，使成一体，使结合

[例] The teachers are trying to integrate all the children into society. 教师们正设法使所有的孩子都与社会融为一体。

[记] integral n. 【数】整数

integrity [in'tegriti] n. 正直，诚实，完整

[例] The ancient temple and the pagoda are still there, but not in their integrity. 那座古老的庙宇和塔还在，但是不完整了。

intellectual [ˌinti'lektjuəl] a. 智力的；有知识的；n. 知识分子

[例] To protect intellectual property rights, we should ruthlessly crack down on piracy. 要保护知识产权，我们必须严厉打击盗版。

intelligence [in'telidʒəns] n. 智力，智慧

[例] Use your intelligence, and you're sure to succeed someday. 发挥你的聪明才智，有一天你一定会成功。

[记] an intelligence agent 间谍，情报人员 /intelligent a. 有才智的，聪明的

> intelligence quotient (IQ) 智商。还有几个Q当下人们使用频繁：EQ—Emotional Quotient，情商；MQ—Moral Intelligence，道德商数，国外很多名校招生时除了看成绩，也要看是否有做公益的经历，其实就是看MQ了；CQ—Creative Quotient，创商，即“创造力商数”；HQ—Health Quotient，健康商数，现代人为了尽早实现卓越的人生理想、提早退休，往往透支体力，三十几岁的人身体综合素质相当于正常工作的六十岁老人，因此，很多社会学者强调大家要注意HQ。

intelligible [in'telidʒəbl] a. 可理解的，明白易懂的

[例] His theory is not intelligible to us. 他的理论我们无法理解。

intend [in'tend] v. 想要，打算，计划

[例] Today, I intend to finish reading this book. 今天我打算读完这本书。

intense [in'tens] a. 强烈的，剧烈的

[例] What struck Wang Zhizhi after he joined the NBA was the intense competition between the players. 当王治郅加入 NBA 后，队员间激烈的竞争使他震惊。

intensive [in'tensiv] a. 加强的，集中的，密集的

[例] Intensive care in hospitals is given to the seriously ill. 在医院里危重病人得到加强护理。

[记] intensive care unit (ICU)医院的深彻治疗病房 /intensively adv. 深入地

intention [in'tenʃən] n. 意图，目的；打算

[例] We understood her intention. 我们明白了她的心意。

interact [ˌintər'ækt] v. 互相作用，互相影响

[例] All things are interrelated and interact with each other. 一切事物均相互联系并相互作用。

[记] interactive a. 交互式的，互动的

> 前缀 inter- 指“在…之间”。如：inter- 两者之间 +act 举动→相互作用；interchange 彼此交换，轮替；interbreed 两个品种之间繁殖→混种；international 国与国之间的→国际的；intersection 两者相互切断→十字路口。

interbreed [ˌintə'bri:d] v.（使）异种交配，（使）混种

Fish of different shapes are difficult to interbreed. 不同形态的鱼很难混种。

[同义词] hybridize

interdependent [ˌintə(:)di'pendənt] a. 相互依赖的，互助的

[例] There is an interdependent relationship between them. 他们之间有一种相互依赖的关系.

interfere [ˌintə'fiə] v. 干涉，干预，妨碍

[例] The noise interferes with my work. 噪音干扰我的工作。

[记] interfere in/with 干涉，干预

interior [in'tiəriə] n. 内部

[例] Interior decorating is a very promising industry nowadays. 室内装修是当今颇具前途的行业。

interior design 室内装饰业 /[反义词] exterior

intermediate [ˌintə'mi:diət] a. 中间的，中等程度的

[例] Grey is intermediate between black and white. 灰色介于黑色和白色之间。

internal [in'tə:nl] a. **内部的；国内的**
[例] A theory has its internal logic. 每种理论都有其内在的逻辑性。
[反义词] external

interpret [in'tə:prit] v. **解释，说明；翻译**
[例] I interpret his answer as a refusal. 我把他的回答理解为拒绝。
[记] interpreter n. 翻译员，讲解员

interrupt [ˌintə'rʌpt] v. **打断，中断；打扰**
[例] It is rude to interrupt. 打断别人的话是不礼貌的。
[记] interruption n. 中断，打断

intersection [ˌintə'sekʃən] n. **交叉路口，十字路口**
[例] The city lies at the intersection of three motorways. 该城市位于三条汽车道的交叉口。

interval ['intəvəl] n. **(时间、空间上的）间隔，间隙**
[例] There was a long interval before he anwsered the telephone. 隔了好久他才回了电话。

intervene [ˌintə'vi:n] v. **插进，介于中间；干涉**
[例] I shall leave on Sunday if nothing intervenes. 如果没有别的事，我星期天动身。

interview ['intəvju:] n. /v. **面试；采访；会见**
[例] Then they closed the interview. 这时他们结束了会晤。

intestine [in'testin] n. **【解】肠**
[例] Each day, 7-10 litres of water enter the small intestine. 每天有7至10升的水进入小肠。

intimate ['intimit] a. **亲密的，隐私的；n. 密友，至交**
[例] Do you believe these two intimate friends used to be mutual sworn enemies? 你相信这两位亲密朋友过去曾是不共戴天的死敌吗？

intricate ['intrikit] a. **错综复杂的，难理解的**
[例] The watch mechanism is extremely intricate and very difficult to repair. 手表的机械结构非常复杂精细，很难修理。

> intricate 和 trick 同源。trick 指花招，戏法。in（里面） +tric（花招）+ate（形容词词尾）→里面的花招太多了→错综复杂的。

intrinsic [in'trinsik] a. **固有的，本质的，内在的**
[例] The intrinsic value of a coin is the value of the metal it is made of. 一枚钱币的内在价值是造这枚钱币的金属的价值。
[反义词] extrinsic

intrude [in'tru:d] v. **闯入，侵入，强行进入**
[例] Employers should not intrude into the private lives of their employees. 老板不应该干涉雇员的私人生活。
[同义词] infringe, interfere, eoverstep, trespass

intuition [ˌintju(:)'iʃən] n. **直觉**

[例] My intuition turned out to be correct. 我的直觉证明是对的。

invade [in'veid] v. 侵略；侵占

[例] The army invaded the town. 军队侵入了这个城市。

invalid [in'vælid] n. 病人，残废者；a. 有病的，残废的

[记] invalidate v. 使无效

invaluable [in'væljuəbl] a. 极有价值的

[例] Good health is invaluable. 健康的身体是无价之宝。

invent [in'vent] v. 发明，创造；编造，虚构

[例] Do you know who invented the magnetic needle? 你知道指南针是谁发明的吗？

[记] invention n. 发明，创造

inventory ['invəntri] n. 库存；详细目录

[例] We made an inventory of everything in the apartment. 对公寓中的所有物品我们做了一次盘点。

inverse ['in'vəːs] a. 倒转的，反转的；n. 反面；v. 倒转

[例] Evil is the inverse of good. 恶是善的反面。

[记] invert v. 使颠倒 / invert an hourglass使沙漏颠倒 / invert a glass把茶杯扣起来 / reverse v. 颠倒；n. 相反，反面

invest [in'vest] v. 投资，投入

[例] The state has planned to invest two million in the dam. 国家计划投资两百万元修建这个大坝。

> 拉丁语 vestis 指衣服。英语中 vest 指“汗衫，背心”比如救生衣叫 life vest。在古代，别人给你衣服穿，让你 in 进入 vest 衣服，就是 invest “授予，很大一笔投资”的含义啦。给你衣服的人就是 investor，投资者；衣服就是 investment，投入的资本。

investigate [in'vestigeit] v. 调查，研究

[例] To investigate a problem is, indeed, to solve it. 调查问题就是解决问题。

[记] investigation n. 调查，研究

invite [in'vait] v. 邀请

[例] She invited us to her party. 她邀请我们参加她的聚会。

[记] invitation n. 邀请；请柬

Unit 16

invoice ['invɔis] n. 发票，发货清单； v. 开发票

[例] The manufacturer invoiced our company for two typewriters. 制造厂家给我公司开了一张两部打字机的发票。

invoke [in'vəuk] v. 祈求，恳求

[例] I invoked their forgiveness. 我恳求他们原谅。

[记] invoke sb. 's help 恳求某人帮助

involve [in'vɔlv] v. 专心于，忙于；使陷入，使卷入

[例] Don't involve other people in your trouble. 别把别人牵涉进你的麻烦中去。

[记] involve sb. in (doing) sth. 使某人牵涉进某事 /be/get involved in sth. 参与某事

irony ['aiərəni] n. 反话；讽刺

[例] The irony is that some of the poorest countries have the richest natural resources. 讽刺的是一些最贫穷的国家拥有最丰富的自然资源。

[记] ironic a. 反语的；讽刺的

irrelevant [i'reləvənt] a. 不相关的

[例] If he can do the job well, his age is irrelevant. 如果他能干好这工作，年龄是无关紧要的。

[反义词] relevant

irresistible [ˌiri'zistəbl] a. 不可抵抗的；不能压制的

[例] Tax-cutting proposals could prove irresistible to lawmakers. 减税提案对立法者来说势在必行。

irrigation [ˌiri'geiʃən] n. 灌溉

[例] The water used for irrigation was piped in from the mountain. 用来灌溉的水是用管子从山里引来的。

irritate ['iriteit] v. 激怒, 使急躁；刺激

[例] The noise of the children was irritating me. 孩子们的吵闹使我恼火。

[记] be irritate by/at. . . 被…弄得恼火 /irritant n. 刺激物；a. 刺激的 /irritation n. 激怒；【医】刺激

isolate ['aisəleit] v. 使隔离，使孤立，使脱离

[例] The farm is isolated; the nearest house is 30 kilometers away. 这个农场与世隔绝，离它最近的住家在 30 公里以外。

> 岛 island 在拉丁语里叫 *insula*，意大利语里叫 *isola*。所以单词 insulate 隔离，绝缘；insulator 绝缘体；isolate 使孤立；isolation 隔离；都含“岛”的特点：被海包围，远离大陆，孤立隔绝。

issue [ˈiʃuː] n. 问题，论点；v. 发行，颁布

[例] The economist will address the economic issues. 那位经济学家将就经济问题发言。

item [ˈaitəm] n. 项目，条款；（新闻等的）一条

[例] There was an interesting item in the newspaper today. 今天的报纸上有一条有趣的新闻。

itch [itʃ] v. /n. 发痒, 渴望

[例] I've got an itch on my back. 我的背上很痒。

[记] itch for 渴望

itinerary [aiˈtinərəri] n. 路线，旅程；旅行计划，旅行指南

[例] He has some more places to visit on his itinerary. 他在旅途中还有几个地方要游览。

jail [dʒeil] v. 监禁；n. 监狱

[例] He was jailed for two years. 他被囚禁了两年。

jam [dʒæm] n. 拥挤，堵塞；果酱

[例] The road is jammed up with motorcars. 路上汽车挤得水泄不通。

> traffic jam 交通阻塞；a jar of jam 一瓶果酱；jam 作动词是“使劲往里塞”的含义，比如扣篮这个动作就叫 jam（或 slam dunk）；one-handed jam 单手扣篮。Michael Jackson 和 Michael Jordan 合作拍过一部 MTV：*Jam*。

jar [dʒɑː] n. 广口瓶

[例] This jar of pure honey weighs 350 grams net. 这瓶纯蜂蜜净重三百五十克。

jargon [ˈdʒɑːgən] n. 行话，专业术语

[例] When you first learn about computers, there is a whole lot of jargon to understand. 当你第一次学习电脑时，有一大堆专业术语需要了解。

jealous [ˈdʒeləs] a. 嫉妒的，妒忌的

[例] He is jealous of their success. 他妒忌他们的成就。

[记] be jealous of sb. /sth. 妒嫉某人或某物

jean [dʒin] n. 牛仔裤, 裤子, 细斜纹布

[例] Jeans are made of jean, denim, or another durable fabric. 牛仔裤是用粗斜纹布或其他耐磨纤维织物制成的。

jeopardize [ˈdʒepədaiz] v. 危害

[例]If you are rude to the boss, it may jeopardize your chances of success. 如果你对老板没有礼貌，就可能危害到你的成功。

[同义词] endanger

jewellery [ˈdʒuːəlri] (=jewelry) n. 〈总称〉珠宝，镶嵌有宝石之饰物

[例]She wears a lot of gold jewelry. 她戴着许多金首饰。

jigsaw ['dʒigsɔː] n. 拼图

[例] A jigsaw is a very good toy for children. 拼图是非常好的儿童玩具。

[记] jigsaw puzzle n. 七巧板，智力拼图玩具

jog [dʒɔg] v. 慢跑

[例] The old bus jogged up and down. 那辆旧公共汽车上下颠簸地行驶。

[记] jogger n. 跑步锻炼的人

joint [dʒɔint] a. 共同的，联合的；n. 接合处，关节

[例] Our arms and legs bend at the joints — the elbows and knees. 我们的胳膊和腿在关节处，即胳膊肘和膝盖处弯曲。

[记] joint venture n. 合资

journal ['dʒəːnl] n. 期刊；日志

[例] The professor is always writing articles for academic journals. 这位教授经常给学术杂志撰稿。

[记] journalism n. 新闻业；新闻工作 /journalistic a. 新闻业的；新闻工作的

> "jour" 在法语中表示"一天"，因此"journal"表示"日志、日记；日报"，"期刊、杂志"的含义是后来引申得来的；进而，"journalism"表示"把每天发生的事情都记录下来的行业"。journalist 新闻记者

journey ['dʒəːni] n. 旅行，旅程；历程

[例] We wish you a pleasant journey. 我们祝你旅途愉快。

judgment ['dʒʌdʒmənt] n. 审判，判决；判断

[例] You shall use you own judgment as to whether you should start work or study for a master's degree. 你应当运用自己的判断力，决定是开始工作还是攻读硕士学位。

[记] judge n. 法官；裁判员；v. 审理；判断；判决

junction ['dʒʌŋkʃən] n. 连接，汇合点，交叉口

[例] The power station stands at the junction of two rivers. 发电站在两条河流的汇合处。

jungle ['dʒʌŋgl] n. 热带丛林

[例] This little town is located in a jungle. 小镇位于丛林中。

[记] jungle law 弱肉强食的（丛林）原则

junior ['dʒuːnjə] a. 级别（职位）较低的；n. 较年幼者；大学三年级学生

[例]He is the junior partner in the firm. 他是这家公司地位较低的合伙人。

junk [dʒʌŋk] n. 废旧杂物；垃圾食物；v. 把…当作废物丢掉

[例] He junked all his old furniture before moving into his new home. 他在搬入新居之前把所有的旧家具都当废物丢掉了。

> junk food 垃圾食品，如 hamburger, potato chips, soft drink 等；junk mail 垃圾邮件，另一个词 spam 指"网上垃圾邮件"用得更

多。Spam原是美国一种猪肉罐头的商标，曾是美军的配给之一，二战期间，把美军吃得快疯掉了。许多人恨死了Spam罐头，却又不得不吃；你多么讨厌网络垃圾，你还得挂在网上。我们总是这样左右为难。

jury ['dʒuəri] n. 【律】陪审团，评判委员会

[例] The jury of the Miss World competition is illegal. 这个世界小姐选美大赛的评判小组是不合法的。

justice ['dʒʌstis] n. 正义，公正；法律制裁

[例] The justice of these remarks was clear to everyone. 人人都明白这些话是公正的。

[记] treat sb. /sth. with justice秉公对待某人/某事 /injustice n. 不公平，不讲道义

justify ['dʒʌstifai] v. 证明…是正当的

[例] The course of events fully justifies our views. 事情的发展完全证明我们的意见是正确的。

[记] justified a. 有正当理由的，合理的

"just"是形容词，表示"正义的、正直的"，后边加上"-ify"变成动词。体会下边一句话的含义："The ends justify the means."——只要能达成目的，一切手段都是正确的。即"为达到目的可以不择手段"。

juvenile ['dʒu:vinail] a. 青少年的；n. 青少年

[例] The problem of juvenile delinquency drew attention from the whole of society. 青少年犯罪的这个问题引起了全社会的注意。

kangaroo [ˌkæŋgə'ru:] n. 袋鼠

[例] Kangaroos are Australian animals. 袋鼠是澳大利亚的动物。

英国航海家库克James Cook船长登陆澳洲，第一次见到袋鼠，问当地土著人What' s that? 土著人不懂英文，回答："Kangaroo"。从此，土著语中的kangaroo（意为：I don't know）进入英文字典。

keen [ki:n] a. 强烈的，敏锐的，渴望的

[例] They are rather keen on your new-type woolens. 他们对你的新型毛织品颇感兴趣。

kidnap ['kidnæp] v. 绑架，勒赎

[例]Two businessmen have been kidnapped. 两个商人被绑架了。

kidney ['kidni] n. 【医】肾，肾脏

kin [kin] n. 家人，亲戚；a. 有亲属关系的；同类的

[例] All his kin were at the wedding. 他的家人和亲戚都参加了婚礼。

kiosk ['ki:ɔsk] / [ki:'ɔsk] n. 亭，报刊亭，公用电话亭

[例]I got a magazine and some cigarettes from a kiosk on the station platform. 我在火车站月台的售货亭里买了一份杂志和一些香烟。

来自墨西哥土语，原意是午休，(用草帽盖住脸，躺倒晒太阳)，引申为小卖部。

kit [kit] n. 工具包，用品箱，成套用具

[例]We made a model plane out of a kit. 我们用一套零件做了一个模型飞机。

kneel [niːl] v. 跪，跪下

[例] Christians often kneel down to say their prayers. 基督教徒通常跪着做祷告。

knight [nait] n. 骑士；v. 授以爵位

[例] He was knighted for his war services. 他因战功而被封为爵士。

国际象棋chess中knight代表马。车rook/castle，相bishop，兵pawn。从chess和Chinese chess看东西方文化差异：chess中的king可以到处走，而中国象棋里的king不出"宫"。Chess里有Queen，可横竖斜着满棋盘跑，威力无穷骠悍泼辣。西方历史上女王的统治屡见不鲜，著名的如埃及女王、英国女王、丹麦女王等。而中国象棋里根本没有"后"这个棋子，象征中国的父权封建历史。将(帅)旁边两个士，喻意我国封建社会的一夫多妻制。

knit [nit] v. 编织，针织

[例] My grandmother knitted me some socks. 祖母给我织袜子。

knob [nɔb] n. 球形把手，旋钮

[例] Turn the door knob to open the door. 拧门把手开门。

knot [nɔt] n. （绳索的）结；节（即1,853米/小时，船和飞机的速度单位）；v. 打结

[例] Will you knot the rope round the post? 请你把这根绳子拴在柱子上好吗？

knowledge ['nɔlidʒ] n. 知识，学问

[例] We go to school to get knowledge about many different things. 我们上学是为了获得关于各种事物的知识。

knowledgeable ['nɔlidʒəbl] a. 有知识的；博学的

[例] He made some knowledgeable remarks at the meeting. 他在会上的发言颇有见地。

label ['leibl] n. 标签，标记，商标；v. 贴标签于，标注

[例] An attractive label is very necessary. 具有吸引力的标签非常必要。

[记] label sb. /sth. as. . . 把某人/某物称作… /[同义词] tag

laboratory ['læbrətɔːri] (=lab) n. 实验室

[例] Bell's laboratory is a well-equipped telecom research center. 贝尔实

验室是个设备齐全的电信研究中心。

labour ['leibə] (=labor) n. 劳动，体力劳动

[例] Many women do hard manual labour. 很多妇女从事重体力活。

> 字根 labor 指"工作 to work"。如：laboratory 工作的地方→试验室; labored 吃力的，困难的; collaborate一起工作→合作; elaborate 努力工作出来的(e-)→精心制作，精巧的。

lack [læk] n. /v. 缺乏，不足

[例] Serious lack of circulating funds forced the closure of the company. 公司因严重缺乏流动资金而被迫关闭。

[记] lack in 在…缺少 /lack of 缺少

lag [læg] n. 落后；a. 最后的；v. 缓缓而行；落后于

[例] He lagged behind us. 他落在我们后面。

lame [leim] a. 瘸的，跛的；(解释或借口)无说服力的

[例] The lame child lagged behind. 跛足的孩子落在后面。

lament [lə'ment] n. 悲伤；哀悼；悼词；v. 哀悼；悔恨

[例] He lamented his thoughtless acts. 他非常懊悔自己轻率的举动。

landfill ['lændfil] n. 垃圾掩埋法，垃圾

[例]That is a new kind of landfill. 这是一种新的垃圾掩埋法。

landmark ['lændmɑːk] n. 地标；里程碑

[例] He orientated himself by finding a familiar landmark. 他靠找寻熟悉的路标确定了方向。

landscape ['lændskeip] n. 风景，地貌；v. 做景观美化

[例] The trees and mountains made the landscape very beautiful. 树木和山脉使风景变得很美。

lane [lein] n. 乡间小道，小巷；行车道；跑道，泳道

[谚] It is a long lane that has no turning. 路必有弯; 事物有变。

laptop ['læpˌtɔp] n. 便携式电脑

[例] The executives are coming with their laptops. 主管们带着他们的手提电脑纷纷而至。

larva ['lɑːvə] (复数为 larvae)n. 幼虫

[例] The tadpole is the larva of the frog. 蝌蚪是蛙的幼体。

latitude ['lætitjuːd] n. 纬度

[例] Our position is latitude 40 degrees north. 我们的位置是北纬40度。

latter ['lætə] a. （通常指两者之间）后者的

[例] Of the two, the latter is far better than the former. 两者中后者比前者好得多。

[记] the latter half of the year 下半年 /the latter years of one's life 晚年

launch [lɔːntʃ] v. /n. 发射；开办，首创；发起（运动等）

[例] Full market research is needed before the launch of new products. 新产品投产之前需要充分的市场调查。

laundry ['lɔːndri] n. 洗衣店；要洗的衣服

[例] There's a lot of laundry in the basket. 筐子里有许多要洗的衣服。

lava ['lɑːvə] n. 熔岩，火山岩

[例] We can see a stream of lava far away. 我们从很远的地方都能看到熔岩流。

> 字根 lav/lau 指“洗”。如: laundry 洗的地方；lava 冲洗山的流体；lavatory 洗手的地方→盥洗室，厕所；lavish 象水流一般的→浪费的。

layer ['leiə] n. 层，阶层

[例] There is a layer of dust on the dressing-table. Clean it before the guest arrives. 梳妆台上落有一层灰尘,在客人来之前,把它擦干净。

layoff ['leiˌɔːf] n. 临时解雇，失业期；活动停止期间

[例] There are more lay-offs in the car industry. 汽车业停业的更多。

layout ['leiˌaut] n. 设计；布置；版面设计

[例] The new page layout is appealing to teenagers. 这个新的版面设计非常吸引青少年。

leaflet ['liːflit] n. 广告单页，传单

[例] Students can earn some money by distrshoting leaflets. 学生们可以通过派发传单挣点钱。

leak [liːk] n. 漏洞，裂缝 ；v. 泄漏

[谚] A small leak will sink a great ship. 小洞沉大船；小患不治成大灾。

lean [liːn] n. 靠；倾斜； 依赖 a. 瘦的;贫乏的

[例] She leaned against his shoulder. 她靠在他的肩上。

[记] lean on 依赖，依靠 /lean toward 有…倾向

leap [liːp] v. / n. 跳，跳越，飞跃

[例] The dog leapt over the fence. 狗跳过了围栏。

lease [liːs] n. 租借，租赁；v. 出租；租得

[例] The firm leases an office near the river. 公司租到一处靠近河边的办事处。

[同义词] charter, hire, let, rent

leather ['leðə] n. 皮革，皮革制品

[例] The sofa is covered in real leather. 这沙发是真皮的。

[记] leather shoes 皮鞋 /leather gloves 皮手套

lecture ['lektʃə] n. /v. 演讲，讲座

[例] I am going to lecture to my students today. 今天我准备给学生们讲课。

legacy ['legəsi] n. 遗赠(物)，遗产

[例] She received a small legacy from her aunt. 她从姑姑那儿得到了一笔小小的遗产。

legal ['liːgəl] a. 合法的；法律上的

[例] The general manager of a company usually is also the legal person of the company. 公司的总经理通常也是公司的法人。

[记] legal aid 法律援助（免费提供律师服务）/legal affairs法律事务 / legal adviser法律顾问

legend ['ledʒənd] n. 传说，传奇；图例

[例] The legend was passed down from age to age. 这个传说一代一代地传下来。

> 联想集团因“Legend”一词使用频率太高，甚至在海外存在商标注册冲突，改名为Lenovo。Lenovo是新造词，其中“le”取自原先的“Legend”，承继“传奇”之意；“novo”来源于拉丁语，代表创新，Lenovo即有“创新的联想”之意。另一知名IT企业Acer独立出一新品牌Benq，意为“Bring Enjoyment and Quality (to life)”，看来IT界不乏造词高手。

legendary ['ledʒəndəri] a. 传奇式的

[例] Her patience and tact were legendary. 她的耐心机智被传为佳话的。

legible ['ledʒəbl] a. （字迹等）清楚的，易读的

[例] Her scripts are barely legible. 她的字迹很难辨认。

legislate ['ledʒisleit] v. 制定法律；用立法实现

[例] It is the job of the Parliament to legislate. 立法是议会的工作。

[记] legislation n. 立法；法律 /legislative a. 立法的 /legislator n. 立法者

> 西方国家的所谓三权分立指立法、司法、执法三权分立，这三方面所对应的英文分别是legislative, judicial and executive。

leisure ['leʒə] n. 空闲，闲暇 a. 空闲的，有空的

[例] What do you do in your leisure time? 你空闲时间做些什么？

[记] at leisure 从容地，有空

lemon ['lemən] n. 柠檬；a. 柠檬色的

[例] Mary's favourite fruit is lemon. 玛丽最喜欢的水果是柠檬。

> lemonade 柠檬汽水。酸涩的柠檬通常用来代表生活中“苦涩”的事情：lemon car 柠檬汽车，质量差的汽车；lemon market 不是卖柠檬的水果市场，而是一个重要的信息经济学概念“次品市场”，George Akerlof教授通过对lemon market的分析获得了2001年的Nobel Prize。

lenient ['li:njənt] a. 宽大的，仁慈的，慈悲为怀的

[例] School examiners say that marking has become more lenient in recent years. 学校主考官说这几年来打分变得更宽松了。

lens [lenz] n. 透镜，镜头

[例] When viewing through the lens, we can see the thing clearer, larger or smaller. 通过透镜，我们可以把物体看得更清楚、更大或更小。

lessen ['lesn] v. 变小，减少
[例] The pain was already lessening. 疼痛正在减轻。

lesser ['lesə] a. 较少的，更少的，次要的
[例] They originally asked for $5 million, but finally settled for a lesser sum. 他们原先要价五百万，最终以较少的金额成交。

lethal ['li:θəl] a. 致命的 n. 致死因子
[例] The closure of the factory dealt a lethal blow to the town. 那家工厂的关闭是对该镇的致命打击。

> 好莱坞著名影星兼导演Mel Gibson早年拍摄的电影《致命武器》的英文原名即为“Lethal Weapon”。

lettuce ['letis] n. 生菜，莴苣
[例] I prefer a lettuce and tomato salad. 我喜欢生菜番茄沙拉。

lever ['levə] n. 杆, 杠杆；v. 抬起
[例] I levered the lid off the box with a stick. 我用一根棍子撬开了箱盖。

levy ['levi] v. 征收，征召；n. 征收额，税款
[例] There is a departure tax levied on all travelers. 所有乘客都要被征收离境税。

liability [ˌlaiə'biliti] n. 责任，义务；倾向
[例] Bad pronunciation is a liability in being a narrator. 不良的发音是做解说员的不利条件。
[记] assets and liabilities 资产和负债

liable ['laiəbl] a. 有责任的；有…倾向的，可能的
[例] He is liable to come today. 他今天很可能要来。
[记] be liable for对…应负责任 /be liable to (do sth.)易于(得病等)；有做某事的倾向

liberal ['libərəl] a. 慷慨的，大方的；自由主义的
[例] My father gives me a liberal amount of money every week. 每周我父亲给我很多的钱。
[记] liberal arts 大学文科

> 字根liber指“自由的”。Liberal party 自由党；liberate 使自由，使解放；People's Liberation Army 人民解放军。其实 liber 起源自正义女神手中的天平 Libra。现在英国法院的门口还站着她的雕像：左手拿 Libra 象征权衡平等，右手执宝剑象征裁决的力量，眼睛被布蒙住，象征绝对的公正无私。十二星座中的天秤座即是Libra。

license ['laisəns] (=licence) n. 执照，许可证；v. 发给执照
[例] A doctor is licenced to practice medicine. 医生行医需要获得许可。
[记] give full licence to do sth. 授权放手做某事 /apply for a driving

licence 申请驾照

lift [lift] v. 提，抬，提升；n. [英]电梯 (=[美]elevator)

[例]This box is too heavy for me to lift. 这箱太重我搬不起来。

likelihood ['laiklihud] n. 可能，可能性

[例] Do you think there is any likelihood of his agreeing to it? 你认为他有可能同意此事吗?

[同义词] possibility

likewise ['laik,waiz] adv. 同样地，照样地

[例] Paul always finishes his work, you should do likewise. 保罗总是能完成他的工作，你应该也一样。

lightning ['laitniŋ] n. 闪电；a. 闪电般的，极快的

[例] During the storm flashes of lightning appeared in the sky. 风暴来临时天空中出现很多道闪电。

[记] lighten v. 减轻;（使）发亮 /lighter n. 打火机 /lightly adv. 轻轻地;轻松地

Unit 17

linger ['liŋgə] v. 逗留，闲荡；拖延

[例] We lingered away the whole summer at the beach. 我们在海滩上消磨掉整个夏天。

linguist ['liŋgwist] n. 通晓多种外语的人；语言学家

[例] The linguist went to study tribal language in the field. 语言学家们去实地研究部落语言了。

[记] linguistic a. 语言的；语言学的

> 字根 lingu 指"舌头，tongue"。所以，linguist 就是玩舌头的人→语言学家；linguistic 语言学的；bilingual 两条舌头→双语者；multilingual 好多舌头→通多国语言者。

link [liŋk] v. 连接；n. 环节，连接物

[例] The two towns are linked by a railway. 这两个城镇由一条铁路连接起来。

[记] link up 联接，结合 /link... with/and... 把…与…连接或联系起来

liquid ['likwid] n. 液体；a. 液态的

[例] If you add too much liquid the mixture will not be thick enough. 加入液体太多，混合液的浓度就不够。

[记] liquid assets 流动资产

literacy ['litərəsi] n. 有读写能力，有文化

[例] A literacy campaign is very necessary. 扫盲运动是非常有必要的。

[记] a literacy class 扫盲班 /illiteracy n. 文盲 /literate n. 学者；a. 有文化的

> 字根 liter 指"letter，文字"。illiteracy 不认字的→文盲

literally ['litərəli] adv. 照字面意义，逐字地

[例] To translate literally is not always the closest to the original meaning. 逐字翻译不一定最接近原义。

literature ['litəritʃə] n. 文学，文学作品，文献

[例]Literature stands related to man as science stands to nature. 文学对于人的关系正如科学对于自然的关系一样相关联。

litter ['litə] n. 垃圾，废弃物；v. 乱丢东西

[例] Never litter anywhere. 千万不要到处乱扔果皮纸屑。

load [ləud] n. 负荷，重担，负载；v. 装载；使担负

[例] The truck was carrying a load of bananas. 这辆卡车装着一车香蕉。

loaf [ləuf] n. 一条面包；游荡；v. 游荡，虚度光阴

[谚] Half a loaf is better than no bread. 有比没有好。

loan [ləun] n. 贷款，借出；v. 借出

[例] Does the loan carry any interest? 这笔贷款是否带利息？

lobby ['lɔbi] n. 大厅，休息室；v. 进行游说，疏通

[例] He will wait for me in the lobby of the hotel. 他会在饭店的大堂等我。

> 每逢美国国会开会，不同地区和不同行业都纷纷派代表到Washington，为自己集团的利益对议员进行游说。这些人不能去议员开会的地方，只能在饭店的大堂lobby和楼道里等候。等议员们回来就见缝插针去游说。于是lobby有了“游说”之意，而lobbyist（大厅人）就是“说客”。

locality [ləu'kæliti] n. 位置，地点

[例] They are trying to point the ship's exact locality. 他们正设法确定轮船的确切位置。

[同义词] location

locate [ləu'keit] v. 位于，坐落于；查找. . . 的地点

[例] The new hospital is to be located near your college. 这所新医院将建在你们学院附近。

[记] be located in/on/at. . . 位于…地方，坐落于…

lodge [lɔdʒ] v. 租住，寄宿；n. 小屋

[例] Where we lodge is the problem. 我们在哪儿住宿是个问题。

log [lɔg] n. 木头，原木；航行日志

[例] The young pioneers lived in a little log cabin in the mountains during the summer camp. 夏令营期间少先队员们住在山里的一间小木屋里。

logical ['lɔdʒikəl] a. 逻辑学的，符合逻辑的

[例] It is logical that people who earn more money should pay higher taxes. 挣钱多的人应该缴纳更多的税，这是合情合理的。

[记] a logical thinker 思想有逻辑性的人

logistics [lə'dʒistiks] n. 后勤学；后勤

[例] None of these ideas requires much in the way of money or logistics.

logo ['lɔgəu] n. 标识；公司标志

[例] His costume had the Superman logo across the chest. 他的服装在胸前有“超人”的标记。

longitude ['lɔndʒitju:d] n. 经度

[例] The captain determines the latitude and longitude of his ship position. 船长测定船位置的经纬度。

[记] latitude n. 纬度

long-term [ˌlɔŋ'tə:m] a. 长期的

[例] I hesitated before making a long-term commitment of this importance. 我犹豫了一下，然后才作出如此重要的长期承诺。

loom [luːm] v. 隐约出现

[例] A hard struggle looms ahead. 一场苦斗迫在眉睫。

> loom 的拼写形式很有意思。loo 像数字 100，m 就是米。在 100m 开外的事物，若隐若现。loom 作名词有“织布机”的含义，也好记：织布机每天织布 100 米。

loop [luːp] v. /n. 环；环形

[例] The plane flew round and round in wide loops. 飞机绕着大圈一圈一圈地飞。

loosen [ˈluːsn] v. 解开，松开；放宽

[例] My belt is too tight; I must loosen it. 我的腰带太紧，我必须松开。

lotion [ˈləuʃən] n. 洗液，洗剂

[例] This lotion should help clear your skin of spots. 这种药水有助于去除你皮肤上的斑。

lottery [ˈlɔtəri] n. 彩票，抽彩给奖法

[例] Marriage is a lottery. 婚姻是一桩难以预测的事。

> 现在流行的什么“福利彩票”，“体育彩票”，“双色球”等等，就是 lottery，或同义词 lotto，中文音译“乐透”，随机开奖对号码。如果要表达简单的“抽签，抓阄”的含义，英文是：draw straws (抽稻草)，或 decide by lot。

lounge [laundʒ] n. 闲逛；休闲室；长沙发；v. 闲荡；懒洋洋地躺卧；虚度光阴

[例] Don’t lounge away your time. 不要虚度时光。

loyal [ˈlɔiəl] a. 忠贞的，忠实的，忠诚的

[例] The prince remained loyal throughout. 王子自始至终忠贞不渝。

[记] loyalty n. 忠诚，忠心

lubricate [ˈluːbrikeit] v. 润滑；加润滑剂

[例] My throat needs lubricating. 我需要润润嗓子。

[记] lubricant oil 润滑油

lucrative [ˈluːkrətiv] a. 有利的；赚钱的

[例] We need a lucrative marketing strategy. 我们需要能赢利的市场策略。

[记] a lucrative business 赚钱的生意

luggage [ˈlʌgidʒ] n. 〈总称〉行李 ([美] baggage)

[例] I’ve just been informed that my luggage has already arrived. 我刚接到通知说我的行李已经运到了。

lull [lʌl] n. 暂停；麻痹；v. 使入睡；使休息

[例] The monotonous voice of the movement of the train lulled me to sleep. 火车行驶时单调的声音使我昏昏欲睡。

lump [lʌmp] n. 块（尤指小块）；v. 使成块状

[例] There is a nasty lump on her neck. 她脖子上有一个大肿块。

lung [lʌŋ] n. 肺

[例] A lot of patients are suffering the pain of lung cancer. 很多病人都在承受肺癌之苦。

lure [ljuə] v. 引诱

[例] Many young Japanese engineers have been lured to the Middle East by the promise of high wages. 在高薪允诺的引诱下,许多年轻的日本工程师去了中东。

[同义词] allure

luxurious [lʌg'zjuəriəs] a. 奢华的，豪华的

[例] This car is our most luxurious model. 这是我们最豪华的汽车型号了。

[记] a luxurious hotel 一间豪华旅馆

lyric ['lirik] n. 抒情诗；歌词；a. 抒情的

[例] He is good at lyrics. 他擅长写抒情诗。

> 古希腊诗歌是在七弦琴lyre伴奏下吟唱的，这也是lyric(抒情诗)一词的起源。lyre是古希腊一种类似小竖琴的乐器，相传由宙斯之子把琴弦缠绕在乌龟壳上制成。据说lyre的琴声可使人忘忧，使奔腾的大河停流，使静止的山峦趋步，使凶顽的猛兽驯服，使沉默的石头开口……后化为星空中的天琴座：Lyra。

macro ['mækrəu] a. 宏观的，巨大的；n. 【计】宏

[例] You can run a macro to change to US spelling. 你可以启动宏指令变成美式拼写。

[反义词] micro /macroeconomics n. 宏观经济学 /microeconomics n. 微观经济学

magic ['mædʒik] n. 魔法；a. 魔术的；有魔力的；不可思议的

[例] They believed that it was all done by magic. 他们相信那都是魔法造成的。

[记] magical a. 魔法的 /magician n. 魔术师

magma ['mægmə] n. (有机物或矿物的)稀糊, 岩浆

[例] Different minerals in the magma create different structures. 岩浆中不同的矿物造成了不同的结构。

magnet ['mægnit] n. 磁铁，吸铁石

[例] A magnet attracts iron. 磁石吸铁。

[记] magnetic a. 磁的，有磁性的；有吸引力的

magnify ['mægnifai] v. 放大，夸大

[谚] Fame is a magnifying glass. 名誉是放大镜。

> 字根magn/maj/max都指“壮大的great”。如：magnifier 放大镜；major 主修，较大的；majority 多数，大半；maximum 最大限度。

> 而单词magnet磁铁，与“大”无关，来源于地理名词——小亚细亚的一个古城马格内西亚，magnet意思是“马格内西亚的石头”。

magnificent [mæg'nifisnt] a. 华丽的，高尚的，宏伟的

[例] The magnificent view of the ancient pagoda dissolved in mist. 那古塔雄伟的景色在雾中消失了。

magnitude ['mægnitju:d] n. 巨大，重要性

[例] I want to know the magnitude of this equipment. 我想知道这个设备的大小。

maiden ['meidn] n. 少女；姑娘

[例] She was a tender, watchful maiden. 她是一个温柔而警觉的少女。

mainstream ['meinstri:m] n. 主流

[例] He likes studying the mainstream of political thought. 他喜欢研究政治思潮的主流。

maintain [mein'tein] v. 维持，维修；主张

[例] He failed again and again simply because he had maintained his defeatist attitude. 因为他一直坚持失败主义的态度，所以失败了一次又一次。

[记] maintenance n. 维持；维修；保养

majesty ['mædʒisti] n. 威严；陛下

[例] I enjoyed all the majesty of royal ceremonies. 我欣赏了皇家仪典的富丽堂皇。

[记] majestic a. 宏伟的，庄严的

major ['meidʒə] a. 主要的，重大的；n. （大学专业的）主修科目

[例] One of the major aims of the air raid was the complete demolition of all means of communications. 这次空袭的一个主要目的是彻底摧毁敌人的通讯设施。

[反义词] minor

majority [mə'dʒɔriti] n. 大多数，大半

[例] The majority of children in our class have brown eyes; only three have blue eyes. 我们班大多数孩子是棕色眼睛，只有三个是蓝眼睛。

[反义词] minority

malfunction [mæl'fʌŋkʃən] v. 发生故障

[例] The computer malfunctioned and printed out the wrong words. 计算机出了毛病，打印的字有问题。

> 字根mal指“坏的，有害的”。malnutrition营养不良；maltreat虐待。

mall [mɔ:l] n. 购物商场，商业街，林荫路

[例] It has sprouted shopping malls, discos and nightclubs, beauty salons, gymnasia, news kiosks, and coffee shops. 购物中心、迪斯科舞厅、夜总会、美容院、健身房、书报亭以及咖啡馆都迅速发展起来了。

mammal ['mæməl] n. 哺乳动物

[例] Human beings are mammals. 人类也属于哺乳动物。

mandatory ['mændətəri] a. 命令的，强制性的，必须履行的

[例] A reply to this letter is mandatory. 这封信非答覆不可。

[记] mandate v. /a. 命令，要求

> 字根 mand 指“命令”。如：command 命令；demand 需求，请求（没有命令，就应该主动请求）；mandate 命令，要求。

manifest ['mænifest] a. 显然的，明了的；v. 显示，表明

[例] He doesn't manifest much interest in his studies. 他表现出对学业没多大兴趣。

manipulate [mə'nipjuleit] v. （熟练地）操作，操纵

[例] He uses his credits to manipulate his supporters. 他用他的信用控制他的拥戴者。

[记] manipulation n. 巧妙的操作

manoeuver [mə'nu:və] n. 策略，巧计；演习

[例] The army is on manoeuvres on the sea. 部队正在海上演习。

> 法语词 maneuver，表示一种很巧妙的动作或手法，魔术师们有 maneuver，政客们也会玩 maneuver。英式英语中 maneuver 拼写为 manoeuvre。

mansion ['mænʃən] n. 大厦，官邸；公寓

[例] This old mansion became a large hospital. 这所老公寓变成了一所大医院。

mantle ['mæntl] n. 斗篷；披风；（地球的）地幔；v. 覆盖

[例] Parents often use a mantle for their baby to keep warm. 父母经常用披风给婴儿御寒。

[记] core 地核 /mantle 地幔 /crust 地壳

> 中文成语“衣钵相传”原为佛家用语。英文相应表达为 take over the mantle （接收披风），语出圣经。先知以利亚曾用自己的披风 mantle 分开约旦河水。后来他被接引上天后留下了披风，他的继承人凭借此衣同样能分开约旦河水。所以 mantle 被西方看作法力或权利传承的媒介。西方魔术师的标准行头就少不了一件 mantle。

manual ['mænjuəl] a. 手工的；n. 手册，指南

[例] You have to change gear manually in this car, it's not automatic. 你得用手动挡，这部车不是自动换档的。

[记] manually adv. 用手地；手工地

manufacture [ˌmænju'fæktʃə] v. 制造，加工；n. 制造，产品

[例]Plastic is an important manufacture. 塑料是种重要产品。

manuscript ['mænjuskript] n. 手稿，底稿，手抄本

[例] When a manuscript has been accepted for publication, it is passed to an editor for detailed scrutiny. 当原稿被采用出版时，便将它交与一名编辑进行仔细校阅。

marathon ['mærəθən] n. 马拉松赛跑；耐力的考验

[例] Garcia ran the marathon in just under three hours. 加西亚在三小时以内跑完马拉松。

marble ['mɑːbl] n. 大理石；(玩具)弹球；a. 大理石的；冷酷无情的

[例] They used marble to build the steps. 他们用大理石修建台阶。

margin ['mɑːdʒin] n. 边沿，边缘；余地

[例] There is no margin for error in our plan. 我们的计划中没有误差的余地。

marine [mə'riːn] a. 海的；海中的；n. 水兵

[例] It is true that a lot of people like marine plants as their food. 确实有很多人喜欢吃海产植物。

> 字根 mari 指“海”。mariner 水手；submarine 海底的，潜水艇。

maritime ['mæritaim] a. 海上的；海事的

[例] That maritime peril happened at night. 那个海难发生在夜晚。

mark [mɑːk] n. 标记，分数；v. 标志着；打分数；作记号

[例] It is dangerous to swim beyond this mark. 超出这个标志游泳是危险的。

marketing ['mɑːkitiŋ] n. 市场营销

[例] Mike is working in the Marketing Department of IBM. 迈克在IBM的市场推广部工作。

marvel ['mɑːvəl] v. 感到惊讶，钦佩；n. 奇迹

[例] I marvel at how it can be so. 我感到惊异，事情怎会如此。

[记] marvelous a. 不可思议的，非凡的

masculine ['mɑːskjulin] a. 男性的，男子气概的；n. 男子

[例] She looks rather masculine in that suit. 她穿着那套衣服看上去很有些男孩子气。

> 反义词 feminine a. 娇柔的，女子的；相应词形变化：masculinity n. 阳性，雄性；femininity n. 阴性。“阳刚气十足的男子”英文中称为 macho。

masquerade [mæskə'reid] n. 化装舞会；假面舞会；v. 伪装

[例] She masqueraded as a shepherd. 她在假面舞会上化装成了牧羊人。

massacre ['mæsəkə] n. /v. 残杀，集体屠杀

[例] The massacre of Jews by Nazi in World War II was appalling. 二次世界大战中德国纳粹分子对犹太人的杀戮是骇人听闻的。

[同义词] decimation, slaughter

massive ['mæsiv] a. 大块的，大而重的；大规模的，大量的

[例] There are massive mineral resources in the west part of China. 中国西部地区有着大量的矿产资源。

[记] mass n. 团；众多 /massively adv. 大规模地

masterpiece ['mɑːstəpiːs] n. 杰作，名著

[例] Each artist dreams of having some masterpieces to be remembered by. 每一位艺术家都希望自己的杰作能被后代牢记。

mate [meit] n. 伙伴；同伴

[例] Where are you going, mate? 老兄，你去哪儿？

[记] workmate 同事 /classmate 同学 /roommate 室友 /mating n. 交配；结婚；a. 相配的

material [mə'tiəriəl] n. 材料，原料；可塑之材 a. 物质的

[例] There is singer material among these young girls. 在这些年轻姑娘中有些是歌唱家的人才。

maternal [mə'təːnl] a. 母亲的，母系的

[例] She shows great maternal affection to her students. 她对她的学生表现出深厚的母爱。

[反义词] paternal

matrix ['meitriks] n. 模型；矩阵

[例] They cannot find the matrix for the competition. 他找不到参加比赛的模型了。

> 电影《黑客帝国》*the Matrix*，英文喻意人们生活在由数字组成的矩阵世界中，一切都是虚幻的，受电脑程序所控制。这部片子很有深度，融入了大量的宗教和神学元素，下面的单词遇到再提。

mattress ['mætris] n. 床垫，空气垫

[例] Mattresseses are filled with feathers, cotton, or straw. 床垫里塞满了羽毛、棉花或草。

mature [mə'tjuə] a. 成熟的；v. 成熟

[例] You are a mature man now; you are no longer a boy. 你现在是成人了，不再是孩子了。

[反义词] immature

maximise ['mæksimaiz] (=maximize)v. 最大化，使增加（或扩大）到最大限度

[例] You should maximize your opportunities to find a good job. 你应该充分利用机会找一份好工作。

maximum ['mæksiməm] n. 最大限度，最大量，最大值

[例] The maximum load for this truck is ten tons. 这辆卡车最大载重量是 10 吨。

meadow ['medəu] n. 草地，牧场

[例] In the countryside, large working farms interrupted a landscape of mountains, meadows, marshland, and abandoned quarries. 在乡村，大片农场影响了山、草地、沼泽地以及闲置采石场的景貌。

mean [miːn, min] a. 低劣的；吝啬的；平均的；v. 想要；n. 平均数；中间
[例] He's no mean teacher. 他可不是个差劲的教师。

measure [ˈmeʒə] v. 测量；n. 测量；措施，办法
[例] There are no words to express the full measure of my gratitude. 任何语言都无法表达我的感激之情。
[记] take measures 采取措施

> 莎士比亚 Shakespeare 名剧《一报还一报》*Measure for Measure*，出自《圣经·马太福音》：For with what judgment you judge, you shall be judged; and with what measure you measure, it shall be measured to you.

mechanism [ˈmekənizəm] n. 机械装置；机构，机制
[例] The bones and muscles are parts of the mechanism of the body. 骨骼和肌肉是人体的组成部件。

media [ˈmiːdiə] (medium 的复数)n. 媒体
[例] The scandal was widely reported in the national media. 这一丑闻在全国的媒体中广为报道。

mediate [ˈmiːdieit] v. 仲裁，居中调停
[例] He mediated a settlement between labor and management. 他通过调停达成劳资双方间和解。

medical [ˈmedikəl] a. 医学的，医疗的
[例] Before you join the company, you will have to have a medical examination. 进本公司前,你得先做体格检查。

medieval [ˌmediˈiːvəl] a. 中世纪的；老式的
[例] The parents with a medieval attitude toward dating are not popular with the young. 对于约会有守旧态度的父母是不受年轻人欢迎的。

medium [ˈmiːdiəm] n. 媒体，方法；a. 中间的，中等的
[例] Commercial television is a medium for advertising. 商业电视是一种广告媒介。

melody [ˈmelədi] n. 悦耳的音调；【音】旋律
[例] I like that song; it has a pleasant melody. 我喜欢那首歌，它有悦耳的旋律。

> 中文音译“麦乐迪”，成为了一家 Karaoke 连锁店名。

melt [melt] v. 融化；熔化
[例] Iron melts at a great heat. 铁在高温下熔化。

memorandum [ˌmeməˈrændəm] (=memo)n. 备忘录；便函；买卖契约
[例] They agreed on the memorandum. 他们就这份买卖契约达成了一致。

[记] memorandum book 备忘录，备查簿

mental ['mentl] a. 精神的，思想上的；智力的

[例] He got the answer by mental arithmetic. 他用心算得出了答案。

mentor ['mentɔː] n. 导师，指导者

merchandise ['məːtʃəndaiz] n. 商品

[例]We often call these goods merchandise. 我们通常把这些货物叫做商品。

mercury ['məːkjuri] n. 水银，汞；温度计

[例]The mercury stood at nearly 40℃. 水银柱几乎升到了摄氏四十度。

> Mercury 罗马神话中墨丘利神。他天生飞毛腿，不但身上长着一双翅膀，在他的帽子、鞋子上、甚至魔杖上都有翅膀。Mercury 自然成为了在众神间传递消息的信使，也成为了是商业、旅行及盗窃的守护神。有趣的是水星是太阳系九大行星中离太阳最近的一颗，绕太阳公转速度最快，是地球的4倍。用跑得最快的神 Mercury 来命名真是再贴切不过了。

Unit 18

mercy ['mə:si] n. 仁慈，宽恕，怜悯

[例] We were treated with mercy. 我们受到仁慈的待遇。

merger ['mə:dʒə] n. 合并，归并

[例] The proposed merger between two of the largest software companies has been passed. 所提议的两大软件公司的合并被通过。

merit ['merit] n. 优点；价值；v. 有益于

[例] There's little merit in passing the driving test if you don't have a car of your own. 如果你没有自己的汽车，通过驾驶考试也没什么价值。

[反义词] demerit

mesmerize ['mezməraiz] v. 吸引住；施催眠术

[例] We stood by the lake, mesmerized by the flashing colours of the fish. 我们站在湖边,被鱼身上闪烁的色彩迷住了。

> 来源于近代催眠鼻祖、奥地利医生 Mermer 的名字。另一单词 hypnosis 也表示“催眠”，则来自希腊神话中的睡神 Hypnos。所以“催眠师”是 hypnotist；“使…催眠”是 hypnotise。

mess [mes] n. 混乱，脏乱；v. 弄乱

[例] Your books and magazines are almost in a mess; go and put them in order. 你的书和杂志简直是乱七八糟,去把它们整理一下。

[记] mess up 搞乱，弄脏

metabolism [me'tæbəlizəm] n. 新陈代谢

[例] Some people's metabolism is more efficient than others. 某些人的代谢作用要比另一些人更为有效。

[记] metabolic a. 新陈代谢的 /metabolize v. 新陈代谢

meteorology [ˌmi:tjə'rɔlədʒi] n. 气象学；气象状态

[例] Nowadays, few people like to study meteorology. 现在，很少有人愿意学气象学。

method ['meθəd] n. 方法

[例] Our teacher is showing us a new method of writing. 老师告诉我们一种书写的新方法。

[记] methodology n. 方法论

metropolis [mi'trɔpəlis] n. 主要都市；首府

[例] Young people prefer working in a metropolis. 年轻人喜欢在大城市上班。

[记] metropolitan a. 大城市的，大都会的

microscope ['maikrəskəup] n. 显微镜

[例] The light microscope magnifies the object 1000 times. 这架光学显

微镜把物像放大一千倍。
[记] microphone n. 麦克风，话筒 /microwave n. 微波炉；微波 /microbe n. 微生物

migrate ['maigreit] v. 移居，迁移
[例] Some birds migrate to find warmer weather. 有些鸟迁徙以寻找更温暖的气候。
[记] migration n. 迁徙；移居

mild [maild] a. 温和的，不严重的
[例] The weather is mild today; it is neither hot nor cold. 今天天气很温暖，不冷也不热。

milestone ['mailstəun] n. 里程碑，重大事件，转折点
[例] The invention of the computer was a milestone in the history of man. 计算机的发明是人类历史上的一件大事。

> mile（英里）是拉丁语*mille*（千）的复数形式。古罗马军团行军一千步的距离即为mile。古罗马的广场上竖有一中央石碑，以此为起点向城外每一千步竖立一块石头，用以标明罗马到某地的距离，milestone 即千步石，里程碑。

military ['militəri] a. 军事的，军用的
[例] According to the Constitution of the country, all the young men do a year's military service. 根据该国的宪法规定，所有的男青年都要服一年兵役。

millennium [mi'leniəm] n. 一千年，千年期
[例] What did you do to celebrate the millennium? 千禧年你是如何庆祝的?

mimic ['mimik] v. 模仿
[例] He mimicked the teacher's voice. 他模仿老师的声音。
[同义词] imitate, mime, mock, model

mineral ['minərəl] n. 矿物
[例] China is rich in minerals. 中国的矿产丰富。

miniature ['minjətʃə] n. 缩小的模型；缩影；a. 微型的；缩小的
[例] The locket contained a miniature portrait of her late husband. 小坠盒里有她已故丈夫的微型肖像。

minimal ['miniməl] a. 最小的，最小限度的
[例] Fortunately, the storm only did minimal damage to the crops. 幸好，暴风雨对农作物只造成很小的损失。

minimise ['minimaiz] (=minimize) v. 最小化，使减少（或缩小）到最低限度
[例] The polar explorers took every precaution to minimize the dangers of their trip. 极地探险者十分小心谨慎，以便使旅途的危险性减少到最小。
[反义词] maximise

minimum ['miniməm] n. 最少量，最小值，最低限度

[例] You must get a minimum of 40 questions right to pass the examination. 你最少必须答对 40 道题才能通过考试。
[反义词] maximum

ministry ['ministri] n.（政府的）部门；牧师
[例] Her father used to work in the Ministry of Agriculture. 他的父亲过去任职于农业部。
[记] the Ministry of National Defense 国防部

minor ['mainə] a. 较小的；不重要的；n. 未成年人；副修科目
[例] The young actress was given a minor part in the new play. 这个年轻女演员只分到这出新戏中一个较次要的配角色。

minority [mai'nɔriti] n. 少数；少数民族
[例] The minority nationality concert lasted two hours. 少数民族音乐会持续了两个小时。
[反义词] majority

mint [mint] n. 薄荷，薄荷糖；造币厂；v. 铸造（硬币）
[例] We sat in the back row, sucking mints. 我们坐在后排，嘴里嚼着薄荷糖。

> 希腊神话中的天后赫拉 Hera 在罗马神话中名字变成了 Juno Moneta。她曾多次警告罗马人即将出现的危险，帮助他们度过难关，成为了罗马人的警告女神。罗马人为 Juno Moneta 建了一座神庙，后来又把造币厂设在了神庙里，希望女神能守护他们的财富，同时随时警告他们不为金钱而迷失。英语中 money 和 mint 都是源自女神的姓氏 Moneta。可现代人有多少能记得手里的 money 有"警告"的含义呢。

minus ['mainəs] a. 负的，零以下；prep. 减（去）
[例] The temperature was minus 20 degrees. 温度是零下 20 度。
[反义词] plus

miracle ['mirəkl] n. 奇迹；奇事
[例] The car hit the child, but by a miracle, he was unhurt. 汽车压着了这个小孩，但他却没有受伤，真是奇迹。

miscellaneous [ˌmisi'leinjəs] a. 混杂的，各种各样的
[例] He bought miscellaneous food to welcome her. 他为了欢迎她，买了各种各样的食物。

miserable ['mizərəbl] a. 极不愉快的，痛苦的
[例] It's raining again — what miserable weather! 又下雨了，多烦人的天气！
[记] misery n. 痛苦；不幸

mishap ['mishæp] n. 灾祸
[例] A mishap prevented him from attending the routine company meeting . 他遇到一件不幸的事，因而不能来参加公司的例会。

[同义词] misfortune

missile ['misail] n. 导弹，发射物

[例] The missile hit the target, but failed to explode. 导弹击中了目标，但却没有爆炸。

mission ['miʃən] n. 任务，使命

[例] It seems to be his mission to help others. 他的天职好像就是帮助别人。

[记] missionary n. 传教士

mitigate ['mitigeit] v. 减轻

[例] Nothing could mitigate the cruelty with which she had treated him. 她对他太残暴了，实在是罪无可恕。

mixture ['mikstʃə] n. 混合（物）

[例] His new play is a mixture of sadness and humour. 他的新剧本融悲哀和幽默于一体。

moan [məun] n. 呻吟；哀悼；v. 抱怨；呻吟

[例] The sick child moaned a little, and then fell asleep. 这个生病的孩子呻吟了几声，后来就睡着了。

mobility [məu'biliti] n. 活动性；灵活性；流动性

[例] The key to the army's effectiveness is its mobility. 军队效率的关键是它的机动性。

[记] mobile a. 可移动的 /mobile phone 手机

mock [mɔk] v. 嘲笑，嘲弄；a. 模拟的；非真实的

[例] They mocked my timidity. 他们嘲弄我的胆小。

[记] mock exam 模考

mode [məud] n. 方式，模式

[例] This fever will return from time to time, if it follows its usual mode. 一般情况，这种热病每隔一阵子就会再发作。

> 字根 mod 指“方式，方法”。如：model 成为一种方式→模型，模特；modest 做人最好的方式→谦虚；modify 改变方式→修改，变更。

model ['mɔdl] n. 样品，模型；模特儿；v. 模仿

[例] This student is a model of diligence. 这学生是勤勉的模范。

moderate ['mɔdərit] a. 适度的，适中的

[例] The wind was strong all day, but it became moderate in the evening. 一整天来风都刮得很厉害,但到傍晚时有所减弱了。

modest ['mɔdist] a. 谦虚的，谦逊的

[例] She is very modest about the prizes she has won. 她对自己获奖非常谦虚。

modify ['mɔdifai] v. 修改，更改

[例] The equipment may be modified to produce VCD sets. 这设备可以经过改装用来生产光碟机。

[记] modification n. 修改，修正

module ['mɔdju:l] n. 模块；登月舱

[例] They found out that they needed a software module. 他们发现他们需要一个软件模块。

moist [mɔist] a. 潮湿的，湿润的

[例] His eyes were moist with tears. 他的眼睛泪水汪汪。

moisture ['mɔistʃə] n. 潮湿，潮气

[例] The sun dries the moisture on the ground. 太阳晒干了地上的潮气。

monitor ['mɔnitə] v. 监控；n. 监控，监视器；班长

[例] We have been monitoring the enemy's radio broadcasts to try to find out their secret plans. 我们一直在监听敌方的电台广播,设法查探他们的秘密计划。

molecule ['mɔlikju:l] n. 【化】分子

[例]There is a molecule separator in the lab. 这实验室有台分子分离器。

monopoly [mə'nɔpəli] n. 垄断，独占；垄断者

[例] A university education shouldn't be the monopoly of the minority whose parents are rich. 大学教育不应是少数富家子弟的专利。

> 前缀 mono- 指"单一"。如：monochrome 单色；monograph 专论；monorail 单轨铁路；poly- 则表示"多个，多元的"。如 polychrome 多色彩的。那么 monopoly 就是"使多元的单一化"→垄断；polypoly 多元对多元→多头垄断；那再猜猜这个词 Polygram？ *

monsoon [mɔn'su:n] n. 雨季；季风

[例] The monsoon brings rain for us. 季风给我们带来了降雨。

monument ['mɔnjumənt] n. 纪念碑

[例] The work is one of the great monuments of English literature. 此作品是英国文学的不朽名作之一。

[记] the Monument to the People's Heroes 人民英雄纪念碑

mop [mɔp] n. 拖把；v. 用拖把拖洗

[例] She mopped up the water. 她把水擦干净了。

moral ['mɔrəl] a. 道德(上)的；精神的；n. 道德

[例] The old gentleman claimed himself to be a very moral man, who had never told a lie in his life. 这位老先生称自己是个很有道德的人,他一生中从未说过一次谎。

[记] moral principles 道德原则 /moral standards 道德标准 /morality [mɔ'ræliti] n. 道德；道德观

morphine ['mɔ:fi:n] n. 吗啡

[例] Morphine, like cocaine, is addictive. 吗啡和可卡因一样，容易使人上瘾。

> morphine 和 marijuana（大麻）都是 opium（鸦片）的提取物。morphine 有麻醉镇定的作用，源于希腊神话中梦神的名字

Morpheus。梦神是睡神Hypnos的儿子，掌管人们的梦境。而在电影*The Matrix*中，黑人演员饰演的Morpheus双手握有一红一蓝药丸，让男主人公Neo选择梦境与现实，有异曲同工之妙。

mortal ['mɔːtl] a. 必死的，致命的；n. 凡人，人类

[例] It is an indisputable fact that man is mortal. 人都会死，这是无可争辩的事实。

[记] a mortal wound致命伤 /mortal combat决斗 /[反义词] immortal a. 不朽的，流芳百世的

mortgage ['mɔːgidʒ] v. /n. 抵押

[例] It is easy to get a mortgage on a house. 办理房屋抵押很容易。

mortify ['mɔːtifai] v. 克服；苦修；使苦恼

[例] He was mortified by his inability to answer the question. 他因为自己答不出这个问题而感到羞怒。

mosquito [məs'kiːtəu] n. 蚊子

[例] The mosquito is an annoying creature. 蚊子是一种讨厌的生物。

motion ['məuʃən] n. 动作；运动

[例] She made motions to him to follow. 她向他招手要他跟上来。

motivate ['məutiveit] v. 激发，激励

[例 Examinations do not motivate a student to seek more knowledge. 考试不能促使学生去追求更多的知识。

motive ['məutiv] n. 动机，（行动的）缘由

[例 His motive for working so hard is that he needs money. 他这么卖命干，因为他需要钱。

motto ['mɔtəu] n. 座右铭，格言

新航道学校motto：I will persist until I succeed. 我坚持，我成功。I will be likened to the raindrop which washes away the mountain; the ant who devours a tiger; the star which brightens the earth; the slave who builds a pyramid. I will build my castle one brick at a time for I know that small attempts, repeated, will complete any undertaking. I will persist until I succeed.

mould [məuld] (=mold)n. 霉；模具；v. 发霉

[例] The walls were black with mould. 墙因发霉而变黑。

mount [maunt] v. 渐渐增加；爬上；登上；n. 山

[例] The old lady can mount the stairs only with difficulty. 这位老妇人上楼梯十分艰难。

[记] mountaineer n. 登山运动员 /mountaineering n. 登山运动

mow [mau] v. 收割庄稼；扫除；n. 干草堆

[例] I want to have my garden mowed. 我想请人来给我的花园除草。

[记] mow the lawn 修剪草坪

muffle ['mʌfl] v. 使（声音）减弱

[例] The sound of the bell was muffled by the curtains. 铃声被帘子蒙住而压低了。

multiply ['mʌltiplai] v. 乘，使相乘；增加；繁殖

[谚] Friendships multiply joys and divide grieves. 友谊增进欢乐,分担忧愁。

mundane ['mʌndein] a. 世俗的，平凡的

[例] The mundane task of setting the table can be fun on holidays. 摆桌子这种平常的任务在假日里会很有意思。

municipal [mju(:)'nisipəl] a. 市政的，市立的；地方自治的

[例] He went to a municipal university. 他考上了一所市立大学。

the municipal government 市政府

murmur ['mə:mə] v. 小声说，咕哝

[例] The child murmured in her sleep. 这个孩子在睡梦中喃喃自语。

muscle ['mʌsl] n. 肌肉

[例] He is a man of muscle. 他是个大力士。

> muscle和mouse同源。当你鼓起你的肱二头肌时，肌肉块就像小老鼠，古罗马人就是这样联想的。另一单词mussel，指我们常吃的一种海味：淡菜、贻贝，也是因为它在颜色和形状上同小老鼠有几分相似。

muscular ['mʌskjulə] a. 肌肉发达的；壮健的

[例] The player is big and muscular. 这个运动员长得魁梧强壮。

mushroom ['mʌʃrum] n. 蘑菇 v. 成蘑菇状

[例] The smoke mushroomed into the sky. 烟呈蘑菇状扩散到天空中。

mustard ['mʌstəd] n. 芥菜；芥末

[例] I don't like mustard; it's too hot. 我不爱吃芥末,这东西太辣了。

> 日本料理中的常见东东。日文中芥末叫wasabi，寿司sushi，生鱼片sashimi。

mute [mju:t] a. 哑的，无声的；n. 哑巴

[例] He turned on the "mute" key of the TV in order to hear me clearly. 他把电视调到无声以便听到我的话。

mutual ['mju:tʃuəl] a. 相互的，彼此的；共同的

[例] You need mutual belief to set up your cooperation. 你们需要相互信任来进行合作。

[记] mutually adv. 相互地

mystery ['mistəri] n. 神秘，神秘的事物

[例] It's a mystery to me. 这对我来说是个谜。

myth [miθ] n. 神话

[例] The myth that elephants never forget. 那个虚构的关于大象的故事令人难忘。

[记] mythology n. 神话，神话学 / [区别] theology [θi'ɔlədʒi] n. 神学

nail [neil] n. 指甲；钉子；v. 钉

[例] Please hammer a nail into the wall. 请在墙上钉个钉子。

naive [nɑːˈiːv] a. 天真的，幼稚的，经验不足的

[例] You weren't so native as to believe him, were you? 你没有轻易相信他，是吧？

naked [ˈneikid] a. 裸体的，赤条条的

[例] He rushed out naked. 他赤身裸体地冲了出来。

the naked facts 明显的事实

[记] the naked truth 原原本本的真理

> 在国外如果看到海边沙滩处的牌子写着"Naked Beach" or "Nudist Beach"，不是说沙滩上没有树，是光秃秃、裸露的沙滩，而指天体浴场。英语中的"裸奔"和"裸泳"却没有用 naked 一词：go skinny-dipping 去裸泳；streaking 裸奔。

namely [ˈneimli] adv. 即，那就是

[例] Only one person can do the job, namely you. 只有一个人能做这项工作，那就是你。

narrate [næˈreit] v. 讲（故事），叙述，讲述

[例] The sailor narrated the story of his life to me in the tavern. 那水手在这酒店里向我讲述了他的一生。

narrow [ˈnærəu] a. 狭窄的；有限的；n. 海峡；v. 变狭窄；收缩

[例] Living in the countryside has narrowed him. 居住在乡下使他眼光短浅了。

[记] narrow down 减少，限制

national [ˈnæʃənəl] a. 国家的，民族的

[例] The national emblem of England is the rose. 英国的国徽是玫瑰花。

[记] nationalism n. 爱国心；民族主义 /nationality n. 国籍

native [ˈneitiv] n. 本地人；a. 本国的；出生地的

[例] The white people here don't mix socially with the natives. 这里的白人不与当地人交往。

naughty [ˈnɔːti] a. 淘气的，顽皮的

[例] Those naughty boys have been acting up again. 那些淘气的男孩子又在调皮捣蛋了。

navigable [ˈnævigəbl] a. 可通航的，可航行的

[例] The river was navigable. 这河流是可以通航的。

> 字根 nav/nau 指"航行，船"。如：navy 船队，海军；naval 海军的；navigate 航行；nausea 船在海上航行→晕船；astronaut 星际航行者→太空人。

navigate [ˈnævigeit] v. 航行，飞行

[例] He was the first man to navigate the Atlantic alone. 他是第一位单

独横渡大西洋的人。

navigation [ˌnæviˈgeiʃən] n. 航行；航海；航空

[例] Navigation is a game for brave people. 航海是勇敢者的游戏。

[记] navigator n. 航海家；导航员，领航员

neat [niːt] a. 有序的；整洁的；灵巧的

[例] A neat work schedule will make us more efficient than before. 合理安排工作表可以让我们更加有效率。

necessity [niˈsesiti] n. 必要性；必需品，必不可少的事物

[例] Water is a necessity of life. 水是生命必不可少的。

[记] necessary a. 必须的；必要的

negate [niˈgeit] v. 否定，打消

[例] He negated all the work we have done. 他否定了我们所做的一切。

negative [ˈnegətiv] a. 否定的，相反的，消极的；n. 否定，底片

[例] He has a very negative attitude to his work. 他的工作态度很消极。

[反义词] positive

neglect [niˈglekt] v. 忽视，疏忽 n. 疏忽，遗漏

[例] In course of time, old customs and observances tend to fall into neglect. 随着时间的推移，旧风俗习惯有被忽略的趋势。

[记] neglect of 疏忽

> 字根neg指“否定”。如：negative；字根lect指“集中”，如collect收集。neglect拒绝集合→忽视。

negligible [ˈneglidʒəbl] a. 可以忽略的，不予重视的

[例] In buying a suit, a difference of ten cents in prices is negligible. 买一套衣服价钱只差一毛钱是无所谓的。

negotiate [niˈgəuʃieit] v. 商议，谈判，磋商

[例] He is now negotiating with his supplier. 他现在正与供应商谈判。

[记] negotiation n. 谈判；协商

nerve [nəːv] n. 神经；紧张，焦虑

[例] She gets nerves before every examination. 每次考试前她都很紧张。

[记] nervous a. 焦虑的；紧张不安的

network [ˈnetwəːk] n. 网络；广播网，电视网

[例] President Bush's speech was broadcast on state networks and from locations. 布什总统的演说由全国广播系统传播并经过地区电视台转播。

> net n. 网，网状物；v. 用网捕；a. 纯粹的。我们上网经常使用的MSN即是Microsoft Network。当然，护理学硕士（The Master of Science in Nursing）的缩写也是MSN。

*

Polygram 宝丽金唱片公司

polygram n. 多字母(组合)

Unit 19

neutral ['nju:trəl] a. 中立的；中立国的

[例] She is neutral in this argument; she doesn't care who wins. 在这场辩论中她保持中立，不在乎谁赢谁输。

nevertheless [ˌnevəðə'les] conj. 然而，不过

[例] She was very tired, nevertheless she kept on working. 她虽然很疲倦，可仍在继续工作。

[同义词] but, however, yet, although, notwithstanding

New Zealand [nju: 'zi:lənd] n. (=NZ)新西兰(太平洋南部岛国)

[例] New Zealand is an island country in the southern Pacific Ocean southeast of Australia. Wellington is the capital and Auckland the largest city. Population, 3,265,300. 新西兰是澳大利亚东南的一个岛国，位于太平洋南部。首都惠灵顿，最大的城市奥克兰。人口 3265300。

nightmare ['naitmɛə] n. 恶梦，梦魇

[例] This mid-term exam is a nightmare. 这次期中考试真是一场恶梦。

> mare 一词指“母马”。但在 nightmare 一词中，mare 指古时传说中的“梦淫妖”，是趁人在睡梦中与之交合的妖怪。中世纪人们认为做恶梦是因为此妖怪坐在睡眠者身上使其窒息的原故。另外，谚语“Money makes the mare go. 有钱能使鬼推磨”，这个 mare，也是鬼。

nobility [nəu'biliti] n. 高贵，贵族

[谚] Virtue is the only true nobility. 万事不如美德高。

[记] noble a. 贵族的；高贵的；n. 贵族

nocturnal [nɔk'tə:nl] a. 夜的，夜间活动的

[例] Hamsters are nocturnal creatures. 仓鼠是夜间活动的动物。

> 字根 noct 指“夜晚 night”。noctambulist 夜间（noct）四处游荡（ambul）的人，梦游者。中文里把晚上特别能熬夜的人称为“夜猫子”，对应的英语是 night owl（猫头鹰）。与之相反，晚上不熬夜，早晨起来精神饱满的人被形容为“fresh daisy”，来自短语“as fresh as a daisy in the morning”，像早上的雏菊一样清新。

nominate ['nɔmineit] v. 提名；推荐；任命

[例] He was nominated (as) Minister of Finance. 他被提名为财政部长。

[记] nominate sb. for…提名某人为…的候选人

nonetheless [ˌnʌnðə'les] adv. 尽管如此；不过

[例] The main stream of the world's situation is peace; nonetheless, local conflicts never stop. 尽管世界形势的主流是和平，但是地区冲突从

未停止过。

norm [nɔːm] n. 标准，规范

[例] You must adapt to the norms of the society you live in. 在社会生活中要遵循社会行为准则。

[记] social norms 社会准则

normal [ˈnɔːməl] a. 正常的，正规的，规范的

[例] The normal price of a ticket is $230! 一张票的正常价格是 230 美元。

nostalgia [nɔsˈtældʒiə] n. 乡愁；向往过去，怀旧之情

[例] She often falls into the mood of nostalgia. 她经常陷入怀旧的情绪中。

> 来自希腊语，nostos → returning home；algos → pain。葡萄牙语同义词 saudade（这个发音比较经典，自己体会）。

notable [ˈnəutəbl] a. 值得注意的，显著的；著名的

[例] The difference in contrast is notable. 差别对比是显著的。

noticeable [ˈnəutisəbl] a. 显而易见的；值得注意的

[例] The hole in your trousers is not noticeable. 你裤子上的洞不明显。

notify [ˈnəutifai] v. 通知，通告

[例] I notified him that the meeting had been postponed. 我通知他会议已经延期。

[记] notice n. 通知；布告；注意；v. 注意到

notion [ˈnəuʃən] n. 概念，观念

[例] He has no notion of what I mean. 他不明白我的意思。

notorious [nəuˈtɔːriəs] a. 臭名昭著的，声名狼藉的

[例] He was notorious for drawing a long bow. 他因吹牛皮而远近闻名。

[反义词] celebrated, famous, renowned, well-known

notwithstanding [ˌnɔtwiðˈstændiŋ] adv. /conj. / prep. 尽管

[例] Notwithstanding his objections, the marriage took place. 尽管他有异议，婚礼还是进行了。

nourish [ˈnʌriʃ] v. 滋养，给…以营养

[例] Milk nourishes a baby. 牛奶供给婴儿养料。

novelty [ˈnɔvəlti] n. 新奇的事物

[例] Its novelty rapidly wore off. 它的新鲜劲儿很快就消失了。

> 字根 nov 指“新的，new”。如：novel a. 新奇的；n. 小说。novelist 小说家；innovation 革新；novice 新手。

novice [ˈnɔvis] n. 新手，初学者

[例] He is a novice at swimming. 他是一个游泳新手。

noxious [ˈnɔkʃəs] a. 有害的

[例] Increasing tax on petrol would encourage people to drive smaller cars with fewer noxious emissions. 增加汽油税往往会鼓励人们开排气量排污量小的车。

nuclear ['nju:kliə] a. 核的，核能的

[例] Nowadays more and more people prefer a nuclear family to an extended family. 现在越来越多的人喜欢核心家庭而不喜欢大家庭。

> nuclear family (仅由父母及子女组成的)核心家庭；核弹 nuclear bomb；核能 nuclear energy；核燃料 nuclear fuel；核反应堆 nuclear reactor。核武器 nuclear weapons；核裁军 nuclear disarmament。

nuisance ['nju:sns] n. 讨厌或麻烦的人或事物

[例] Don't make yourself a nuisance to others. 不要做一个令人讨厌的人。

> 法语词。公共标志中：Commit No Nuisance 意思是"禁止小便"。

numerous ['nju:mərəs] a. 众多的，无数的，许多的

[例] Those birds have become more numerous lately. 近来那种鸟变得越来越多了。

nursery ['nə:səri] n. 托儿所

[例] The nursery teacher made the children sit bolt upright. 幼儿园的老师让孩子们笔直地坐着。

[同义词] playgroup, kindergarten 幼儿园 /nursing home 敬老院

nurture ['nə:tʃə] n. /v. 养育，培养

[例] The two sisters had been nurtured very differently. 这姊妹俩接受过极不相同的教育。

[记] Nature vs. Nurture 先天与后天

nutrition [nju:'triʃən] n. 营养，营养物

[例] A balanced diet provides nutrition for your body. 均衡的食物使你的身体获得营养。

nylon ['nailən] n. 尼龙

[例] This dress is 80% nylon. 这件连衣裙的料子 80% 是尼龙。

oasis [əu'eisis] (复数为 oases） n. (沙漠中) 绿洲

[例] Oases symbolize hope in desert areas. 绿洲在沙漠地区象征着一种希望。

oath ['əuθ] n. 誓言，宣誓

[例] He swore an oath to support the king. 他宣誓支持国王。

[记] take/swear an oath 宣誓

obese [əu'bi:s] a. 肥胖的，肥大的

[例] She has become obese and lazy. 她变得肥胖而且懒惰。

> 必背疾病单词：obesity 肥胖症；insomnia 失眠；hypertension 高血压；heart disease 心脏病；arthritis 关节炎；diabetes 糖尿病；diarrhea 腹泻；heatstroke 中暑；asthma 阿诗玛→哮喘。

obey [ə'bei] v. 服从，顺从
[例] The students obey the new teacher without hesitation. 学生们毫不犹豫地服从这位新老师。

obedient [ə'bi:djənt] a. 服从的，顺从的
[例] He is an obedient and well-behaved child. 他是个顺从而循规蹈矩的孩子。

objection [əb'dʒekʃən] n. 反对，不赞成；异议
[例] He has a strong objection to getting up early. 他强烈反对早起。

objective [əb'dʒektiv] n. 目标，宗旨；a. 客观的
[例] My objective this summer is to learn swimming. 我今年夏天的目标是学习游泳。
[反义词] subjective a. 主观的, 个人的

obligation [ˌɔbli'geiʃən] n. 义务，职责，债务
[例] We are under an obligation to help. 我们有义务帮忙。

oblige [ə'blaidʒ] v. 迫使，责成；施恩惠于；使感激
[例] I will oblige any sincere request. 我会答应任何诚意的请求。

oblivious [ə'bliviəs] a. 遗忘的，健忘的
[例] She was oblivious to our warnings. 她忘了我们的提醒。

obscure [əb'skjuə] a. 难理解的，晦涩的；v. 搞混，使难理解
[例] His success obscured his failures. 他的成功使他的失败显得微不足道。

observation [ˌəbzə:'veiʃən] n. 观察，观测；言论，评论
[例] Give me your observations on what's happened. 把发生的事情给我报告一下。

observe [əb'zə:v] v. 观察，观测；遵守；评述
[例] I observed him going out. 我看见他出去了。

obsess [əb'ses] v. 迷住, 使困扰
[例] He became absolutely obsessed with the girl in red. 他被红衣少女完全迷住了。
[记] be obsessed by /with 被…缠住，迷住心窍

obsolete ['ɔbsəli:t] a. 荒废的；过时的
[例] Many skills will become obsolete in the next century. 许多技能在下个世纪将会被淘汰。

obstacle ['ɔbstəkl] n. 障碍，障碍物
[例] Her father's opposition remained only their obstacle. 她父亲的反对是他们唯一的障碍。

obstruct [əb'strʌkt] v. 阻隔，阻碍
[例] The road was obstructed by a fallen tree. 路被一棵倒下的树堵住了。

字根struct指“建筑to build”。如: structure 建筑物, 结构; construct 一起来build→建造, 创立; destruct 使建筑物倒下→破坏; instruct

在心里面建造→指导；instructor 大学讲师；obstruct 阻止(ob-=against)建筑→阻隔。

obstruction [əb'strʌkʃən] n. 障碍物，阻塞物

[例] It took three weeks for the workers to clear the obstructions from the river. 工人们用了三个星期清除河中的障碍物。

obtrusive [əb'tru:siv] a. 突出的；令人厌恶的；过分炫耀的

[例] Try to wear something less obstrusive. 穿衣服不要太显眼。

obvious ['ɔbviəs] a. 显然的，明显的

[例] It is obvious that even if we can save much energy, we can only delay the energy crisis. 很明显,即使我们能节约很多能量,我们也只能推迟能源危机的到来。

[记] obviously adv. 明显地

occasion [ə'keiʒən] n. 场合；时机，机会

[例] A wedding is a very happy occasion. 婚礼是个非常愉快的盛会。

[记] on occasion 有时，不时 /occasionally adv. 偶而，时而

occupy ['ɔkjupai] v. 占用，占有

[例] The company occupies the whole building. 这个公司占用了整个大楼。

[记] be occupied in 正在(做某事) /occupation n. 工作，职业

occur [ə'kə:] v. 发生，出现

[例] The accident occurred at five o'clock. 事故发生在五点钟。

occurrence [ə'kʌrəns] n. 发生的事，出现

[例] Robbery in New York is an everyday occurrence. 在纽约，抢劫每天都在发生。

odd [ɔd] a. 临时的；奇怪的；奇数的

[例] Why do they want odd jobs — jobs usually requiring little skill and knowledge? 为什么他们会干这种一般没有什么技术和知识的零工呢？

必背数学单词：add/plus 加；subtract 减；multiply/times 乘；divide 除；odd number 奇数；even number 偶数；integer 整数；fraction 分数；decimal 小数；angle 角；plane 平面；square 正方形，平方；rectangle 长方形；triangle 三角形；circle 圆。

odds [ɔdz] n. 可能的机会

[例] The odds are in favour of the diligent ones. 机会青睐勤奋者。

[记] against all (the) odds 尽管有极大的困难

odour ['əudə] (=odor) n. 气味；意味，迹象

[例] The odour summoned up memories of my childhood. 这气味使我回忆起孩提时代。

official [ə'fiʃəl] a. 正式的，官方的

[例] The mass media demanded that all the official documents concerning the sale of this land be made public. 大众媒体要求公布有关出售这块

土地的全部正式文件。

officious [ə'fiʃəs] a. 爱发号施令的，好管闲事的

[例] He's an officious little man and widely disliked in the company. 他是一个好管闲事的小男人，在公司里人们普遍不喜欢他。

[记] an officious statement 非正式声明

off-season ['ɔf'siːzn] n. 淡季

[例] The businessman waited until the off-season to take a holiday. 这个商人等着生意淡季去度假。

[反义词] midseason n. 旺季

offset ['ɔfˌset] v. /n. 补偿，抵消

[例] He has to offset his small salary by living economically. 他只好以节俭的生活来抵消其低微的收入。

[记] offset sth. by(doing) sth. 以某物补偿或抵消某物

offspring ['ɔfspriŋ] (单复数同形)n. 子女，子孙，后代

[例] They have two offspring. 他们有两个孩子。

[同义词] child, descendant

olive ['ɔliv] n. 橄榄，橄榄树

> olive branch 橄榄枝，和平、希望的象征。《圣经》记载：当 flood（洪水）淹没整个大地，按照上帝意志所有的动物与人类都成对地进入 ark（方舟）中。40 天后，Noah（诺亚）从方舟窗户放出一只 raven（乌鸦），去查看洪水是否退去，结果 raven 一去无踪影。又放出一只鸽子 dove（不是德芙巧克力），最后 dove 回到诺亚方舟上，嘴里衔着新拧下的橄榄枝，表明洪水已退，大地恢复生机。

omit [əu'mit] v. 遗漏，省去，删去

[例] The secretary omitted the date when typing the contract. 秘书在打印合同时漏掉了日期。

ongoing ['ɔngəuiŋ] a. 进行中的

[例] The discussions are still ongoing. 讨论仍在进行。

ooze [uːz] v. 渗出；泄漏

[例] Blood oozed from his wound. 鲜血慢慢流出伤口。

[同义词] seep

opacity [əu'pæsiti] n. 不透明性

[例] They have chosen the frosted glass owing to its opacity. 他们选择了这种磨砂玻璃，因为它是不透明的。

[反义词] transparence n. 透明，透明度

opaque [əu'peik] n. 不透明物；a. 不透明的

[例] This is a chemical solution opaque to x-rays. 这是一种X光不能穿透的化学物质。

operate ['ɔpəreit] v. 起作用；操作；运转

[例] These reasons operated on the mind of the audience. 这些道理在听众的思想上产生了作用。

[记] operation n. 运转，操作；手术；军事行动

opinion [ə'pinjən] n. 意见，看法；评价

[例] He asked for his father's opinion about his plans. 他征求爸爸对他的计划的意见。

opponent [ə'pəunənt] n. 对手，敌手，反对者

[例] We beat our opponents at football. 我们在足球赛中击败了对手。

[同义词] adversary, competitor, contender, rival

opposite ['ɔpəzit] a. 对面的，相对的，相反的；n. 相反的事物

[例] Her house is opposite to mine. 她的房子在我的房子对面。

[记] be opposite to 在…对面; 与…相反 / just the opposite 恰恰相反

> 如果有人问："你是不是对那个女孩子有兴趣？"你不想否认也不愿承认，可以轻描淡写地说：Opposites attract. 异性相吸，很正常。

oppress [ə'pres] v. 压迫，压抑

[例] A sense of trouble ahead oppressed my spirits. 对今后困难的预感使我情绪低落。

[记] oppressive a. 压制性的，压迫的

opt [ɔpt] v. 选择

[例] I opted for early retirement. 我选择提早退休。

[记] opt for(从多种方案中)作出选择

optical ['ɔptikəl] a. 眼的；视力的；光学的

[例] The magician performed several optical illusions. 魔术师表演了几个视觉上的幻术。

[记] optical instruments 光学仪器 /optical fibre 光导纤维

optimal ['ɔptiməl] a. 最佳的，最理想的

[例] This is the optimal season for the growth of plants. 这是植物生长的最佳季节。

optimistic [ˌɔpti'mistik] a. 乐观的；乐观主义的

[例] We are optimistic about its future. 我们相信前景是乐观的。

[记] optimism n. 乐观（主义）/optimist n. 乐观主义者 /[反义词] pessimistic a. 悲观的

option ['ɔpʃən] n. 选择，选择权；选项

[例]The government has two options: to reduce spending or to increase taxes. 政府只有两种选择,不是削减开支便是增加税收。

orchestra ['ɔːkistrə] n. 管弦乐队；乐队演奏处

[例] The orchestra played the Chinese national anthem. 乐队演奏了中国国歌。

> 源自希腊，orchestra 原指"露天舞蹈场地"，后来戏剧多在室内

上演，英国人把剧场内的前排座位叫作了orchestra。而法国人则把这些位置安排给乐师们。所以orchestra从原来的“舞蹈场”变成了今天的“管弦乐队，交响乐团”。

orbit [ˈɔːbit] n. 轨道；v. 绕轨道运行，做圆圈飞行
[例] The earth orbits the sun once every 365. 25 days. 地球每365. 25天绕太阳轨道一圈。

order [ˈɔːdə] n. 次序，顺序；命令；订单； v. 命令；订购
[例] Please order for me. 请替我点菜。

ore [ɔː(r)] n. 矿石
[例] This mountain area is rich in iron ore. 这儿的山区富含铁矿。

organism [ˈɔːgənizəm] n. 生物体，有机体
[例] Reproduction is one of the essential properties of a living organism. 繁殖是有生命的生物最重要的特性之一。
[记] organ n. 器官

organise [ˈɔːgənaiz] (=organize) v. 组织，安排
[例] Jane organised the party. She asked people to come and bought the food and drinks. 简组织了这个聚会。她请大家参加，并买了食品和饮料。

oriental [ˌɔ(ː)riˈentl] a. 东方的；n. 东方人，亚洲人
[例] Oriental art is becoming more and more popular. 东方艺术越来越受到欢迎。

字根ori指“升起，rise”。oriental太阳升起的地方→东方的；origin升起的地方→起源；originator发起人；orientate使向东，引申为定方向；国外大学新学期开学前有一周叫O-week，即Orientation Week，给新生介绍大学的各种情况，让他们摸清方向，尽快适应。

original [əˈridʒənəl] a. 起初的，原来的；n. 原作；原物
[例] The original owner of the house was the Duke of Wellington. 这房子本来的主人是威灵顿公爵。

originate [əˈridʒineit] v. 发源，开始；创始，创造
[例] This painting style originated in Italy. 这种绘画风格源自意大利。

ornament [ˈɔːnəmənt] n. 装饰品，点缀物，饰物；v. 装饰
[例] Several ornaments were lined up on the table. 桌上摆放着几个装饰品。
[同义词] decorate, adorn

orthodox [ˈɔːθədɔks] a. 正统的，传统的；习惯的
[例] His ideas are very orthodox. 他的想法非常正统。
[记] Eastern Orthodox church 东正教

otherwise [ˈʌðəwaiz] adv. 以另外方式，在其他方面

[例] He is noisy, but otherwise a nice boy. 他爱吵闹，但在其他方面却是个好孩子。

ounce [auns] n. 盎司；少量

[谚] An ounce of prevention is worth a pound of cure. 预防为主，治疗为辅。

> 法语词，简写为 oz，重量等于 1/16 磅 (pound)，小于 1 两，不到 6 钱，反正很少。

outcome ['autkʌm] n. 结果，结局

[例] The outcome was not what he expected. 结果并不像他天真地希望的那样。

[同义词] consequence, result

outfit ['autfit] n. 用具；配备；v. 配备，装备

[例] The football team were wearing orange outfits. 这个足球队的队员穿着清一色的橘黄色运动服。

outlet ['autlet] n. 出口，出路

[例] The shoe manufacturer had several outlets. 那家制鞋厂商有几家代销店。

outline ['autlain] n. 外形，轮廓；大纲

[例] He drew the outline of a house on the paper. 他把房子的轮廓画在纸上。

output ['autput] n. 产量；输出

[例] After the reform they doubled their output. 改革后他们的产量翻了倍。

outset ['autset] n. 开端，开始

[例] The novel fascinates readers from the outset. 这部小说一开头就把读者迷住了。

outstanding [aut'stændiŋ] a. 突出的，杰出的

[例] He would become an outstanding writer someday. 将来他会成为一名杰出的作家。

outweigh [aut'wei] v. 比…更重要；比…更有价值

[例] The advantages of the plan outweigh its drawbacks. 那计划的优点胜过缺点。

> 想迅速增加单词量可以从 out 做起。out 构成合成词时指“在…上超过”。outnumber, outscore, outrank, outwit, outsmart, outrun, outwalk, outsell, outspeed, outsing, outshout, outsail, outsit, outsoar, outsleep, outstare

overall ['əuvərɔːl] a. 全部的;全面的

[例] The overall cost of the trip was about $ 1,000. 旅行的全部费用大约一千美元。

overcome [ˌəuvəˈkʌm] n. 战胜，克服

[例] She tried her best to overcome her weakness. 她努力克服自己的弱点。

[同义词] conquer, surmount

overdue [ˈəuvəˈdjuː] a. 迟到的，延误的

[例] The train is overdue. 火车误点了。

overlap [ˌəuvəˈlæp] v. 复叠，部分相同

[例] The style in these two books largely overlaps. 这两本书的文体有许多处是一致的。

overlook [ˌəuvəˈluk] v. 俯瞰，耸出，远眺；没注意到

[例] The house on the hill overlooks the village. 从小山上的房子可以俯瞰村庄。

Unit 20

overseas [ˌəuvəˈsiːz] a. 海外的，国外的；adv. 海外

[例] Overseas students are concerned about the destiny of their motherland. 海外留学生关心着祖国的命运。

oversee [ˈəuvəˈsiː] v. 监督，监管

[例] The teacher oversaw the students while they took the exam. 学生们考试时这位老师监考。

overshadow [ˌəuvəˈʃædəu] v. 遮蔽，使…失色

[例] He overshadowed all his comrades. 他使所有同僚都黯然失色。

overtime [ˈəuvətaim] n. 超时；加班；a. 加班的；adv. 加班地；v. 使超时

[例] Her boss often asks her to do overtime. 她的老板经常叫她加班。

> over的构词能力也极强，over表示"在…之上，越过"。如overrun超支，overwork过度操劳。现在各个行业里都有人觉得自己为公司做了很多事，但是公司没有在薪金上给予足够的认可，这个时候他们总会说自己"overworked but underpaid"。

overwhelming [ˌəuvəˈwelmiŋ] a. 势不可挡的，压倒性的

[例] The general impression of the painting is overwhelming. 这幅画给人总的印象是很有气势。

owe [əu] v. 欠；感激；把…归功于

[例]We owe our parents a lot. 我们对父母感恩不尽。

[记] owe sth. to 把…归功于

ownership [ˈəunəʃip] n. 所有权，物主身份

[例] The equity ownership ought to be protected. 业主权益(产权)应该得到保护。

oxide [ˈɔksaid] n. 【化】氧化物

[例] The oxide mineral content of the rocks is generally low, at 5-10 percent. 岩石中氧化矿物质的含量通常较低，在5%到10%左右。

ozone [ˈəuzəun] n. 臭氧

[例] The ozone layer cuts off most of the ultraviolet radiation from the sun. 臭氧层阻挡了大部分来自太阳的紫外线辐射。

[记] ozone layer 臭氧层

pace [peis] n. 一步；速度；步调；v. 踱步

[例] Are wages keeping pace with inflation? 工资的提高能否与通货膨胀同步？

[记] at a good pace 相当快地 /set the pace 为别人定步调; 树榜样

pacific [pəˈsifik] a. 平静的，和平的

[例] What a beautiful pacific place this is! 这是一个多么美丽而平静的

地方啊！

> the Pacific 太平洋；Atlantic 大西洋；arctic 北极；antarctic 南极；Asian-Pacific region 亚太地区；Asia Pacific Economic Cooperation 亚太经合组织 APEC，不要和 OPEC 弄混了：欧佩克，石油输出国组织 Organization of Petroleum Exporting Countries。

package ['pækidʒ] n. 包裹；包；v. 包裹，包装

[例] He packaged up the presents he had got for his birthday and put them in the cupboard. 他把收到的生日礼物包成一包放在橱里。

packaging ['pækidʒiŋ] n. 包装

[例] The consumers always complain that too much packaging increases the cost of the food. 消费者总是抱怨过多的包装增加了食品的费用。

pagoda [pə'gəudə] n. 宝塔（尤指东方佛塔）

[例] The pagoda looks magnificent. 这个宝塔看起来非常宏伟。

[区别] tower n. 塔，铁塔；高楼

painstaking ['peinsteikiŋ] a. 辛勤的，辛苦的

[例] The mastery of a language requires painstaking effort. 要学好一种语言，必须下苦功。

palm [pɑ:m] n. 手掌；棕榈树，棕榈叶；v. 与…握手

[例] He put the insect on the palm of his hand. 他把虫子放在他的手掌心。

> What tree do fortune tellers like to look at? 算命先生喜欢看什么树？当然是 palm 了。“看手相” 叫 to read one’s palm；看手相的人：palmist。

pamphlet ['pæmflit] n. 小册子

[例] I took a few pamphlets from the travel-agency. 我从旅行社拿了几本小册子。

[同义词] booklet, brochure, leaflet

panel ['pænl] n. 座谈小组

[例] Each panel focused on a different subject. 每个小组集中讨论不同的主题。

panic ['pænik] n. /v. 惊恐，惊慌

[例] When the theater caught fire, there was a panic. 剧院失火时，引起一阵恐慌。

> 希腊神话中森林之主潘神 Pan，人身羊足，头上有角，居住在森林之中。常藏在隐蔽处，猛然跳出，把旅行者吓得魂不附体，以此为乐。panic一词指“pan引起的恐惧”。口语中常说Don’t panic. 不要惊慌。

paperback ['peipəbæk] n. 平装本，纸面本

[例] This bookshop only sells paperbacks. 这书店只出售平装书。
[反义词] hardcover 精装本，硬皮书

parachute ['pærəʃu:t] n. 降落伞
[例] Parachutes in the air look like white mushrooms. 空中的降落伞看起来像白色的蘑菇。

parade [pə'reid] v. /n. 游行；炫耀
[例] The Olympic Games began with a parade of all the competing nations. 奥运会以参赛各国运动员的列队行进开始。

paradise ['pærədaiz] n. 天堂
[例] This club is a sportsman's paradise. 这个俱乐部是运动爱好者的乐园。

> 英国诗人 John Milton 名著《失乐园》Paradise Lost 取材于《圣经》，是描写 Adam 与 Eve 因偷吃 forbidden fruit 被逐出伊甸园 (Garden of Eden 的长诗)。Heaven 也表示"天堂"，人间天堂就是 a heaven on earth 或 earthly paradise，相当于陶渊明笔下的世外桃源、美国作家 James Hilton 在 Lost Horizon 中虚构的喜马拉雅山谷 Shangri-la、英国小说家们写的 Utopia (乌托邦) 和 Erehwon (nowhere 的反写)。

paradox ['pærədɔks] n. 自相矛盾的事物；似非而是的论点
[例] It is a paradox that in such a rich country there should be so many poor people. 这样一个富国中有那么多穷人，这是一种矛盾的现象。

paragraph ['pærəgrɑ:f] n. (文章的) 段落，节
[例] Read from the book, starting at the second paragraph. 念书，从第二段开始。

parallel ['pærəlel] n. 平行线；a. 平行的；v. 平行，相似
[例] There are few parallels between American football and European football. 美国足球和欧洲足球没有什么相似之处。
[记] unparalleled a. 无比的，无双的

paralyse ['pærəlaiz] (=paralyze)v. 使麻痹，使瘫痪，使无助
[例] The electricity failure paralysed the train service. 电力中断使得列车无法运行。
[记] paralysis n. 瘫痪 /paralysed a. 麻痹的，瘫痪的

parameter [pə'ræmitə] n. 参数，起限定作用的因素
[例] This document makes clear the parameters we can operate within. 这份文件阐明：我们操作范围的参数。

paramount ['pærəmaunt] a. 至高无上的，极为重要的
[例] This duty is paramount to all the others. 没有比这更重要的义务了。

> Paramount 派拉蒙电影公司。看看下面品牌的含义：robust 精力充沛的；rejoice 欣喜；safeguard 捍卫；nestle 安居；canon 教规，作家的真作；Daphne 为逃避阿波罗而变成月桂树的女神；dove

鸽子，也有人说是：Do you love me?

paraphrase ['pærəfreiz] v. /n. 解释，改述

[例] The teacher asked his students to paraphrase the long sentence. 老师让学生解释这个长句子。

parasitic [ˌpærə'sitik] a. 寄生的

[例] Don't be parasitic upon the labor of others. 不要依靠他人的劳动过寄生生活。

[记] parasite n. 寄生虫

parlour ['pɑːlə] n. 客厅

[例] The parlour has been decorated delicately. 客厅装饰得很精美。

partial ['pɑːʃəl] a. 部分的，局部的；偏袒的，不公平的

[例] I'm very partial to sweet foods. 我特别喜欢甜食。

participate [pɑː'tisipeit] v. 分享；参与

[例] If only I could participate in your good fortune. 要是我能分享你的好运就好了。

[记] participate in 参加，参与 /participant n. 参与者 /class participation 课堂参与

particle ['pɑːtikl] n. 颗粒，微粒；极小量

[例] Particles of dust are everywhere. 到处是尘埃。

particularly [pə'tikjuləli] adv. 特别，尤其

[例] We've been particularly busy these days. 这些日子我们特别忙。

partner ['pɑːtnə] n. 伙伴，同伙；搭档

[例] He was considered a partner in the crime. 他被认为是同谋。

passion ['pæʃən] n. 激情，热情

[例] His skills as a player don't quite match his passion for the game. 他的水平与他对这项游戏的酷爱程度不太相配。

[记] passionate a. 充满热情的

> 注意：当大写 Passion 时，特指圣经中记载的耶稣在最后的晚餐之后，直到被钉死在十字架上这段时期内所受的苦难。Passion play，应正确翻译为受难剧；Passion Sunday 耶稣受难日。经典的宗教片《耶稣受难记》The Passion of the Christ，被有的片商误译为“最后的激情”。

passive ['pæsiv] a. 被动的，消极的

[例] In spite of my efforts the boy remained passive. 不管我怎么努力，那男孩还是很消极。

[反义词] active

pastime ['pɑːstaim] n. 消遣；娱乐

[例] Watching TV is a popular pastime. 看电视是一种流行的消遣。

[同义词] amusement, diversion, enjoyment, recreation, relaxation

patent ['peitənt] n. 专利，专利权；v. 得到专利权

[例] The invertor patented his device. 发明者为他的发明申请了专利。

patriot ['peitriət] n. 爱国者

[例] A true patriot will never betray his country. 一位真正的爱国者永远不会出卖自己的国家。

[反义词] traitor n. 叛徒，叛国者

> 字根 patr 指“父亲的”。paternal 父亲的；patron 赞助人，老顾客（商家的衣食父母）；patronise 资助（像父母资助孩子读书一样）；patriot 词义延伸指爱父亲、祖先之国的人。

patrol [pə'trəul] v. 出巡；巡逻；n. 巡逻

[例] Every hour a policeman patrolled our street. 每隔一小时就有一名警察在我们这条街上巡逻。

patron ['peitrən] n. 赞助人；顾客，主顾

[例] A wealthy patron has promised to send him to study abroad. 一个富有的资助人答应要送他出国留学。

pattern ['pætən] n. 模范；式样；v. 模仿

[例] You can make a dress from this paper pattern. 你可以用这个纸样儿做一套衣服。

pause [pɔ:z] n. /v. 暂停，中止

[例] When he had run up the hill, he paused for a minute to rest. 他跑上小山时，停下来休息了一会儿。

payroll ['peirəul] n. 工资表

[例] Every month she has to prepare the staff payroll. 她每月都得准备全体员工的工资表。

peak [pi:k] n. 山峰，巅，顶点；v. 达到最大值

[例] The mountain peaks are covered with snow all the year. 山顶上终年积雪。

peculiar [pi'kju:ljə] a. 奇怪的；特有的，独特的

[例] He behaves in a very peculiar way sometimes. 他的行为有时很奇特。

pedal ['pedl] n. 踏板；v. 踩…的踏板

[例] One of the pedals has come off my bicycle. 我那自行车的踏脚板有一个已脱落了。

pedestrian [pe'destriən] n. 步行者；a. 徒步的

[例] In the accident, a pedestrian and a cyclist were injured. 在这场事故中，一位行人和一位骑车人受了伤。

[记] pedestrian crossing/zebra（斑马）crossing 人行横道

peel [pi:l] v. 剥；削；剥落

[例] My skin always peels when I've been in the sun. 我晒过太阳后总是脱皮。

peep [pi:p] v. 窥视，偷看；n. 窥看，隐约看见

[例] I peeped through the window to see if she was there. 我从窗子看了看她是否在那里。

> peeping Tom 偷窥狂。古时考文垂 Coventry 领主横征暴敛，他的妻子为民请命，与丈夫打赌，某日自己裸体骑马绕城一周，丈夫就要降低税率。全城百姓出于感激，自觉回避。只有一裁缝 Tom 在窗口偷窥，后双目失明。Tom 因此而名垂艳史，现在考文垂城中还有一尊他的雕像。peephole 门上的窥视孔。

peer [piə] v. 凝视；盯着看；n. 同等地位的人；同辈
[例] The new postman peered through the mist, trying to find the right house. 新来的邮递员在雾中仔细张望,设法寻找到他要找的那一家。

penalty ['penlti] n. 惩罚；刑罚；罚款
[例] What is the penalty for dangerous driving? 对危险驾车给予什么处罚?
[记] on penalty of 否则受…处罚；违者处以…刑罚

penetrate ['penitreit] v. 刺入，穿透；识破；洞察
[例] Western ideas penetrate slowly through the East. 西方观念逐渐传入东方。

penguin ['peŋgwin] n. 企鹅
[例] The penguin is popular with people. 企鹅广为人爱。

penicillin [ˌpeni'silin] n. 青霉素
[例] They have injected him with penicillin. 他们已给他注射青霉素。

penny ['peni] n. 便士
[例] It won't cost a penny. 它一文不值。

pension ['penʃən] n. 养老金，退休金
[例] The old man lives on a pension. 那位老人靠养老金生活。

per [pəː] prep. 每（一）
[例] How much do you earn per week? 你每周挣多少钱?
[记] per day/month/year 每天 / 月 / 年

perceive [pə'siːv] v. 感知，察觉；认识到
[例] I perceived that I could not make her change her mind. 我发觉我不能使她改变主意。

percent [pə'sent] n. (单复数同) 百分之…
[例] I am 100 percent in agreement. 我百分之百同意。

> 字根 cent 指“一百”。century 是百年，一个世纪；百分数就是 percent；一元钱有 100 cents；水从固点到沸点有 100 度，每一度是百分之一等级，即是 centigrade，摄氏度℃；而单词 centipede 中 ped=foot，所以 centipede 就是一百只脚→蜈蚣。

percentage [pə'sentidʒ] n. 百分比，百分率
[例] The hecklers constituted only a small percentage of the audience. 质

问者只是一小部分听众。

perennial [pə'renjəl] a. 终年的，常年的，长期的

[例] Politics provides a perennial subject for argument. 政治是一种长期争论不休的话题。

performance [pə'fɔːməns] n. 履行，执行；表现；表演

[例] The theater gives two performances a day. 这座剧场一天演出两场。

peril ['peril] n. 危险

[谚] Preparedness averts peril. 有备无患。

period ['piəriəd] n. （一段）时间，时期；句号

[例] Picasso's early career is divided into his blue period and rose period. 毕加索的早期生涯被分为忧郁期和得意时期。

periodical [ˌpiəri'ɔdikəl] a. 周期的，定期的；n. 期刊，杂志

[例] This is a monthly periodical. 这是月刊。

[记] learned periodical 学术期刊 /periodically adv. 周期性地; 定期按时

peripheral [pə'rifərəl] a. 外围的；n. 外围设备

[例] The peripheral part of the city is poor. 这个城市的周边地区很穷。

[记] periphery n. 外围，周边

perish ['periʃ] v. 毁灭，消亡；腐烂

[例] Flowers perish when frost comes. 霜降时花枯萎。

> 西方学术界有一句很有名的话"Publish or Perish!"表示从事研究的人，如果在一段时期之内没有按照要求在规定的期刊杂志上发表一定数量的论文或学术文章，那只能另谋高就或者干脆没饭吃了。

permanent ['pəːmənənt] a. 永久（性）的

[例] I have a permanent job here. 我在这里有一个永久的工作。

permissible [pə'misəbl] a. 允许的，许可的，准许的

[例] Her request is permissible. 她的要求可以准许。

permit [pə'mit] v. 允许，许可，准许；n. 执照，许可证

[例] The words hardly permit doubt. 这些话简直不容置疑。

[记] permission n. 允许；许可

perplex [pə'pleks] v. 使为难；使困惑；使混乱

[例] Modern men are often perplexed by what to do. 现代人常常感到非常困惑，不知如何是好。

[同义词] puzzle, confuse, bewilder

persevere [ˌpəːsi'viə] v. 坚忍，坚持

[谚] To persevere means victory! 坚持就是胜利！

persist [pə'sist] v. 坚持不懈，持续

[例] On the top of very high mountains snow persists throughout the year. 高山顶上，积雪终年不化。

[记] persist in doing sth. 坚持做某事 /persistence n. 坚持，持续 / persistent a. 坚持的，持续的

personality [ˌpəːsəˈnæliti] n. 个性，品格

[例] The boy is developing a fine personality. 这孩子的个性在往良好的方面发展。

personnel [ˌpəːsəˈnel] n. 人员，职员

[例] New personnel are needed for next project. 我们的下一个项目需要新人员。

[记] personnel agency 职业介绍所

perspective [pəˈspektiv] n. 前景，（观察问题的）视角，观点，想法

[例] In his book, he looks at China from a fresh perspective. 在他的这本书中，他用新的角度看中国。

persuade [pəˈsweid] v. 说服，(使)相信；劝某人做(不做)某事

[例] He persuaded her to go to school, even though she did not want to. 即使她不想去上学，他还是说服了她。

pertinent [ˈpəːtinənt] a. 有关系的，相关的

[例] The reporter asked two pertinent questions. 记者问了他两个相关问题。

pervade [pəˈveid] v. 弥漫于，遍及，遍布

[例] The smell of cooking pervaded the room. 房间里充满了烹调食物的气味。

[记] pervasive a. 遍布的；普遍的

> 字根 vade 指“行走”。in- 进来 +vade 走→走进来→ invade 侵略；e- 向外 +vade 走→ evade 逃避；per- 全面的 +vade 走→ pervade 遍布，弥漫。

pessimistic [ˌpesiˈmistik] a. 悲观的；悲观主义的

[例] He is pessimistic about the future. 他对未来感到悲观。

pest [pest] n. 害虫；有害动物

[例] Insects which eat crops are pests. 吃庄稼的昆虫是害虫。

[记] pests of society 害群之马，社会败类 /pesticide n. 杀虫剂

petition [piˈtiʃən] n. 请愿（书）；v. 请求

[例] The villagers all signed a petition asking for a hospital to be built. 村民们都在请愿书上签名要求建一所医院。

> 字根 pet 指“寻求”。appetite 寻求的情绪→欲望，食欲；compete, competition 一起寻求一样东西→竞争； repetition 再次寻求→重复；impetus 内部寻求→动力，刺激；petitioner 寻求的人→请愿人。

petroleum [piˈtrəuliəm] n. 石油

[例] Petroleum is an important natural resource. 石油是一种重要的自

然资源。

> 字根 petr 指“石头”。如：petrology 岩石学；petroleum 石油。还记得 surprise, amaze, astonish, astound 这些表示“惊奇”的词吗？要表达最高程度的“惊奇”，就是 petrify 使石化，吓呆。

pharmacy [ˈfɑːməsi] n. 药店；药剂学

[例] In the West you probably don’t go to the hospital; you go to the pharmacy or drug store. 西方人买药时经常不去医院，而是到药房或杂货店。

[记] pharmacist 药剂师 /pharmaceutical company 制药公司

phase [feiz] n. 阶段，时期；方面

[例] What phase of mathematics are you studying now? 你在学习哪一方面的数学？

[同义词] aspect, stage

phenomenon [fiˈnɔminən] (复数为 phenomena)n. 现象

[例] Snow in Egypt is an almost unknown phenomenon. 在埃及，雪几乎是一个不为人知的现象。

[记] the phenomena of nature 自然现象 /a social phenomenon社会现象

philosophy [fiˈlɔsəfi] n. 哲学

[例] Her second major is philosophy. 她的第二专业是哲学。

[记] philosopher n. 哲学家，哲人

> 拉丁文中 phil 指爱，soph 指智慧。pilosophy 就是爱智慧，据说该词由希腊哲人毕达哥拉斯创造。他曾创造了数的平方、立方等概念，提出了毕达哥拉斯定理（相当于我国勾股定理）。但他认为自己远远不够智慧，如果人们非要把智慧 soph 和他联系在一起，那么就请称呼他 philosopher 爱智慧的人吧。

physical [ˈfizikəl] a. 身体的，物质的；物理的

[例] Physical fitness is having a strong healthy body. 身体健康就是有一个强壮健康的身体。

[记] physics[ˈfiziks] n. 物理学

physician [fiˈziʃən] n. 医师，内科医师

[例] I have had myself carefully examined by physicians. 我已请医生给我仔细检查过了。

[区别] physicist n. 物理学家

physiology [ˌfiziˈɔlədʒi] n. 生理学

[例] I am not interested in physiology. 我对生理学不感兴趣。

[记] physiological a. 生理学的

picnic [ˈpiknik] n. 野餐 vi. (去)野餐

[例] We had a picnic by the sea. 我们在海边搞了一次野餐。

Unit 21

picturesque [ˌpiktʃə'resk] a. 如画的；独特的

[例] I was attracted by the picturesque scene on the West Lake. 我被西湖如画的风景迷住了。

> 形容词尾-que指“风格”。如：unique一种风格→唯一的；antique以前的风格→古代的，古董；arabesque 阿拉伯风格→阿拉伯图案的，蔓藤花纹。

pie [pai] n. 馅饼

[例] Would you like another piece of apple pie? 你想再来一块苹果派吗？

[记] pie chart 饼状图

pierce [piəs] v. 刺穿，刺破，穿透；深深感动

[例] The needle pierced the material. 这根针刺穿了织物。

pigment ['pigmənt] n. 色素；颜料

[例] We need the lead-free pigment. 我们需要无铅颜料。

[记] dye n. 染料；v. 染色

pill [pil] n. 药丸；丸剂

[例] The doctor told him to take six pills a day until he fully recovered. 医生嘱咐他每天服六粒药，直到痊愈。

pillar ['pilə] n. 【建】柱子；栋梁，重要的支持者

[例] The roof of the church was supported by stone pillars. 这座教堂的屋顶由石柱支撑着。

pimple ['pimpl] n. 粉刺；脓疱

[例] He has a lot of pimples on his face. 他脸上有很多粉刺。

> pimple 青春（痘）、脸上的小豆豆；dimple 酒涡；mole 痣；freckle 雀斑；wrinkle 皱纹

pinpoint ['pinˌpɔint] v. 精确指示；n. 针尖；极小的事物

[例] His refusal to help simply pinpointed his cowardice. 他拒绝帮助正显示出他的胆小。

pioneer [ˌpaiə'niə] n. 先锋，先驱

[例] His grandfather was one of the pioneers of flying. 他的外祖父是飞行的先驱者之一。

pirate ['paiərit] n. 海盗；盗版者；v. 盗版；掠夺

[例] The terrible pirates attacked a merchant ship. 可怕的海盗袭击了一个商船。

pitfall ['pitfɔːl] n. 陷阱；未料到的危险（或困难）

[例] He gave me advice on how to avoid the pitfalls of the legal process. 他给我提出了建议,告诉我如何避免法律程序中的陷阱。

> Pit 坑;俗语:A fall into a pit, a gain in your wit. 吃一堑,长一智。

pivot ['pivət] n. 枢轴,支点;中心点,重点

[例] The mother is often the pivot of family life. 母亲往往是家庭生活的中心人物。

placement ['pleismənt] n. 放置,安置;布局

[例] The placement of the buttons and knobs in the car is well thought out. 车中按钮和旋钮的布置考虑得很周到。

plagiarism ['pleidʒiərizəm] n. 剽窃,剽窃物

[例] The journal accused the professor of plagiarism. 那种刊物指控这位教授剽窃。

plague [plei] n. 瘟疫

plain [plein] n. 平原,草原;a. 简单的,明白的

[例] He made it plain that he did not like me. 他很明白地说他不喜欢我。

[区别] plane n. 平面,飞机;a. 平的

plastic ['plæstik] n. 塑料,塑料制品;a. 有可塑性的,塑料的

[例] The supermarket used paper bags instead of plastic ones. 这家超市使用纸袋而非塑料袋。

plateau ['plætəu] n. 高原,高地

[例] The atmosphere is thin on the Tibetan plateau. 西藏高原空气稀薄。

> 法语字母组合 eau,借入到英语中仍然保留其拼写,如:plateau 高原,bureau ['bjuərəu](政府机构的)局,tableau ['tæbləu]场面,beau [bəu]纨绔子弟,nouveau [nuː'vəu]暴发户,等。

platform ['plætfɔːm] n. 平台;站台;讲台

[例] He spoke to us from a platform in the school hall. 他站在学校礼堂的讲演台上给我们演讲。

plausible ['plɔːzəbl] a. 似是而非的

[例]Her explanation sounds fairly plausible to me. 我听她的解释似乎合情合理。

plea [pliː] n. 辩解;恳求,请求

[例] Her plea was that she did not see the signal. 她的辩解是说她没看见信号。

[记] make a plea for 主张,请求

pledge [pledʒ] n. 保证,誓言;v. 保证

[例] The unions made a no-strike pledge. 工会保证不会罢工。

plentiful ['plentiful] a. 许多的,大量的

[例] Opportunities to practice the language are plentiful. 练习语言的机会很多。

plight [plait] n. 境况，困境

[例] He began to tell about his plight. 他开始讲述他的困境。

plot [plɔt] n. （小说、戏剧等的）情节；阴谋，（秘密）计划

[例] They are plotting to rob a bank. 他们正在策划抢银行。

plum [plʌm] n. 李子

[例] An ambassadorship is granted as a political plum. 大使职位被视为政治美差。

[记] plum job 美差，肥缺

> 英文中很多水果名称有固定的喻义。如前面学过的lemon；plum比喻最好的东西；peach因其形状优雅比喻出色、优秀的人或物；tomato颜色鲜红外表光洁，比喻迷人漂亮的女人；cherry 樱桃比喻童贞，处女；pepper 辣椒则比喻活力、精力。如：There was a lot of pepper left in the old man. 那位老人依然精力充沛。

plume [plu:m] n. 羽毛；大羽

[例] This is the long plume of a heron in the breeding season. 这是处在繁殖季节的一只鹭的长羽毛。

plummet ['plʌmit] v. 垂直落下，（价格、水平等）骤然跌落

[例] The damaged aircraft plummeted down to earth. 损坏的飞机垂直坠落于地上。

plunge [plʌndʒ] v. /n. 跳入，投入；猛冲

[例] He plunged into the water to save the child. 他跳入水中救小孩。

plus [plʌs] prep. 加上；a. 正的，加的

[例] Intelligence plus wit makes for an interesting person. 智慧加上机智就会造就一个有趣的人。

poet ['pəuit, 'pəuet] n. 诗人

[例] I like plays which are written in poetic form. 我喜欢用诗的形式写成的剧本。

[记] a romantic poet 浪漫主义诗人 /poem n. 诗 /poetic a. 诗的

policy ['pɔlisi] n. 政策，方针

[例] It is the policy of the government to improve education. 改进教育是政府的政策。

polish ['pɔliʃ] v. 擦光，擦亮；使完美，改进

[例] Silver polishes easily with this special cloth. 用这块特殊的布很容易把银擦亮。

poll [pəul] n. 民意测验

[例] A public-opinion poll shows that most people in Taiwan are in favor of the "one country, two systems" policy. 一项民意调查显示，大多数台湾人支持"一国两制"政策。

[记] take a poll 投票表决

英语中的“人头税”叫 poll tax，美国英语叫 head tax。poll 来源于德语，指“人头”。过去人们聚集在一起，一眼望去只能看见人头攒动，只有数人头来计数。时间一长，poll 演变为“投票数，民意测验”。a heavy / light poll 高（低）得票率

pope [pəup] n. 罗马教皇，主教
[例] The election of a new pope is coming. 新教皇的选举即将到来。

popularity [ˌpɔpjuˈlæriti] n. 流行，普及，声望
[例] That record increased the singer's popularity. 那张唱片提升了歌手的声望。
[记] popular a. 流行的；通俗的

porcelain [ˈpɔːslin] n. 瓷器；a. 瓷制的，精美的
[例] The porcelain teacups belong to the shop owner. 这些瓷茶杯是店主的。

pore [pɔː] n. 毛孔；小孔；气孔；v. 熟读，凝视；沉思
[例] The graduates pored over the classified ads in search of a job. 大学毕业生们仔细阅读分类广告栏以寻找工作。

pornography [pɔːˈnɔgrəfi] (=porno) n. 色情文学；色情描写
[例] Two trucks full of hard-core pornography were seized by customs officials today. 今天海关官员查封了装满两卡车的赤裸裸的黄色作品。
[记] pornographic websites 色情网站

portable [ˈpɔːtəbl] a. 手提式的，轻便的，便携的
[例] The portable telephone is very popular now. 现在这种手提电话非常流行。

portfolio [pɔːtˈfəuljəu] n. 文件夹；公事包
[例] She has forgotten her portfolio on a chair. 她把文件夹落在椅子上。
[记] briefcase n. 公文包

字根 port 指“运送 / 港口”。portable 可运送的→便携的；porter 运送之人→脚夫，搬运工；portfolio 搬运纸（folio 指对开纸，对折纸）的东西→公事包。port 作“港口”，如：passport 通过港口必要的东西→护照；transportation 在两个港口间往来→交通，运输（古时交通主要是通过天然河道，船运为主）；opportunity 当船队靠近港口，就可能获得补给，开展贸易，大发一笔→机会。

portion [ˈpɔːʃən] n. 一部分，一份
[例] She only eats a small portion of food. 她只吃分得的一小部分食物。

portray [pɔːˈtrei] v. 描绘，描述
[例] It is difficult to portray feelings in words. 感情很难用言语来描写。
[同义词] depict, describe

pose [pəuz] n. 姿势、姿态；v. 摆姿势
[例] His brave words are merely a pose. 他勇敢的言词仅仅是做样子而已。

ending pose （表演的）结束造型

positive ['pɔzətiv] a. 肯定的；积极的；正的
[例] It was a positive delight to hear her sing so beautifully. 听她美妙的歌声绝对是一种享受。
[反义词] negative

possess [pə'zes] v. 占有，拥有
[例] He possesses two cars. 他有两辆汽车。

possession [pə'zeʃən] n. 所有物，财产；拥有，占有
[例]The portrait was his proudest possession. 那肖像是他最为珍贵的东西。

postage ['pəustidʒ] n. 邮资
[例] Stamps show how much postage has been paid. 邮票表明已付了多少邮资。
[谚] postcode 邮递区号

postgraduate [ˌpəust'grædjuit] n. 研究生
[例] He made up his mind to be a postgraduate. 他决定做一名研究生。

postpone [pəust'pəun] v. 延迟，使延期
[例] We postponed the match from March 5th to March 19th. 我们把比赛从 3 月 5 日推迟到 3 月 19 日举行。

postulate ['pɔstjuleit] v. 假定；推测；n. 假定；假设
[例] The expert has postulated that the cancer can be cured in the next century. 专家们推测在下个世纪癌症将能被治愈。

potent ['pəutənt] a. 有效力的，强有力的
[谚] Beauty is potent, but money is more potent. 美貌固有力，金钱力更大。
[反义词] impotent 无力的；阳痿的

potential [pə'tenʃəl] n. 潜力，潜能；a. 潜在的，可能的
[例] Every seed is a potential plant. 每粒种子都可能长成植物。

pour [pɔː] v. 灌注，倾泻，往…倒；下倾盆大雨
[例] Tears poured from her eyes. 泪水从她眼中涌出。

> downpour n. 倾盆大雨。"倾盆大雨"的表达法很多，比如大家都很熟悉的：It's raining cats and dogs. 字面意思是"雨大得下猫下狗"，出自于北欧神话传说。在北欧神话中，猫狗都是暴风雨之神奥丁 Odin 的侍从，它们一起出动时往往风雨大作。所以猫和狗分别被人们视为大雨和狂风的象征。

poverty ['pɔvəti] n. 贫穷，贫困
[例] Poverty and starvation caused by pollution, desertification and deforestation mean we cannot survive. 由污染、土壤沙化以及乱砍滥伐引起的贫穷和饥饿使我们无法生存下去。
[记] poor a. 贫穷的，可怜的

practical ['præktikəl] a. 实践的，实际的，应用的

[例] He is very practical -- he can make or mend almost anything. 他很能干，他几乎可以制造或修理任何东西。
[反义词] theoretical a. 理论的

preach [priːtʃ] v. 鼓吹
[例] He was always preaching exercise and fresh air. 他总是倡导运动和呼吸新鲜空气。
[记] preach at/to sb. 对某人谆谆告诫

precaution [priˈkɔːʃən] n. 预防措施
[例] Safety first, precaution crucial. 安全第一，预防为主。

precede [priˈsiːd] v. 领先(于)，在…之前，先于
[例] The host preceded his speech with a welcome to the guests. 主人讲话前先对来客表示欢迎。

precedent [priˈsiːdənt] n. 先例，前例
[例] There is no precedent for this situation. 对这一情况是没有先例的。
[记] preceding a. 在先的；在前的 /the preceding night 前一晚

precise [priˈsais] a. 精确的，准确的
[例] A lawyer needs a precise mind. 律师需要极清楚的头脑。
[记] at that precise moment 恰恰在那个时刻 /precisely adv. 正好，恰恰

predator [ˈpredətə] n. 掠夺者，食肉动物
[例] These predators of the African grasslands live on mice and rabbits. 这些非洲草原上的肉食动物以捕食老鼠、兔子为生。
[反义词] prey n. 被掠食者

predict [priˈdikt] v. 预言，预料，预报
[例] She predicted that he would marry a doctor. 她预言他将娶一位医生。

predominant [priˈdɔminənt] a. 主导的，支配的；占绝大多数的
[例] Which party is predominant in the election? 哪个政党在选举中占上风?
[记] predominate v. 支配，压倒 /predominantly adv. 大多数，主要的

preference [ˈprefərəns] n. 偏爱，优先选择
[例] A teacher should not show preference for any one of his pupils. 老师不应偏爱任何一个学生。

prefix [ˈpriːfiks] n. 前缀
[例] The word appears to consist of prefix and stem. 这单词包括前缀和词干。
[记] suffix n. 后缀 /root n. 词根

pregnant [ˈpregnənt] a. 怀孕的；富有意义的
[例] The health centre provides milk and vitamins for pregnant women.

健康中心为孕妇们提供牛奶和维生素。
[记] get pregnant 怀孕 /pregnancy n. 怀孕

prejudice ['predʒudis] n. 偏见，成见 v. 使存偏见，使有成见
[例] These facts prejudiced them against her. 这些事实促使他们对她有偏见。

> 2004年BBC在英国发起投票，选出对女性影响最大、改变女性世界观的文学作品，Jane Austen的《傲慢与偏见》Pride and Prejudice名列榜首，不可不读。

preliminary [pri'liminəri] a. 预备的，初步的
[例] There are a lot of preliminaries to go through before you can visit Italy. 在你访问意大利之前，有许多准备工作要做。

premise ['premis] n. 前提
[例] If your premise is established, your conclusions are easily deducible. 如果你的前提成立,那么就很容易推断出你的结论了。

premium ['primjəm] n. 保险费；奖金；奖励
[例] He paid premiums on his life insurance last year. 他去年付了人寿保险费。

prerequisite [pri:'rekwizit] n. 先决条件，前提
[例] A sense of humour is prerequisite to understanding her work. 要理解她的作品就必须具有幽默感。

prescribe [pris'kraib] v. 指示，规定；开处方；开药
[例] The doctor prescribed total abstinence. 医生嘱咐病人戒酒。

prescription [pri'skripʃən] n. 处方，药方
[例] What's your prescription for a happy marriage? 你认为幸福婚姻有什么秘方?

> 必须要有医生开的处方才能买到的药叫Prescription Drug 处方药;而不需要医生的处方就可以自己购买的药叫Nonprescription Drug 非处方药，或Over the Counter 可在柜台上买到的药，全球通用简称－OTC。

presence ['prezns] n. 出席，到场；存在
[例] Your presence is a great compliment. 承蒙光临，不胜荣幸。

presentation [ˌprezen'teiʃən] n. 陈述；赠送；表演，演出
[例] There is a presentation of a new play tonight. 今晚有一场新戏演出。
[记] give a presentation of 对…作陈述

preserve [pri'zə:v] v. 维护，保护；保存；n. 果酱；蜜饯
[例] Ice helps to preserve food. 冰有助于保存食物。

press [pres] n. 记者，新闻界；新闻报道；出版社
[例] The power of the press is very great. 新闻界的力量非常大。

> 字根press指“压”。单词press作动词即有“压，压平”的含义；

compress 大家一起压→镇压，压缩；depress 向下压→压下，使沮丧，使萧条；express 挤压出来→表达，快递；impress 压进去→盖印，留下印象。

pressure ['preʃə] n. 压力，压迫
[例] Do not put much pressure on the handle; it may break. 不要在把柄上太用力了，它会坏的。

prestige [pres'tiːdʒ] n. 威望，声望
[例] The old universities of Oxford and Cambridge enjoy a lot of prestige. 历史悠久的牛津大学和剑桥大学享有很高的声望。

presume [pri'zjuːm] v. 假定，假设
[例] I presume from your speech that you are a foreigner. 根据你的谈话，我还以为你是个外国人呢。

prevail [pri'veil] v. 盛行，流行；获胜，占上风
[例] Truth will ultimately prevail. 真理终究会胜利。
[记] prevail over/against 压倒，战胜

prevalent ['prevələnt] a. 普遍的，流行的
[例] The habit of travelling by aircraft is becoming more prevalent each year. 坐飞机旅行一年比一年普遍了。

previous ['priːviəs] a. 以前的，先前的
[例] He has had no previous experience of this kind of job. 他从前没有做这种工作的经验。
[记] previously adv. 以前，先前

prey [prei] n. 被掠食者，牺牲者；v. 捕食，掠夺
[例] Snakes track their prey by its scent. 蛇通过猎物的气味来追踪。
[反义词] predator

primary ['praiməri] a. 主要的，首要的；原来的；初等的；小学的
[例] The primary cause of his failure was his laziness. 他失败的主要原因是懒惰。

prime [praim] a. 最佳的；首要的，首位的
[例] Spring is the prime time for planting trees. 春天是植树的最好时间。
[记] the prime minister 首相 /prime time（广播、电视的）黄金时间 / primer 启蒙读本

primitive ['primitiv] a. 原始的，远古的
[例] Primitive man made tools from sharp stones and animal bones. 原始人用尖石块和动物的骨头制造工具。

principal ['prinsəp(ə)l] a. 主要的，首要的；n. 负责人；中（或小）学校长
[例] Once the principal contradiction is grasped, all problems will be readily solved. 一旦抓住了主要矛盾,一切问题就迎刃而解。

principle ['prinsəpl] n. 原则，原理；（行为）准则
[例] On the basis of the five principles for peaceful coexistence there can be a reasonable dialogue between any two governments. 以和平共处的

五项原则为基础任何两国政府间都可以进行合理的对话。

prior ['praiə] a. 在先的，在前的

[例] I have a prior engagement and so can't go with you. 我预先有约会，所以不能跟你去。

[记] prior to 在…之前

priority [prai'ɔriti] n. 优先考虑的事，优先（权）

[例] The highest priority of governments has been the problem of heavy traffic. 政府已经优先考虑交通拥挤的问题。

[记] prioritize v. 以优先顺序安排处理

privacy ['praivəsi] n. 隐私；独处

[例] We must respect other's privacy. 我们应该尊重别人的隐私。

> 字根 priv 指“私有的”。private 私人的；privatise 民营化，使私有化；privilege 限于一个人的法律（字根 leg 指法律）→特权；deprive 从个人处夺走→剥夺。

privilege ['privilidʒ] n. 特权

[例] The privilege was abused. 这一特权被滥用了。

prize [praiz] n. 奖赏，奖金，奖品；v. 珍视，重视

[例] We prize honor above money. 我们珍视荣誉甚于金钱。

probe [prəub] n. 探针，探测器；v. 探查，查明

[例] She tried to probe my mind and discover what I was thinking. 她试图探查我的心意,想知道我在想什么。

procedure [prə'siːdʒə] n. 手续，步骤，程序

[例] The new work procedure is a great improvement on the old one. 新工序比起老工序来是一个巨大的改善。

proceed [prə'siːd] v. 继续进行

[例] The interview proceeded in a most friendly atmosphere. 会见在极友好的气氛中进行。

> 前缀 pro- 常见含义为“向前”和“在...之前”。如：proceed 向前走（ceed=go）；prolong 向前长→延长；produce 向前引出→生产；prohibit 在习惯 habit 形成之前→禁止。

process ['prəuses] n. 过程，进程

[例] The firm is now in the process of moving the main equipment to a new place. 公司目前正在把主要设备迁到新地址去。

produce [prə'djuːs] v. 生产；产生

[例] That factory produces cars. 那家工厂生产小汽车。

productivity [ˌprɔdʌk'tiviti] n. 生产力；生产率

[例] The factory is looking for ways of improving productivity. 工厂正设法提高生产率。

Unit 22

professional [prə'feʃənl] n. 专业人员；a. 专业的，职业的
[例] For professional footballers, injuries are an occupational hazard. 对于职业足球运动员来说,受伤是职业本身带来的危险。
[记] profession n. 职业，专业 /professor n. 教授

proficiency [prə'fiʃənsi] n. 熟练，精通
[例] You need some proficiency in book – keeping for this job. 干这项工作你需要会熟练记账。

profile ['prəufail] n. 侧面；概况；人物简介
[例] Her beautiful profile impressed the audience very much. 她漂亮的侧面轮廓给观众留下很深的印象。

profit ['prɔfit] n. 利润，赢利；收益；v. 得益
[例] This new invention will bring you great profits. 这项新发明会像一座金矿一样给你们带来利润。

profound [prə'faund] a. 深刻的，极深的
[例] We had a profound lesson in ideological education yesterday. 昨天我们上了一堂深刻的思想教育课。

programme ['prəugræm](=program) n. 方案，程序；节目；v. 编程序；安排节目
[例] There was an interesting programme on TV yesterday. 昨天有个很有趣的电视节目。
[记] programmer n. 【计】程序员

progress ['prəugres] n. /v. 前进，进步
[例] The building of the largest bridge across a river in Asia is in progress. 这座亚洲最大的跨江大桥正在建设中。
[记] in progress 正在进展中

prohibit [prə'hibit] v. 禁止，阻止
[例] Smoking is strictly prohibited in the process of handling explosive materials. 在处理易爆物时,严格禁止吸烟。
[记] prohibit sb. from doing sth. 禁止某人做某事

project ['prɔdʒekt] n. 项目；计划，方案
[例] It is an elaborate project that answers many purposes. 这是一项适用于多方面需要的精心完成的设计。
[记] overhead projector 幻灯机，投影仪

proliferate [prəu'lifəreit] v. 增生扩散
[例] They suffer from the fears that nuclear weapons might proliferate . 他们忍受着核武器扩散引起的恐慌的折磨。
[记] prolific a. 多产的；丰富的

prolong [prə'lɔŋ] v. 延长

[例] We must prolong the runway of the airfield. 我们必须加长机场跑道。

prominent ['prɔminənt] a. 突出的，显著的，卓越的

[例] A single tree in a field is prominent . 田地里一棵孤零零的树是很显眼的。

> 单词 eminent 表示“出来，伸出”，基本含义为“在众多竞争者或同类中脱颖而出”，作为形容词引申含义为“卓越的、杰出的”。而 prominent 在前边又加上了“pro”，进一步加强了向前突出的意思，因此从表达程度上来讲，prominent 要重于 eminent。

promising ['prɔmisiŋ] a. 大有希望的，有前途的

[例] The weather is promising. 天气可望好转。

promote [prə'məut] v. 促进；提升，晋升

[例] Our teacher has been promoted to headmaster. 我们的老师已被提升为校长了。

[记] promotion n. 促进；晋升；促销

prompt [prɔmpt] v. 促使；使下决心；a. 迅速的，即时的

[例] What prompted you to do such a thing? 什么促使你做出这种事?

prone [prəun] a. 倾向于，易于

[例] Children of poor health are very prone to colds in winter. 体弱的孩子在冬天易患感冒。

[记] prone to 倾向于…

proofread ['pru:fri:d] v. 校正，校对

[例] He has some books which I edited and proofread. 他有几本我编辑校对的书。

[记] proofreader n. 校对者

propel [prə'pel] v. 推动；推进；驱动

[例] His addiction to drugs propelled him towards a life of crime. 他吸毒成瘾促使他走向犯罪的道路。

property ['prɔpəti] n. 所有物，财产；房产；特性

[例] This car is my property. 这车是我的财产。

prophet ['prɔfit] n. （基督教、犹太教、伊斯兰教的）先知

[例] Mohammed is the prophet of the Muslims. 穆罕默德是穆斯林的先知。

> pro- 指“在…之前”，prophet 事先说话（phe）之人→先知。prophecy 预言。

proponent [prə'pəunənt] n. 建议者，支持者

[例] He is one of the leading proponents of the project. 他是这个计划的主要倡议者之一。

[反义词] opponent

proportion [prə'pɔːʃən] n. 比例

[例] This door is narrow in proportion to its height. 这扇门就其高度的比例而言窄了些。

proposal [prə'pəuzəl] n. 提议，建议

[例] The proposal of new terms for a peace treaty has been raised. 缔结和平条约新条款的建议已经提出。

[记] propose v. 提议，建议

prosecute ['prɔsikjuːt] v. 告发，起诉

[例] He was prosecuted for robbery. 他因抢劫而被起诉。

[记] prosecution n. 起诉 / prosecutor n. 原告；起诉人 /[区别] persecute v. 迫害 /persecution n. 迫害

prospect ['prɔspekt] n. 景色，前景；期望；v. 寻找，勘探

[例] There's not much prospect of Mr. Smith's being elected as Congressman. 史密斯先生被选为议员的希望不大。

[记] prospective a. 未来的；预期的 /perspective n. 透视；远景；前景；观点

prosper ['prɔspə] v. 成功；兴旺，繁荣

[例] The coastal areas prasper thanks to overseas trade. 由于海外贸易，沿海地区繁荣兴旺。

[记] prosperity n. 繁荣，昌盛

prosperous ['prɔspərəs] a. 兴旺的，繁荣的，成功的

[例] He ended up being a prosperous businessman. 他最终成为一个成功的企业家。

protein ['prəutiːn] n. 【生】蛋白质；a. 蛋白质的

[例] They were weakened by a diet that was low in protein. 他们日常饮食中蛋白质含量不足，因而身体虚弱。

protest [prə'test] n. /v. 主张，断言，拒付

[例] The tourists protested about the bad service at the restaurant. 旅客们对那家饭店低劣的服务表示不满。

[记] protest against 抗议，反对

protocol ['prəutəkɔl] n. 草案，协议；礼仪

[例] The companies said they would share technology and develop a standard set of communication protocols. 这些公司说，他们将分享技术，开发一套标准的交流协议。

> 前缀 proto- 指 "first"。如：protocol 最先粘上去的→草案，协议；比如计算机网络的 TCP/IP 协议：Internet Protocol 和 Transmission Control Protocol。prototype 第一个形式→原型；prototype horse 始祖马；prototype bird 始祖鸟。

prototype ['prəutətaip] n. 原型；模型

[例] The prototype for a future school building was shown in the library.

未来学校的模型在图书馆中展出。

proverb ['prɔvəːb] n. 谚语，格言

[例] “Don’t put all your eggs in one basket” is a proverb. “切忌孤注一掷”是一句谚语。

provided [prə'vaidid] a. 如果，倘若

[例] They provided their guests with dainties. 他们为客人提供美味食品。

province ['prɔvins] n. 省；（动植物生长的）地区

[例] China is divided into numerous provinces. 中国被分成了许多省份。

provision [prə'viʒən] n. 条款，规定；供应品

[例] Both sides have to act according to the provisions of the agreement. 双方都应按照协议条款办事。

provoke [prə'vəuk] v. 激怒，挑拨；驱使

[例] Mind you, that dog is very dangerous when provoked. 当心，那条狗被激怒时是很危险的。

[记] thought-provoking a. 引起思考的，发人深省的

proximity [prɔk'simiti] n. 接近，邻近

[例] Our school buildings are in close proximity to each other. 我们学校的房子一座挨着一座。

[记] in the proximity of 在…附近 /proximate a. 接近的

psychology [sai'kɔlədʒi] n. 心理学

[例] The professor is a specialist in studying a criminal’s psychology. 这位教授是位研究罪犯心理的专家。

> psycho- 表示“灵魂，精神”，源于一则美丽的古罗马传说：凡人少女Psyche和爱神丘比特Cupid相恋，每晚在一座宫殿里相会。Cupid一再嘱咐不要探究他的身份，不要窥看他的容貌。Psyche忍不住好奇，一天夜里在他熟睡时点上蜡烛偷看，方知与她相爱之人竟是众神中最俊美的爱神。她惊喜交加，手不禁一颤，一滴烛油滴落，Cupid顿时惊醒，旋即离去，从此不见。Psyche悲恸欲绝，悔恨不已，开始四处漂泊，寻找情人。后经历了无数劫难之后终于与Cupid重聚，结为夫妇，并成为灵魂、精神之神。送给大家一句话：Love could not dwell where there is no trust. （Cupid离开Psyche时如是说）

publication [ˌpʌbli'keiʃən] n. 出版物；出版，发行

[例] The collection of the theses is ready for publication. 这本论文集已准备好可以出版了。

[记] public n. 公众；a. 公众的

publicity [pʌb'lisiti] n. 引起公众关注；宣传

[例] There has not been much publicity about this conference at the top

level. 对这次高级会议没有作什么宣传。
[记] seek publicity 求名，出风头

publish ['pʌbliʃ] v. 公布；出版，发行
[例] News of the general's sudden death was not published for several days. 那个将军突然死亡的消息有好几天没有公布。

pulse [pʌls] n. 脉搏，脉冲
[例] The doctor felt her pulse on her wrist. 医生在她的手腕上号脉。
[记] impulse n. 冲动，刺激；v. 推动

pump [pʌmp] n. 泵，抽水机；打气筒；v. (用泵)抽，抽吸；打气
[例] A bicycle pump puts air into the tires. 自行车打气筒把空气打进轮胎里。

punctual ['pʌŋktjuəl] a. 准时的，守时的
[例] Try and be punctual. 要努力遵守时间。

> 以下单词都源自拉丁文 *punctum*，意思是"点，point"。puncture 刺一个点→刺破，小孔；acupuncture 针灸；punctuate 加标点，强调；punctual 遵守时间上的一点→准时的；punch 打孔，拳打，殴打。上班打卡是 punch in，下班打卡是 punch out，都在卡上打上一点或一个小孔作记号。

purchase ['pə:tʃəs] v. /n. 购买
[例] The new couple spent some money purchasing of the furniture necessary for their new house. 这对新婚夫妇花了一些钱购买新房子里必需的家具。

purity ['pjuəriti] n. 纯洁，纯净
[例] A lily symbolizes purity. 百合花象征纯洁。
[记] purify v. 使纯净，净化 /purified water 纯净水

pursuit [pə'sju:t] n. 追求；追赶；工作，事业
[例] They did all this for the pursuit of profit. 他们所做的这些都是为了追求利润。
[记] the pursuit of higher education 追求高等教育 / in pursuit of 追踪；追求

puzzle ['pʌzl] n. 难题；谜；v. (使)迷惑，(使)为难
[例] It's a puzzle where all my money goes each week. 我感到迷惑，不知道每星期的钱都到哪儿去了。

pyramid ['pirəmid] n. 金字塔；棱椎
[例] The ancient pyramids in Egypt are one of the world wonders. 古埃及金字塔是世界奇迹之一。
[记] Pharaoh n. 法老 /mummy n. 木乃伊

quadruple ['kwɔdrupl] a. 四倍的；n. 四倍；v. （使）成四倍
[例] Our profits have quadrupled in ten years. 10 年里我们的利润翻了两番。

quake [kweik] v. 震动，颤动；n. 地震
[例] The ground quaked under his feet. 大地在他的脚下震动。
[记] earthquake 地震

qualification [ˌkwɔlifiˈkeiʃən] n. 资格，资历，条件；资格证明
[例] What qualifications have you got to apply for this job? 申请这个工作你所具有的条件是什么？

qualify [ˈkwɔlifai] v. 使适合，使胜任；使具有资格
[例] Do you qualify for the vote? 你有投票资格吗？

qualitative [ˈkwɔlitətiv] a. 性质的; 定性的
[例] We need both qualitative and quantitative analysis. 我们需要做定性和定量分析。

quality [ˈkwɔlifai] v. 使适合，使胜任；使具有资格
[例] Do you qualify for the vote? 你有投票资格吗？

quarantine [ˈkwɔrəntiːn] v. 隔离；检疫；n. 隔离检疫期
[例] James was quarantined for three weeks when he had scarlet fever. 詹姆士患猩红热后被隔离了三个星期。

> 4 的拉丁文数字写法为 quar，quarantine 原指 40 天时间。古代把得了传染病的地区封闭隔离起来40 天，叫 quarantine。为什么是40 天呢？ 40 是一个神圣的数字，《圣经》中上帝降洪水，暴雨 40 天 40 夜；摩西带领犹太人出埃及，穿越沙漠，历时 40 年；摩西在西奈山接受十诫，40 天；基督在荒野斋戒 40 天，所以早期罗马天主教徒的苦行期也定为 40 天。

quarrel [ˈkwɔrəl] v. /n. 吵架, 争论
[例] We had a quarrel about money. 我们因为钱的问题争吵起来。
[记] quarrel with 跟…吵架

quartz [kwɔːts] n. 石英
[例] Have you bought the quartz clock? 你把石英钟带来了吗？

> 也和 4 有关：石英（SiO_2 二氧化硅）是四面体的晶体造型。

query [ˈkwiəri] n. /v. 疑问，询问
[例] I have several queries about the work you gave me. 我有几个问题是关于你给我的工作的。

questionnaire [ˌkwestʃəˈnɛə] n. 调查表，调查问卷
[例] Of nearly 5,000 questionnaires that were sent out, only 428 were returned. 发出近 5000 份问卷，只收回了 428 份。

queue [kjuː] v. 排队（等候）；n. （排队等候的）队列
[例] We had to queue for hours to get in. 我们必须排几个小时的长队才能进去。

> 法语词。原指“尾巴”，后指“辫子”。queue up at the box office 在售票处排队，就是在售票窗口外组成一条长长的尾巴。美国

英语中“排队”是 Please stand in line.

quit [kwit] v. 放弃；离开；辞职

[例] He has not quit smoking, but has cut down to three cigarettes a day. 他并没有戒烟,但是已减到每天只抽三支烟了。

quiz [kwiz] n. 问答比赛；小测验，小考

[例] The quiz was a good opportunity for the exhibition of his knowledge. 这次测验是他显示知识的好机会。

据说 quiz 一词由一家剧院经理所创。他同别人打赌说他可以在一夜之间造出一个新的、毫无意义的、人们却又不能不接受的词。他花钱雇了一些顽童，连夜在城中的每一面墙壁上用粉笔写上“quiz”的字样。第二天一早，人们发现了这个词，但谁也不知道它的意思，争相打听。于是这个毫无词义的“quiz”不久就有了“智力测验”、“恶作剧”等词义。

quota ['kwəutə] n. 配额, 限额

[例] No boat is allowed to catch more than its quota of fish. 任何船都不允许捕获超过限量的鱼。

quote [kwəut] v. 引用，引述；报价 n. 引号

[例] The author frequently quoted Shakespeare. 作者经常引用莎士比亚作品里的话。

[记] in quotes 在引号中 / quotation n. 引用语, 价格, 行情表

race ['reis] n. 赛跑，速度竞赛；人种，种族

[例] The horse is racing against five others. 这匹马正在和其他5匹马比赛。

[记] the human race 人类

radiate ['reidieit] v. 辐射；发散；传播

[例] Four avenues radiate from the square. 四条林荫大道从那广场向四方延伸。

[记] radiation n. 发射；辐射

radical ['rædikəl] a. 激进的；根本的

[例] His opinions are very radical. 他的观点很偏激。

[记] radicalism n. 激进主义 /radically adv. 根本上；以激进的方式

radius ['reidjəs] n. (圆的)半径

[例] They searched within a radius of one mile of the school. 他们在学校周围 1 英里内寻找。

[记] diameter 直径

rage [reidʒ] n. 盛怒，狂怒

[例] My father was in a rage last night. 我父亲昨天晚上十分生气。

[记] be the rage 流行，风靡一时 /in a rage 一怒之下

road rage 开车嚣张，无视交通法规，对他人造成威胁的驾驶行为。air rage 坐飞机时闹事，或对 stewardess（空中小姐）找茬的行为。这种人就是 air-rage passengers。如打电话时遇到自动语音服务系统：找某分公司请拨 1，某部门再拨 12，然后一段音乐…phone rage。

ragged ['rægid] a. 破旧的

[例] A man in ragged clothes was begging on the corner. 一名衣着破烂的男人在角落里乞讨。

[记] be run ragged 因过度使用而破旧 /[同义词] shabby

raid [reid] n. 突袭，袭击

[例] A security guard was killed in the car raid. 这次汽车劫案中有一名保安遇害。

raincoat ['reinkəut] n. 雨衣

[例] He had no raincoat on when the rain started. 开始下雨时他没穿雨衣。

random ['rændəm] a. 随机的，任意的 n. 随意，任意 adv. 胡乱地

[例] The winning numbers are drawn at random. 中奖数字是随意抽取的。

[记] randomly adv. 随便地 /at random 随便地；碰运气地；随机存取

range ['reindʒ] v. 把…分类，使成系列 n. 行列，一系列；范围；山脉

[例] Prices ranged from 5 dollars to 10 dollars. 价格自五美元至十美元不等。

[记] in range 在射程内 /in the range of 在…范围内，在射程内 /ranger 在一定范围内走来走去的人→巡逻者。

ranking ['ræŋkiŋ] n. 排名，地位，等级

[例] She is now fifth in the world ranking. 她现在全世界排名第五。

rash [ræʃ] a. 草率的，鲁莽的

[例] Don't go making any rash decisions about your future. 不要对你的未来作任何草率的决定。

[记] a rash decision 轻率的决定

rate [reit] n. 比率，率；速度

[例] The rate of inflation decreased to 10% last year. 去年通货膨胀率降低为百分之十。

ratio ['reiʃiəu] n. 比（率）

[例] The ratios of 1 to 3 and 30 to 90 are the same. 1 与 3 之比和 30 与 90 之比相同。

[记] in direct ratio 按正比例 /in inverse ratio 按反比例

rational ['ræʃənl] a. 理性的，合理的；推理的；n. 【数】有理数

[例] Man is a rational being. 人类是有理性的动物。

[记] a rational suggestion 合理的建议 /rationality 合理性

raw [rɔː] a. 天然的，未加工的；（数据等）原始的

[例] Many people don't like to eat oysters raw. 许多人不喜欢生吃牡蛎。

[记] raw material 原料

> raw talent 未加工的天才。相当于中文里说某人是一块璞玉，有很好的天赋，但有待雕琢磨炼，将来可成大器。

razor ['reizə] n. 剃刀；v. 剃

[例] He razored his face clean of his beard. 他用剃刀将脸上的胡须刮干净。

[记] electric razor 电动剃须刀 /eraser 橡皮擦

react [ri'ækt] v. 作出反应，反应

[例] An acid can react with a base to form a salt. 酸和碱起化学反应成盐。

[记] react on 对…起作用 /react to 对…作出反应 /reaction n. 反应，反作用

realistic [riə'listik] a. 现实的，实际的

[例] She gave us a realistic appraisal of our chances. 她对我们的机会做了一个实际的评估。

reality [ri(ː)'æliti] n. 真实，事实

[例] Your observations do not seem to be about reality. 你的意见看上去并不实际。

[记] realism n. 现实主义 /realist n. 现实主义者

realm [relm] n. 领域

[例] Such idea only belongs in the realm of science fiction. 这样的理念只适合科幻领域。

[同义词] domain, field, range, region

reap [riːp] v. 收割，收获

[谚] We reap what we sow. 种瓜得瓜，种豆得豆。

> 英国小说家 Charles Reade 如此理解耕耘和收获：
> Sow a thought, reap an act;
> sow an act, reap a habit;
> sow a habit, reap a character;
> sow a character, reap a destiny.

rear [riə] n. 后部，后面；v. 培养；栽种；饲养

[例]There is a motorcycle at the rear of the house. 房子后面有一辆摩托车。

reasonable ['riːznəbl] a. 合理的；通情达理的

[例] It's not reasonable to expect a child to understand sarcasm. 希望孩子明白讽刺的意义这未免太脱离实际。

[记] reasonably adv. 适度地；相当地 /reasoning n. 推理；a. 推理的

reassure [ˌriːəˈʃuə] v. 使安心，使放心，安慰

[例] When the child was afraid in the storm, his parents reassured him. 孩子害怕风暴时，他的父母安慰他。

recall [riˈkɔːl] v. 回忆，回想起；召回

[例] Recall the misery of the past and contrast it with the happiness of today. 想想过去的苦,比比今天的甜。

recede [riˈsiːd] v. 后退，倒退；变模糊

[例] His hair is beginning to recede from his forehead. 他的头发开始从前额往后秃了。

receipt [riˈsiːt] n. 发票，收据；收到

[例] When you have paid for something, a receipt is given to you. 当你付了某样东西的钱时，你就会拿到收据。

reception [riˈsepʃən] n. 前台，接待处；接待；欢迎会

[例] Leave your key at the reception. 你把钥匙留在接待处。

[记] receptionist 前台接待员

recession [riˈseʃən] n. （经济）衰退

[例] This country was in a trade recession. 这个国家处于贸易萧条时期。

recipe [ˈresipi] n. 烹饪法，食谱；秘诀

[例] In the recipe, it says that I must use two eggs. 这个食谱上说我必须用两个鸡蛋。

recital [riˈsaitl] n. 独奏会，独唱会；叙述，背诵

[例] His violin recital wasn't as good as they had hoped. 他的小提琴演奏会不像他所希望的那样好。

Unit 23

reckless ['reklis] a. 不计后果的

[例] Such reckless spending is a crime. 如此挥霍是一种罪恶。

[记] be reckless of 不注意

reckon ['rekən] v. 估计，判断；以为，认为

[例] We reckon on your support. 我们希望得到你的支持。

recognize ['rekəgnaiz] v. 认识，辨认出；正式承认，认可

[例] I recognized Peter although I hadn't seen him for 10 years. 虽然我有10年没看到彼得了，但我认出了他。

recollect [ˌrekə'lekt] v. 记起，想起

[例] I recollect hearing his speech then. 我记得那时候听过他的演说。

[同义词] recall, remember

> 字根lect指"集合to gather"。如：collect一起集合→收集；recollect重新收集到一起→记起，想起；lecture 把大家集合到一起→演讲；lecturer 演讲者；select 把集合在一起的分离出来(se-=apart)→挑选；neglect 没有加入集合→忽视，漏做。

recommend [ˌrekə'mend] v. 推荐，介绍；劝告，建议

[例] I recommend you to wait. 我劝你等一等。

recommendation [ˌrekəmen'deiʃən] n. 推荐，推荐信，介绍信；建议

[例] They bought the car on his recommendation. 他们因他的推荐而买了这辆车。

reconcile ['rekənsail] v. 使和解，使和谐，使顺从；和解

[例] The estranged couple were reconciled after a year. 翻脸的那对夫妻一年以后又和好了。

[记] be reconciled with sb. 同某人言归于好

recover [ri'kʌvə] v. 重新得到；恢复（健康、知觉、情绪等），使复原

[例] She soon recovered herself and stopped crying. 她很快就恢复了常态，不哭了。

[记] recovery n. 恢复，痊愈，防御

recreation [ˌrekri'eiʃən] n. 消遣，娱乐

[例] He is in charge of recreation. 他负责娱乐活动。

> Recreation Ground/Amusement Park 游乐场，猜猜对应的英语单词：过山车，碰碰车，摩天轮，旋转木马。都是现在小学四年级英语课本下册收录的词汇：roller coaster, bumper car, Giant Wheel, merry-go-round。

recruit [ri'kru:t] v. 招募；n. 新兵；新成员

[例] They are recruiting new staff. 他们正在招募新人。
[记] recruitment n. 招聘；征募新兵

rectangle ['rektæŋgl] n. 长方形，矩形
[例] The plate itself is a small rectangle of metallic material. 这只盘子本身就是个小长方形，是用金属材料做的。

rectify ['rektifai] v. 纠正，矫正，改正
[例] I hope I can find a way to rectify your opinion of my behavior. 我希望能设法使你改变对我行为的看法。

recycle ['ri:'saikl] v. 使再循环；回收利用，反复应用
[例] I plan on recycling old warehouses as condominiums. 我打算把旧仓库改建成公寓。

> cycle 循环，轮转。mono 单一 +cycle 轮→ monocycle 独轮车；bi 二 +cycle 轮→两轮车→ bicycle 自行车；tri 三 +cycle 轮→ tricycle 三轮车；motorcycle 摩托车；cyclist 骑自行车或摩托车的人；re-重来 +cycle 循环→ recycle 回收利用。

redeem [ri'di:m] v. 赎回；挽回；补偿
[例] You botched the last job but can redeem yourself on this one. 你把上次的工作搞糟了，但可以通过这次的工作挽回声誉。
[记] to redeem one's promise 履行诺言

reduce [ri'dju:s] v. 减少，缩小；降低
[例] They've reduced the prices in the shop, so it's good time to buy . 商店已经降低了商品的价格，看来现在是买东西正合适。

redundant [ri'dʌndənt] a. 多余的
[例] As the economy weakens, more and more workers will be made redundant. 随着经济疲软，越来越多的岗位不得不裁员。
[记] redundancy n. 冗余

reef [ri:f] n. 暗礁，珊瑚礁
[例] They look as although they belong in a warm and sunny tropical coral reef rather than the dark and cold abyss. 看来它们适合温暖阳光的热带珊瑚礁，而不是阴暗寒冷的深渊。

reel [ri:l] v. 旋转，眩晕；n. 卷轴；(磁带等的)一盘
[例] My head reeled with the facts and figures. 我的脑子被一堆事实和数据搞得一片混乱。
[记] reel off 熟练地、一口气地背出

reference ['ref(ə)rəns] n. 证明；参考；提及，涉及
[例] When I was looking for a job, I asked my head teacher to give me a reference. 我找工作时，向我的班主任要了一份关于我情况的证明。

> Letter of Recommendation 表达同一含义，英联邦国家喜欢用 Reference，北美则倾向用Letter of Recommendation。

refine [ri'fain] v. 提炼，精炼，精制

[例] Reading good books helps to refine one's speech. 阅读好的书籍有助于一个人的言谈文雅。

reflect [ri'flekt] v. 反射；反映；反省

[例] A mirror reflects a picture of you when you look in it. 当你照镜子时，镜子映出你的形象。

[记] reflection n. 反射；映象；倒影

reform [ri'fɔːm] n. /v. 改革，改进

[例] He promised to reform if given another chance. 他答应只要再给他一个机会就一定改过。

[记] the reform and opening-up policy 改革开放的政策

refreshing [ri'freʃiŋ] a. 消除疲劳的，提神的；令人耳目一新的

[例] This dish tastes very refreshing. 这道菜很爽口。

[记] refresh v. 更新 /refreshment n. 点心，饮料

refund [riː'fʌnd] n. /v. 退款

[例] We can refund the price difference. 我们可以退还差价。

refuse [ri'fjuːz] v. 拒绝，谢绝

[例] Joan's mother refused to consent to let her go abroad. 琼的母亲不答应让她出国。

[记] refusal n. 拒绝，推却

refute [ri'fjuːt] v. 驳斥，反驳

[例] I refuted him easily. 我很容易就驳倒了他。

[记] refute one's argument / claim 驳斥某人的论点 / 说法

regard [ri'gɑːd] n. 敬爱，尊重；问候；方面；v. 看待

[例] You can't regard him as a friend but a business associate. 你不能把他看作朋友，他只是个生意合伙人。

[记] in/with regard to 关于

regarding [ri'gɑːdiŋ] prep. 关于，至于，就…而论

[例] I wrote a letter regarding my daughter's school examinations. 我写了一封关于我女儿学校考试的信。

regardless [ri'gɑːdlis] a. 不管，毫不顾及的 adv. 不顾地，不管

[例] I protested, but she carried on regardless. 我极力反对，但她置之不理仍一意孤行。

regime [rei'dʒiːm] n. 政治制度，政权

[例] The regime got rid of most of its opponents. 这一政权铲除了多数反对者。

> 字根 reg 指"统治，管理"。如：regime 政体，政权；region 统治的地区→区域，领域；regular 有管理的，受统治的→有秩序的，规则的；regulate 管理，控制；regulation 规定；irregular 不规则的。

region ['ridʒən] n. 地区，地带，区域

[例] My hometown is in the southern region of China. 我的家乡在中国的南部地区。

[记] regional a. 地方的，区域的

register ['redʒistə] v. 登记，注册，挂号；n. 登记簿

[例] The teacher kept a register of the names of the children. 这个老师保留了一份孩子们的名册。

registration [ˌredʒis'treiʃən] n. 登记，注册，挂号

[例] At the beginning of a new term, every student must complete registration. 新学期一开始，每个学生都必须注册。

regular ['regjulə] a. 定期的，有规律的，经常的

[例] She could hear the regular tick of the clock. 她听得见钟有规律的嘀嗒声。

[记] regularity n. 规律性 /regularly adv. 有规律地，定期地

regulate ['regjuleit] v. 管理，控制，调节

[例] The speed of the machine may be automatically regulated to pace the packing operation by an inner microcomputer. 机器的速度可通过内部的微型电脑自动调节得同包装速度一致。

regulation [ˌregju'leiʃən] n. 规章，规则，规定

[例] The rules and regulations should be made to be manifest to all staff. 规章制度应该让全体员工都明白。

rehearsal [ri'hə:səl] n. 排演，演习

[例] This play will need a lot of rehearsal. 这剧需要多次排演。

[记] in rehearsal 在排演中，在排练中 /dress rehearsal 彩排；预演

reimbursement [ˌri:im'bə:smənt] n. 偿还；赔偿，补偿

[例] Who do I see about reimbursement of travelling expenses? 我该向谁报销旅行费用？

[记] reimburse v. 偿还 /reimburse sb. for a loss 赔偿某人的损失

> 单词 burse=purse 指钱包；re 重新 +im(im-=in)进入 +burse 钱包，把拿出来的钱重新放入钱包→ reimburse 报销；赔偿。

reinforce [ˌri:in'fɔ:s] v. 增援；增强，加强

[例] The news reinforced her hopes. 这个消息增强了她的希望。

reject [ri'dʒekt] v. 拒绝

[例] We rejected his idea for a music club, and decided to have an art club instead. 我们没有采纳他关于成立音乐俱乐部的想法，而是决定成立艺术俱乐部。

related [ri'leitid] a. 有关系的，相关的

[例] She is related to me by marriage. 她和我有姻亲关系。

relatively ['relətivli] adv. 相对地，比较而言

[例]A relatively small number of people disagreed. 不同意的人相对来

说还是比较少的。

relax [ri'læks] v. 使松弛，放松；使轻松，休息

[例] Don't worry about it; just try to relax. 不要为这事担心，放松些。

[记] relaxation n. 放松；消遣

release [ri'li:s] n. 释放，解除；发布

[例] I released the horse and it ran away. 我放了这匹马，让它跑走了。

relevant ['reləvənt] a. 有关的，切题的

[例] Color and gender are hardly relevant when one applies for a job. 申请工作时，肤色和性别几乎与之无关。

[记] relevance n. 中肯，适当 /[反义词] irrelevant

reliable [ri'laiəbl] a. 可靠的，可信赖的

[例] It's not reliable to judge a man only by his looks. 单凭容貌来判断一个人是不可靠的。

[反义词] unreliable

relief [ri'li:f] n. 安慰；减轻，缓解

[例] I felt great relief when I heard I had passed the examination. 听说我已经通过了考试，我如释重负。

religious [ri'lidʒəs] a. 宗教的；虔诚的

[例] Hans was a very religious man. He behaved in a Christian way to all people including his enemies. 汉斯是个虔诚的宗教信徒，所以他用基督教的方式对待一切人，包括他的敌人。

[记] religion n. 宗教

> 字根lig指"绑to bind"。religion就是把自己重新绑回神的身边→宗教，信仰。所以oblige指"去绑"，就有"迫使"的含义。当你对别人施与恩惠，从情感上绑住了对方，也叫oblige，be obliged to sb. 就是"感谢某人"；口语表达"Much obliged!"绑得太多，绑得太紧，当然就是谢谢的意思啦。

reluctance [ri'lʌktəns] n. 不情愿，勉强

[例] She made a great show of reluctance, but finally accepted our offer. 她表现得很不情愿，但最后还是接受了我们的提议。

[记] reluctant a. 勉强的；不愿意的

rely [ri'lai] v. (on, upon)依靠，依赖；信赖

[例] You can't rely on him. 你别信任他。

[记] rely on 依靠; 信任, 信赖

remainder [ri'meində] n. 剩余部分；【数】余数

[例] I will go ahead with three of you, and the remainder can wait here. 我将和你们三个向前走，剩下的人可以在这里等着。

remarkable [ri'mɑ:kəbl] a. 值得注意的；非凡的，卓越的

[例] He has a remarkable memory. 他有惊人的记忆力。

remedy ['remidi] n. 药物，治疗物；补救（法）

[例] Your only remedy is to go to court. 你唯一的补救法是诉诸法律。

remind [ri'maind] v. 提醒，使想起

[例] These photos remind me of my childhood. 这些照片使我想起了我的童年。

remote [ri'məut] a. 遥远的；偏僻的，偏远的

[例] She came from a remote village. 她来自一个偏远的乡村。

[记] remote control n. 遥控器

remuneration [riˌmju:nə'reiʃən] n. 报酬

[例] He received a small remuneration. 他得到少量报酬。

[记] remunerate v. 报酬

render ['rendə] v. 给予，提供；翻译

[例] You have rendered great service. 你们帮了很大的忙。

replace [ri'pleis] v. 代替，取代；替换

[例] We'll get someone or other to replace him. 我们会找别人来代替他。

[记] replace with 以…代替，替换为

replenish [ri'pleniʃ] v. 补充

[例] The music will replenish my weary soul. 音乐使我疲惫的精神充满活力。

represent [ˌrepri'zent] v. 代表着，象征

[例] We chose a committee to represent us. 我们选出一个委员会来作我们的代表。

[记] representative n. 代表；a. 典型的，有代表性的

reproach [ri'prəutʃ] n. 责备，指责

[例] His manners are beyond reproach. 他的举止无可厚非。

reptile ['reptail] n. 爬行动物

[例] It is said that he hates reptiles. 据说他讨厌爬行动物。

[记] reptant a. 匍匐的, 爬行的

> 生命基本单位：protein 蛋白质，gen 基因，cell 细胞；低等水生：fish，shellfish 贝，甲壳类；爬行：reptile，insect 昆虫；飞行 bird；哺乳：mammal，monkey，人：human being。

reputable ['repjutəbl] a. 著名的，享有声望的

[例] Most of the college students hope to work in highly reputable firms. 多数大学生都希望在著名的公司工作。

reputation [ˌrepju'teiʃən] n. 名誉，名气

[例] It is hard to make a good reputation. 取得一个好名声是很难的。

[记] have a reputation for/of sth. 因…而著名, 以…闻名 /reputed a. 有名气的

request [ri'kwest] n. /v. 要求，请求

[例] We shall give your request our careful consideration. 我们将仔细考虑你的要求。

require [ri'kwaiə] v. 需要；命令，规定

[例] You are required by law to wear a seat belt. 法律规定你要系安全带。

[记] requirement n. 需求，要求，必要条件

rescue ['reskjuː] v. 拯救，营救；救援

[例] We rescued the boy who fell into the river. 我们救起了掉进河里的小孩。

research [ri'səːtʃ] n. 研究，调查；探索

[例] It is a good idea to do some research before you buy a house. 买房子之前作些调查，这个主意不错。

resemblance [ri'zembləns] n. 相似，类似

[例] There was a distant resemblance between them. 他俩有隐约相似的地方。

resemble [ri'zembl] v. 像，与…相似

[例] She resembles her mother in the way she moves her hands when she talks. 她说话时打手势的动作像她妈妈。

> 字根 sembl 指“类似”。assemble 使相似，聚集相似者→集合，聚集；dissemble 使不相似→掩饰，假装；resemble 再次感觉相同→相似。

reserve [ri'zəːv] n. 储备（物），储备金；v. 预定；保留；储备

[例] I have reserved a room for you at the hotel. 我已在旅馆为你预订了一个房间。

reservoir ['rezəvwɑː] n. 水库

[例] This reservoir provides water to the whole city. 这个水库供全城用水。

reside [ri'zaid] v. 居住

[例] That city that I reside in is most beautiful. 我居住的那个城市极其美丽。

[记] residence n. 居住, 住处 /residential a. 住宅的, 与居住有关的

resign [ri'zain] n. 辞去(职务)；v. 辞去, 辞职

[例] Some resigned from the board of directors. 有几个人从董事会中辞职。

[记] resign from 辞职

resignation [ˌrezig'neiʃən] n. 辞职；辞呈

[例] We acquiesced with his resignation. 我们默许了他的辞职。

resist [ri'zist] v. 抵抗，抵御；反抗

[例] She could hardly resist laughing. 她真忍不住要笑。

[记] resistance n. 反抗, 抵抗 /irresistible a. 不可抵抗的

resolution [ˌrezə'ljuːʃən] n. 决定，决议，决心；解决

[例] She's always making good resolutions. 她决心总是下得很好。

resolve [ri'zɔlv] v. 决心，决定

[例] He wes resolved that he would study. 他下定决心要好好学习。

> 字根solv指"松开to loosen"。如：solve 松开→解决，溶解；absolve 去松绑放出来→赦免，免除；dissolve 分解开来(dis-=apart)→溶解，解散；insolvable 不能松开的→不能解决的，无法溶解的；resolve 重新松开恢复原状→分解，溶解，解决，决定。

resort [ri'zɔːt] n. 度假胜地；v. 求助，采用，诉诸

[例] I'm sorry you have resorted to deception. 我很遗憾你竟用欺骗手段。

resource [ri'sɔːs] n. 资源

[例] The local library is a valuable resource. 当地图书馆是一个宝贵的资料库。

respect [ris'pekt] n. /v. 尊敬，敬重

[例] You should know how to respect yourself before you can get respect from others. 你该先知道如何尊重自己然后你才能得到别人的尊重。

[记] respectable a. 可敬的

respond [ris'pɔnd] v. 回答，响应，作出反应

[例] I offered him a drink but he didn't respond. 我请他喝酒，但他没什么反应。

respondent [ris'pɔndənt] n.（民意测验等的）调查对象

[例] Only 60 percent of respondents said they were satisfied. 只有60%的民意测验被调查对象说他们很满意。

response [ris'pɔns] n. 回答，响应

[例] I've had no response to my letter. 我还没有收到回信。

responsible [ris'pɔnsəbl] a. 负有责任的，可靠的，可依赖的

[例] You'll be held personally responsible. 惟你是问。

retain [ri'tein] v. 保持, 保留

[例] Old as she is, she still retains an appearance of youth. 尽管上了年纪，她仍然保有年轻的外貌。

[区别]obtain v. 获得 /contain v. 包含 /maintain v. 维持 /sustain v. 支持

restore [ris'tɔː] v. 恢复；归还；修复

[谚] It's hard to restore a broken mirror. 破镜难重圆。

[记] restore sth. to. . . 把某物还给…

restrain [ris'trein] v. 抑制，遏制

[例] I can't restrain my anger when I hear of people being cruel to animals. 当我听到人们残酷地对待动物时，我抑制不住愤怒。

> 字根strain和strict指"拉紧"。如：strain拉紧，扭伤，紧张；constrain强迫，拘束；overstrain过度紧张，工作过度；strict使拉紧，紧张→严格的，严厉的；constrict一起拉紧→压缩，收缩；restrict往回拉紧→限制，限定；district被拉开的部分→区域，地区，行政区。

restrict [ris'trikt] v. 限制，约束，限定

[例] Don't restrict her proper activities. 不要限制她的正当活动。

[记] restriction n. 限制，约束

result [ri'zʌlt] n. 结果，后果；v. 导致，产生

[例] As a result, there is often trouble in American families. 因此，美国家庭中常常会出现麻烦事。

[记] as a result of 作为…的结果，由于… /result from 由于 /result in 导致

resume [ri'zju:m] n. 摘要；履历；v. 再继续，重新开始

[例] The dog resumed its post by the door. 那只狗再次占据了门边的位置。

résumé [ˌrezju:'mei] n. (求职者等的）简历；摘要

[例] Please send your personal résumé to us before sitting a written test. 参加笔试之前，请将个人简历寄给我们。

retail ['ri:teil] n. 零售 a. 零售的 v. 零售, 转述 adv. 以零售方式

[例] These shoes retail at $ 10. 这鞋零售价是每双 10 美元。

[记] retailing 零售业 /retailer n. 零售商 /wholesaler n. 批发商

retain [ri'tein] v. 保留，保持

[例] This small village still retains its old-world character. 这个小村庄仍然保持着古色古香的特点。

retreat [ri'tri:t] v. /n. 后退，撤退，撤回

[例] They watched his retreating figure. 他们看着他走远的身影。

retrieve [ri'tri:v] v. 重新得到，收回；n. 找回

[例] Henry did his best to retrieve the situation. 亨利尽力挽回局势。

retrospect ['retrəuspekt] n. 回顾

[例] It was, in retrospect, the happiest day of her life. 回想起来，那是她一生中最幸福的日子。

[记] retrospective a. 回顾的

reveal [ri'vi:l] v. 展现, 显示, 暴露

[例] He was glad it was to him that she had revealed her secret. 他很高兴她把自己的秘密告诉了他。

revenge [ri'vendʒ] n. /v. 报仇，复仇

[例] Hamlet sought revenge for his dead father. 哈姆雷特为他死去的父亲报仇。

[记] be revenged on sb./revenge oneself on sb. 向某人报仇

> 古语“报仇”为 venge。所以单词 avenge 和 revenge 都指“报仇”了。从单词构成来看，avenge 中 a-=to，指“对（向）某人报仇”；revenge 中 re-=again，指“再一次报仇”。好比你上次找我报了仇，这次我还要再一次报复回来。颇有冤冤相报何时了的味道。好词！ avenger n. 复仇者。

revenue ['revinju:] n. 收入；国家的税收

[例] State universities in the U. S. get most of their revenue from taxes. 在

美国的州立大学大部分收入是靠税款。

reverse [ri'və:s] v. 颠倒；改变；n. 相反，对立面；a. 相反的，颠倒的；

[例] He is reversing the car. 他正在倒车

[记] reversal n. 颠倒

Unit 24

review [ri'vjuː] n. /v. 回顾；复习；评论

[例] We must make a careful review of political events. 我们必须谨慎地回顾政治事件。

revise [ri'vaiz] v. 修订，校订，修改

[例] He was revising what he had written. 他正在修改他所写的东西。

[记] revision n. 修订，校订，修改

revive [ri'vaiv] v. (使)苏醒；(使)复兴；(使)复活

[例] The fresh air soon revived him. 新鲜空气使他很快就苏醒过来了。

revolution [ˌrevə'luːʃən] n. 革命运动；旋转

[例] The army officers led a revolution against the king. 军官们领导了一次反对国王的革命。

reward [ri'wɔːd] n. 报酬，奖品，奖金；v. 报答，酬谢，奖励

[谚] Virtue is its own reward. 善即善报，为善最乐。

[记] reward sb. for sth. 为某事报答某人 /as a reward for 作为(对某事的)报酬

rhythm ['riðəm] n. 节奏，韵律

[例] I can't dance to music without a good rhythm. 没有好的节奏我不能跟着音乐跳舞。

> 整个单词里只有一个元音字母“y”，要注意它的读音。目前较流行的音乐曲风 R&B 指的就是“Rhythm and Blues”，即“节奏布鲁斯”；其形容词形式为 rhythmical。

ribbon ['ribən] n. 缎带，丝带，带子

[例] Her hair was tied up with a ribbon. 她的头发用一条丝带扎着。

riddle ['ridl] n. 谜，谜语

[例] See if you can solve this riddle. 看看你是否能解开这个谜。

> 除了人人皆知的 Sphinx's riddle 外，Plato 的《理想国》*The Republic* 中也有个著名的 riddle：
> A man who's not a man
> Saw but didn't see a bird that wasn't a bird
> Sitting on a branch that wasn't a branch
> And hit him but didn't hit him
> With a rock that wasn't a rock.
> 一个不是男人的男人看见又没看见，用一块不是石头的石头打又没打，一只站在不是树枝的树枝上的不是鸟的鸟。(这是一个什么场景？猜猜。) *

ridge [ridʒ] n. 背脊；屋脊；山脊，山脉；v. 起皱

[例] The ridges of the European and American nose are taller than those of the Chinese. 欧美人的鼻梁比中国人的要高些。

ridiculous [ri'dikjuləs] a. 荒谬的，可笑的

[例] Who made this ridiculous rule? 这条荒唐的规则是谁定的?

rigid ['ridʒid] a. 固执的；严格的；刚硬的

[例] Old men are always very rigid in their ideas. 老人的想法总是十分固执。

rigorous ['rigərəs] a. 严格的，严厉的，一丝不苟的

[例] We should follow rigorous discipline. 我们必须遵守严格的纪律。

[同义词] rigid, severe, strict

rim [rim] n. （圆形物的）外缘，边缘

[例] Mike liked the golden rims of his glasses very much. 麦克很喜欢眼镜的金色镶边。

ripe [raip] a. 熟的；时机成熟的

[例] This fruit isn't ripe yet. We can't eat it. 这水果还没有熟，我们不能吃。

risk [risk] n. 危险性，风险

[例] He took a risk when he crossed the old bridge. 他冒险过了这座旧桥。

[记] at risk 有危险 /at one's own risk 自担风险

ritual ['ritjuəl] n. 典礼,(宗教)仪式；a. 典礼的；(宗教)仪式的

[例] My household chores have become a morning ritual. 家务已经成了我早晨的例行公事。

rival ['raivəl] n. 竞争者，对手；v. 竞争

[例] She and I are rivals for the swimming prize. 我和她是游泳比赛奖项的竞争对手。

[记] rivalry n. 竞争，敌对状态

> rival和river有些渊源。rival来自拉丁语rivalis，意为“住在河对岸的人，共饮一江水的人”。不是表达“我住长江头，君住长江尾。日日思君不见君，共饮长江水”的相思情意，而是指一种原始的竞争关系。古往今来，一江一河的占用权、用水权、捕鱼权曾使多少近邻变成了竞争对手。

roar [rɔː] v. 吼叫，呼啸

[例] You need not roar. 你不必那么大声嚷嚷。

robust [rə'bʌst] a. 强壮的，强健的

[例] His robust strength was a counterpoise to the disease. 他身体强壮抵住了这疾病。

rock-bottom ['rɔk'bɔtəm] a（物价、贫困等的）最低点，最低水平

[例] Prices have reached the rock bottom. 价格降到了最低点。

role [rəul] n. 角色，作用，任务

[例] He played the role of the old king in our school play. 他在我们学校演的剧中扮演老国王的角色。

romantic [rə'mæntik] a. 浪漫的，充满传奇色彩的

[例] His memoirs were criticized as offering a fascinating but thoroughly romantic view of the past. 他的回忆录被指责为展示了过去美丽的向往但完全是虚构的。

> romantic, romance都是从roman (罗马人)一词变化而来。romance最初指罗马人广为流传的一首歌曲或一则传奇故事。内容大都是描写骑士为了心中的爱人甘愿奉献一切。于是romance就转化为“风流传奇”、“浪漫文学”等含义，中文音译“罗曼史”；而romantic 音译为“罗曼蒂克”。

roster ['rəustə] n. 花名册，登记表

[例] He is on the roster for tomorrow night. 他在明晚活动的名单上。

rotate [rəu'teit] v. （使）旋转，（使）转动

[例] You can rotate the wheel with your hand. 你可用手转动轮子。

rough [rʌf] a. 粗糙的，粗略的，大致的

[例] The monkey’s skin has a rough feel. 猴子的皮肤有一种粗糙感。

rouse [rauz] v. 唤醒；激励，使振奋

[例] We should rouse ourselves up. 我们要振奋起来。

route [ru:t] n. 路线；途径，渠道

[例] We came by a longer route than usual. 我们走了一条比通常要长的路来的。

routine [ru:'ti:n] n. 例行公事，日常工作，常规；a. 日常的，惯例的

[例] Will you go to the routine meeting instead of me? 你代我去参加这次例会好吗?

row [rəu] v. 划(船); n. 一排，一行

[例] You should learn to row a boat. 你该学习划船。

[反义词] column n. 一栏

royal ['rɔiəl] a. 王室的，皇家的；第一流的；高贵的

[例] Practice is the royal road to success when learning a language. 练习是学习语言的捷径。

[记] royalty n. 皇室，王权

ruin ['ru:in] v. 使毁灭；n. 毁灭；废墟

[例] The storm ruined the crops. 暴风雨毁坏了庄稼。

rumour ['ru:mə] n. (=rumor)流言，谣言

[例] The rumour soon gained currency. 谣言很快传开了。

> 注意拼写：rumour = rumor；humour = humor。联想记忆：rude humour 粗鲁的幽默→rumour 谣言。区别：gossip 流言，八卦。Entertainment and Gossip 就是“娱乐与八卦新闻”。

rural ['rurəl] a. 农村的，乡村的，田园的

[例] Crops are grown in rural areas. 庄稼种在乡村地区。

[反义词] urban a. 城市的

rust [rʌst] v. 生锈；n. 锈，铁锈

[例] If you leave your metal tools outside in the rain, they will rust. 如果你在雨天把金属工具放在外面，它们会生锈的。

[记] rusty a. 生锈的

sacred ['seikrid] a. 神的；神圣的

[例] He considered it a sacred duty to fulfill his dead father's wishes. 他认为实现父亲的遗愿是神圣的义务。

[记] be sacred from 免除，不受

sacrifice ['sækrifais] n. /v. 牺牲；献祭

[例] I would never dream of asking you to make such a sacrifice. 我决没想到要你做出这样的牺牲。

[记] sacrifice A for B 为B而牺牲A /make all sacrifices 不惜一切牺牲 /sacrifice. . . for 为…而牺牲

> 字根 sacr 指“神圣的”。如：sacred 神圣的；sacrifice 使成为神圣的东西→牺牲，献祭。人们相信为信仰奉献生命之后，灵魂和精神将成为神圣的；古代以活人献祭神灵，是最原始的牺牲。

safeguard ['seifˌgɑːd] v. /n. 保护，保卫

[例] Keeping clean will safeguard you against disease. 保持清洁能预防疾病。

[同义词] shield

safety ['seifti] n. 安全，平安

[例] They ran to safety, away from the fire. 他们跑到安全的地方，远离了大火。

saga ['sɑːgə] n. 传奇，长篇英雄传奇

[例] His biography is a saga of scientific expeditions. 他的传记是一部科学探险的纪实。

salad ['sæləd] n. 沙拉

[例] Have some salad. 吃点沙拉吧。

[记] mixed salad 什锦色拉

> 字根 sal 指“盐 salt”。盐在古代被视为珍品，古罗马军队曾发盐给士兵做为薪饷。所以 salary 食盐配额→薪水。desalt 脱盐处理；salted 盐腌的，老练的；salad 被加过盐的→沙拉（生菜加了盐或其他调味品后凉拌，不就是沙拉吗）。

salon ['sælɔːŋ] n. 沙龙

[例] She started a beauty salon near her home. 她在自己家附近开了一家美容院。

[记] a beauty salon 美容院

sample ['sæmpl] n. 样品，样本；v. 抽样调查

[例] Samples are presented free in the company. 本公司样品免费赠送。

sandwich ['sænwidʒ] v. 夹入中间；n. 三明治，夹心面包

[例] I was sandwiched between two fat men. 我被夹在两个胖子中间。

> Sandwich 原为英格兰地名。此地有一伯爵生活荒淫无度，且极为好赌。赌瘾一来便整日整夜坐在赌桌旁，他吩咐仆人在用膳时间只需给他送夹有烤牛肉的夹心面包片。他的赌友们将这种食品戏称为当地土特产：sandwich，从此流传。

sane [sein] a. 心智健全的；理智的

[例] He is a very sane person. 他是一个很有头脑的人。

[反义词] insane

sanitary ['sænitəri] a. 卫生的，清洁的

[例] Hospital operating instruments must be sanitary. 医院的手术器械必须是消过毒的。

[记] sanitation n. 卫生，卫生设施

saturate ['sætʃəreit] v. 使饱和，浸透；使充满

[例] The air was saturated with the perfume of flowers. 空气中充满着花的芬芳。

[记] saturate oneself (in)埋头在…中，精通 /[反义词] unsaturated a. 不饱和的

savage ['sævidʒ] a. 野蛮的，凶猛的；v. 用暴力对付；n. 粗鲁的人

[例] He has a savage temper. 他脾气粗暴。

scaffold ['skæfəld] n. 【建】脚手架；绞刑台

[例] Spacing the scaffolds opens up the tree so light can penetrate, which encourages fruit production. 挪开脚手架让那棵树展开，这样就可以吸收阳光以促进结果。

scale [skeilz] n. 刻度；规模；天平，磅秤；鱼鳞；v. 测量；攀登

[例] A machine for weighing people has a scale from one pound to 300 pounds on it. 称体重的机器上有从 1 磅到 300 磅的刻度。

[记] on a big/large scale 大规模的（地）

> 一词多义，记住"刻度"的含义即可。古人在树上划一道道的刻度，记录自己有多高，那是最原始的"秤，测量"的含义。古人把鱼捞起来一看"哇，这种动物刻痕累累，身体上自带刻度！"要想攀登一座高山，古人没有工具，只能借助山壁上的一道道刻痕，用手扣住石缝往上爬。所以 scale 有"攀登"之意。

scan [skæn] v. /n. 浏览；扫描，反复察看

[例]I usually scan the morning papers while eating breakfast. 我经常吃早饭时浏览晨报。

[记] scanner n. 扫描器 扫描仪

scar [skɑ:] n. 疤痕，伤疤

[例] The wound left a scar. 那伤口留下了一个疤。

scarce [skɛəs] a. 不足的，缺乏的

[例] Many natural materials are becoming scarce. 许多天然原料越来越少。

scarcely ['skɛəsli] adv. 不足地；几乎不，简直没有

[例] He is scarcely trustworthy. 他不值得信赖。

scatter ['skætə] v. 撒，使散开

[例] Don't scatter your strength. 不要分散精力。

scenario [si'nɛəriəu] n. 事态，局面

[例] Imagine a scenario where only 20% of people have a job. 想象一下只有 20% 的人有工作是什么样的局面。

> scenario: 本是一个意大利语戏剧类名词，指剧情说明或歌剧、电影的脚本。英语中的文艺词汇多从意大利语引进，常以o, a结尾。如：aria 咏叹调；diva 歌剧女主角；sonata 奏鸣曲，北京现代轿车索纳塔。

scene [si:n] n. 情景，景色;现场;（戏剧的）一场

[例] The scene is a perfect dream when you see the sun rising slowly in the east. 看着太阳从东方慢慢升起，这种景色确实太美了.

scent [sent] n. 气味；香味 v. 使香

[例] The scent of the flower hung in the air. 花的芳香在空气中荡漾。

sceptical ['skeptikəl] a. 怀疑论的，怀疑的

[例] His attitude towards all religion is sceptical. 他对所有宗教的态度持怀疑态度

schedule [skedʒu:l] n. 时间表，日程安排表

[例] The next thing on our schedule is to telephone our friends. 我们的日程安排中要做的下一件事是给我们的朋友打电话。

[记] ahead of schedule比时间表提前 /behind schedule落后于时间表 / on schedule 按时间表，准时

> 汉语拼音记忆：s（是）+ che（车）+ du（堵）+ le（了），使我不能 on schedule 准时。

scheme [ski:m] n. 计划，方案，谋划

[例] All the schemes and intrigues are doomed to failure. 一切阴谋诡计都是注定要失败的。

scholarship ['skɔləʃip] n. 奖学金；学问，学识

[例] For a few, scholarships were sources of support. 奖学金是少数人接受教育的学费来源。

[记] fellowship 奖学金

scold [skəuld] v. 责骂，斥责

[例] Don't scold the child without reason. 不可无缘无故地责骂小孩。

score [skɔː] n. 分数，成绩

[例] The score in the football game was 4 : 1. 足球比赛的比分是四比一。

> 古义指"二十"。《圣经》上有 three score and ten，即"人生七十古来稀"。古代牧羊人数羊总是二十二十的数，每数二十便在木头上划一凹痕 making a score。后引申为"计数，得分"等含义。

scratch [skrætʃ] n. 乱写；抓痕；擦伤；v. 乱涂；擦；刮；搔

[例] He scratched the insect bite on his leg (with his nails). 他(用指甲)在他腿上搔虫咬的地方。

script [skript] n. 手稿；笔记；剧本；试卷

[例] I received a letter from him in his neat script. 我收到了他一封字迹工整的信件。

[记] scriptwriter n. (电视、电影)脚本作者

scrutinize ['skruːtinaiz] v. 详细检查，仔细审查

[例]The jeweler scrutinized the diamond for flaws. 宝石商人仔细察看钻石有无瑕疵。

[记] scrutiny n. 详细审查

sculpture ['skʌlptʃə] n. 雕刻，雕塑；雕塑品

[例] The college offers classes in sculpture. 学院开设雕塑课。

seal [siːl] n. 海豹；封条；印，图章；v. 密封

[例] We seal the back of envelopes. 我们把信封的背面封上。

secondary ['sekəndəri] a. 中等教育的；第二的，次要的

[例] Price is the most important factor for us — location is a secondary issue. 价格对我们最重要，其次才是场地问题。

[记] a secondary cause 次要原因

section ['sekʃən] n. 部分；片断；章节

[例] One section of the class was reading and the other section was writing. 班上的一部分人在看书，另一部分人在写东西。

> 字根 sect 指"切割"。如：sect 宗教教派，流派；bisect 平分，一分为二；insect 躯体分割成一节一节的→昆虫；intersection 相互切割，纵横切割→ 交叉，十字路口；vivisect 切割活的东西→活体解剖。

sector ['sektə] n. 部分，部门

[例] At the sectors where accidents are most likely to take place, trains always travel at a moderate speed. 在事故好发地段，火车总是以中速行驶的。

secular ['sekjulə] a. 长期的，现世的，物质的，非宗教的

[例] Knowledge is no longer sacred but secular. 知识不再是神圣的而是

为大众所接受的。

secure [si'kjuə] a. 安全的，放心的，无忧虑的
[例] I don't feel secure when I am alone in the house. 我一个人在家时感到不安全。
[记] be secure of 对…有把握，确信

security [si'kjuəriti] n. 安全；债券，证券
[例] The government looks after the security of the country. 政府保障国家的安全。
[记] Security Council (联合国)安全理事会

sediment ['sedimənt] n. 沉淀，沉积；沉积物
[例] The sediment of coffee will settle. 咖啡渣会沉淀下去。

seek [si:k] v. 寻找，寻求，探索
[例] They are seeking the most reasonable diet which will do good to their health. 他们在寻找有益于健康的最合理的饮食。
[记] seek after 寻找，追求

seep [si:p] v. 渗出，渗漏
[例] Rain seeped through the roof. 雨水从房顶往下漏。
[同义词] ooze

segment ['segmənt] n. 部分；切片；片断
[例] Different segments of the panel are painted different colors. 各段护墙板被漆上不同的颜色。
[记] in segments 成段, 分节

segmentation [ˌsegmən'teiʃən] n. 分割
[例] The second way in which imperfect competition can affect trade is through market segmentation. 不完全竞争影响商业的第二种方法是通过市场细分。

segregate ['segrigeit] v. 隔离
[例] The doctor segregated the child sick with scarlet fever. 大夫把患猩红热的孩子隔离起来。
[同义词] separate

seize [si:z] v. 抓取，夺取
[例] Uncontrollable laughter seized us. 我们不由自主地大笑起来。
[记] seize on 猛扑,抓住; 利用

seismic ['saizmik] a. 地震的，地震引起的
[例] The discovery of seismic activity suggests geological activity, which could provide large amounts of heat and minerals. 地震活动的发现表明地质运动可以提供大量的地热和矿物质。

select [si'lekt] v. 选择，挑选，选拔；a. 精选的
[例] They were selected from many applicants. 他们是从许多报名者当中选出来的。
[区别] elect v. 选举

selection [si'lekʃən] n. 选择，挑选，选拔

[例] This shop has a huge selection of contemporary novels. 本店精选大量当代小说出售。

[区别] election n. 选举

semester [si'mestɑ] n. 学期

[例] There are two semesters in a year. 一年中有两个学期。

[同义词] term

> 源于德语，德语中也是写做 semester，指大学里面的一个学期，也就是半个学年。但其实德语是从于拉丁文*semestris*，由sex（六）和 mensis（月）组成，意思是“六个月的时期”。

seminar ['seminɑː] n. 研讨会；讨论课

[例] Why didn't you come to yesterday's seminar? 你昨天讨论课怎么没来?

[记] a seminar course 讨论式的课程 /workshop 实习

> 字根semin指“种子seed”。如：semination播种，传播；disseminate扔下种子→传播，散布；seminar 种子会，孕育思想种子的地方→研讨会。

senior ['siːnjə] n. 大学四年级学生；a. 较年长的，较高级的

[例] He is my senior by three years. 他比我大三岁。

sensational [sen'seiʃənəl] a. 使人感动的, 非常好的

[例] We attended a sensational concert — one never to be forgòtten. 我们参加了一个壮观的音乐会——决不会被忘记的音乐会。

[记] sensation n. 感情；感动，耸人听闻

sensible ['sensəbl] a. 明智的，有判断力的

[例] If you are sensible, you will study for another year. 如果你明智的话，你就再学习一年。

sensitive ['sensitiv] a. 敏感的

[例] She is sensitive to what people think of her. 她对人们对她的看法是很敏感的。

[记] be sensitive to 对…敏感, 易感受…

sensor ['sensə] n. 传感器

[例] Place the sensor on a flat surface and rotate it slowly through 360°. 把传感器放在一个平面上慢慢转动 360 度。

[记] sensory a. 感觉的, 感官的

separate ['sepərit] a. 分开的，单独的；v. ['sepəreit] 分开；分别

[例] The children sleep in separate beds. 孩子们分别睡在各自的床上。

[记] separately adv. 分别地，各自地 /be separated by 被…隔断 /be separated from 和…分离开, 和…分散 /separate into 分离成

sequence ['siːkwəns] n. 次序，顺序；连续，一连串

[例] Let me tell you about these events in historical sequence. 让我来按历史顺序给你们讲这些事。

[记] in sequence 顺次，挨次 /consequence n. 结果 /sequential a. 连续的；结果的

> 字根 sequ 指“跟随”。如：sequential a. 随之而来的，连续的；consequence n. 结果；subsequence n. 随后，后来。

series ['siəri:z] n. 连续，一系列

[例] He saw a series of white arrows painted on thc road. 他看见马路上画有一连串白色箭头。

[记] a series of 一系列, 许多 /in series 连续, 逐次

session ['seʃən] n. 会期；开庭

[例] The general session approved the report of the investigation committee. 全会批准了调查委员会的报告。

*

谜语：一个独眼太监用一块轻石片打一只停在芦苇上的蝙蝠，没中。

Unit 25

severe [si'viə] a. 严厉的；严重的，剧烈的

[例] The severe teacher has gone abroad. You can breathe freely again. 要求苛刻的教师已经出国了，你可以完全放心了。

sewerage ['sjuəridʒ] n. 排水设备；污水处理

[例] We need to make a plan for dealing with sewerage. 我们需要制订一个计划处理污水问题。

sex [seks] n. 性行为；性别

[例] Which sex is your cat?你的猫是公的还是母的?

> gender 和 sex 在指“性别”时，可以互换，没有区别。西方表格在填写性别一栏时，Sex 和 Gender 通用。

sexual ['seksjuəl] a. 性的，与性有关的；性爱的

[例] Birds have developed a sexual difference in the colours of their feathers. 鸟类已经发展到羽毛颜色不同，体现两性区别。

[记] sexy a. 性感的

shabby ['ʃæbi] a. 破旧的,低劣的,卑鄙的,不公平的

[例] He looks shabby. 他的样子寒酸。

shadow ['ʃædəu] n. 影子，阴影

[例]The willow's shadow falls on the lake. 垂柳的影子倒映在湖面上。

[记] shade n. 阴暗处；v. 遮蔽；使阴暗；使渐变

shallow ['ʃæləu] a. 浅的；肤浅的，浅薄的

[例]The sea is shallow here. 这儿的海水很浅。

[记] shallow-brained/shallow-headed a. 肤浅的；知识浅薄的 /shallow-hearted a. 薄情的

shape [ʃeip] n. 形状，外形；体形；使成形

[例]He shaped a pot out of the clay. 他用黏土塑成一只罐子。

shatter ['ʃætə] n. 粉碎，碎片；v. 打碎，粉碎

[例] A rare piece of porcelain is now in shatters. 一件稀有的瓷器现在已经支离破碎了。

shed [ʃed] v. 流出；散发；脱落；n. 小屋，工棚

[例] I shed 25 pounds as a result of my new diet. 使用新食谱后，我减去了 25 磅。

sheer [ʃiə] a. 全然的，纯粹的，绝对的，彻底的；v.（使）避开，偏航

[例] I'll never forget the look of sheer joy on her face. 我永远忘不了她脸上那种纯粹的快乐的表情。

shelf [ʃelf] n. 架子，搁板

[例] Like any other journal, its popularity will last for a moment, but it will remain on the shelves. 与其他杂志一样，这本杂志只会红极一时而后无人问津。

[记] be on the shelf 束之高阁，废弃的

shelter ['ʃeltə] n. 掩蔽处；v. 掩蔽，躲避

[例]Their cabin in the woods served as a retreat from the pressures of business. 林中的小木屋是他们躲避生意压力的隐居处。

shift [ʃift] n. /v. 转换，转移，变换

[例]The wind shifted to the north. 风转向北吹。

[记] make shift 代用；将就使用 /the day-shift 日班 /on the night-shift 值夜班

shiver ['ʃivə] v. 颤抖，哆嗦，发抖

[例] We shivered as we waited for him in the cold car. 当在车里等他时，我们冻得哆嗦。

> 动词以 -er 结尾，表示一种反复状态。如：batter 连续的用 bat 击打→连续敲击；chatter 反复的 chat →喋喋不休；flicker 摇曳，闪烁不定； teeter 蹒跚，摇摇欲坠；teeter-totter 反复的摇摇欲坠→跷跷板。

shortly ['ʃɔ:tli] adv. 立刻，不久，马上

[例]Shortly afterwards, the police stopped the car and both men were arrested. 过了没有多久,警察截住了那辆汽车,两个贼都被抓获了。

shower ['ʃauə] n. 淋浴；阵雨

[例]Postcards showered on her. 大批明信片雪片似地向她飞来。

[记] take a shower 冲个澡

shrink [ʃriŋk] v. 退缩，收缩；减少，贬值

[例] The dress shrank when I washed it. 这件衣服洗后缩水了。

shuffle ['ʃʌfl] n. 洗纸牌；混乱；蒙混；v. 洗牌；拖曳；搅乱

[例]With sore legs and an aching chest he shuffled over to the bathroom. 拖着病腿忍着胸痛，他缓慢地走进浴室。

[记] shuffle cards 洗纸牌 /reshuffle n. 改组；公司重组

> 象声词。仔细听听洗扑克牌时的声音。“洗纸牌”叫做 shuffle cards。那么 reshuffle 就是“重新洗牌”，引申为“改组，公司重组”。另外一像声词 shuttle，指“列车飞机等穿梭往返”，shuttle 发音本身就可体会“呼啸，穿梭”的含意。

shutter ['ʃʌtə] n. 百叶窗；快门；v. 关上

[例] They shuttered the store for the holiday. 他们节日期间关店门。

sibling ['sibliŋ] n. 兄弟姐妹，同胞

[例] Most young smokers are influenced by their friends' and older siblings' smoking habits. 多数低龄吸烟者是受到其朋友或兄长吸烟习惯的影响。

siege [siːdʒ] n. /v. 包围，围攻；长期努力

[例]The TV station has been under siege from irate viewers phoning in to complain. 电视台被愤怒的观众们的投诉电话围攻。

sign [sain] n. 标记，符号；征兆，迹象

[例]He made a sign for me to follow him. 他向我示意跟着他（走）。

[记] sign up 签字参与某事

signal ['signl] n. 信号，暗号

[例] A red light is usually a signal of danger. 红灯通常是危险的信号。

significant [sig'nifikənt] a. 有意义的，重大的

[例] There has been a significant rise in the firm's profits. 公司利润有了很大增长。

[记] significantly adv. 意味深长地

signpost ['sainpəust] n. 路标，指示牌

[例] A signpost indicated the right road for us to follow. 路标指给我们应走的路。

silt [silt] n. 淤泥；残渣；v. (使)淤积

[例] River sediments gradually silted the harbor. 河流的沉积物逐渐淤积在港口。

similar ['similə] a. (to)相像的，类似的

[例] My new dress is similar to the one you have. 我的新衣服和你的那件相似。

[记] be similar to 与…相似 / [区别] be fimiliar with 对…熟悉

> 字根 simi 和 simu 指"相似 like"。如：simile 类似的东西→直喻；similar 类似的；assimilate 使成为类似→吸收，同化；dissimilate 使变得不同，异化；simulate 类似，假装；simultaneous 同时发生的。

similarity [ˌsimi'læriti] n. 类似，相似之处

[例] A similarity can be observed between them. 它们之间可以看到相似之处。

simplify ['simplifai] v. 简化，精简

[例] Try to simplify your explanation for the children. 设法解释得简单些，好让孩子们听得懂。

simulate ['simjuleit] v. 模拟；假装，冒充

[例] We can use computers to simulate many conditions. 我们可以用计算机模拟各种情况。

[记] simulate rain 人工降雨 /simulative a. 假装的

simultaneously [ˌsiməl'teiniəsli] adv. 同时发生地，同时进行地

[例] We all arrived simultaneously at the same spot. 我们最终不约而同地到达了同一地点。

sin [sin] n. 罪，罪过

[例] It's a sin to tell lies. 说谎是一种罪恶。

sincere [sin'siə] a. 真诚的，诚挚的

[例] Please accept my sincere congratulations. 请接受我最衷心的祝贺。

> 据说该词可追溯到意大利文艺复兴renaissance时期，奇才米开朗基罗Michelangelo生活的那个时代。Michelangelo成名前在采石场工作。当时的采石工人常常在大理石上涂蜡，遮掩瑕疵，以图卖个好价钱。后来元老院颁令，凡大理石不得涂蜡，换言之，大理石必须“无蜡”。用拉丁文表示为sine cera（没有蜡）。两部分合成英文单词sincere，由“无蜡的”引申为“纯粹的”，“真诚的，真挚的”。现在的英文信常见落款：
>
> Yours sincerely
>
> Harvey

site [sait] n. 地点，场所

[例] The construction site of a new school was a hive of activity. 新学校的建筑工地上一片繁忙紧张的景象。

situated ['sitjueitid] a. 位于…的，坐落在…的

[例] The school is situated in the suburbs. 这所学校位于郊外。

situation [ˌsitju'eiʃən] n. 情况，处境，形势

[例] Due to poor management, they finally got into a difficult financial situation. 由于经营不善，他们最终陷入财政困难。

skeleton ['skelitən] n. 骨骼，骨架；框架，提要

[例] A long illness made a skeleton out of him. 长期的卧病使他骨瘦如柴。

> 源自希腊语skeletos干枯的。当肉体干枯之后，就只剩下骨架了。中文里的“骷髅”一词，也是skeleton。历史之父希罗多德的著作中曾描述古埃及有一习俗：凡重大的宴会(feast)都要在席上显眼处安放一具骷髅(skeleton)，借此提醒众宾客居安思危，不忘苦难。所以英文中有skeleton at the feast的表达，但意思已变为指“扫兴的家伙”了。

sketch [sketʃ] n. /v. 素描，速写，草图

[例] He sketched the cat. 他给猫画了个速写。

[记] sketch out 画出…的轮廓，简略地描述

skill [skil] n. 技能，技巧

[例] The trained teacher managed the children with skill. 这位训练有素的教师很熟练地管理儿童们。

[记] skill in 对…熟练 /skilled worker 技术工人 /skillful a. 灵巧的，熟练的

skim [skim] v. 浏览，略读；轻轻掠过

[例] The swallows were skimming over the water. 燕子掠过水面。

[记] skim through 浏览，翻阅一下

skip [skip] v. 跳跃；遗漏；悄悄离开

[例] A newspaper reader can select what he is interested in and skip what he thinks is boring or irrelevant. 报纸读者可以选择自己感兴趣的新闻，略过自己认为是枯燥的或无关的消息。

[记] to skip school 逃学

skull [skʌl] n. 头脑，头骨

> Yale 耶鲁大学著名神秘组织：Skull and Bones 骷髅头和人骨会，简称“骷髅会”。成立于1832年，宗旨在于扶植盎格鲁萨克逊菁英后代，取得财富和权力，美国许多名门望族都加入了“骷髅会”，其中最著名的当属布什家族，包括小布什和老布什总统在内。

slender ['slendə] a. 苗条的，纤细的，微弱的

[例] Sobs shook her slender frame. 她抽泣着，苗条的身体在颤动。

[区别] slander v. /n. 诽谤

slice [slais] n. 薄片；v. 把…切成（薄片），切削

[例] I sliced the bread. 我把面包切成片。

> 厨房动词集合：slice 切片，dice 切丁，shred 切丝，chop 切碎，boil 煮，fry 煎，deep-fry 炸，steam 蒸，roast 烤，bake 烘，shell 剥皮，peel 削皮，beat 打；toss 拌，mash 捣（成泥）。

slide [slaid] v. 滑行，滑动；n. 滑动；幻灯片

[例] The book slid off my knee. 书从我膝盖上滑落。

[记] slide into 不自觉地陷入(某种状态)

slightly ['slaitli] adv. 少量地，轻微地

[例] I knew him slightly. 关于他我只知道一点儿。

slim [slim] a. 苗条的，修长的

[例] The chance of success is slim. 成功的机会很小。

slippery ['slipəri] a. 滑的，滑溜的

[例] The floor is slippery. 道路很滑。

[记] as slippery as an eel 难于应付的，滑头的 /slippers 拖鞋

slogan ['sləugən] n. 口号，标语

[例] The advertising slogan was a play on words. 那条广告口号是双关语。

> 古苏格兰氏族部落土语，意为“战斗时的呐喊”。在英语中第一次有记录的使用是1813年美国海军同英国舰队的战斗中，美军舰长要求水兵把“Don't Give Up the Ship”一语印在一面旗帜上，系在桅杆顶。并对水兵们说：The cry “Don't Give Up the Ship” will be our slogan.

slope [sləup] v. 倾斜，有坡度；n. 斜坡

[例] He ran up the slope to the top of the hill. 他爬上斜坡到了山顶。

slothful ['sləuθful] a. 偷懒的 n. 懒惰

[例] Fatigue had made him slothful. 疲劳使他懒散。

[记] sloth n. 懒惰；【动】树獭

sluggish ['slʌgiʃ] a. 行动迟缓的

[例] If you don't eat breakfast, you'll feel tired and sluggish. 如果不吃早餐，你就会感到疲劳和动作迟缓。

[记] a sluggish market 不景气的市场

slum [slʌm] n. 贫民窟

[例] I grew up in the East London slums. 我是在东伦敦贫民窟长大的。

smash [smæʃ] v. 打碎；猛撞，猛击；（打球时）扣杀

[例] Although the bed was smashed to pieces, the man was miraculously unhurt. 虽然床摔碎了,人却奇迹般地没有受伤。

smog [smɔg] n. 烟雾

[例] The smog was so bad that schoolchildren were advised to stay indoors. 烟雾太大建议小学生们呆在室内。

> 英文中混合构词法：smoke+fog → smog；motor+hotel → motel 汽车旅馆；helicopter+airport → heliport 直升飞机场；breakfast+lunch → brunch 早午餐

smuggle ['smʌgl] n. /v. 走私，偷带

[例] He was caught smuggling cameras into the country. 他向这个国家走私照像机被抓住。

[记] smuggler n. 走私者

snack [snæk] n. 快餐，小吃

[例] She fixed us a snack. 她为我们准备了点心。

snatch [snætʃ] v. 一把抓住，攫取

[例] He snatched the book from my hands. 他一把从我手里抢走了书。

soak [səuk] v. 浸泡，湿透

[例] Sponges readily soak up water. 海绵容易吸水。

soap [səup] n. 肥皂

[例] Many different companies sell soap, tires, and so on. 许多不同的公司出售肥皂、轮胎等等。

[区别] soup n. 汤

> soap opera 肥皂剧，因当初赞助商为一家肥皂公司得名；sitcom (situation comedy) 情景喜剧，配音经常加入观众笑声，如 *Friends*，*Sex and the City* 等；drama 电视剧，如 *The X-Files*；Serial 连续剧。

soar [sɔː] v. 高飞，翱翔；剧增

[谚] The eagle soared over the valley in search of food. 鹰在村子的上空翱翔,寻觅食物。

so-called [ˌsəuˈkɔːld] a. 所谓的；号称的

[例] I went to see the playwright's so-called masterpiece and were very disappointed. 我去看了该剧作家的所谓大作，非常失望。

social [ˈsəuʃəl] a. 社会的；社交的，爱好交际的

[例] She has a social nature. 她天生好交际。

software [ˈsɔftwɛə] n. 【计】软件

[例] This is a computer software shop. 这是一家计算机软件商店。

[反义词] hardware n. 五金器具；【计】硬件

solar [ˈsəulə] a. 太阳的，日光的

[例] This toy is operated by solar energy. 这个玩具是太阳能驱动的。

[记] solar system 太阳系 / solar energy 太阳能

solicitor [səˈlisitə] n. 律师，法律顾问

[例] We asked a solicitor for advice. 我们向一位律师咨询。

solo [ˈsəuləu] n. 独奏曲；a. 单独的

[例] She sang a solo at the party last night. 她昨晚在聚会上独唱了一支歌。

sole [səul] a. 唯一的；n. 鞋底，脚底；基础

[例] You have to follow the guide whose sole interest is to cover all spots according to his strict schedule. 你得跟着导游走,而导游的唯一兴趣就是按照他那一成不变的时间表,走过所有风景点。

solid [ˈsɔlid] a. 固体的；牢固的，质地坚实的

[例] The new office building is a very solid construction. 新建的写字楼非常坚固。

solution [səˈljuːʃən] n. （问题等的）解决办法；溶液，溶解

[例] What is the solution to your trouble? 你解决困难的办法是什么?

[记] solute n. 溶解物，溶质 /soluble a. 可溶的，可溶解的

somewhat [ˈsʌmwɔt] ad. 有点，稍微

[例] I was somewhat surprised. 我有点惊讶。

sophisticated [səˈfistikeitid] a. 精密复杂的，尖端的；老练的，富有经验的

[例] They should win with their sophisticated weapons. 他们的武器精良，应该能赢。

> 字根 soph 指“智慧”。如：philo 爱 +sophy 智慧→ philosophy 哲学；sophisticated 智慧的，世故的，老练的；一半聪明 sophos + 一半愚笨 moros → sophomore 大学二年级学生。freshman 大一学生，junior 大三学生，senior 大四学生。

sorrow [ˈsɔrəu] n. 悲伤，悲痛

[例] He told me with sorrow that his mother was very ill. 他悲伤地告诉我，他的母亲病得很厉害。

sort [sɔ:t] n. 种类，类别；v. 把…分类
[例] He is the a sort of persen who is incapable of deceiving you. 他是那种不会欺骗你的人。
[记] a sort of 稍稍地；有几分 /of all sorts 各种各样的

sound [saund] a. 健全的；合理的；n. 声音；v. 发出声音；听起来
[例] The book is full of sound advice. 这本书里有很多好的建议。
[记] a sound sleep 酣睡

source [sɔ:s] n. 来源，根源
[例] I've heard from reliable sources that the company is in trouble. 我听到来源可靠的消息说公司遇到了麻烦。
[记] outsourcing 外部采购 /[区别] resource n. 资源

souvenir ['su:vəniə] n. 纪念品
[例] Please accept this little gift as a souvenir. 请接受这个小小的礼物作为纪念。

spacious ['speiʃəs] a. 宽敞的，广阔的
[例] The hotel is neither spacious nor comfortable. 这旅馆既不宽敞也不舒服。

span [spæn] n. 跨度，间距；持续的时间
[谚] Life is but a span. 人生苦短。

spare [spɛə] a. 多余的，剩下的 v. 节约，节省
[例] If you have a spare bed, may I stay tonight? 如果你有空床的话，今晚我可以留下吗？
[记] spare no efforts 不遗余力 /spare time 空闲时间

spark [spɑ:k] n. 火花，火星
[谚] A single spark can start a prairie fire. 星星之火，可以燎原。
[记] sparkle v. 发火花；(使)闪耀；用眼神表达

spawn [spɔ:n] n. (鱼等的)卵，幼苗；v. 产卵；造成，引起
[例] The computer industry has spawned hundreds of new companies. 电脑行业中已有几百家新公司涌现。

> Spawn（再生侠）在美国、欧洲都是一个家喻户晓的名字。他与 Spiderman（蜘蛛人），Batman（蝙蝠侠），Superman（超人）等漫画人物齐名。

specialist ['speʃəlist] n. 专家，专科医生
[例] She is a specialist in e-business. 她是电子商务专家。
[记] specialty n. 专业；专长 /specialize v. 专门从事

species ['spi:ʃiz] n. [单复同] 物种，种类
[例] Some species of animals have become extinct because they could not adapt to a changing environment. 有一些动物已经灭种了，因为它们不能适应环境的变化。

specific [spi'sifik] a. 详细的，明确的，详尽的

[例] I want a specific answer. 我想要一个明确的回答。
[记] specifically adv. 确切地；特别地

specify ['spesifai] v. 具体指定，详细指明
[例] Can you specify the reasons? 你能确切说明原因吗？

specimen ['spesimən] n. 样本，样品
[例] He collects specimens of all kinds of rocks and minerals. 他采集各种岩石和矿物的标本。
[同义词] sample

spectacle ['spektəkl] n. 观览物，展览物，奇观，景象
[例] Viewed from the top of Mount Tai, the sunrise was indeed a spectacle. 从泰山顶上看去，日出真是个奇观。
[记] a pair of spectacles 一副眼镜

spectacular [spek'tækjulə] a. 引人入胜的，壮观的
[例] We saw with our own eyes the spectacular display of fireworks. 我们亲眼目睹了放焰火的壮观景象。

spectator [spek'teitə;'spekteitə] n. 观众
[例] The match attracted over 40,000 spectators. 这场比赛吸引了40000多观众。
[区别] audience n. 观众（听众，室内，强调“听”）/spectator n. 观众（旁观者，露天，强调“看”）

spectrum ['spektrəm] n. 光谱；系列，范围，幅度
[例]The exam is supposed to cover the whole spectrum of ability. 考试应该覆盖所有能力范围。

> 字根spect指“看to see”。如：spectacle用来看的东西→景象，眼镜；prospect向前看→前途，期望；inspect往里看→检查，视察；respect再一次看，一再注视→重视，尊敬；suspect向下看，像看到外表现象以下的东西→怀疑；retrospect往回看→回顾，反省；spectrum看得到的→光谱。大千世界都是因为有光才可见。第一次对spectrum的研究是牛顿发现太阳光（白光）通过玻璃棱镜后分解成从红光到紫光的各种颜色光谱。

spell [spel] n. 魅力；v. 拼写；意味着
[例] Pupils should know how to spell commonly used words. 学生们应当知道如何拼写常用词。

sphere [sfiə] n. 球体；范围，领域，半球
[例] We move in different spheres. 我们在不同的领域里活动。

spice [spais] n. 香料，调味品
[例] Variety is the spice of life. 多彩的生活才有情趣。
[记] dry spice 干五香料 /ground spice 五味粉 /The Spice Girls 辣妹组合

spill [spil] v. 溢出；溅出，洒落
[例] Take heed not to spill milk on the rug. 当心别把牛奶洒在地毯上。

[记] spillage n. 溢出, 溢出量

spin [spin] v. 旋转, 纺, 纺纱; n. 旋转

[例] We took a spin around town. 我们乘车出去绕城转了一圈。

spiritual ['spiritjuəl] a. 精神上的

[例] Sometimes spiritual happiness is more important. 有时精神上的快乐更为重要。

split [split] v. 劈开; 使分裂, 使分离

[例] The crowd split into several groups. 人群分成几组。

spoil [spɔil] v. 损坏, 损害; 溺爱; 变质

[例] Our holidays were spoilt by bad weather. 我们假日的乐趣被恶劣天气所破坏。

sponge [spʌndʒ] n. 海绵; 棉球; 纱布; v. 用海绵吸

[例] Don't sponge off the table. 不要用海绵擦桌子。

sponsor ['spɔnsə] n. 发起者, 主办者; 赞助者; 赞助商; v. 发起, 主办; 赞助

[例] The company had sponsored the football match. 该公司已为这场足球赛提供了赞助。

[记] class sponsor 班主任

Unit 26

spot [spɔt] n. 斑点，污点；地点，现场
[例] She had spots on her face when she was ill. 当她生病的时候，她脸上有斑点。
[记] on the spot 立刻；现场，当场

spotlight ['spɔtlait] n. 聚光灯
[例] He likes to be in the spotlight. 他喜欢出风头。
[记] be in the spotlight 成为注意的中心，处于显著地位

spouse [spauz] n. 配偶（指夫或妻）
[例] They get free tickets for their spouses. 他们为家属领到了免费的票。

> 古希腊商人签订合同叫 *spendo*，古罗马结婚时有一习俗，男女双方的亲友需聚在女方父亲家中签订婚约 *sponsalia*。spouse 拥有婚约的人→配偶。单词 sponsor（主办者）也源于此。

sprawl [sprɔːl] n. /v. 四肢伸开躺卧（的姿势）；伸展，蔓延
[例] He lay there in a sprawl. 他四肢伸开躺在那里 。

spray [sprei] v. 喷雾；喷洒
[例] The seeds were sprayed over the ground in huge quantities by aeroplanes. 飞机把这些草籽大量地撒在地面上。

spring [spriŋ] n. 春天；弹簧；泉；v. 跃出
[例] The spring has run down. 钟表发条走完了。
[记] spring up 发生，萌芽；生长；出现

> spill, spring, spray 三个单词体会发音来区别词义。spill 发音短促，感觉几滴水珠"泼溅"出来；spring 发音是一股气流涌出，春天冰雪消融，"泉水涌出"；spray 发音时体会口腔扁平，水流泼散面积更大，所以指"喷洒"。家里喷洒用的空气清新剂，杀小强的喷雾器等，都叫 sprayer。

sprout [spraut] v. 萌芽；n. 幼芽
[例] Buds sprout in the spring. 幼芽在春天萌发。

spur [spəː] n. 踢马刺；刺激物；v. 鞭策，刺激
[例] Pride spurred the man to fight. 自尊心刺激他去决斗。

squash [skwɔʃ] n. 南瓜；【体】壁球；v. 压扁，压制
[例] The fruit at the bottom of the box had been squashed. 箱底的水果已经压烂了。

squeeze [skwiːz] v. 挤压，压榨；n. 压榨，拥挤
[例] He squeezed an orange to get the juice out. 他挤压橘子以便榨出橘汁。

put the squeeze on sb. 对某人施加压力
[记] squeeze out 榨出，挤出

stabilize ['steibilaiz] v. （使）稳定，(使)稳固
[例] The family is a stabilizing element in society. 家庭是社会的一个稳定因素。

stable ['steibl] a. 稳定的；n. 畜栏，马厩
[例] Markets are flourishing and prices are stable. 市场繁荣，物价稳定。
[记] stability n. 稳定

> stable 古义专指“马厩”。驰骋奔腾的骏马一但进入 stable，就变得安静稳定，乖乖地吃草了，最多尾巴扫两下。马厩 stable 引申为“稳定”之义。establish v. 固定，建立，设立；establishment n. 确立，建筑物。

stadium ['steidiəm] n. 露天体育场
[例] The crowd surged out of the stadium. 人群从体育场涌出。
[记] football stadium 足球场

staff [stɑːf] n. 全体职员，全体员工；全体教员
[例] The department has a staff of 38. 本部门有 38 个员工。

stage [steidʒ] n. 舞台；时期，阶段
[例] The first stage of our journey to Xi' An will be the flight from Dalian to Beijing. 我们去西安的第一段路程将乘飞机从大连到北京。
[记] at a later stage 后来 /on the stage 在舞台上 /stage by stage 一步一步地

stagnant ['stægnənt] a. 停滞的，不流动的
[例] The moss grows in stagnant pools of water. 不流动的水池里产生青苔。

stain [stein] v. 染污，沾污；n. 污点，瑕疵
[例] The coffee stained his shirt brown. 咖啡把他的衬衫染上了棕色。
[记] stainless a. 无瑕疵的；不锈的 / stainless steel 不锈钢

stake [steik] n. 赌注；树桩；v. 赌
[例] I'd stake my all on it. 我拿我的一切打赌。
[记] at stake/risk 在危急之中

standard ['stændəd] n. 标准，规范；a. 标准的
[例] Your work is not up to standard. 你的工作不够标准。
[记] living standard 生活水平 /standardize v. 使标准化

staple ['steipl] n. 钉书钉；主要产品(或商品)；a. 主要的
[例] Rice is the staple food in many Asian countries. 大米是许多亚洲国家的主食。
[记] stapler n. 订书机

stare [stɛə] v. 凝视，盯着看
[例] He stared at the word trying to remember what it meant. 他盯着这

个单词，努力想记起它的意思。
[记] stare at 凝视，盯住

> 拉丁文 *stare* 指“站立 to stand”。英语中 sta- 即有“站立，持续，固定，静止”等含义。英语单词 stare 指 gaze fixedly，固定的看着→凝视，盯着；station 一直站立的地方→车站；statue 站立的，持续固定的东西→雕像。

starve [stɑːv] v. 挨饿；饿死
[例]They tried to starve the army into surrender. 他们试图使守军因饥饿而投降。
[记] starve for news 渴望消息

statement ['steitmənt] n. 声明，陈述
[例]The government's statement on the present situation in the Middle East was soon carried all over the world by TV. 我国政府关于中东局势的声明通过电视迅速传遍全世界。

state-of-the-art a. 最先进的
[例] This is the state-of-the-art digital television. 这是最先进的数字电视。

static ['stætik] a. 静态的，静力的
[例] This cloth material has static electricity. 这种布料带有静电。

stationary ['steiʃənəri] a. 静止的，停滞的；稳定的
[例] Wait until the bus is stationary before you get off. 你要等公共汽车停稳了再下车。

stationery ['steiʃənəri] n. [总称]文具
[例] This shop handles paper and stationery. 这家商店经营纸张文具。

statistic [stə'tistik] a. 统计（学）的
[例] The statisticdata comes from a study recently conducted by the British government. 统计数据来自英国政府最近进行的一项研究。

statistics [stə'tistiks] n. 统计学
[例] Remember that these statistics describe college freshmen in 1972. 要记住,这些统计数据是关于 1972 年时的一年级新生的。

statue ['stætjuː] n. 雕像，塑像
[例]The Statue of Liberty was presented to the United States of America in the nineteenth century by the people of France. 自由女神雕像是法国人民在 19 世纪送给美国的。

status ['steitəs] n. 地位，身份
[例]Being an engineer gives him a high social status. 做工程师给了他很高的社会地位。
[记] social status 社会地位 /status quo 现状

stature ['stætʃə] n. 身高，身材；(精神、道德等的)高度
[例] Bernard was short in stature, with a large head. 伯纳德身材矮小脑袋大。

steadfast ['stedfəst] a. 坚定的

[例] He was a steadfast bachelor and intended to remain so. 他是一个坚定的单身汉而且还要一直坚持下去.

steady ['stedi] a. 稳的，平衡的，稳定的

[例] That ladder doesn't look very steady. 那架梯子看上去不太牢固。

[记] steadily adv. 平稳地；逐渐地

steep [sti:p] a. 陡峭的，陡直的

[例] The steep rock seems to be growing at an angle. 这块陡直的岩石似乎在以一定角度生长。

steer [stiə] v. 驾驶，掌舵；操纵

[例] He steered the ship carefully between the rocks. 他小心地在礁石间驾驶船。

> steer 古意也表示"站立"，后来又派生出"站立着的事物"的意思。古代航行站立在船头的人就是 steerer，舵手。steerable a. 可驾驶的，易操纵的；steering n. 操纵，掌舵。

stem [stem] v. 起源于，基于，由…造成；n. 茎，干

[例] Correct decisions stem from correct judgments. 正确的决定来源于正确的判断。

[记] stem from 源自，起源于

stereotype ['stiəriəutaip] n. 老一套；陈腔滥调，刻板模式

[例] He's the stereotype of an army officer. 他属于那种老派军官。

[记] stereo n. 立体声；a. 立体的，立体感觉的

steward ['stjuəd] n. (轮船、飞机等)乘务员；(聚会的）筹备人；管家

[例] He is the steward of that great estate. 他是那一大笔财产的管理人。

stick [stik] v. 钉住，粘住

[例] The wheels of the car stuck in the mud and we could not go on. 车轮陷入泥里，我们不能前进了。

[记] sticker n. 不干胶贴纸

stiff [stif] a. 硬的，僵直的；呆板的；艰难的

[例] Her fingers were stiff with cold. 她的手指冻僵了。

[记] a stiff examination 难度大的考试

stimulate ['stimjuleit] v. 刺激，激励

[例] I'm trying to stimulate him to study harder. 我试图激励他更加用功读书。

stimulus ['stimjuləs] n. 〈复数为 stimuli〉刺激物，促进因素，刺激

[例] Light is a stimulus to growth in plants. 光是植物生长的促进因素。

> 原来是指驱赶动物往前走的一头削尖的小木棍子 stick，引申为"刺激，刺激物"。stimulus 的同义词 spur（踢马刺），引申也有"刺激"的含义。另外，拉丁文 *goad* 直接进入英语，指的就是那根"赶牛棒"，引申为"刺激"，成为 GRE 考试词汇。看来人们

要想达到目标 goal，后面真需要有 goad。

stipulate ['stipjuleit] v. 规定，保证

[例] We have stipulated a date of payment and a price. 我们规定了偿付日和价格。

[记] stipulation n. 规定，约定

stir [stəː] v. 搅动，搅拌；引起，煽动

[例]You had better stir yourself. 你最好迅速行动起来。

store [stɔː] n. 商店；v. 贮藏，储备

[例] I stored all the apples from our trees. 我把树上收的苹果都存放起来了。

straight [streit] a. 直的，直接的，坦率的；立即，马上

[例]The smoke rose straight upwards. 烟一直向上升。

straightforward [streit'fɔːwəd] a. 正直的，坦率的，直截了当的

[例]We took a straightforward route to the beach. 我们取直道到海滩去。

strain [strein] n. 过度疲劳；紧张；v. 扭伤；拉紧

[例] I strained my back when I lifted the box. 我抬箱子的时候扭了背。

strand [strænd] n. 绳，线，串；河岸；v. 搁浅；使陷于困境

[例]I was stranded in the strange town without money or friends. 我困在那陌生的城市，既没有钱，又没有朋友。

strangle ['stræŋgl] v. 扼杀，压制；使窒息

[例] Mills argues that high taxation strangles the economy. 米尔斯反驳说高额征税压制了经济。

strategy ['strætidʒi] n. 战略，策略，行动计划

[例] Mao Zedong was skilled in military strategy. 毛泽东善于制定军事战略。

[记] strategic a. 战略上的 /strategy and tactics 战略与战术

streamline ['striːmlain] a. 流线型的；n. 流水线工作；v. 使成流线型；使简化

[例] We're taking steps to streamline operations and increase productivity. 我们正在采取措施使操作流水线化，提高生产力。

strenuous ['strenjuəs] a. 奋发的，紧张的

[例] Sherry's been making a strenuous effort to lose weight. 雪利一直在竭尽全力减肥。

后缀-ous 指"充满了…"。strenuous 充满了 strength 力量→发奋的；furious 充满了 fury 愤怒→愤怒的；glorious 充满了 glory 光荣→显赫的，光荣的；laborious 充满了 labor 劳动→勤劳的，艰辛的。

strengthen ['streŋθən] v. 加强，巩固

[例]We must strengthen the weak links. 我们要加强薄弱环节。

[记] strengthen unity 加强团结

stress [stres] n. 压力，重压，紧张；v. 着重，强调

[例]In fact, stress isn't the bad thing it is often supposed to be. 事实上，压力并不像人们所认为的那样是一件坏事。

[记] lay/place/put stress on 把重点放在…上

stretch [stretʃ] v. 伸展，伸长

[例] He stretched his arms for a book. 他伸出手臂去拿一本书。

strict [strikt] a. 严格的，严厉的

[例] Our teacher is strict; we have to do what she says. 老师很严格，我们不得不按她说的去做。

[记] be strict with sb. 对某人严厉

stride [straid] v. 迈大步走，大踏步走

[例] They are striding forward both in English and in mathematics. 他们的英语和数学都在大踏步地取得进展。

strike [straik] v. 打，敲，击；袭击；n. 罢工；打击

[例] The workers were on strike because they wanted more money. 工人们在罢工，因为他们要求增加工资。

[记] air strike 空袭 /be on strike 举行罢工

striking ['straikiŋ] a. 显著的，惊人的

[例] There is a striking contrast between the two different interpretations on the same case. 对同一件事，两种解释截然不同。

strip [strip] v. 剥，剥去，脱去

[例] He stripped the paper off the wall. 他把墙上的纸撕了下来。

[记] stripper n. 脱衣舞表演者

strive [straiv] v. 努力，奋斗

[谚] Wit and will strive for victory. 智慧加毅力，拚搏能胜利。

[记] strive after/for 为…奋斗

stroke [strəuk] n. (网球等)一击，(划船等)一划，(绘画等)一笔

[例] With one stroke of his ax, he had cut the tree down. 他一斧子就砍倒了这棵树。

> 游泳的各种泳姿：仰泳 backstroke，蛙泳 breaststroke，自由泳 freestyle/front crawl，蝶泳 butterfly stroke。

stubborn ['stʌbən] a. 顽固的，固执的

[例] She won't do what I ask — she's very stubborn. 她不按我的要求去做，她很固执。

studio ['stjuːdiəu] n. 画室；照相室；演播室；摄影棚；工作室

[记] art studio 美术工作室 / a TV studio 一间电视演播室

stuff [stʌf] n. 东西，物品，材料；素材

[例] There's some white stuff on this plate. 这个盘子上有些白色的东西。

stunt [stʌnt] v. 阻碍发展；n. 矮小的人(或物)；惊人表演，绝技

[例] Lack of sunlight will stunt the plant's growth. 缺少日照会使植物发育迟缓。

> stunt man 身怀绝技的人→特技演员，(电影中) 替身。区别单词 stun v. /n. (使) 惊吓，晕倒。那么 stun man 即是经常使别人目

瞪口呆之人，所以也指“特技演员，替身”，与 stunt man 通用。

sturdy ['stə:di] a. 强健的；坚定的

[例]The child had sturdy legs. 这个孩子有健壮的双腿。

style [stail] n. 风格，类型

[例] Jack has a strange style of walking: he walks with one shoulder a little higher than the other. 杰克走路的样子特别：他走路时一只肩比另一只高一点。

[记] come into style 变得时髦；流行起来 /out of style 不时髦的 /stylish a. 新式的；时髦的 /stylistic a. 风格上的

subject ['sʌbdʒekt] n. 主题，题目；学科，科目；a. 服从的；易受…影响的

[例] I was the subject of their talk. 我是他们谈论的话题。

[记] be subject to 倾向于…；易于…

前缀sub-指“在…下under”。原来sub-=sup-是指“高”(如sublime崇高的)，但它的比较级为 super，最高级为 supreme，跟它们相比，sub-就“低”了。所以：subject 往下投掷(ject)→从属的，服从的；subconscious 意识之下→潜意识；substance 表相之下→本质，实质；subtitle 标题(title)之下→副标题；subway 地下铁。

subjective [sʌb'dʒektiv] a. 主观的

[例] Subjective judgments are often wrong. 主观判断常常是错的。

[反义词] objective a. 客观的；n. 目标

subjugate ['sʌbdʒugeit] v. 使屈服，使服从，克制

[例] Her own needs had been subjugated to the needs of her family. 她自己的需要得服从她家庭的需要。

submit [səb'mit] v. 提交，呈递；服从

[例] I hope you can submit you term papers before the deadline. 我希望你们能在最后限期之前交上你们的学期论文。

[记] submit to 服从于，屈从于；把…提交给…

subordinate [sə'bɔ:dinit] n. 部属，下级；a. 次要的，下级的

[例] The minority is subordinate to the majority. 少数服从多数。

subscribe [səb'skraib] v. 订阅（杂志等）；签署；捐款

[例] You can subscribe to the magazine for as little as $32 a year. 每年只要花 32 美金就可以订阅该杂志。

[记] subscribe to 预订；同意；订阅

subsequent ['sʌbsikwənt] a. 随后的，后来的

[例] Subsequent events proved her wrong. 后来发生的事证明她错了。

[记] subsequently adv. 随后

subsidy ['sʌbsidi] n. 津贴，补贴

[例] The government has decided to increase subsidies for agricultural products. 政府决定增加对农产品的补贴。

substance [记] subsidise v. 资助，津贴

['sʌbstəns] n. 物质；实质

[例] Salt is a substance we use in cooking. 盐是我们做菜时用的东西。

substantial [səb'stænʃəl] a. 大量的；真实的

[例]They have made substantial improvement. 他们已经做了很大的改进。

substitute ['sʌbstitju:t] n. 代替者，替代品；v. 代替

[例] He substituted as the typist in the office. 他代替做这个办公室的打字员。

[记] substitute A for B 用 A 代 B /substitute sb. by another 用别人替换某人

> 球场上的候补队员或板凳队员，就是 substitute. 另一种调侃的说法是 bench warmer，板凳温暖者。因为当某球星被候补球员替换下场时，该球星会坐在候补队员刚坐过的、还有余温的凳子上。

subtitle ['sʌbtaitl] n. 副标题；对白字幕；v. 给…加标题、字幕

[例] This is the film that was subtitled for English-speaking audiences. 这是一部给说英文的观众加了字幕的电影。

subtle ['sʌtl] a. 微妙的，细致的

[例] There are some subtle differences between the two. 二者之间有细微差别。

subtract [səb'trækt] v. 减去，减少

[例] The little girl has begin to learn to add and subtract. 这小女孩已在学做加减法了。

suburb ['sʌbə:b] n. 郊区，市郊

[例] They proposed setting up a school in the suburb. 他们建议在这个郊区成立一所学校。

[记] urban areas 市区

successor [sək'sesə] n. 后继者，继任者；后续的事物

[例] He is the successor to the throne. 他是王位的继承人。

[记] successive a. 继承的, 连续的

succinct [sək'siŋkt] a. 简洁的，简明的

[例] Please give a succinct summary of your points. 请简要总结你的观点。

succumb [sə'kʌm] v. 屈服，屈从；死于

[例] He succumbed to TB. 他死于肺结核。

[记] succumb to 屈服

suck [sʌk] v. 吸，吮；吸取

[例] The baby was sucking milk from its mother. 婴儿在吮吸母亲的乳汁。

sue [sju:] v. 控告，提出诉讼；向…请求

[例] The company is suing the former president. 公司正在起诉前任总裁。
[记] sue sb. for 控告某人违反… / [同义词] litigate, prosecute

sufficient [sə'fiʃənt] a. 足够的，充足的
[例] Sufficient data has been collected for the building project. 有关这项建筑工程已经收集了充分的资料。
[反义词] insufficient, deficient, inadequate

suffix ['sʌfiks] n. 【语】后缀，词尾
[例] The word is usually, with the suffix -ly in a different color. 这个单词是 usually,后缀 ly 用不同的颜色标出。

suicide ['sjuisaid] n. 自杀
[例] It is professional suicide to involve oneself in illegal practices. 从事非法活动即是专门的自毁行为。
[记] a suicide squad 敢死队 /suicide bombing 自杀性炸弹袭击

sum [sʌm] n. 总数，总和
[例] Father has decided to give his son a huge sum of money to make him independent from the family. 父亲决定给儿子一大笔钱让他离家自立。

summary ['sʌməri] n. 摘要，概要
[例] The chemistry book had a summary at the end of each chapter. 那本化学书每章末尾均附有一概要。

summit ['sʌmit] n. 最高点，顶点；顶峰；最高级会议
[例] He has reached the summit of his ambition. 他已达到了他野心的极致。

sundial ['sʌndaiəl] n. 日规；日晷
[例] The sundial is an ancient device for telling the time. 日晷是古代的计时器。

superb [sju:'pə:b] a. 极好的，最佳的，杰出的
[例] The construction built out of natural materials looks superb. 这个由天然材料建成的建筑物非常雄伟。

superior [sju:'piəriə] a. 较高的，上级的；较好的
[例] He is superior to me at work, while he is inferior to me in intelligence. 他在工作上是我的上级，而他的智力却不及我。
[记] a superior court 上级法院 / be superior to胜过，比…好 / [反义词] inferior

superstition [ˌsju:pə'stiʃən] n. 迷信
[例] A common superstition considered it bad luck to sleep in a room numbered 13. (西方)一种普遍的迷信认为在 13 号房间睡觉是不吉利的。

> 星期五和 13 历来被认为不吉利。这是从神话、《圣经》、风俗习惯产生的联想。据《圣经》上讲，上帝创造了第一个男人亚当，然后从亚当身上取下一根肋骨造了女人夏娃。亚当是在星期五

被造出来的，他和夏娃吃禁果也在星期五，他俩死的日子也是星期五。英国从前常常在星期五处死罪犯。北欧神话中，13个人坐在一起聚餐是不吉利的。圣经中耶稣和其12门徒的最后的晚餐正好是13人。耶稣在星期五被钉死在十字架上。复活节前的星期五叫 Black/Good Friday 耶稣受难日。

supervise ['sju:pəvaiz] v. 监督，管理，指导

[例] This kind of project ought to be supervised by the management. 这种工程应该由资方来监管。

supervisor ['sju:pəvaizə] n. 主管，监督人

[例] The examination will be inspected by the special supervisor. 这次考试将由专家来监察。

Unit 27

supplement ['sʌplimənt] v. 增补，补充；n. 补充（物），增刊

[例] I supplemented my income by taking a night job. 我靠做夜工增加收入。

supplementary [ˌsʌpli'mentəri] a. 补充的，增补的

[例] The supplementary estimates are not exact. 追加的预算不够确切。

supply [sə'plai] v. 供给，供应，提供；n. 供应品，补给

[例] Domestic consumers were supplied with enough necessities by companies. 公司给住户提供了足够的生活必需品。

[记] in short supply 短缺 /supply... to 把…供给 /supply... with... 供应…

suppose [sə'pəuz] v. 假定；认为；应该…，本该

[例] Suppose a company has a new breakfast cereal that it wants to sell. 假设有个公司想出售一种新的早餐麦片粥。

[记] be supposed to do sth. 被期望或要求做某事；应该做某事

supreme [sju:'pri:m] a. 最高的，至高无上的

[例] The most important law court is called the Supreme Court. 最重要的法院叫做最高法院。

surface ['sə:fis] n. 表面，地面，水面

[例] The surface of bamboo feels so smooth. 竹子的表面摸上去很光滑。

surge [sə:dʒ] n. /v. 汹涌，澎湃

[例] The fans surged forward to see the movie star. 影迷们汹涌地奔去看那个影星。

surgery ['sə:dʒəri] n. 外科；手术；诊疗室

[例] Cancer usually requires surgery. 癌症通常需要动手术。

[记] surgeon n. 外科医生

surmount [sə:'maunt] v. 战胜；超越；克服；在…顶上

[例] The church steeple surmounts the square. 教堂的尖塔高耸在广场之上。

> 前缀 sur- 是 super- 的变体，都表示“在…上 over, above”。sur-(over)+ mount (mountain)→ surmount 山之上，引申为“战胜，克服”；sur-+name → surname 名字之上→姓，姓氏；surpass (=overpass)胜过，超过；sur-(over)+vey(see)→ survey(=oversee)俯瞰，调查；sur-(over)+vive(to live)→比谁活得长→ survive 幸存。

surpass [sə:'pɑ:s] v. 超过；胜过

[例] The beauty of the scenery surpassed my expectations. 该处风景之秀丽超出了我的想象。

surplus ['sə:pləs] a. 剩余的，过剩的

[例] During that period of time, Brazil had a surplus of coffee. 那时，巴西的咖啡供过于求。

surrender [sə'rendə] v. 投降；放弃

[例] Thousands of illegal immigrants have surrendered to police. 数以千计的非法移民已经向政府自首。

[记] surrender oneself to 向…投降；沉迷在；听任…摆布

surrounding [sə'raundiŋ] a. 周围的，环境的；n. 环境

[例] The retired old men have to try to adapt themselves to the surroundings. 退休的老人们不得不尽量使自己适应周围的环境。

[记] social surroundings 社会环境

survey ['sə:vei] n. / v. 调查，检验

[例] According to a recent survey, in Shanghai alone there are more than 2. 5 million migrant workers. 根据最近的一项调查，仅上海就有250多万外来民工。

survive [sə'vaiv] v. 幸存，活下来

[例] The man was very ill, but he survived. 这个人病得很厉害，可是他活下来了。

[记] survival n. 生存，幸存 / survivor n. 幸存者，生还者

susceptible [sə'septəbl] a. 易受感动的，易受影响的

[例] We are all susceptible to advertising. 我们都容易受广告的影响。

[记] be susceptible to 对…敏感的；容易受到…

suspect [səs'pekt] v. 怀疑；['səspekt] n. 嫌疑犯

[例] I suspect that the computer has been infected by viruses. 我怀疑电脑可能受到了病毒的侵袭。

[记] suspect sb. of sth. 疑心某人干某事 /doubt v. 怀疑

> suspect 与 doubt 在意义和用法上的区别：suspect 后的从句用 that 引导，that 从句表达的内容可能是存在的。doubt 后的从句用 if 引导，if 从句表达的内容的真实性受到怀疑。如：I doubt if the computer has been infected by viruses. 电脑是否受到了病毒的侵袭，对此我表示怀疑。

suspend [səs'pend] v. 吊；悬挂；v. 延.缓

[例] Tom is suspended from school for a week for bad conduct. 汤姆因为行为不端被停学一周。

suspicious [səs'piʃəs] a. 怀疑的，可疑的，引起怀疑的

[例] The affair doesn't look more suspicious than we suspected. 这事看来没有我们猜测的那么可疑。

sustain [səs'tein] v. 支撑，撑住，维持

[例] There is not enough air to sustain life in this room. 屋里空气稀薄，快憋死了。

[记] sustainable a. 可以忍受的 /sustainable development 可持续性发展

swallow ['swɔləu] v. 吞咽；吞下；n. 燕子

[例] Most snakes swallow their prey whole. 多数蛇都是囫囵吞下它们的猎物。

swap [swɔp](=swop) v. /n. 交换

[例] He swapped his watch for a box of cigars. 他用他的手表换了一盒雪茄。

swarm [swɔːm] n. （蜜蜂等）一大群；（迅速移动的）人群

[例] A researcher observed a swarm of bees migrating with a queen bee to establish a new colony. 一位研究人员观察到了一群有蜂后的蜜蜂建立一个群落。

sway [swei] v. （使）摇摆，（使）摆动，（使）摇晃

[例] Swaying hips properly is the basis of the heel-and-toe walking race. 正确地摆动臀部是竞走的基本要素。

[同义词] swing

swear [swεə] v. 诅咒，咒骂；起誓保证

[例] He swore that his story was true. 他发誓说他的故事是真实的。

sweep [swiːp] v. 扫，打扫；扫过，掠过

[例] I saw the tops of trees moving in circles, and pieces of wood were swept up into the air. 我看见树梢来回摆动，木块被风吹上了天空。

> 短语 sweep the board，指“大获全胜”，源于赌博。board 指“赌桌”。当在一轮赌博中庄家 banker 独胜，他会用一把长木尺将桌面上所有的筹码和钱一扫 sweep 而空。Sweep the board 就是汉语中“通吃，通杀”的含义，引申为“大获全胜”。

swell [swel] v. 肿胀；膨胀；增大

[例] These small items help to swell the total greatly. 这些小数目使总额增加不少。

[同义词] bulge, enlarge, expand, inflate

swift [swift] a. 迅速的；敏捷的

[例] She is swift to reply. 她立刻答复。

switch [switʃ] n. 开关，电闸；v. （突然地）转换，转变

[例]There is a switch on the wall for turning on the lights. 墙上有一个开电灯的开关。

[记] switch on 开 /switch off 关 /switch to 切换到（另一电视频道等）

Sydney ['sidni] n. 悉尼（澳大利亚）

[例] Sydney is the important financial, industrial and educational centre in Australia. 悉尼是澳大利亚重要的金融、工业及教育中心。

syllabus ['siləbəs] n. 教学大纲，课程提纲

[例] The syllabus changes every year. 教学大纲每年都有变化。

> 由印刷错误而产生的单词。古罗马政治家 Ciero 一篇文稿中有个词 sittybas 目录，被印刷工误排成 syllabos，后演变为 syllabus，

仍然指目录，后引申为课程大纲等义。

symbol ['simbəl] n. 符号，记号；象征
[例] The dove is the symbol of peace. 鸽子是和平的象征。

symbolise ['simbəlaiz](=symbolize) v. 象征，是…的象征
[例] The Red Cross symbolizes humanitarianism. 红十字象征着人道主义。

symmetry ['simitri] n. 对称（性）；匀称
[例] The wound on the left side of his forehead spoiled the symmetry of his face. 他前额左方的伤口破坏了他脸部的匀称美。
[反义词] asymmetry

sympathetic [ˌsimpə'θetik] a. 同情的，有同情心的
[例] The volunteers felt sympathetic to the victims. 志愿者对罹难者表示同情。
[记] sympathy n. 同情，同情心

symphony ['simfəni] n. 交响乐，交响曲
[例] A tape deck played a Beethoven symphony and children played with Fisher-Price toys. 一边是录音机播放着贝多芬的交响乐曲，一边是孩子们在玩费歇尔价格指数玩具。

symposium [sim'pəuziəm] n. 专题报告会；专题论文集
[例] Later, a symposium on lipstick shades. 随后，关于唇膏的专题论文集渐渐地发生了变化。

源自希腊语，字面意思为“大家一起来喝酒”。古希腊人流行在饭后一边喝着小酒，一边讨论知识方面的问题。比现在大学里的 symposium 惬意多了。

symptom ['simptəm] n. 症状，征兆
[例] A persistent cough may be a symptom of tuberculosis. 持续的咳嗽可能是肺结核的症状。

synergy ['sinədʒi] n. (=synergism)协同，配合
[例] The benefits of cost savings, greater efficiency and synergy are being realised. 人们正在意识到节省费用、高效以及协作的好处。

前缀 sym-/syn- 指“一起，同时”。如：symbol 总是在一起的→（事物的）象征；sympathy 一起共有的感情→同情；symphony 同时的声音→交响乐；syndicate 企业在一起→企业联合，财团，辛迪加；syndrome 一起出现的病症→综合症，症候群；synthetic 放在一起的→综合的，合成的；synergy 大家一起干活 → 协同配合。

synonymous [si'nɔniməs] a. 同义的
[例] Nixon's name has become synonymous with political scandal. 尼克松的名字成了政治丑闻的同义词。
[反义词] antonymous

synthetic [sin'θetik] a. 合成的，人造的；综合的

[例] This synthetic dress material does not crush. 这种合成纤维衣料不会皱。

system ['sistəm] n. 系统；制度，体制

[例] The old administration system is under greater and greater challenge. 旧的行政管理体制正受到越来越大的挑战。

systematic [ˌsisti'mætik] a. 系统的，有条理的

[例] The systematic attempt is no longer what it used to be. 有计划的行为与以往大不一样了。

tab [tæb] n. 易拉罐拉环；标签，铭牌

tablet ['tæblit] n. 药片；碑，牌匾

[例] They put up a marble tablet in memory of his father. 他们建了一座大理石碑来纪念他的父亲。

[记] memorial tablet 纪念碑

taboo [tə'buː] n. 禁忌；忌讳 a. 禁忌的

[例] Things that are taboo in some cultures may be perfectly acceptable in others. 在一些文化中是属于禁忌的事物在另一些文化中可能是可以完全接受的。

[记] a taboo subject 一个忌讳的话题

> 源于汤加语 tabu，现已成为一个国际性词语，如法语 tabou，德语 Tabu，西班牙语 tabu，印尼语 tabu 等。英语除在人类学中拼为 tabu，一般多为 taboo。

tackle ['tækl] n. 用具，装备；v. 着手处理，对付，解决

[例] Everyone has his problems to tackle. 每人都有一些问题要去解决。

tactic ['tæktik] n. 策略，战略

[例] He's threatening to sue us? That's a tactic he's used before. 他威胁起诉我们？那是他过去用过的伎俩。

[记] a delaying tactic 拖延的战术 /strategy n.战略

tag [tæg] n. 标签，标牌

[例] Tags should be stuck into the goods to show their prices clearly. 标签应该醒目地贴在商品上以标示价格。

[记] a price-tag 价格标签

tailor ['teilə] n. 裁缝；v. 剪裁，适应

[例] This novel was tailored to popular taste. 这本小说被改编成迎合大众的口味了。

takeaway ['teikəwei] a. 供外卖的；n. 外卖餐馆

[例] Eat in or takeaway? 店内吃或带走？（快餐店服务员常问）

talent ['tælənt] n. 天赋，才能；天才

[例] My sister has a talent for music. 我妹妹有音乐才能。

[记] literary talent 文学才能 /special talent 特殊才能 / 人才

原为希腊货币单位。马太福音有一则寓言：一主人在出门前把金钱托付给他的三位仆人打理。第一位分到 5 talents，第二位 2 talents，第三位 1 talent。当主人回来后，头两位仆人的钱已经翻倍，主人很高兴。而第三位还是只有 1 talent，因为他怕丢失把钱埋起来了，没有做生意，甚至没有存银行，连利息都没有。主人非常生气，把这 1 个 talent 收回并奖赏给了第一位仆人。马太的寓意是：上帝赋予的天赋和才能人人都有义务去加以发挥。talent 遂引申为“天赋、才能”。

tally ['tæli] v. **符合，吻合** n. **比分，得分**

[例] The report tallies with your description of the accident. 报导和你对该事故的描述相吻合。

[记] tally with 与…相符合、一致

源于拉丁文 *tallia* 枝条。中世纪英国计数工具，原指一根狭长的木签，上刻有痕迹表示数额，整个木签从中劈开相耦合的两半，交易双方各执一半为凭。有点类似于中国古代帝王授予大将兵权的信物：虎符 Tally of Tiger。调发军队时，需持虎符左右两半验合。

tame [teim] a. **平淡的；枯燥乏味的；驯服的**

[例] The tame lions can communicate and dance together with the actors. 驯服的狮子可以与演员交流并同台共舞。

tangible ['tændʒəbl] a. **切实的，确实的，真实的；可触摸的**

[例] We need tangible evidence if we're going to take legal action. 如果要采取法律行动，就需要实实在在的证据。

[记] tangible asset 有形财产

tap [tæp] v. **轻拍，轻叩，轻敲；** n. **水龙头**

[例] She tapped him on the shoulder. 她轻轻拍了拍他的肩膀。

[记] tap at/on the door 敲门

tape [teip] n. **带子；磁带**

[例] We use sticky tape to stick things together. 我们用胶纸把东西粘在一起。

target ['tɑ:git] n. **靶子，目标，对象**

[例] The hunter's target was a wild animal. 这个猎人的目标是一只野兽。

[记] on target 击中要害的；完全准确的 /hit a target 达到目标

tariff ['tærif] n. **关税；收费表，价目表**

[例] There is a very high tariff on jewelry. 宝石类的税率很高。

[记] agreement tariff 关税协定

关税与贸易总协定GATT (General Agreement on Tariff and Trade)，它与国际货币基金组织 IMF (the International Monetary Fund)，世界银行 (the World Bank) 一起，构成了当代世界经济体系的三大支柱。

taxation [tæk'seiʃən] n. **征税，课税；税款**

[例] The government has decided to increase taxation. 政府决定提高税收。
[记] taxation bureau 税务局

tease [ti:z] v. 取笑；嘲弄
[例]If you always tease others like that, you'll forfeit the good opinion of your friends. 你如果老是那样捉弄别人，你就会丧失朋友们对你的好感。

technical ['teknikəl] a. 技术的，技能的，工艺的
[例] To build this machine，you must have technical ability. 要造这台机器，你们必须有技术能力。
[记] technical know-how 技术知识；技术诀窍

technique [tek'ni:k] n. 技巧，技术
[例] I want to learn the latest techniques for making toys. 我想学习制作玩具的最新技能。

technological [ˌteknə'lɔdʒikəl] a. 技术上的
[例] I am amazed at the technological advances in the past twenty years. 对 20 年来技术的发展我感到非常惊讶。

technology [tek'nɔlədʒi] n. 技术
[例] Life is made so much easier with modern science and technology. 有了现代科学技术，生活变得多么惬意。
[记] technology-intensive a. 技术密集的

tedious ['ti:diəs] a. 冗长乏味的；单调枯燥的
[例]The tedious job simply ate me up. 那单调乏味的工作简直把我烦死了。

teenager ['ti:nˌeidʒə] n. 十几岁的青少年
[例] The survey shows that four out of five teenagers have experimented with illegal drugs. 调查显示十几岁的青少年中每五人就有四人尝试过非法毒品。
[记] teen a. 少年的；少女的；十几岁的

temper ['tempə] n. 脾气，情绪，心情；v. 调节
[例] He's in a temper today. 他今天在闹情绪。

> temper 古意为“节制，中庸之道”。人们的脾气都应该是有节制的，中庸的。如果失去了节制，就是 lose one's temper “发火，生气”，保持节制就是 keep one's temper “忍住气，不发火”。

temperate ['tempərit] a. 温和的；不极端的，有节制的
[例]Britain has a temperate climate. 英国的气候温和。
[记] temperate criticism 温和的批评

temple ['templ] n. 庙，寺；教堂；鬓角
[例] The library is often considered as a temple of learning. 图书馆常被人们认为是知识的殿堂。

tempo ['tempəu] n. （音乐）速度，节拍
[例] The long strike has upset the tempo of production. 这次长时间的

罢工已经破坏了生产进度。

temporary ['tempərəri] a. 暂时的，临时的

[例] The loss of electrical power was only temporary. 停电只是临时的。

[记] temporary employment 临时的工作

temptation [temp'teiʃən] n. 引诱，诱惑

[例] Jack cannot resist the temptation of the sight of the purse on the counter. 杰克无法抵抗柜台上钱包的诱惑。

[记] fall into temptation 受诱惑 /resist temptation 抵制诱惑

tenant ['tenənt] n. 房客；租户

[例] He threatens to take the tenant to court or to have the tenant evicted. 他威胁将租户送上法庭或逐出。

[反义词] landlord n. 房东

tend [tend] v. 趋向，有某种倾向；照管

[例] People under some stress tend to demonstrate their full range of potential. 处于压力下的人容易发挥自己全部的潜力。

[记] tend to 趋向 /tend on 招待，照料

tendency ['tendənsi] n. 趋势，趋向

[例]There is a growing tendercy to marry later. 晚婚是一种日益增长的趋势。

[记] have a tendency to/towards 有…的倾向

tender ['tendə] a. 脆弱的；温柔的；软弱的；v. （正式）提出；投标

[例] My finger is tender because I cut it yesterday. 我的手指一碰就疼，因为昨天割破了。

[记] tender for v. 投标

> 世界摇滚第一人“猫王”Elvis Presley 经典名曲 Love me tender: Love me tender, love me sweet; Never let me go. You have made my life complete. And I love you so. . .

tense [tens] a. 拉紧的，绷紧的

[例] The players were tense at the start of the game. 队员们在比赛开始时很紧张。

tension ['tenʃən] n. 紧张，不安，拉紧（状态）

[例] The tension in the Far East is building up again. 中东的形势又逐步紧张起来。

tent [tent] n. 帐篷；帐棚

[例] I went into her tent and she told me to sit down. 我进了她的帐篷，她让我坐下。

term [tə:m] n. 名称；期限，学期；条款，条件

[例] He was made captain of the football team for a term of one year. 他被推选为足球队队长，任期一年。

terminate ['tə:mineit] v. 停止，结束，终止

[例] Jane's unhappy married life terminated in divorce. 珍妮的不幸婚姻以离婚而告终。

> 施瓦辛格 Arnold Schwarzenegger 经典电影《终结者》系列，英文名 *Terminator*。

terminology [ˌtəːmiˈnɔlədʒi] n. 术语学

[例] It is important that lawyers use the correct terminology when they prepare contracts. 律师制定合同时使用正确的术语很重要。

terrace [ˈterəs] n. 梯田；平台 v. 使成梯形地

[例] They made a terraced garden. 他们造了一个梯形花园。

terrain [ˈterein] n. 地形

[例] He climbed a tree to view the surrounding terrain. 他爬上一棵树来察看周围的地形。

terrestrial [tiˈrestriəl] a. 陆地的；陆栖的

[例]Elephants are terrestrial animals. 大象是陆地的动物。

[记] terrestrial animals 陆栖动物 /terrestrial interests 名利心

> 我们把外星人称作 ET，即是 the Extra-Terrestrial。中国古时的术数家拿十二种动物来配十二地支，组成十二生肖属相，英文译为 Twelve Terrestrial Branches and Symbolic Animals。"天干"则被译为 Celestial Stems。

terrify [ˈterifai] v. 使恐怖，恐吓

[例] Her husband's violence terrified her. 丈夫的暴力使她感到恐怖。

[记] terrifying a. 极大的, 可怕的 /terrorist n. 恐怖分子 /terror n. 恐怖 / terrorism n. 恐怖主义

terrific [təˈrifik] a. 极好的，极棒的；令人恐怖的

[例] The drunken man drove at such a terrific pace that an old couple were knocked down. 这醉汉驾车速度极快，结果撞倒了一对老年夫妇。

territory [ˈteritəri] n. 领土，版图，地域

[例] Wild animalr often mark their territory with scent.野生动物通常用气味标记它们的领地。

tertiary [ˈtəːʃəri] a. 第三的，第三位的；高等教育的

[例] There are three main types of prevention, known as primary, secondary and tertiary. 有三种预防，即第一级预防，第二级预防和第三级预防。

[记] primary a. 第一位的；小学的 /secondary a. 次要的，第二的；中学的

testify [ˈtestifai] v. 作证；证明，证实

[例] I won't testify against my friend. 我不想作对我朋友不利的证言。

[记] testify against 作不利于… 的证明 /testify to 证明, 证实

testimony [ˈtestiməni] n. 证词，宣言，陈述

[例] In his testimony, he denied that the company had ignored safety procedures. 他在证词中否认公司忽视了安全防范程序。

> 在提供证词之前，法庭要求证人发誓，对于无神论者，问题是："Do you solemnly affirm that the evidence to be given by you shall be the truth, the whole truth, and nothing but the truth?" 证人回答 "Yes." 或 "I do."。

thaw [θɔː] n. /v. 解冻，融解，融化

[例] The sun thawed the ice and melted the snow. 阳光下冰消雪融。

[记] thaw out(使)解冻，融化

theft [θeft] n. 偷，偷窃

[例] He was put in prison for theft. 他因为偷窃被关进监狱。

[记] thief n. 小偷

theme [θiːm] n. （谈话、讨论、文章等的）主题，题目

[例] Stamp collecting was the theme of his talk. 集邮是他谈话的主题。

Unit 28

theoretical [θiə'retikəl] a. 理论上的

[例] Equality between men and women in our society is still only theoretical. 男女平等在我们这个社会还只停留在理论上。

[记] theoretically adv. 在理论上；理论地

theory ['θiəri] n. 理论，原理

[例] One theory about the moon is that it is a piece broken off the earth. 有一种关于月球的理论认为它是从地球分离出的一部分。

thereby [ˌðεə'bai] adv. 因此，从而

[例] He became a citizen, thereby gaining the right to vote. 他成了公民，因此有投票权。

thesis ['θiːsis] n. 论点；论文

[例] Their main thesis was that the rise in earnings was due to improvements in education. 他们的主论点是收入的增加应该归功于教育水平的提高。

texture ['tekstʃə] n. 质地；结构；构造

[例] We can see the orderly texture of matter through an electron microscope. 我们可以通过电子显微镜看到物质的有序结构。

therapy ['θerəpi] n. 治疗

[例] The physical therapy alternates with a chemical one. 理疗和化疗交替进行。

[记] therapist n. 治疗学家；治疗师

thermal ['θəːməl] a. 热的，热量的

[例] We have bath water from thermal springs. 我们用温泉水洗浴。

> therm(o)- 是"热的"意思。比如 thermodynamics 热力学，thermonuclear 热核的，热核反应的，thermostat 自动调温器，恒温器，thermos 暖水瓶。

thigh [θai] n. 大腿，股

[例] Fat tends to accumulate around the hips and thighs. 脂肪多在屁股和大腿周围囤积。

thorough ['θʌrə] a. 十分的，彻底的

[例] They made a thorough search for the lost ring, but didn't find it. 他们仔细地寻找过那枚丢失的戒指，可是没有找到。

thoughtful ['θɔːtful] a. 认真思考的，考虑周到的；体贴的

[例] It was thoughtful of you to warn me of your arrival. 你来之前先通知我，真是考虑周到。

threaten ['θretn] v. 威胁，恐吓；危害到；预示

[例] The expansion of the deserts seriously threatens the survival of wildlife. 沙漠的扩大严重地威胁着野生动物的生存。

[记] threaten to do sth. 威胁要做某事

threshold ['θreʃhəuld] n. 门槛；开端；最低限度

[例] The sound was so loud it was on the threshold of pain. 声音大得开始使人无法忍受。

> 在东西方婚礼的习俗上有一点是共通的：新郎抱新娘过门槛(carry the bride over the threshold)古罗马人认为新娘第一天进新家被门槛绊脚很不吉利，干脆由新郎bridegroom抱进去吧。另外注意西方婚礼新娘站在新郎的左边，男右女左。这个习惯是由于古代抢亲成风，新郎左手护住新娘，右手必须腾出来握剑，随时跟上来抢亲的人拼杀！

thrift [θrift] n. 节省，节俭

[例] To practice thrift is a virtue. 节俭是美德。

[记] thrifty a. 节约的

thrive [θraiv] v. 繁荣，兴旺发达，茁壮生长

[谚] First thrive and then wive. 先立业，后成家。

tide [taid] n. 潮，潮汐；潮流，趋势

[例] It was their first victory. The tide had turned. 这是他们的第一次胜利。他们开始转好运了。

[记] tidal a. 潮汐的 /tidal wave 海啸

tidy ['taidi] a. 整齐的，整洁的

[例] Everybody wants the house tidy, but nobody wants to tidy it himself. 谁都想让房子整洁，可谁也不愿意亲自整理。

tilt [tilt] v. (使)倾斜, (使)翘起

[例] I tilted the cup to drink out of it. 我斜起杯子以便喝里面的水。

timber ['timbə] n. 木材，木料

[例] We must safeguard forest timber. 我们必须保护森林。

[同义词] lumber, wood

time-consuming ['taimkən,sju:miŋ] a. 耗时的

[例] All this begging for money was time-consuming and degrading so I decided to concentrate on finding work. 乞讨又耗时又没面子，因此我决定一心一意找工作。

timely ['taimli] a. 及时的，适时的

[例] We greatly appreciate your timely help. 我们非常感谢你们的及时帮助。

timetable ['taimteibl] n. 时间表

[例] A timetable lists the times at which certain events, such as arrivals and departures at a transportation station, are expected to take place. 时刻表列出了某些事情比如车站里交通工具到达和离开的预计时间。

[同义词] schedule

timid ['timid] a. 胆小的, 羞怯的

[例] You are every inch as timid as a mouse. Just speak up! 你真是十足的胆小如鼠。大声说出来吧!

[同义词] cowardly, fearful

tiny ['taini] a. 极小的, 微小的

[例] He carved so many characters on a tiny piece of marble. 他将那么多字刻在一小块大理石上。

tip [tip] n. 小费; 提示; 尖端; 倾斜; v. 使倾斜, 给小费

[例] I gave a tip to the man who carried my cases. 我给了那个替我拿箱子的人一点小费。

[记] have (sth.) on the tip of one's tongue 话到嘴边（却想不起来了）

tissue ['tisjuː] n. 餐巾纸; 棉纸; 【生】组织

[例] She used paper tissues to blow her nose. 她用棉纸擤鼻子。

[同义词] napkin

titanic [tai'tænik] a. 巨大的, 力大无比的

[例] I could scarcely imagine such a titanic event. 我几乎想象不出这事件之重大。

> 希腊神话中泰坦巨人Tians, 力大无穷。titanic是其派生的形容词, 表示“巨大的”。如著名的泰坦尼克号游轮Titanic以此为命; 德国化学家Klaproth发现的金属元素命名为钛titanium, 因为他认为钛的超强度和超高的耐熔度正与泰坦神的伟大相辉映。羽毛球拍、网球拍等都以含Ti而价高。

toast [təust] n. 烤面包（片）; v. 祝酒, 干杯; 烤, 烘

[例] We toasted the bride and bridegroom. 我们为新娘新郎干杯。

> 英国莎士比亚时代有一流行习俗: 人们饮酒时, 喜爱把加有香料的烤面包片toast放入酒中, 据说能使酒的味道更美。在当时drink a toast意思是: 喝了那个面包片。所以有了我们现在的说法: Let's drink a toast to sb.（来, 为某人干一杯!）, toast也有了“干杯, 祝酒”的词义。

toil [tɔil] v. 长时期地苦干, 辛苦劳作

[谚] Pleasure comes through toil. 苦尽甘来。

token ['təukən] n. 象征; a. 象征的, 表意的

[例] We shook hands as a token of our friendship. 我们握手以表示我们的友谊。

[记] subway tokens 地铁代币

tolerance ['tɔlərəns] n. 忍受, 容忍; 宽容

[例] We should always try to show tolerance to other people. 我们应当始终对他人表示宽容。

[记] tolerate v. 忍受 /tolerable a. 可忍受的 /tolerant a. 宽容的

toll [təul] n. 通行费；代价；钟声；丧钟（宣布死亡）

[例] The accident took a heavy toll of lives. 事故中人员伤亡惨重。

topic ['tɔpik] n. 话题，题目

[例] Choose one from the three topics. 从三个题目中任选一个。

[记] write on the topic of 以…为题目而写

torch [tɔːtʃ] n. 手电筒；火把；火炬

[例] He used a torch to see into the dark cupboard. 他用一只手电筒照看黑暗的橱柜。

> 奥林匹克火炬接力Olympic Torch Relay, 奥运圣火 Olympic Flame。在传说中，奥运火炬的起源是来自希腊神话，是普罗米修斯从天界取得了火种送至人间的。

toss [tɔs] v. 扔，掷，掷

[例] They tossed the ball to each other. 他们把球互相扔来扔去。

[记] toss for sth. 掷钱币以决定某事

total ['təutl] a. 总的，全部的；n. 总数

[例] In total, over 150,000 people were killed in the violent tsunami. 在这次强烈海啸中丧生的人总计超过了150,000。

tough [tʌf] a. 艰难的；坚强的，坚韧的

[例] You need to be tough to survive in a society full of competition. 要在充满竞争的社会中生存就要有坚韧不拔的意志。

[记] a tough policy 强硬的政策

tournament ['tuənəmənt] n. 锦标赛，联赛，比赛

[例] The tournament took five days. 邀请赛历时五天。

tow [təu] n. /v. 拖，拖曳；牵引

[例] We towed the car to the garage. 我们把车子拖到了汽车修理间。

towel ['tauəl, taul] n. 毛巾；v. 用毛巾擦

[例] We need a new towel. 我们该换毛巾了。

[记] throw in the towel 认输

toxic ['tɔksik] a. 有毒的，有毒性的

[例] All medicines are toxic. 所有药物都有毒性。

> 来源于希腊语里的toxon，意为弓箭。荷马史诗《伊利亚特》*Iliad*中还能寻到踪迹。后来战争中人们普遍在箭头上涂上毒药，提高弓箭的杀伤力，字根tox就有了“毒”的含义。如：toxicant 毒物，毒药；detoxify 解毒；toxicologist 毒物学家(比如欧阳锋)；intoxicate 心里中毒→使陶醉。

trace [treis] v. 追踪，追溯 n. 痕迹；足迹；少许

[例] They traced the criminal to a house in the city. 他们追踪罪犯到了城里的一座房子里。

[记] a trace of 一丝，少许

track [træk] n. 足迹，轨迹，车辙；v. 跟踪，追踪

[例] The hunter followed the animal's tracks. 猎人追踪动物的足迹。

[记] trace back to 追溯到，追究到，追查到

tradition [trə'diʃən] n. 传统，惯例

[例] It is a tradition that the young look after the old in their family. 在他们家，年轻的照顾年长的是一个传统。

tragedy ['trædʒidi] n. 悲剧；灾难，不幸

[例] I prefer comedy to tragedy. 我喜欢喜剧而不喜欢悲剧。

[反义词] comedy

trail [treil] v. 拖，拉；跟踪；n. 踪迹，痕迹

[例] The carriage left a trail of dust. 马车后扬起了一路灰尘。

trait [treit] n. 特性，品质

[例] Thousands of years later people are still arguing vehemently against each other over whether personality traits are born or learned. 数千年后，人们依然在热烈争论，究竟个性是先天就有还是后天习得的。

[记] a trait of 一点点，少许，微量

tramp [træmp] n. 流浪者，游民；长途跋涉

[例] The tramp begged for food. 那流浪汉乞讨食物。

tranquil ['træŋkwil] a. 安静的

[例] The old enjoy the tranquil life in the country. 老年人喜欢乡村平静的生活。

transaction [træn'zækʃən] n. （一笔）交易，业务

[例] Sellers and buyers manage business transactions by keeping in touch with each other. 买卖双方通过保持联系来管理业务。

> 前缀 trans- 指“越过，贯穿 across”。如：trans- 贯穿往来 +action 行动→transaction 交易；transit 经过，通行；translate 越过到了对面→移动，翻译；transparent 穿过来穿过去两边都清楚明显 (apparent)→透明的；transform 变形；transformer 形状变来变去的人→美国动画片变形金刚。

transcribe [træns'kraib] v. 转录

[例] Thousands of pages of testimony were transcribed at a cost of $ 2. 50 a page. 数千张的证言材料以每张 2.5 美金的价格让别人抄写。

[记] transcript n. 抄本

transfer [træns'fəː] v. 迁移，转移，调动

[例] The dog has transferred his affection to his new master. 那只狗已把它的感情转移给它的新主人了。

[记] transfer to 转移；转学

transform [træns'fɔːm] v. 使变形，使改观

[例] She transformed the room by painting it. 她油漆了房间使它为之一新。

transit ['trænsit] n. /v. 经过，通行，中转

[例] Transit passengers please go to the lounge. 中转旅客请到休息厅。

[记] in transit 在运输中 /transition n. 过渡 /transitional a. 过渡时期的

translate [træns'leit] v. 翻译；转化

[例] No matter how well a poem is translated, something of the spirit of the original work is lost. 无论一首诗翻译得多好，原创作品中的一些神韵也会丢失。

[记] translator n. 翻译者 /[同义词] interpret

transmit [trænz'mit] v. 传送；传播；遗传

[例] Parents transmit some of their characteristics to their children. 父母把一些特有的素质遗传给儿女。

transparent [træns'pɛərənt] a. 透明的；可穿透的

[例] Not all glass is transparent. 并非所有玻璃都是透明的。

transplant [træns'plɑːnt] v. 移植

[例] He patiently showed us how to transplant rice. 他耐心地教我们插秧。

transport ['trænspɔːt] n. /v. 运输，运送，传送

[例] Before it could be transported to the United States, a site had to be found for it and a pedestal had to be built. 在雕像可以运往美国之前，必须给它选个场地，还要建一个雕像底座。

[记] transportation n. 交通，运输

trap [træp] n. 陷阱，圈套，诡计

[例] The police set a trap for the thieves. 警察设下了圈套捉小偷。

trauma ['trɔːmə] n. 外伤；身体上的伤；精神上的创伤

[例] Multiple-personality disorder is usually caused by early childhood trauma. 多重个性紊乱经常是由童年早期的精神创伤造成的。

[记] traumatic a. 外伤的；创伤的 /psychotrauma n. 心理创伤

treasure ['treʒə] n. 金银财宝，宝藏；v. 珍爱

[例] He treasures the watch his mother gave him. 他珍爱母亲送给他的表。

[记] treasury n. 财政部, 国库

> 《金银岛》*Treasure Island* 是 19 世纪出生在英国苏格兰爱丁堡，著名的文学作家罗伯特 · 路易斯 · 斯蒂文森（Robert Louis Stevenson）一生最畅销的小说之一。如果说中国的孩子是看着《西游记》长大的，那么美国的孩子就是看着 *Treasure Island* 长大的，*Treasure Island* 可算是有史以来最好看的海盗小说。

treatise ['triːtiz] n. （专题）论文，专著

[例] His treatise claimed our attention. 他的论文引起我们的注意。

treatment ['tri:tmənt] n. 治疗，疗法；待遇；处理（方式）

[例] A proper treatment will do great good to both his body and his psychology. 正确的治疗对他的身心都大有裨益。

treaty ['tri:ti] n. 条约

[例] The two countries signed a treaty in which they agreed to help each other. 两国签署了同意互助的条约。

[记] a peace treaty 和平条约

tremble ['trembl] v. /n. 战栗，颤抖

[例] There was a tremble in her voice. 她的声音颤抖着。

tremendous [tri'mendəs] a. 巨大的，极大的；惊人的

[例] We went to a tremendous party. 我们参加了一个盛大的聚会。

trench [trentʃ] n. 沟渠，壕沟；v. 掘壕沟；围以沟，隔绝

[例] The firemen trenched the fire by pulling down houses. 消防队员拆倒房屋来隔绝火势的蔓延。

trend [trend] n. 趋势，倾向；v. 伸向；倾向

[例] The trend of modern living is to exercise regularly and eat wisely. 有规律的锻炼、有节制的饮食是现代生活的趋势。

trespass ['trespəs] v. 侵入；n. 过失；非法侵入

[例] The farmer said we were trespassing. 这个农民说我们未经许可进入了他的土地。

trial ['traiəl] n. 审讯；考验，磨炼；试验；试用

[例] Life is full of trials. 人生充满着磨难。

[记] on trial 试用；试验中；审讯中

triangle ['traiæŋgl] n. 【数】三角形；三角关系

[例] The three places form a triangle. 三个地方构成一个三角。

tribe [traib] n. 部落，部族

[例] Some African tribes have no written language. That's why they are so backward. 一些非洲部落没有书面语言，这正是他们落后的原因。

> 卢梭在《社会契约论》中曾提到了 tribe 一词的来源：古罗马成立时，人民由阿尔班人 Alban，萨比奈人 Sabine 和外国人三部分构成，故称为 tribe，tri+be 三个存在。而向古罗马捐献财物、进贡就是 tribute。其他同源词还有 contribute 捐献、捐赠；distribute 分发；attribute 归结于，属性；tributary 从属的。

tributary ['tribjutəri] a. 附庸的，从属的，支流的；n. 进贡国，附庸国；支流

[例] The major tributaries are described below. 主要的几个支流会在下面描述。

trick [trik] n. 骗局，花招，诡计；诀窍，技巧

[例] He got the money from me by a trick. 他用诡计骗走了我的钱。

[记] tricky a. 狡猾的，机警的

trifle ['traifl] n. 琐碎事；小事

[例] Don't trifle with you health. 不可把健康当儿戏。

trigger ['trigə] n. （枪等的）扳机；v. 引发，触发

[例] He accidentally triggered his rifle. 他无意中扣发了他步枪的扳机。

trim [trim] v. 修剪，整理；a. 整齐的，整洁的

[例] A bird trims its feathers. 鸟整饰它的羽毛。

triple ['tripl] a. 三倍的，三重的；n. 三倍；v. 使增至三倍

[例] He tripled his income. 他使他的收入增加两倍[增至三倍]。

triumph ['traiəmf] n. 胜利，成功；v. 获得胜利

[例] It was a great triumph when our team won the race. 我们队赛跑赢了，这是一个很大的成功。

> 古罗马时期将军打了胜仗回到罗马城，要举行盛大的凯旋仪式，拉丁文叫做 *triumphus*，triumph 即源于此。Arch of Triumph 法国凯旋门；trump 扑克牌中王牌。

trivial ['triviəl] a. 微不足道的，没有价值的

[例] Don't always quarrel over trivial matters! 你们别总为了一些的琐碎小事争吵！

[记] trivial matters 无关重要的事情 /trivia n. 琐事；电影的花絮

> tri 三 + via 路 +al 形容词尾→ trivial 三条路的会合点，三岔路口。古罗马妇女从市场 shopping 归来，喜欢停在三岔路口同人闲聊，内容自然是诸如谁家的蔬菜水果新鲜啦，谁家的价格便宜啦等无关紧要的琐事。名词形式 trivia，还指"电影的花絮"。

tropic ['trɔpik] n. 热带地区 a. 热带的

[例] He lives in the tropics. 他住在热带地区。

trunk [trʌŋk] n. 大旅行箱；树干；躯干

[例] Can she move that trunk by herself? 她自己能搬动那只大箱子吗？

[记] live in one's trunks 总穿着旅行服装；老在旅行

trustworthy ['trʌstˌwəːði] a. 值得信赖的，可靠的

[例] The firm is one of our most trustworthy concerns. 该公司为我方最值得信赖公司之一。

tube ['tjuːb] n. 管，管子，电子管，显像管；地铁

[例] She passed me a tube of toothpaste. 她递给我一管牙膏。

tuition [tjuː'iʃən] n. 学费

[例] Foreigners pay a much higher tuition than the locals. 外国人所付学费比本国人高得多。

turbulent ['təːbjulənt] a. 动荡的，混乱的；汹涌的

[例] The sea was too turbulent for us to be able to take the boat out. 大海波涛汹涌，我们无法出海。

[记] turbulence n. 骚乱，动荡

turmoil ['təːmɔil] n. 骚动，混乱

[例] The demonstration turned into turmoil. 示威演变成骚乱。

turnout ['tə:naut] n. 聚集人数，到会人数

[例] There was a disappointingly poor turnout to hear such a well-known speaker. 只有很少的人来听这么著名的演讲者的演讲。

turnover ['tə:nˌəuvə] n. 流通量；营业额

[例] Annual turnover is about $9 billion. 年营业额约为 90 亿美元。

tutor ['tju:tə] n. 家庭教师；（大学中的）导师

[例] Her tutor teaches her at home. 她的家庭教师在家里教她。

tutorial [tju:'tɔ:riəl] n. 大学导师的个别指导时间，辅导课

[例] My tutor gives a tutorial every week. 我的辅导老师每周辅导一次。

[记] individual tutorial 个别辅导 /laboratory tutorial 实验辅导课

twilight ['twailait] n. 暮色；曙光

[例] Bats flit about in the twilight. 蝙蝠在暮色中四处飞翔。

[记] twilight of the gods 诸神的末日(北欧神话)

> 前缀 twi- 指 two，twilight 即是在明暗二者之间的光，所以既指"暮色"，也可以指"曙光"；两个(tw)孩子在妈妈肚子里(in)→twin 双胞胎；twig 小树枝，树杈（一分为二的，分叉的）；twist 两个拧在一起→缠绕，扭曲。

twin [twin] a. 双的；n. 双胞胎

[例] The plan has a twin purpose. 这个计划有双重目的。

twinkle ['twiŋkl] v. 闪烁，闪耀

[例] We could see the distant twinkle of the harbour lights. 我们可以看见港湾的灯光在远处闪烁。

> 你的记忆深处还有这首儿歌吗：一闪一闪亮晶晶，满天都是小星星。挂在天上放光明，好像许多小眼睛。Twinkle, twinkle, little star. How I wonder what you are. Up above the world so high. Like a diamond in the sky. . .

twist [twist] n. /v. 拧，扭曲；缠绕

[例] Twist the lid to open it. 拧这盖儿打开它。

typical ['tipikəl] a. 典型的，有代表性的

[例] He is a typical pupil; he is like most of the other pupils. 他是一个有代表性的学生，他和大多数其他学生一样。

Unit 29

ubiquitous [juːˈbikwitəs] n. 到处存在的，普遍存在的

[例] Plastic packaging is ubiquitous nowadays. 现在到处都是塑料包装。

[记] ubiquity n. 到处存在

ultimate [ˈʌltimit] a. 最后的，最终的；根本的

[例] Their ultimate destination was Paris. 他们最终的目的地是巴黎。

ultimately [ˈʌltimətli] adv. 最后，最终，终于

[例] Truth will ultimately prevail. 真理终究会胜利。

umpire [ˈʌmpaiə] n. 裁判员，仲裁人

[例] Mark was thrown out of the game for hitting an umpire. 马克因为殴打裁判被逐出比赛。

[同义词] referee

> 英语中有一种构词现象比较特殊，是由于发音的原因而词形拼写发生变化。比如：原来“一名裁判员”是a noumpere，后来不定贯词a和单词的首字母n结合，写成了现在的an umpire。同样情况的还有：apron围裙，a napron→an apron; orange橙，a norange→an orange; adder蝰蛇，a dder→adder; nickname绰号，an ickname→a nickname，等。

unanimous [juːˈnæniməs] a. 全体一致的，一致同意的，无异议的

[例] We are in unanimous agreement. 我们全体意见一致。

unconditional [ˌʌnkənˈdiʃənəl] a. 无条件的

[例] The general said he would fight on until the enemy agreed to an unconditional surrender. 将军说他将战斗到底，除非敌人同意无条件投降。

underestimate [ˈʌndərˈestimeit] v. 低估，看轻；n. 低估

[例] Never underestimate the power of the press. 永远不要低估新闻界的力量。

[反义词] overestimate

undergo [ˌʌndəˈgəu] v. 经历，遭受

[例] I underwent so much suffering in early years that I am afraid of nothing today. 早年我经历了如此多的苦难，所以现在什么都不怕。

undergraduate [ˌʌndəˈgrædjuit] n. 大学本科生

[例] The undergraduates of Oxford come from all over the world. 牛津大学的学生来自世界各地。

[记] undergraduate 本科学生，还未毕业；postgraduate = graduate students 研究生；如果 单说 graduate，指本科毕业生。

underground [ˈʌndəgraund] a. 地下的；秘密的；n. 地铁

[例] There is an underground room in the old house. 在老房子里有一个地下室。

> 地铁在美国叫做subway，英国通常称underground，伦敦和悉尼简称为Metro。

underlie [ˌʌndəˈlai] v. 位于…之下；成为…的基础

[例] Social problems and poverty underlie much of the crime in today's big cities. 社会问题与贫困成为了现今大城市严重犯罪的基础。

underline [ˌʌndəˈlain] v. 在…的下面划线；强调

[例] I underlined the idiomatic expressions in the passage to catch your eye. 我在文章中的习惯用语下面划了线，以便引起你的注意。

undermine [ˌʌndəˈmain] v. 暗中破坏，逐渐损坏

[例] The constant criticism was beginning to undermine her confidence. 持续的批评开始逐渐削弱她的自信。

undertake [ˌʌndəˈteik] v. 担任；许诺，保证

[例] The developed countries should undertake the main responsibility of global air pollution. 发达国家应担当起全球空气污染的主要责任。

undone [ˈʌnˈdʌn] a. 未做完的；松开的

[例] Your zip's undone. 你的拉链没有拉上。

unfold [ʌnˈfəuld] v. 展开，打开，摊开；展示

[例] As the story unfolds, we learn more about Max's childhood. 随着故事情节的展开，我们知道了有关马克斯童年更多的事。

unfortunate [ʌnˈfɔːtʃənit] a. 不幸的；令人遗憾的

[例] The unfortunate expedition brought them few achievements. 运气不佳的探险使他们收获甚微。

uniform [ˈjuːnifɔːm] n. 制服；a. 一致的；一贯的

[例] Do you have to wear a uniform if you work at McDonald's? 在麦当劳工作必须穿制服吗？

unify [ˈjuːnifai] v. 使成一体，使联合，统一；使一致

[例] Music serves to identify and unify members of the group. 音乐有鉴别和团结其成员的作用。

[记] unity n. 团结，统一

union [ˈjuːnjən] n. 联合，结合；联盟

[例] The largest teachers' union supports the education reforms. 最大的教师联盟支持教育改革。

[记] trade union <英>/ labor union<美> 工会

> union（联合）和onion（洋葱）不仅形似而且同源，都来自拉丁语unio，表示联合。洋葱onion之所以有“联合”之意，是因为它是由若干层包裹而成的一个整体圆球。onion在古代极受青睐，据说能激发性欲，增强体力。建造金字塔的古埃及工人们吃过，亚历山大大帝的军队也吃过。

unique [ju:'ni:k] a. 独一无二的，唯一的

[例] Each person's fingerprints are unique. 每个人的指纹都是独一无二的。

unite [ju(:)'nait] v. 联合，团结

[例] Workers of the world, unite! 全世界无产者，联合起来！

universal [ˌju:ni'və:səl] a. 普遍的；全世界的；全面的

[例] Love is a subject of universal interest. 爱情是一个普遍感兴趣的问题。

universe ['ju:nivə:s] n. 宇宙，世界

[例] The incurable disease did disable him to live the life of this kind he had always dreamt of, but made him work harder at his explorations of the universe . 不治之症的确使他不能过他梦寐以求的生活，但使他加倍地致力于宇宙探索工作。

> 字根 vers 指“转，转向”。adverse 去转向 → 反向的，敌对的；conversation 一起转向，面对面 → 交谈；universe 万物旋转成为一体 → 宇宙。

unlikely [ʌn'laikli] a. 未必的，不大可能的，不大可靠的

[例] It seems unlikely that the wonder we have been expecting will appear. 看来，我们一直在期待的奇迹不大可能出现了。

unofficial [ˌʌnə'fiʃəl] a. 非官方的，非正式的

[例] “Take Me Home, Country Road" became West Virginia's unofficial state song. “乡村之路”成为西弗基尼亚非正式的州歌。

unprecedented [ʌn'presidəntid] a. 无前例的，空前的

[例] Such hurricanes were quite unprecedented and caused widespread damage. 这种飓风前所未有，造成了广泛的损失。

update [ʌp'deit] v. 更新，使跟上时代

[例] Our e-mail addresses are unlikely to be updated every day. 我们的电子邮件地址不可能天天更新。

upgrade [ʌp'greid] v. 使升级，提升

[例] The anti-virus software should often be upgraded. 杀毒软件应当经常升级。

[记] on the upgrade 改善的，进步的

uphold [ʌp'həuld] v. 支持，坚持，维护；维持

[例] The appeal court upheld the sentence. 上诉法庭维持了判决。

upset [ʌp'set] v. 弄翻；使心烦意乱，使不适

[例] The wind will upset the boat. 风会把船吹翻。

upside down [ʌpsaid'daun] adv. 颠倒, 混乱

[例] The house was turned upside down by the burglars. 那间房被窃贼翻得乱七八糟。

[记] inside out 彻底地；（衣服）里面穿到了外面 /ups and downs 起伏，兴衰沉浮

urban ['ə:bən] a. 城市的，市内的
[例] Both urban and rural areas are more and more prosperous. 都市和乡村都越来越繁荣了。
[记] urbanise v. 使城市化 /urbanization n. 城市化

urgent ['ə:dʒə:nt] a. 紧急的，急迫的
[例] The report called for urgent action to reduce lead in petrol. 这份报告呼吁采取紧急行动减少汽油中的含铅量。
[记] urge v. 催促，力劝；n. 强烈欲望

utensil [ju:'tensl] n. 器皿，用具（尤指厨房用具）
[例] The cooking utensil were frozen up in the ice. 炊具都给冻在冰里了。

utility [ju:'tiliti] n. 效用，有用
[例] Demonstrations allow customers to get an immediate idea of a product's utility. 使用示范让消费者立刻了解产品的功用。
[记] utilities 水电气杂费 /Does your rent include utilities? 房租里包括水电气费吗？（租房场景）

utilize ['ju:tilaiz] v. 利用
[例] We must consider how best to utilize the resources we have. 我们必须考虑如何最好地利用我们已有的资源。
[记] utilization n. 利用, 使用

utmost ['ʌtməust] a. 极度的，最大程度的；n. 极限，最大可能
[例] I overheard two girls talk in utmost seriousness about the exams. 我无意中听到两个女孩子极其严肃地谈论着考试。
[同义词] extreme

utterly ['ʌtəli] adv. 完全地，彻底地
[例] Whether you like her or not is utterly irrelevant. 这跟你喜不喜欢她没有一点关系。

vacancy ['veikənsi] n. 空，空白，空缺，空闲
[例] The vacancy has been filled. 空缺已有人补上。

vacant ['veikənt] a. 空的，未被占用的；空缺的
[例] Are there any rooms vacant in this hotel? 这家旅馆有空房吗？

vacation [və'keiʃən] n. 休假，假期；v. 度假
[例] I worked in a small beachside restaurant during the summer vacation. 暑假我在一家小的海滨餐馆打工。

vaccinate ['væksineit] v. 进行预防接种；种痘；n. 被接种牛痘者
[例] Has your child been vaccinated against smallpox? 你的小孩接种牛痘疫苗了吗？
[记] vaccination n. 种痘，接种疫苗

vacuum ['vækjuəm] n. 真空；空白；空虚
[例] Her death left a vacuum in his life. 她的去世给他的生活留下一片真空。

[记] vacuum cleaner 真空吸尘器

vague [veig] a. 含糊的，不清楚的

[例] In a fog everything looks vague. 在雾中一切东西都显得模糊。

vain [vein] a. 徒劳的，无结果的；自负的

[例] We protested in vain. 我们抗议但没有结果。

[记] in vain 徒然，枉然

valentine ['vælәntain] n. 情人；情人节礼物

[例] One of the symbols of St Valentine's Day is the Roman god of love – Cupid. 情人节的标志之一是罗马爱神—丘比特。

[记] Saint Valentine's Day 圣瓦伦丁节，情人节（2 月 14 日）

> 古罗马的战事连绵，暴君下令适龄男子必须从军，不许举行婚礼。有修士 Valentine 不忍见一对对情侣生离死别，为前来求助的情侣秘密地主持结婚典礼。后来消息走漏，Valentine 被捕入狱，于公元 270 年 2 月 14 日在地牢里受尽折磨而死。情人节来历版本甚多，取此文愿天下有情人终成眷属。

valid ['vælid] a. 具有效力的；有根据的，有理的

[例] My passport is valid for 10 years. 我的护照有效期是十年。

[记] validity n. 有效性 /validate v. 使有效 /[反义词] invalid

value ['vælju:] n. 价值；v. 估价；重视，珍视

[例] I have always valued his advice. 我一向尊重他的意见。

van [væn] n. 厢式货车

[例] You will certainly need to make arrangements for the sitting of the outside broadcast van and the laying of cables. 你肯定需要安排好实况转播车的停放位置和电缆的铺设。

vanilla [vә'nilә] n. 香草

[例] Many children don't like vanilla-flavoured ice-cream. 许多孩子不喜欢香草味冰激淋。

> 汤姆 · 克鲁斯 Tom Cruise 主演的电影《香草天空》Vanilla Sky。
> vanilla ice-cream 香草冰淇淋 / ice-cream cone 甜筒 / ice candy 冰棒 / milk-shake 奶昔 / sundae 圣代

vanish ['væniʃ] v. 消失；突然不见

[例] I thought it would rain, but the clouds have vanished and it's a fine day. 我原以为天要下雨的，可是云消失了，是个好天。

[同义词] disappear, fade, perish

vapour ['veipә] n. 蒸汽；水蒸气

[例] Water can change from liquid state into ice or vapour. 水能从液态变成冰或水蒸汽。

variable ['vɛәriәblz] n. 变量，可变因素；a. 可变的

[例] There are some variables that can change our plans. 有一些不定因

素会改变我们的计划。

variation [ˌvεəri'eiʃən] n. 变更，变动，变化

[例] This recipe makes an interesting variation on the traditional Christmas cake. 这种配方改变了传统的圣诞蛋糕。

variety [və'raiəti] n. 变化，多样化，各类

[例] Variety is the spice of life. 变化是生活的调味品。

[记] a variety of 各种各样的，品类繁多的

various ['vεəriəs] a. 不同的，各种各样的

[例] There are various colors to choose from. 有各种各样的颜色可供选择。

vary ['vεəri] v. 变化，使多样化

[例] Driving regulations vary from state to state. 各国的驾驶规则是不同的。

vast [vɑːst] a. 广阔的，广大的；大量的

[例] The refugees come across the border in vast numbers. 大量的难民越过边境。

vegetarian [ˌvedʒi'tεəriən] n. 素食者，素食主义者

[例] I've become used to a vegetarian diet. 我已经习惯了吃素。

> 并非来自于蔬菜 vegetable，而是源于拉丁文 *vegetus*— 是精力旺盛、生气蓬勃、活力充沛的意思。

vegetation [ˌvedʒi'teiʃən] n. 〈总称〉植物，植被

[例] They made their way through the thick vegetation in the valley. 他们穿过峡谷里茂密的草木丛。

vehicle ['viːikl] n. 工具，手段；交通工具，车辆

[例] Language is the vehicle of human thought. 语言是人类表达思想的工具。

velocity [vi'lɔsiti] n. 速度，速率；迅速

[例] There will be strong winds tonight with velocities of 60 miles an hour and more. 今晚将有大风，时速达 60 英里以上。

venom ['venəm] n. 毒液；恶意；v. 放毒，使恶毒

[例] The viper paralyses its prey by injecting it with venom. 毒蛇是通过给猎物注射毒液而使其瘫痪。

> venom 这个词一开始是 wen，意为希望，一支分出导致了 win 赢，胜利；另一支演化成和"爱"有关的单词，如：venery 性欲，venerate 尊崇，venin 媚药。单词 venom 和 venin 现在已经成为"毒素"的含义了。也许，古人们早就认识到，任何诱发虚假爱情的事物，本质上都是毒药。

venture ['ventʃə] n. 冒险，投机；v. 冒险，冒险行事

[谚] Nothing ventured, nothing gained. 不入虎穴，焉得虎子。

venue ['venjuː] n. 发生地点，举行场所

[例] They have already told us the venue of tomorrow's match. 他们已

告诉我们明天比赛的地点。

verbal ['və:bəl] a. 口头的；动词的

[例] A verbal report will usually be enough. 通常一个口头汇报就可以了。

[同义词] oral

verge [və:dʒ] n. 边缘，边沿

[例] He was on the verge of bankruptcy. 他濒临破产。

[同义词] edge

verify ['verifai] v 证实，核实，查清

[例] He tried in every way to verify this theory. 他想一切办法来验证这个理论。

[同义词] certify, confirm, prove

versatile ['və:sətail] a. 多才多艺的；有多种用途的

[例] Nylon is a versatile material. 尼龙是一种有多种用途的材料。

[记] versatility n. 多功能性

version ['və:ʃən] n. 版本；一种说法

[例] I have heard two versions of the accident. 我已经听到关于这个事故的两种说法了。

versus ['və:səs] (=Vs.) prep. （诉讼、比赛等中）对

[记] China versus Italy 中国队对意大利队

vertebrate ['və:tibrit] a. 有脊椎的，脊椎动物的；n. 脊椎动物

[例] Mammals and reptiles are both vertebrates. 哺乳动物和爬行动物都是脊椎动物

[记] backbone n. 脊柱；骨干 /[反义词] invertebrate

vertical ['və:tikəl] a. 垂直的，直立的

[例] In some places the cliff was almost vertical, and much too dangerous to climb. 在一些地方悬崖几乎是垂直的，非常危险不能攀登。

[反义词] horizontal

vessel ['vesl] n. 船；容器，器皿；血管，脉管

[谚] Empty vessels make mast sound. 满瓶不响，半瓶晃荡。

veterinary ['vetərinəri] (=vet) n. 兽医；a. 兽医的

veto ['vi:təu] n. 否决，否决权；v. 否决，禁止

[例] Jenny wanted to invite all her friends, but I quickly vetoed that idea. 詹妮想邀请她所有的朋友，但我很快否决了。

via ['vaiə] prep. 经，通过

[例] I sent a message to Mary via her brother. 我托玛丽的兄弟带个口信给她。

viable ['vaiəbl] a. 可行的；可望成功的；能养活的

[例] It seems as if your proposal is not really economically viable. 好像你的提议在经济上不可行。

vibrate [vai'breit] v. 使振动；摇摆

[例] Some insects? wings vibrate so fast that the movement is invisible to the human eye. 一些昆虫的翅膀摆动很快，以至于人们用肉眼都无法察觉。

[记] vibration n. 振动，摆动

vice versa ['vaisi 'vɜːsə] adv. 反之亦然

[例] The boys may refuse to play with the girls, and vice versa. 男孩可能不愿同女孩玩，反之亦然。

vicinity [vi'siniti] n. 邻近，附近地区

[例] The stolen car was found in the vicinity of the station. 被偷走的车在车站附近找到了。

[记] in the vicinity of 在…附近

vicious ['viʃəs] a. 邪恶的，不道德

[例] She was shocked by the vicious criticism. 她被恶意的批评吓住了。

victim ['viktim] n. 受害者，牺牲品

[例] One of the bombing victims was dead on arrival at hospital. 一名炸弹爆炸的受害者刚送到医院就死了。

[记] victim of crime 犯罪的受害者

victory ['viktəri] n. 胜利，成功

[例] The school football team has had three victories this month against other schools. 校足球队这个月三次战胜其他学校。

> 罗马神话中胜利女神Victory，希腊神话中胜利女神则是Nike，耐克运动品牌以此为命。西方男孩名字 Victor 维克多；女孩名字 Victoria维多利亚；人们伸出右手的食指和中指，比划作V形，都表示“胜利”的含义。

vigorous ['vigərəs] a. 强有力的

[例] Environmentalists have begun a vigorous campaign to oppose nuclear dumping in this area. 环保主义者展开了一次强有力的运动反对在该地区倾倒核垃圾。

[记] vigor n. 精力，活力

villa ['vilə] n. 别墅，城郊小屋

[例] I want to buy a villa outside the city. 我想在城外买幢别墅。

violate ['vaiəleit] v. 违反，违背；侵犯

[例] The sound of guns violated the usual calm of Sunday morning. 炮声破坏了平常星期日早晨的宁静。

[记] violate a law 犯法 /violation n. 违反，违背

violence ['vaiələns] n. 猛烈，强烈；暴力，暴行

[例] They will meet violence with violence. 他们将用暴力来对付暴力。

[记] violent a. 猛烈的，狂暴的

virgin ['vəːdʒin] n. 处女；a. 处女的，童贞的，纯洁的

[记] the Virgin Mary 圣母玛利亚

> 正义女神 Astraea 在希腊神话中的黄金时代末期，由于人类触犯了她，大怒之下返回天庭，化身为天空中的处女座 Virgo。单词Virgin即源于此。

Unit 30

virtual ['və:tjuəl] a. 实际上的，事实上的；虚的

[例] She is the virtual president, though her title is secretary. 虽然她的头衔是秘书，她是实际上的董事长。

[记] VR (Virtual Reality) 【计】虚拟现实 /virtually adv. 事实上，实质上

virtue ['və:tju:] n. 美德，德行；优点

[例] Patriotism, respect and patience are always virtues . 爱国、尊敬和忍耐永远都是美德。

virus ['vaiərəs] n. 病毒

[例] The disk was accidentally infected with a virus called Trojan Horse. 这张磁盘不小心感染了木马病毒。

visa ['vi:zə] n. 签证

[例] You are allowed to apply to the Consul for an exit visa. 你可以向领事申请出境签证。

> 字根 vis 指"看见 see"。visa 看见的、出示的证件→签证；visible 可见的；visit 去看→拜访；revise 重新看→修改，校订。

visible ['vizəbl] a. 看得见的，可见的

[例] The comet is visible to the naked eye. 肉眼就可以看见彗星。

vision ['viʒən] n. 视力，视觉；幻想

[例] She suffered temporary loss of vision after being struck on the head. 头部被击中后，她经历了暂时的失明。

visual ['viʒuəl] a. 视力的，视觉的

[例] Artists translate their ideas into visual images. 艺术家把他们的思想转化为视觉的形象。

[记] visual arts 视觉艺术 /visualise v. 使显现；使形象化

vital ['vaitl] a. 生命的；生死攸关的，极其重要的

[例] These measures are vital to national security. 这些措施对国家安全极其重要。

> 拉丁文中 vita 指生命 life。而 vivere 指 to live，所以字根 viv 即有"生活，生存"之义，如：vivid 鲜活的，活泼的；revive 复活；survive 幸存，活下来。

vitamin ['vaitəmin] n. 维他命，维生素

[例] Fresh greenstuffs are rich in vitamins. 新鲜蔬菜含有丰富的维生素。

vivid ['vivid] a. 生动的，逼真的，鲜明的

[例] She is girl with vivid red hair and a vivid imagination. 她是一个留着鲜红的头发并且想象力活跃的孩子。

vocabulary [və'kæbjuləri] n. 词汇；词汇表

[例] The vocabulary used in the course book is printed at the back. 这本教科书里要用的词汇表印在书后。

vocational [vəu'keiʃənəl] a. 职业（上）的

[例] There are vocational and technical schools to deal with job training for kids not destined for university. 这里有职业学校和技术学校，为不愿上大学的孩子们提供工作培训。

> career, vocation, occupation, job 的区别。car + er 原意是“车走的跑道”，沿着特定轨道一直走下去，不会改变。所以 career 指长期或终身的、需特殊技能的工作。vocation 中字根 voc，指“呼唤的声音，召唤”，这份工作是上天的召唤，你特别适合，有天分。occupation 来源于 occupy，占据你时间的工作，指为了谋生而规律的工作。job，普通工作，学生打工叫 part-time job。

vogue [vəug] n. 流行，时尚；时髦事物（或人物）

[例] Long hair for men and high boots for ladies are no longer in vogue. 男子留长发、妇女穿高筒靴不再流行了。

[记] in vogue 流行，时髦

void [vɔid] n. 空间，空旷；a. 空的，空闲的，空虚的

[例] The amusement park will fill a void in this town, which has little entertainment for children. 这个游乐场将填补小镇上没有儿童娱乐设施的空缺。

volatile ['vɔlətail] a. 易变的，反复无常的（性格）；易挥发的

[例] People are afraid to change jobs in today's volatile economy. 在当今变化无常的经济形势下人们不愿换工作。

volcano [vɔl'keinəu] n. 火山

[例] The volcano erupted and buried two small towns under meters of hot ash, mud and bits of molten rock. 这次火山爆发将两座小城镇掩埋于两米厚的尘埃、熔岩的泥浆和碎块之下。

> 来自希腊神话中的铁匠兼火神 Vulcan 武尔坎。他的妻子是鼎鼎大名的美神 Venus 维纳斯。后来美神爱上了战神帅哥，红杏出墙，还生下了私生子丘比特！ Vulcan 招惹不起强大的情敌，只好终日躲在地底下打铁。某日，胸中的怒火、妒火、炉火同时喷发：火山爆发 volcano。

volt [vəult, vɔlt] n. 伏特（电压单位）

[记] These batteries are 1.5 volts each. 这些电池每节 1.5 伏。

volume ['vɔljuːm] n.（书）卷，册；体积，容量

[例] The volume of this container is 2 cubic meters. 这个容器的容量是两立方米。

voluntary ['vɔləntəri] a. 自愿的，志愿的

[例] Most charities rely on voluntary contributions from the public. 多数慈善机构都是靠民间的自愿捐助。

volunteer [ˌvɔlən'tiə] n. 志愿者；志愿兵；v. 志愿；a. 志愿的

[例] The four volunteers entered the test chamber on June 12 with a limited supply of air and water. 四个志愿者于6月12日进入了限供空气和水的试测仓。

voucher ['vautʃə(r)] n. 代金券，优惠购物券；证人

[例] The voucher can be used at most major supermarkets. 这张代金券能在大多数大超市里使用。

vow [vau] n. 誓约；v. 宣誓

[例] The couple made their wedding vows at St. Paul's Church. 这对情侣在圣保罗教堂里宣誓结婚。

[同义词] swear, promise, pledge, oath

vulgar ['vʌlgə(r)] a. 粗俗的，庸俗的

[例] Vulgar fashions filled the store windows. 商店的橱窗里摆满了俗气的服装。

voyage ['vɔiidʒ] n. 航海；航空；航行

[例] He accepted the offer by the navy to go on a voyage to explore the Southern Sea in the name of the government on a warship. 他受海军之助，凭借政府权利乘战舰继续在海上探索南海。

> 法语Bonvoyage一路顺风。bon好的，voyage一次旅程。相当于英语Good journey.

vulnerable ['vʌlnərəbl] a. 易受伤的，脆弱的

[例] The young girl looked very vulnerable. 那姑娘看上去十分柔弱。

[记] be vulnerable to 易受影响的 /[同义词] susceptible

wage [weidʒ] n. 工资

[例] The railroad workers have asked for a wage increase. 铁路工人要求增加工资。

wagon ['wægən] n. 货车；四轮马车

> 我们常说的面包车，就是wagon。wagon还有一个不常用的词义，指北斗七星。英国人也称北斗七星为Charles's Wain 查理斯的马车；美国人称之为Great dipper 大杓子。国产家庭用车“北斗星”的原型是铃木公司的Wagon R，取名北斗星，颇有心思。

wander ['wɔndə] v. 徘徊，漫步；精神恍惚

[例] It is fun to wander the world. 漫游世界是非常惬意的。

[区别] wonder n. /v. 惊奇

ward [wɔːd] n. 病房，病室；（尤指未成年人的）被监护人

[例] The physician infected the whole ward with his humour and laughter. 这位内科医生用他的幽默和笑声感染了整个病房的人。

wardrobe ['wɔːdrəub] n. 衣柜；藏衣室；全部服装

[例] Can you hang these in the wardrobe, please? 请你把这些挂在衣柜里。

warehouse ['wɛəhaus] n. 仓库

[记] household goods warehouse 家具仓库

warranty ['wɔrənti] n. 保证书；保证，担保

[例] The car is still under warranty. 这辆车仍在保修期内。

[记] a three-year warranty三年保证期 /warrant v. 担保 /[同义词]guarantee

wax [wæks] n. 蜡；v. 上蜡；增加；月亮渐满

[例] Candles are made from wax. 蜡烛是蜡做的。

> wax 作动词有"上蜡；逐渐增加；月亮由亏转盈"的含义。给汽车养护的一个重要措施就是 waxing 上蜡；月亮由亏转盈逐渐变大，并且越来越亮，就如同不断的上蜡一样。所以月有"阴晴圆缺"就是 wax and wane。waxing moon 上弦月。

weave [wi:v] v. 编织；编造

[例] We are weaving garlands of flowers for heroes. 我们在为英雄编织花环.

weight [weit] n. 重量；体重（尤指肥胖）

[例] It is better to lose weight through exercise. 最好是通过锻炼减肥.

weird [wiəd] a. 怪诞的，古怪的

[例] Her weird dress attracted attention in the small town. 她那奇装异服在这小镇很惹人注目。

> 莎士比亚悲剧《麦克白斯》中的三女巫 Weird Sisters，也是希腊神话中的命运三女神，相当于罗马神话里的 Fates。weird，witch 巫婆，wizard 巫师，都"巫"到一块儿了！

welfare ['welfɛə] n. 福利，幸福

[例] In making this decision, the court's main concern is for the welfare of the children. 法庭做出这一裁决考虑的主要因素是孩子们的幸福。

[记] social welfare 社会福利

well-being ['welbiiŋ] n. 康乐，安乐，福利

[例] Our only concern is the children's welfare. 我们唯一关注的是儿童们的福利。

[同义词] welfare

whale [weil] n. 鲸鱼；v. 捕鲸；猛烈攻击

> dolphin / porpoise 海豚；seal 海豹；walrus 海象；常见鲸鱼有 blue whale 蓝鲸，sperm whale 抹香鲸（体内含有与黄金等价的化妆品原料—龙涎香。）

whereas [wɛə'ræz] conj. 然而，但是

[例] Whereas the city spent over $1 billion on its museums and stadiums, it failed to look after its schools. 这个城市在建博物馆和体育馆上耗资超过 10 亿，然而却无力顾及建筑学校。

whereby [wɛə'bai] conj. 在那个方面；凭这个，由此

[例] The mall created a frequent-shopper plan whereby customers earn discounts. 这个商场对回头客有优惠策略，凭此顾客们享受了打折。

whilst [wailst] conj. 当…时候
[同义词] while

whirl [(h)wəːl] v. (使)旋转；一连串快速的活动
[例] We watched the seagulls whirling and shrieking over the harbour. 我们注视海鸥在港口上空盘旋尖叫。

whisper ['(h)wispə] v. 低声说；耳语
[例] The two girls were whispering in the library. 这两个女孩在图书馆里低声说话。

whistle [(h)wisl] n. 口哨，汽笛声；v. 吹口哨
[例] The referee whistled and the game began. 裁判吹响哨音比赛开始。

wholesale ['həulseil] n. 批发；a. 批发的，大批的
[例] These wholesale dealers earned a large sum of money. 这些批发商大赚了一笔。

wholesome ['həulsəm] a. 有益健康的
[例] Vegetables and fruits are wholesome food. 蔬菜和水果是健康食品。

> whole 古义为“健康的，未受伤的”，引申为“无缺的，完整的，整体”。形容词后缀-some 表示“像…样的，有…倾向的”。wholesome 有健康倾向的→有益健康的；burdensome 沉重的；troublesome 麻烦的；而 handsome 原意也指像手一样的→handy 灵便的，后莎士比亚创造性地用 handsome 表示男子“英俊的”。美国人又用它来表示“可观的”，earn handsome money 赚大钱。

wicked ['wikid] a. 邪恶的；缺德的
[例] It is wicked of you to torment the poor dog. 你折磨那只可怜的狗真缺德。

> wick 灯芯，蜡烛心。《大话西游》中朱茵就是 wick。她和 wicked 其实没有一点关系，wicked 一词和 witch 巫婆同源。

widespread ['waidspred] a. 分布广泛的，普遍的
[例] The disease soon became widespread. 疾病很快蔓延开来。

widow ['widəu] n. 寡妇；v. 使成寡妇(或鳏夫)
[例] She became a widow at twenty-five. 她二十五岁开始守寡。

width [widθ] n. 宽度，广度；宽阔，广阔
[例] In front of the skyscraper is a road of great width. 摩天大楼前有一条宽阔的马路.

wilderness ['wildənis] n. 荒野，不毛之地
[例] From his attic window he looked out over a wilderness of roofs. 从他阁楼的窗户望去, 他看到一大片屋顶.

wildlife ['waildlaif] n. 〈总称〉野生动物；野生动植物
[例] Environmental pollution endangers wildlife. 环境污染威胁着野生

动植物的生存.

windfall ['windfɔːl] n. 意外之财，横财

[例] The merger could mean a $2. 2 billion windfall for shareholders. 这一合并可能意味着股东会获得二十二亿美元的意外之财。

> windfall 大风吹落。被大风吹落的果实，毫不费力地拾起来，即是意外之财，飞来横财。

winding ['waindiŋ] n. 绕，缠；a. 卷绕的

[例] There is a winding path to the village. 有一条弯弯曲曲的小路通向村庄。

wisdom ['wizdəm] n. 智慧

[谚]That's good wisdom which is wisdom in the end. 最后灵验的话才是至理名言；聪明到头才算真。

wit [wit] n. 机智风趣

[例] His writings sparkle with wit. 他的作品闪露着才智。

withdraw [wið'drɔː] v. 收回，撤消；撤退

[例] She withdrew all her savings from the bank. 她把存在银行里的钱都取了出来。

[记] withdraw money from the bank从银行取款 /withdraw a remark收回发言

wither ['wiðə] v. （使）枯萎，凋谢

[例] The flowers withered in the cold. 花在寒冷的天气里凋谢了。

> 来源于 weather 天气，指受阳光、风雨、温度等的影响。weather 不好，植物就会 wither。

withstand [wið'stænd] v. 抵挡，顶住，经受住

[例] The bridge is built to withstand an earthquake of 8. 3 magnitude. 这座桥能经受 8. 3 级的地震。

witness ['witnis] v. 亲眼看见，目睹；n. 目击者，见证人

[例] We witnessed tremendous changes in the city. 我们目击了这个城市的巨大变化。

womb [wuːm] n. 【医】子宫；发源地

[记] from the womb to the tomb 从生到死，一生中

workaholic [ˌwəːkə'hɔlik] n. 工作狂

[例] I do not want to become a workaholic. 我不想成为工作狂。

> work 工作+aholic…迷，嗜…者→workaholic 工作狂。aholic 可以加到另一个词的后面，来表示喜欢或沉迷于某事物的人。比如我们说某人的女朋友是“购物狂”、“碎钞机”，就用 shopaholic 表达；而 webaholic 就是“网络迷”，“网虫”啦。

workforce ['wəːkfɔːs] n. 劳动力

[例] This year ten per cent of the workforce will be made redundant. 今

年有百分之十的人下岗。

workload ['wə:kləud] n. 工作量

[例] We hired another secretary to handle the increased workload. 我们雇用了另一名秘书来处理增加的工作量。

[记] heavy workload 巨大的工作量

workshop ['wə:kʃɔp] n. 研讨会；车间，工场

[例] Are you interested in the summer poetry workshop? 你对暑假诗歌学习班感兴趣吗？

worldwide ['wə:ldwaid] a. 世界范围的，全世界的

[例] The concert attracted a worldwide television audience of over a billion people. 音乐会吸引了全球十几亿的电视观众。

worship ['wə:ʃip] n. 崇拜；（对神的）信奉，礼拜；v. 做礼拜

[例] She gazed at the famous singer with worship in her eyes. 她注视着歌星，眼神里充满着仰慕。

wrap [ræp] v. 裹，包，捆

[例] Wrapped up in this shawl, you look prettier. 围上这围巾你更漂亮。

[rek] v. /n. （船、飞机等）失事，遇难；破坏，毁坏

wreck [例] The tsunami caused wrecks all along the coast. 那次海啸在沿海岸造成了许多船难。

wretched ['retʃid] a. 不幸的，可怜的，悲惨的

[例] I was shocked to see their wretched living conditions. 看到他们恶劣的生活条件我十分震惊。

X-rated ['eks,reitid] (青少年禁看的)X 级片

xerox ['ziərɔks] n. 复印；复印件 v. 复印

[例] Could you xerox it and give me back the original? 你能把它复印了，并把原件还给我吗？

> 前面提到了很多大公司用英语单词作为品牌名称，Xerox 美国施乐公司却是个反例。Xerox 作为世界上第一台静电复印机的品牌名称而家喻户晓，被英语吸收成为常用单词，表示 photocopy。可想施乐过去的辉煌。

Xmas ['krisməs] (=Christmas) n. 圣诞节

[例] We will have a Xmas party this weekend. 这个周末我们将有一个圣诞晚会。

X-ray ['eks'rei] n. X 光

[例] The doctor took some x-ray photographs of Tom's broken arm. 医生给汤姆摔坏的胳膊拍了些 X 光片。

y-axis ['wai'æksis] n. y 轴，纵坐标轴

[例] The wage rates for labour in the two localities are shown on the y-axis. 这两地劳动力的价格在纵坐标轴上有所表现。

yawn [jɔ:n] v. 打呵欠；张开；n. 呵欠

[例] I felt so sleepy I couldn't stop yawning. 我感到很困，止不住地打呵欠。
[记] snore v. 打鼾 /sneeze v. 打喷嚏

yearn [jəːn] v. 渴望，向往
[例] The overseas Chinese yearned to return to their native land. 华侨们渴望回到故乡。
[记] yearn for 渴望

yelp [jelp] v. 狗吠
[例] The dog yelped with pain. 狗疼得叫了起来。

yield [jiːld] v. 生产，产生；投降，屈服；n. 产量；收益
[例] Such investments can yield 20 percent. 这样的投资可生息百分之二十。
[记] yielding a. 易弯曲的；屈从的；n. 让步 /unyielding a. 坚硬的，不屈的

yoga ['jəugə] n. 瑜珈，瑜珈术
[例] Some people learn yoga to keep fit. 有些人学瑜伽健身。

> boxing 拳击，shadowboxing 太极拳，Taekwondo 跆拳道，karate 空手道，judo 柔道，wrestle 摔交，sumo wrestling 相扑。最近流行什么"舍宾"健身。猜猜看是那个英语单词？

yoghurt ['jɔgət] n. 酸奶
[例] I've bought some yoghurt for the salad. 我买了些酸奶，做沙拉用。

yummy ['jʌmi] a. 美味的；n. 美味
[例] This cake is really yummy. 这蛋糕真好吃。
[记] yum int.美味的

youngster ['jʌŋstə] n. 年轻人，小伙子
[例] These youngsters yearn for adventure in the wild. 这些青年人渴望野外冒险。

zeal [ziːl] n. 热心，热情，热忱
[例] Jack served everyone with zeal. 杰克热心地为大家服务。
[记] zealous a. 热心的

zest [zest] n. 情趣，乐趣；热情
[例] The experts showed great zest for the genetically modified food. 专家们对转基因食品表现出极大的兴趣。

> 借自法语 zeste，指柑桔皮、柠檬皮。主要加于饮料中调味，增加香气。现引申为"情趣"等含义。短语 eat with zest，和着柠檬皮一起吃→吃得津津有味。

zigzag ['zigzæg] v. 曲折地前进；adv. 呈之字形地
[例] The road zigzagged through the mountains. 道路曲折地穿过群山。

zone [zəun] v. 将…分区，使分成地带；n. 地带；区域
[例] They zoned the house into sleeping and living areas. 他们把房子分成睡眠和起居的区域。
[记] smokeless zone 禁止吸烟区 /[同义词] area

* 舍宾：shaping 形体塑造

附录一 雅思考试分类词汇表

雅思听力生活类词汇

1. 描述人的外表衣着

gender 性别 medium build 中等身材 average height 不高不矮 slim 苗条的 stout 结实的、矮胖的 plump 丰满的

bald/balding 秃头 hair color 头发颜色 brown 棕色 blond 金发碧眼的 straight/curly/wavy hair 直、卷、波浪发 fair hair 金发 dyed hair 染发 parted in the middle 中分 a pony tail 马尾 long/short plaits 长短辫子

angular（面部）棱角分明的 scar 疤痕 beard 落腮胡子 moustache/mustache 小胡 wearing glasses 戴眼镜 contact lenses 隐型眼镜 tattoo 纹身

trousers 长裤 jeans 牛仔裤 T-shirt T恤 top 上衣 pullover 套头毛衣 suit 西服 套装 sweater 套头衫、运动衫

pink and white striped skirt 粉红色和白色间条裙 spotted shirt 斑点衬衣 checked shirt 格子衬衣

be in red/green/dark 身着红 / 绿 / 黑色衣服 be in/ wear tie 戴领带 bracelet 手镯 stockings 长袜 boots 靴子 high-heel shoe 高跟鞋 sandal 凉鞋 sports shoes 运动鞋

2. 个人信息

full name 全名 surname/family name/last name 姓氏 first/given name 名字 middle initial 中间名缩写

nationality 国籍 passport number 护照号码 visa 签证 ID/identification/identity 身份证 driving/driver's license/licence 驾驶执照 date of birth 出生年月日 age 年龄 blood type 血型 height 身高 weight 体重 marital status 婚姻状况 home address 家庭住址

course applied 申请课程 prefered/favourite food 比较 / 最爱吃的食物 hobbies 爱好 register/enrollment date 注册 / 报到日期 English proficiency 英语水平 first impressions of the city/university 对城市或大学的第一印象 home/office number 家庭 / 办公室电话号码 date of arrival/departure 到达 / 出发日期 signature 签名

3. 租房场景

Student Accommodation Center 学生住宿管理中心 Student Accommodation Officer 学生

住宿管理员 housing coordinator 住宿协调员 newspaper advertisements 报纸广告 real estate agency 房地产中介

landlord 男房东 landlady 女房东 roommate/flatmate/dormmate/housemate 室友

for lease/for rent 出租 for sale 出卖

surroundings 环境 rural areas 乡村 suburb 市郊 downtown 市区 Road(Rd.), Street(St.), lane 小路巷 Avenue 大道 floor number 楼层 room number 房间号

flat/apartment 公寓 dormitory (dorm) 学生宿舍 student hostel 学生旅店 youth hostel 青年旅店 homestay 在当地居民家居住 unit 单元房 townhouse 连排房屋 motel 汽车旅馆

hall/lobby 门厅 bedroom 卧室 a double/twin bedroom 双人间 a single bedroom 单人间 balcony 阳台 bedroom 睡房 kitchen 厨房 laundry room 洗衣室 bathroom 卫生间 shower 淋浴 garage 车库 hallway/corridor 走廊 store room/house 储藏室 yard 院子 garden 花园

stove 炉子 fridge/refrigerator 冰箱 microwave oven 微波炉 washing machine 洗衣机 air-conditioner 空调 electric fan 电风扇 radiator 电暖器 electric stove 电炉

unfurnished 无家具 furnished 有家具 pillow 枕头 pillow case 枕套 bed linen 床单 spread 床罩 sheet 被单被褥 mattress 床垫 blanket 毯子 towel 毛巾 curtain 窗帘 carpet 地毯 wardrobe 衣柜

utilities 水电气费 rent 租金 bond 押金 blackout 停电 pet 宠物 insect infestation 闹昆虫

4. 交通

travel agency 旅行社 book the ticket 订票 motel 汽车旅馆 hostel 青年旅社 passport 护照 visa 签证 make a reservation 预定 confirm a reservation 确认预定 cancel one's reservation 取消预定 frist come,first serve 先到先服务原则 book a room/table 预订房间 / 饭桌 cancel one's reservation 取消预定

timetable 时刻表 fare 票价 toll 通行费 saver ticket 优惠票 open ticket 开放机票 one-way ticket 单程票 round-trip/return ticket 往返票

first class 头等舱 business class 商务舱 economy class 经济舱

layover/stopover 中途停留 non-stop flight 直达航班 connecting-flight 转机 flight number 航班号 take off 起飞 land 降落 check in 办理登机手续

airport tax 机场税 duty-free shop 免税店 excess charge 超重 vacant seat 空座 destination

目的地 extra charge/surcharge附加费 fulling-booked满了 seat arrangement/assignment定座 E.T.A(estimated time of arrival)预计到达时间 E.T.D(estimated time of departure)预计起飞时间
Expressway 高速公路 express train 高速列车 van 中巴 shuttle bus 班车 airport limousine 机场大巴 berth 铺位（火车上）

Ford 福特 Rolls & Royce 劳斯莱斯 Benz 奔驰 BMW 宝马
parking lot/area 停车场 car park 停车场 parking meter 米表 parking permit/sticker 停车许可
pay a fine 罚款 tow away 拖走 clamp the wheel 锁轮胎

5. 旅游场景

credit card 信用卡 driving license/licence 驾照 expire 驾照/护照等过期 platform 站台 book the room(make a reservation)订房间 currency 货币 Canadian dollars 加元 Australian dollars澳币 Pound英镑 Japanese Yen 日元 credit card信用卡 Visa维萨卡 MasterCard 万事达 American Express 美国运通

deserts 沙漠 hilly areas 丘陵地带 wetlands 沼泽地 bushland 灌木丛 tropical rain forests 热带雨林 resorts 胜地 coastal areas 沿海地区 lake 湖 hotsprings 温泉 fountain 泉水，喷泉 beaches 海滩 spotlight tour 聚光灯旅行 four-wheel drive 四驱车 waterfalls 瀑布 castle 城堡 art gallery 画廊 museum 博物馆

public transport公共交通 private transport私人交通 ferry渡船 underground/subway/tube/Metro 地铁 river cruise 巡游 boat trips 乘船游览 hiking 徒步旅行 hitch-hike 搭便车旅行 backpacker 背包旅行

swimming游泳 diving潜水，跳水 scuba diving戴着水下呼吸器潜水 surfing冲浪 skiing 滑雪 water skiing 滑水 hang gliding 悬挂滑翔 water polo 水球 souvenir 纪念品 snake 蛇 stingers 刺痛人的东西 shark 鲨鱼 jellyfish 水母 certain plants 某些植物 beach towel 大浴巾 telescopes望远镜 walking boots步行靴 socks袜子sunscreen防晒霜 long trousers 长裤

6. 打工场景

labour market 劳工市场，劳务市场
Labour exchange/employment exchange 职业介绍所
seasonal work 季节工作
piecework 计件工作
timework 计时工作
position/post 职位
vacancy 空缺，空额
work permit 工作许可证
to apply for a job 求职，找工作
occupational disease 职业病
vocational guidance 职业指导
vocational training 职业训练
personnel/staff 人员

clerk 办公室人员
trainee/apprentice 学徒工
night shift 夜班
trade union 工会 (美作:labor union)
remuneration 报酬
pay/wage/salary 工资
premium/bonus/extra pay 奖励
payday 发工资日，付薪日
pay slip 工资单
payroll 薪水册
pension 养老金
receptionist 接待员
typist/data entry 打字员 / 数据录入者
key puncher 电脑操作员
stenographer 速记员
telephone operator 电话接线员
shorthand typist 速记打字员
delivery boy 送报员
secretary 秘书
model 模特
clerk 店员
mailman 邮差
newspaper boy 报童
milkman 送奶人
florist 卖花人
baker 面包师
guide 导游
window dressing 橱窗装饰
shoplifters 商店扒手
keep an eye on stock 照看货物
coffee break 喝咖啡间休

7. 银行

check(美国)支票 cheque(英)支票 ATM 自动取款机 cashier收银员 loan 贷款 draw/withdraw money 提款 give the money in fives/tens 换成五元或十元面额 pin number/password/code密码 credit card信用卡 open a student account开个学生账户 check the present balance in your account 查询你的账户余额 apply for a personal loan申请个人贷款 change pounds into dollars 把英镑兑换成美元 the current rate 汇率

8. 医疗场景

clinic 诊所 physician 内科医生 oculist/eye doctor 眼科医生 surgeon 外科医生 dentist 牙医 vet 兽医 see a doctor 看病 send for a doctor 请医生 make an appointment 预约

symptom 症状 have/catch a cold 感冒 have a sore throat 嗓子痛 stomachache 胃痛 fever 发烧 cough 咳嗽 headache 头痛 toothache 牙痛 have a runny nose 流鼻涕 depression 沮丧、消沉 vomit/throw up 呕吐 dizzy 头晕 feel chilly 觉得发冷 phlegm 痰

liver trouble 肝炎 pneumonia 肺炎 flu 流感 allergy 过敏症 twisted 扭伤的 asthma 哮喘 diabetics 糖尿病患者 cramps 抽筋 diarrhea 腹泻 have a stuffed nose 鼻子不通 cholera 霍乱 stiff neck 脖子发僵 yellow fever 黄热病 hay fever 枯草热

pills 药丸 tablet 药片 capsule 胶囊 mixture 合剂 eyedrops 眼药水 syrup 糖浆 pad 药棉块 vitamin 维他命 penicillin 盘尼西林 antibiotic 抗生素 ointment 药膏 medication 药物 aspirin 阿司匹林 cold cure 感冒药 sweating medicine 发汗药 febrifuge 退烧药

bandage 绷带 syringe 注射器 stethoscope 听诊器 injection 注射 preventive injection 预防针 gauze 纱布 case history 病历 extract 拔牙 take one's temperature 量体温 feel one's pulse 量脉搏 take one's blood pressure 量血压 give a prescription 开药方 have an operation 动手术

9. 地区介绍

province 省 state 州 county 县

cost of living 生活费用 crime 犯罪 pace of life 生活节奏 interesting 有意思的 boring/dull 烦闷的
main/primary/leading industry 主要产业 manufacturing 制造 processing 加工 farming 种植 sheep and cattle farming 牛羊畜牧业 fishing 捕鱼 fish farming 水产养殖 wine-making 酿酒 transportation 运输 printing 印刷 electronics 电子

climate/weather 气候天气 annual average 年平均 highest/lowest temperature 最高 / 低温度 minus twenty degrees Celsius/Centigrade 摄氏零下 20 度 -20°C wet 潮湿的 windy 多风的 old and wet 湿冷的 rainy 多雨的 cloudy 多云的 flood 洪水 drought 旱灾

language 语言 accent 口音 dialect 方言
main attraction 主要吸引力
wine 葡萄酒 wool 羊毛 cereals 谷物 timber 木材

10. 地理方位

right, left, in front of, behind, rear, next to, at the end of, cross road to, opposite to, the one after
be far from 距离某处很远 be nearby 距离某处很近
go straight across/to/through 径直走过 / 向 / 过
go up/down 向上（北）/ 向下（南） go back/back/back up 向回走
go east/west/south/north 向东 / 西 / 南 / 北
go on/along…till you meet··· 沿···一直走 / 直到···
be on sb's left/right 在某人的左边 / 右边
be the first/second/third from the left/right 从左 / 右数第一 / 二 / 三个
directly opposite 和···相对
be located behind/in front of 坐落在···的后面 / 前面
be on the corner of A street and B street 在 A 和 B 街交汇的拐角处
be in the corner of 在···的角落里

ground floor （英）首层 wing 侧楼
annex 建筑的附属建筑 basement 地下室

twin building 两个完全相同的建筑
landmark 标志性的建筑
block 街区 complex 建筑群
stair 楼梯 step 台阶 aisle 过道
wheel chair access 无台阶的通道（残疾人用）
intersection/crossroad 十字路口
a fork on the road 分叉路口 a T road 丁字路口
intersection/crossroad 十字路口
flyover 立交桥

11. 地名

U.K. /the United Kingdom/Great Britain 英国（大不列颠）
London 伦敦 England 英格兰
Liverpool 利物浦 Manchester 曼彻斯特
Sheffield 谢菲尔德 Birmingham 伯明翰
Coventry 考文垂 Leeds 利兹
Scotland 苏格兰 Glasgow 格拉斯哥
Edinburgh 爱丁堡 Wales 威尔士
Cardiff 加的夫 North Ireland 北爱尔兰
Belfast 贝尔法斯特

Ireland 爱尔兰 Dublin 都柏林

Australia 澳大利亚
Canberra 堪培拉 Queensland 昆士兰州
Brisbane 布里斯班 New South Wales 新南威尔士州
Sydney 悉尼 South Australia 南澳大利亚州
Adelaide 阿德莱德 Victoria 维多利亚州
Melbourne 墨尔本 Western Australia 西澳大利亚州
Perth 珀斯

New Zealand 新西兰 Wellington 惠灵顿

Canada 加拿大
Ottawa 渥太华 British Columbia 不列颠哥伦比亚省
Victoria 维多利亚 Vancouver 温哥华
Alberta 艾伯塔省 Edmonton 埃德蒙顿
Ontario 安大略省 Toronto 多伦多
Quebec 魁北克省 Montreal 蒙特利尔

The United States of America 美国
Washington 华盛顿 New York 纽约
Boston 波士顿 Atlanta 亚特兰大
Seattle 西雅图 Los Angeles/L.A. 洛杉矶
Chicago 芝加哥

雅思听力校园类词汇

1. 新生报到会

admission office 入学办公室 register/enroll 登记、报到 student union 学生会 opening ceremony 开学典礼 orientation meeting 新生介绍会 orientation week (初到校)适应周 lecture 讲演 报告 picnic 野餐 barbecue 烧烤
president 校长 chancellor 名誉校长 principal (中学)校长 headmaster 小学校长 headmistress 小学校长（女）

faculty 教职员工的总称，系 dean 系主任 professor 教授 associate professor 副教授 assistant professor 助理教授 adviser/ mentor 导师 lecturer 讲师 counselor 辅导老师 coordinator 课程协调人 / 班主任

2. 选课场景

Portuguese 葡萄牙语 Italian 意大利语 Russian 俄语 Arabic 阿拉伯语, Mandarin(Standard Chinese) 普通话 Cantońese 广东话 Spanish 西班牙语 French 法语 German 德语 Latin 拉丁语 Greek 希腊语

fundamental/elementary course 基础课 intermediate 中级的 advanced 高级的 selective/ elective/optional course 选修课 required course/compulsory course 必修课 exemption 免修课
applicant 申请人 enrolment 注册 application form 申请表
course arrangement 课程安排
letter of recommendation 推荐信
school 学院 graduate school 研究生院
undergraduate 本科 postgraduate 研究生
School of Arts and Sciences 文理学院
score 成绩 credit 学分 degree 学位 certificate 证书 diploma 文凭

3. 授课场景

literature 文学 philosophy 哲学 history 历史 art 艺术 sociology 社会学 linguistics 语言学 psychology 心理学 engineering 工程学 architecture 建筑学 business 商务 law 法学 economics 经济学 finance 金融学 accounting 会计学 banking 银行学 biochemistry 生物化学

TA(Teaching Assistant)助教 office hour 教授与学生面谈的时间 assessment 对学生的学习情况进行评估
handout 上课老师发的印刷品 assignment 作业 presentation 针对某一专题进行的发言 project 课题 paper/thesis/dissertation 论文/硕士论文/博士论文 essay 短论文 journal 周记/每周要做的作业 class participation 课堂参与 attendance 出勤率 lecture 老师的讲课 tutorial 助教的辅导课 seminar 研讨会 workshop 实习 research 研究 deadline 最后期限 teaching aid教具 laptop笔记本电脑 Powerpoint (ppt.)幻灯软件 overhead projector 放映机 slide 幻灯片

4．图书馆场景

catalogue 目录 reference stacks 书库 library card/admission card 借书卡
date slip/deadline/date of expiry 期限
due 应付费 overdue and pay a fine 过期并交罚款
renew 续借 available 可获得的
out on loan 借出的 closed reserved 只读不借
in circulation 在书库里 out circulation 借走了
not for circulation 不外借 held in the closed reserved 闭馆保存的
classification 分类 category 种类
bibliography 书目（籍者检索目录）
periodical (magazines and journals)定期刊物
return in time 及时归还
interlibrary service 图书馆际服务
open/closed shelves 开架/闭架书库

5．计算机房

computer lab 计算机房 mainframe 主机 monitor 监视器、显示器 screen 屏幕 keyboard 键盘 modem 调制解调器 cable modem 宽带调制解调器 mouse 鼠标 hard disk 硬盘 floppy disk 软盘 disc 光盘 memory 内存 sound card 声卡 graphic card 图形卡、显卡 loudspeaker 扬声器 printer 打印机 scanner 扫描仪 photocopier/copier 复印机 laser printer 激光打印机 dot-matrix printer 针式打印机 color inject printer 彩色喷墨打印机 software program 程序 virus 病毒 copyright law 版权法 copy 复制

6．问卷调查

poll 民意调查 survey 调查 sample 样本 respondent 调查对象 interviewee 被访谈的人 interview 采访、访谈 questionnaire 调查问卷 observation 观察
short answer questions 简答题 multiple choice 选择题 matching 搭配题 rate 打分 rank 排序 classification 分类 gap filling 填空
hypothesis 假设 statistics 统计 statistically valid 统计学上有效的 data/datum 数据 investigation 调查 quantitative 数量的/定量的 significant difference 显著的差异 analyze/analyse data 分析数据 results 结果 conclusion 结论 interpretation 解释/阐释 opinion 观点 private opinions 个人观点 public opinions 公众观点

7．学校生活

campus 校园 common room（英）师生公用的休息室
accommodation 住宿 dorm/dormitory 宿舍
dormmate /roommate /flatmate /housemate 合租一间宿舍 / 公寓 / 房屋的人
canteen 餐厅 dining hall 食堂 cafeteria 自助小餐厅

vegetarian 素食者 pie 馅饼 pudding 布丁果冻 soup 汤
coffee 咖啡 fish and chips 炸鱼和土豆片 greasy 油腻的
parking lot 停车场 parking regulations 停车规定
shopping mall 购物中心
teaching building 教学楼 / 教室楼
lecture theatre 大教室 / 阶梯教室
administrating office/admin office 行政办公室
laboratory/lab 实验室
student union 学生会
club 学生俱乐部 society 学生社团
student account 银行中的学生账户
current account 现金账户
chequebook/checkbook 支票本
withdraw cash 取钱
deposit money in a band 存钱
tuition 学费 midterm 期中考试 final 期末考试

雅思写作名词精选

abolition 废除
absurdity 荒唐；谬论
abuse 滥用
achievement 成就
adaptation 改写；适应
admiration 崇拜
adventurer/explorer 探险者
adverse impact 负面影响
adversity 逆境
affection 友情 / 感情
alienation 疏远
ambition 志向
amusement 娱乐
anecdote 轶事
apathy 冷漠无情
approach 方法
assault 攻击
assessment 评估
association 联想；联合
athlete 运动员
availability 可用性；实用性
barrier 妨碍
behavior 行为
beneficiary 受益人
budget 预算
burden 负担
campaign 运动
candidate 候选人
capacity 能力
celebrity 名人
character 性格
characteristic 特征

charm 魅力
clerk 职员
cohesion 凝聚力
colleague 同事
collectivism 集体主义
comfort 舒适
commercial 商业广告
commercialization 商业化
commodity 商品
companion/partner 同伴
conformity 一致
consultation 咨询
consumption 消费
content 内容
contentment 满意；满足
contribution 贡献
correlation 相关性
costume 服装
creativity 创造性
criteria 条件
cruelty 残忍
customer 顾客
cybercrime 网络犯罪
depression 沮丧；低沉
deprivation 剥夺
descendant 后代
deterioration 恶化
detour 绕道
developed countries 发达国家
developing countries 发展中国家
digestion 消化吸收
dignity 尊严
discipline 纪律
discomfort 不舒服
discontent 不满足
discrimination 歧视；区别
disgust 反感
disorder 无序状态
disorientation 迷失方向感
disposition 部署
distraction 分心的事物
diversity 多样化；多样性
domain 领域
duplication 重复（建设）
duration 持续时间
employee 雇员
employer 雇主
endeavor 努力
enjoyment 享受
enthusiasm 热情；狂热
equality 平等
evaluation 评价
exception 例外
export 出口
feature 特点
fidelity 忠实
flexibility 灵活性
forefather/ancestor 祖先
freedom 自由
frustration 挫折
goodwill 善意
grace 雅致
guardian 监护人
halt 停止；终止
hardship 艰难险阻
heritage 遗产
horizon 地平线
hostility 敌对
humanity 人性
idol 偶像
immunity 免疫力
import 进口
indication 迹象
indifference 不关心
individuality 个性化
industry 工业；行业
inequality 不平等
infrastructure 基础设施
ingenuity 独创性
initiative 主动性
instruction 教导
integrity 完整性
intellectual 知识分子
intelligence 智能

interaction 互相影响
interference 干涉
interpretation 解释
intolerance 不宽容
involvement 参与
jealousy 妒忌
joint effort 共同努力
journalist/correspondent 记者
lack 缺乏
landmark 标志性建筑；里程碑
life expectancy/life span 寿命
literacy 读写能力
manufacturer 制造商
match 匹配
measure 测量；评估
minority 少数人
misconduct 行为不端
morality 道德
motion 运动
norm 准则
notion 观念；想法
obligation 义务
obstacle 障碍物
occupation 职业
opponent 对手
originality 创意
outcome 后果
outlook 观点；景色
participation 参与
pastime 消遣
peer 同龄人
penalty 刑罚；处罚
perseverance 坚定不移
personality 性格
perspective 看法
popularity 普及；流行
popularization 普及
practice 做法
precaution 防范
principle 原则
profession/occupation 职业
proficiency 精通
promotion 提升
prospect 前景
prosperity 繁荣
protocol 协议
prudence 慎重
public opinion 舆论
punishment 惩罚
purity 纯洁性
rebellion 反叛
recovery 恢复
regression 衰退
regulator 监控者
reliability 可性度
remedy/therapy 疗法 补救的方法
remote education 远程教育
revelation 揭示/表现
revenue 总收入
reward 奖赏；报酬
rumor/gossip 谣言；传闻
satisfaction 满足
self-discipline 自律
self-respect/self-esteem 自尊心
shortcoming 缺点
side-effect 副作用
signal 信号
sociologist 社会学家
soul 灵魂
specialty 专业
stability 稳定性
status 地位
stereotype 成见
straightforwardness 直率
strain 压力；过度劳累
strategy 策略
strength 实力
stress 压力
substance 实质
supplement 补充
sympathy 同情
symptom 症状
talent 人才
teenager 青少年

temper 性情；烦躁
temptation 诱惑
threshold 开端
tip 提示；技巧
tolerance 宽容
tragedy 悲剧
trait 特点
trap 陷阱
triviality 琐事
troublemaker 捣乱者
tutor 导师
uniformity 一致
vanity 虚荣心
variety 多样性；种类
vexation 烦恼
victim 受害者
vitality/vigor/energy/vim 活力；精力
void 空虚
warmth 温暖
weakness 缺点
withdrawal 退出；撤退
zeal 热情

雅思写作动词精选

abide by/obey/observe 遵守
abolish 废除
abuse 虐待；滥用
accommodate 供给；调节
acquire 获取
adore 崇拜；爱慕
allocate 分配
alter 改变
attract 吸引
approach 对待；处理
approve of 赞成
arise 出现
arouse 激发
assume 承担（责任）
attach 赋予；粘上
attain/obtain/acquire 获取；得到
attend 参加；就读
ban 禁止
blossom 兴旺发达
boom 繁荣
bring sb./sth. into full play 充分调动…的积极性
censor 审查
characterize 以…为特色
charge 收费
cherish 珍视
claim 宣称
coexist 共存
coincide with 与…相符
collect 收集
commute 来回往返于
condemn 谴责
consult 咨询
contaminate 污染
contribute to 贡献
crack down on 打击；制裁
cultivate 培养
defy 不服从；藐视
degenerate 退化
degrade 使降级
depreciate 贬值
deprive(of) 剥夺
desert 抛弃
detect 察觉
deter 阻止
deteriorate 恶化
determine 决定
disclose 揭露
discourage 使气馁
diversify 使多样化
divert 使分心
dominate 占优势
drop out 退学；放弃
eliminate 消除

endanger 危害
enlighten 启发
enrich 丰富
entertain 招待；娱乐
evaluate 评价
evolve 演变
exaggerate 夸张
exert 施加（压力）
expel 排除；开除
explore 探究
expose 揭露
guarantee 保证；担保
hamper 妨碍；牵制
hinder/impede/block/hamper 阻碍
idealize 理想化
identify 辨认
ignore 无视；不理睬
imitate 模仿
impair 危害；伤害
impose/confine/place restrictions on/
restrict/limit 限制
incur 招致；引发
inherit 继承
innovate 改革创新
install/set up/erect/fix/mount 安装
lavish 浪费
maltreat 虐待
maximize 最大化
minimize 使最小化
mould/build 塑造
neglect 忽视
oblige 强迫
observe/follow 遵从
overcome 克服（困难）
participate 参与
perform 履行；表演
please 取悦
preserve 保留；保护
prohibit 禁止
publicize 宣传
pursue 追求
quit 放弃
quote 引用
refine 精炼
reflect 反映
reform 改革
regulate 管制；调控
rehabilitate 使恢复
release 释放
render 给予
represent 代表
resort to 诉诸于；采取
restore 重建；恢复
restrain 约束
retain 保留
roam 闲逛
sacrifice 牺牲
shun 回避
signify 表示；意味
spoil/indulge 宠坏；溺爱
spread 传播
steer 驶向；掌舵
stick to 坚持
stimulate 刺激
stipulate/set 规定
substitute 代替
supervise 监督
control 控制
surpass 超过
survive 生存
threaten 威胁
tolerate 忍受
treasure 珍视
trigger 引发
underestimate 低估
undermine 危害
unload 摆脱负担
vanish 消失
wither 退化；萎缩

雅思写作形容词精选

absurd 荒唐的
addictive 上瘾的
affectionate 有感情的
aggressive 有上进心的
alert 敏锐的；警惕的
arduous 费劲的
authoritative 权威性的
awkward 尴尬的
balanced 平衡的
cogent 使人信服的
cold-blooded 冷血的
cold-hearted 无情的
compassionate 富有同情心的
compatible 兼容的
complicated 复杂的
confident 自信的
contributive 有贡献的
corrupt 腐败的
demanding 要求高的
detrimental 有害的
devious 偏离正道的
dishonorable 不光彩的
disturbed 受到干扰的
eccentric 古怪的
economical 节约的
enlightened 开明的；文明的
exotic 异国的
fashionable 时髦的
feasible 可行的
fictitious 虚假的
flexile 灵活多样的
fruitful 有成效的
glamorous 富有魅力的
ignorant (of) 无视的；无知的
impressive 令人印象深刻的
inborn 天生的
incompatible 不可调和的
inconceivable 不可思议的
indecent 不妥的；不检点的
indifferent 冷漠的
indispensable 不可或缺的
inexhaustible 取之不尽的
infectious 传染性的
influential 有影响力的
ingrain 根深蒂固的
inhumane 不人道的
initial 首先的
innocent 多管闲事的
instructive 智力的
intellectual 中间的；过渡的
interpersonal 人际关系的
intimate 亲密的
irreparable 不可挽回的
irresistible 不可抵抗的
irritating 恼人的
isolated (from) 隔绝的
laudable 可赞誉的
lavish 大方的
legitimate 合法的
loyal 忠诚的
luxurious 奢侈的
magnanimous 宽宏大量的
mature 成熟的
misleading 误导的
money-oriented 向钱看的
nourished 有营养的
obscure 模糊的
old-fashioned/out of date 过时的
perilous 危险的
permissive 宽容的；许可的
pornographic 色情的
potential 潜在的
practical 实际的；务实的
pressing 紧迫的
prevailing 占主导地位的；流行的
professional 专业的
prosperous 繁荣昌盛的
prudent 谨慎的

psychological 心理上
rational 理性的
reverse 相反的
rewarding 值得的
ridiculous 荒谬的
rigid 严格的
rough 粗略的
self-contemptuous 自卑的
shabby 破旧不堪的
sheltered 受保护的
sociable 好交际的
sole 唯一的
stern/strict 严格的
stressful 有压力的
stringent 严厉的
stylish 时髦的
superficial 表面现象的
tempting 吸引人的
time-honored 久享盛名的
traditional 传统的
typical 典型的
unadvised 轻率的
uncompromising 不妥协的
unconcerned 冷漠的
uneasy 不自在的
unethical 不道德的
unfeeling 冷漠的
unhealthy 不健康的
unified 同一标准的
unique 独特的
unjust 不公平的
unsociable 不善于社交的
untimely 不和时宜的
unwholesome 不健康的
vexing 令人烦恼的
vivid 鲜明的
voluntary 自愿的
vulnerable 易受伤害的
well-grounded 有充足理由的
wholesome 健康的；有益的

雅思写作关联词精选

Sequence 顺序
first / initially / second / etc. / to begin with / then / next / earlier / later / following that / afterwards
Addition 此外
in addition / and / similarly / likewise / as well as / besides / furthermore / also / moreover / too / not only... but (also)... / even / besides this
Reason 原因
since / as / so / because (of) / due to / owing to / the reason why / leads to / thanks to
Consequence 结果
as a result / thus / so / therefore / consequently / it follows that / thereby / eventually / in that case / admittedly
Contrast 对比
however / on the other hand / despite / in spite of / though / although / but / on the contrary / otherwise / yet / instead of / rather / whereas / nonetheless / compared with / in contrast
Certainty 确定
obviously / certainly / plainly / of course / undoubtedly
Condition 条件
if / unless / whether / provided that / for / so that / whether / depending on

Time 时间

before / since / as / until / meanwhile / at the moment / when / whenever / as soon as

Example 举例

for example / for instance / just as / in particular / such as /namely

Summary 总结

in conclusion / in summary / lastly / finally / to sum up / to conclude / in short

附录二 雅思考试逆序词汇表

agenda
pagoda
plea
saga
yoga
media
encyclopedia
nostalgia
insomnia
bacteria
cafeteria
criteria
via
vanilla
villa
formula
drama
magma
dilemma
diploma
trauma
arena
algebra
cobra
era
flora
orchestra
extra
visa
vice versa
data
delta
quota
lava
larva
bonanza
influenza
grab
tab
womb
succumb
dumb
knob
herb
superb
proverb
absorb
suburb
curb
disturb
aerobic
pacific
specific
terrific
magic
allergic
graphic
demographic
ethic
workaholic
dynamic
ceramic
academic
epidemic
mimic
comic
seismic
panic
titanic
picnic
ethnic
clinic
chronic
epic
tropic
topic
fabric
eccentric
lyric
intrinsic
classic
dramatic
systematic
diplomatic
aromatic
automatic
static
aquatic
tactic
hectic
energetic
apathetic
sympathetic
synthetic
aesthetic
anaesthetic
cosmetic
parasitic
gigantic
romantic
authentic
antibiotic
exotic
enthusiastic
elastic
plastic
fantastic
domestic
realistic
pessimistic
optimistic
characteristic
statistic
toxic
ad hoc
bead
proofread
widespread
salad
load
workload
odd
embed
provided
proceed
exceed
heed
breed
interbreed
ragged
wretched
shed
naked
wicked
so-called
coed
sacred
complicated
sophisticated
related
X-rated
situated
unprecedented
assorted
congested
hallowed
aid
raid
bid
forbid
acid
rigid

valid
invalid
solid
amid
pyramid
timid
void
grid
fluid
liquid
vivid
bald
herald
field
yield
mild
bold
scold
fold
scaffold
unfold
uphold
threshold
mould
band
beforehand
New Zealand
gland
demand
command
expand
brand
grand
strand
withstand
bend
ascend
descend
dividend
defend
legend
blend
amend
recommend
depend
append
suspend
trend
tend
intend
contend
attend
extend
bind
remind
grind
bond
almond
respond
correspond
fund
refund
found
profound
compound
background
underground
all-round
sound
astound
method
period
likelihood
bombard
discard
standard
beard
regard
disregard
mustard
safeguard
ward
reward
steward
awkward
straightforward
hazard
haphazard
herd
weird
cord
afford
applaud
fraud
bud
algae
bribe
ascribe
subscribe
describe
prescribe
transcribe
tribe
globe
wardrobe
probe
cube
tube
surface
replace
commonplace
displace
pace
race
embrace
terrace
trace
masterpiece
prejudice
sacrifice
slice
invoice
spice
apprentice
justice
device
novice
enhance
compliance
appliance
resemblance
glance
performance
finance
clearance
appearance
tolerance
fragrance
assurance
nuisance
reluctance
acquaintance
substance
circumstance
instance
advance
allowance
coincidence
confidence
evidence
intelligence
hence
conscience
audience
convenience
condolence
violence
commence
reference
preference
conference
coherence
occurrence
presence

essence
competence
influence
sequence
consequence
convince
province
ounce
announce
scarce
fierce
pierce
commerce
workforce
enforce
reinforce
divorce
source
resource
deduce
reduce
induce
produce
lettuce
decade
fade
parade
masquerade
grade
degrade
upgrade
persuade
evade
invade
pervade
recede
precede
concede
suicide
coincide
glide
collide
slide
stride
reside
tide
worldwide
oxide
code
explode
mode
erode
episode
exclude
crude
intrude
longitude
magnitude
latitude
gratitude
altitude
aptitude
fee
coffee
flee
degree
foresee
oversee
guarantee
committee
wildlife
garbage
baggage
luggage
engage
mortgage
package
camouflage
damage
drainage
rage
average
beverage
coverage
sewerage
discourage
envisage
heritage
disadvantage
percentage
stage
postage
cottage
savage
wage
voyage
badge
edge
pledge
knowledge
acknowledge
dredge
ridge
fridge
lodge
grudge
siege
privilege
allege
oblige
prestige
bulge
indulge
range
arrange
challenge
revenge
fringe
infringe
sponge
plunge
lounge
charge
emerge
verge
forge
gorge
surge
cliché
avalanche
catastrophe
underlie
pie
fake
intake
undertake
stake
quake
hike
strike
stroke
heatstroke
evoke
invoke
provoke
scale
gale
inhale
whale
exhale
female
wholesale
formidable
noticeable
agreeable
knowledgeable
fable
navigable
liable
reliable
variable
viable
remarkable
available

enable
reasonable
capable
comparable
considerable
innumerable
vulnerable
miserable
durable
disable
indispensable
timetable
inevitable
insurmountable
notable
adaptable
portable
stable
reputable
invaluable
conceivable
bubble
feeble
edible
legible
eligible
negligible
intelligible
tangible
feasible
visible
sensible
responsible
accessible
permissible
plausible
compatible
susceptible
irresistible
flexible
gamble
tremble
resemble
assemble
marble
double
miracle
spectacle
obstacle
vehicle
particle
muscle
cycle
recycle
cradle
riddle
handle
dwindle
shuffle
muffle
trifle
smuggle
triangle
strangle
rectangle
jungle
reconcile
crocodile
file
profile
fragile
juvenile
compile
missile
volatile
versatile
reptile
fertile
futile
tackle
twinkle
role
sole
staple
principle
triple
ample
sample
example
temple
pimple
cripple
couple
quadruple
aisle
subtle
subtitle
entitle
mantle
whistle
bustle
battle
molecule
schedule
module
capsule
style
puzzle
fame
lame
blame
flame
tame
scheme
theme
supreme
extreme
regime
crime
prime
maritime
overtime
pastime
programme
overcome
outcome
dome
wholesome
awesome
fume
volume
plume
resume
résumé
presume
consume
assume
costume
mundane
lane
sane
insane
scene
gene
intervene
champagne
combine
define
refine
confine
morphine
decline
deadline
guideline
streamline
discipline
underline
outline
masculine
famine
undermine
determine
marine
quarantine

valentine
destine
intestine
routine
genuine
divine
backbone
cone
undone
clone
postpone
prone
milestone
zone
ozone
airborne
landscape
shape
tape
recipe
ripe
cope
microscope
slope
pope
stereotype
prototype
bare
welfare
declare
glare
nightmare
compare
spare
hectare
stare
aware
software
massacre
sincere
interfere
adhere
sphere
hemisphere
atmosphere
severe
persevere
questionnaire
bushfire
admire
umpire
aspire
inspire
expire
desire
entire
acquire
require
ore
bore
core
score
adore
chore
folklore
explore
furthermore
pore
store
restore
herbivore
carnivore
bizarre
cure
secure
obscure
procedure
endure
figure
brochure
lure
allure
measure
treasure
leisure
ensure
insure
assure
reassure
pressure
feature
creature
miniature
mature
literature
stature
manufacture
lecture
acupuncture
infrastructure
furniture
venture
adventure
capture
sculpture
departure
nurture
gesture
moisture
texture
mixture
cease
lease
release
decrease
tease
chase
purchase
phase
erase
paraphrase
obese
precise
concise
paradise
merchandise
franchise
generalise
symbolise
demise
premise
minimise
maximise
compromise
organise
arise
authorise
comprise
enterprise
treatise
baptise
expertise
advertise
disguise
bruise
cruise
devise
revise
supervise
likewise
otherwise
pulse
license
dense
condense
tense
intense
response
dose
enclose
disclose
diagnose
pose
compose

decompose
suppose
dispose
expose
elapse
collapse
eclipse
glimpse
coarse
adverse
reverse
diverse
universe
inverse
converse
endorse
curse
clause
pause
abuse
accuse
fuse
refuse
diffuse
confuse
amuse
warehouse
greenhouse
spouse
rouse
arouse
analyse
paralyse
debate
eradicate
dedicate
certificate
delicate
duplicate
communicate
fabricate
lubricate
intricate
locate
allocate
advocate
candidate
accommodate
update
delegate
negate
segregate
mitigate
investigate
navigate
subjugate
appreciate
associate
radiate
mediate
intermediate
affiliate
appropriate
initiate
differentiate
negotiate
deviate
alleviate
escalate
dilate
annihilate
violate
isolate
contemplate
legislate
translate
calculate
circulate
regulate
emulate
simulate
stimulate
formulate
accumulate
manipulate
stipulate
insulate
congratulate
postulate
mate
climate
ultimate
intimate
estimate
underestimate
approximate
designate
vaccinate
fascinate
subordinate
coordinate
originate
contaminate
disseminate
eliminate
discriminate
dominate
nominate
terminate
exterminate
innate
donate
unfortunate
anticipate
participate
rate
exhilarate
separate
celebrate
vertebrate
vibrate
deliberate
moderate
proliferate
exaggerate
accelerate
generate
temperate
operate
cooperate
desperate
integrate
migrate
emigrate
pirate
elaborate
collaborate
decorate
ameliorate
deteriorate
commemorate
evaporate
corporate
doctorate
narrate
penetrate
concentrate
demonstrate
frustrate
saturate
compensate
dictate
agitate
facilitate
irritate
hesitate
rotate
devastate
estate
evacuate
graduate
undergraduate
postgraduate
evaluate

equate
adequate
fluctuate
excavate
aggravate
elevate
activate
cultivate
motivate
innovate
delete
athlete
obsolete
deplete
concrete
discrete
bite
cite
elite
granite
finite
definite
infinite
unite
despite
favourite
site
prerequisite
exquisite
opposite
appetite
invite
remote
promote
denote
quote
devote
etiquette
contribute
distribute
attribute
cute
acute
prosecute
execute
refute
parachute
dilute
absolute
mute
route
compute
dispute
substitute
destitute
institute
constitute
barbecue
rescue
due
overdue
queue
colleague
plague
vague
fatigue
catalogue
vogue
value
clue
glue
venue
avenue
revenue
opaque
technique
unique
antique
picturesque
sue
ensue
issue
tissue
statue
virtue
concave
weave
retrieve
naive
conducive
deceive
conceive
perceive
forgive
olive
derive
thrive
deprive
strive
cohesive
defensive
comprehensive
intensive
massive
passive
elusive
obtrusive
negative
informative
native
alternative
lucrative
decorative
curative
qualitative
conservative
effective
objective
subjective
elective
collective
perspective
detective
counterproductive
primitive
cognitive
sensitive
positive
motive
captive
consecutive
revive
survive
resolve
dissolve
evolve
involve
approve
carve
starve
nerve
observe
deserve
reserve
preserve
curve
owe
dye
gaze
amaze
freeze
squeeze
jeopardize
seize
stabilize
utilize
recognize
scrutinize
mesmerize
prize
emphasize
downsize
doze
ooze

loaf
reef
chef
relief
brief
grief
staff
tariff
stiff
layoff
stuff
behalf
shelf
golf
dwarf
lag
brag
tag
zigzag
fang
gang
demanding
notwithstanding
outstanding
winding
surrounding
regarding
well-being
packaging
catching
refreshing
painstaking
striking
ranking
sibling
cling
compelling
overwhelming
forthcoming
time-consuming
lightning
ongoing
spring
offspring
promising
enterprising
hairdressing
fascinating
frustrating
marketing
everlasting
amazing
prolong
lung
jog
log
smog
breach
preach
coach
cockroach
reproach
approach
detach
enrich
sandwich
branch
trench
launch
bunch
arch
research
torch
hatch
snatch
dispatch
scratch
sketch
stretch
itch
switch
outweigh
thigh
rough
breakthrough
thorough
tough
paragraph
triumph
ash
dash
flash
smash
rash
crash
squash
sluggish
establish
publish
embellish
demolish
polish
accomplish
vanish
replenish
diminish
astonish
furnish
cherish
perish
flourish
nourish
distinguish
extinguish
harsh
crush
oath
width
faith
booth
myth
alumni
leak
peak
soak
feedback
paperback
drawback
hijack
lack
snack
crack
track
wreck
trick
stick
block
flock
mock
suck
seek
bulk
blank
link
shrink
junk
trunk
overlook
bark
embark
mark
landmark
benchmark
hallmark
spark
framework
network
risk
kiosk
dusk
global
verbal
radical
medical

periodical
logical
technological
chronological
technical
clinical
typical
empirical
physical
practical
theoretical
sceptical
optical
vertical
pedal
conceal
heal
appeal
cereal
seal
reveal
zeal
legal
lethal
beneficial
official
unofficial
artificial
financial
social
commercial
crucial
sundial
perennial
material
tutorial
trial
terrestrial
initial
substantial
confidential

essential
potential
partial
trivial
decimal
minimal
optimal
mammal
thermal
normal
abnormal
signal
final
original
aboriginal
criminal
diagonal
professional
vocational
national
rational
sensational
unconditional
conventional
maternal
eternal
internal
external
journal
nocturnal
charcoal
goal
municipal
principal
cathedral
liberal
federal
peripheral
mineral
bilateral
moral

neutral
rural
proposal
disposal
rehearsal
universal
colossal
fatal
recital
capital
vital
dental
oriental
mental
fundamental
detrimental
continental
total
mortal
crystal
dual
gradual
individual
manual
visual
intellectual
punctual
habitual
ritual
spiritual
eventual
virtual
mutual
sexual
medieval
rival
festival
approval
interval
loyal
royal

label
cancel
excel
model
kneel
peel
reel
parallel
panel
channel
personnel
compel
propel
expel
barrel
quarrel
vessel
fuel
marvel
towel
hail
jail
nail
trail
detail
retail
entail
prevail
boil
turmoil
spoil
toil
peril
utensil
fossil
distil
tranquil
devil
civil
recall
windfall

pitfall
mall
overall
install
spell
dwell
swell
landfill
fulfill
chill
skill
pill
spill
drill
poll
payroll
toll
dull
skull
lull
symbol
protocol
alcohol
cholesterol
enrol
patrol
whirl
curl
haul
graceful
grateful
slothful
plentiful
thoughtful
foul
crawl
sprawl
dam
beam
mainstream
jam
diagram
deem
redeem
esteem
gem
item
stem
system
rhythm
claim
acclaim
dim
skim
slim
rim
trim
victim
realm
palm
random
condom
wisdom
venom
boom
doom
loom
bloom
groom
mushroom
blossom
atom
symptom
custom
accustom
rock-bottom
charm
alarm
swarm
germ
term
long-term
firm
affirm
confirm
reform
uniform
inform
conform
transform
platform
norm
brainstorm
enthusiasm
criticism
absenteeism
atheism
metabolism
organism
mechanism
plagiarism
memorandum
petroleum
gum
stadium
medium
premium
millennium
aquarium
equilibrium
symposium
consortium
plum
slum
curriculum
asylum
minimum
maximum
forum
spectrum
sum
vacuum
gym
ban
urban
can
scan
dean
jean
lean
mean
slogan
amphibian
physician
guardian
vegetarian
egalitarian
pedestrian
clan
craftsman
loan
moan
span
cosmopolitan
van
maiden
keen
canteen
strengthen
alien
token
specimen
abdomen
barren
loosen
lessen
threaten
heighten
enlighten
fasten
even
campaign
sign
design

resign
assign
bargain
chain
porcelain
plain
domain
terrain
strain
restrain
constrain
retain
retain
maintain
contain
fountain
entertain
stain
sustain
attain
vain
protein
margin
virgin
kin
penicillin
vitamin
heroin
spin
sin
penguin
ruin
twin
condemn
ribbon
falcon
abandon
burgeon
wagon
jargon
marathon

region
fashion
cushion
companion
opinion
union
champion
occasion
collision
vision
provision
mansion
dimension
pension
tension
explosion
version
excursion
passion
recession
depression
session
possession
mission
emission
commission
discussion
conclusion
vacation
qualification
publication
application
recommendation
foundation
accommodation
recreation
obligation
irrigation
navigation
variation
aviation

abbreviation
inflation
constellation
calculation
circulation
regulation
decimation
animation
formation
resignation
discrimination
anticipation
generation
remuneration
aspiration
decoration
exploration
corporation
registration
administration
duration
configuration
civilisation
compensation
vegetation
hesitation
segmentation
documentation
presentation
adaptation
temptation
dissertation
reputation
evaluation
equation
situation
innovation
observation
taxation
fraction
distraction

transaction
affection
objection
selection
section
intersection
diction
fiction
friction
distinction
function
malfunction
dysfunction
junction
auction
obstruction
ambition
tradition
addition
edition
expedition
nutrition
petition
competition
superstition
tuition
intuition
intention
contention
lotion
motion
emotion
notion
reception
conception
exception
prescription
assumption
option
eruption
abortion

portion
proportion
caution
precaution
contribution
solution
resolution
revolution
institution
reckon
salon
nylon
lemon
phenomenon
monsoon
coupon
patron
off-season
comparison
skeleton
badminton
yearn
concern
discern
pattern
govern
stubborn
dawn
spawn
yawn
upside down
drown
ego
logo
cargo
undergo
forgo
echo
studio
portfolio
scenario
ratio
solo
gizmo
volcano
casino
taboo
kangaroo
tempo
macro
veto
mosquito
motto
embryo
handicap
heap
leap
reap
gap
mishap
overlap
kidnap
soap
trap
wrap
tap
swap
peep
creep
seep
steep
sweep
dip
scholarship
ownership
worship
skip
flip
drip
strip
gossip
tip
equip
yelp
camp
damp
tramp
bump
dump
lump
pump
chop
workshop
mop
loop
laptop
grasp
backup
bar
scar
calendar
bear
gear
nuclear
rear
swear
vulgar
familiar
peculiar
jar
similar
pillar
solar
spectacular
secular
extracurricular
muscular
regular
cellular
seminar
roar
soar
fiber
chamber
timber
embroider
bewilder
wander
gender
slender
render
surrender
tender
remainder
hinder
cylinder
order
border
disorder
sheer
pioneer
peer
career
volunteer
steer
defer
differ
infer
confer
transfer
teenager
trigger
endanger
ginger
linger
merger
voucher
decipher
fresher
leather
gather
wither
bother
cashier

barrier
dealer
astronomer
former
inner
partner
per
hamper
temper
whisper
prosper
lesser
cater
crater
character
deter
diameter
parameter
alter
shelter
filter
counter
encounter
chapter
helicopter
charter
disaster
semester
youngster
register
foster
roster
scatter
shatter
latter
flatter
litter
shutter
commuter
conquer
lever

shiver
deliver
cover
recover
turnover
manoeuver
shower
layer
fertilizer
fair
despair
heir
souvenir
reservoir
stir
ambassador
corridor
senior
junior
inferior
superior
interior
exterior
prior
major
bachelor
tailor
chancellor
counsellor
minor
error
supervisor
sensor
sponsor
successor
predator
escalator
spectator
commentator
factor
sector

solicitor
monitor
mentor
ancestor
tutor
razor
occur
amateur
blur
murmur
labour
harbour
odour
behaviour
parlour
glamour
rumour
pour
vapour
downpour
endeavour
flavour
devour
spur
whereas
overseas
bias
atlas
Xmas
logistics
statistics
odds
billiards
Forbes
species
series
metropolis
debris
basis
oasis
thesis

crisis
analysis
arthritis
axis
y-axis
lens
chaos
encompass
surpass
trespass
bypass
harass
embarrass
access
process
excess
confess
bless
regardless
nonetheless
nevertheless
reckless
mess
harness
wilderness
witness
address
congress
progress
press
depress
oppress
stress
distress
mattress
obsess
assess
possess
dismiss
gross
toss

fuss
syllabus
focus
circus
fungus
radius
genius
plus
surplus
calculus
stimulus
minus
bonus
tremendous
gorgeous
miscellaneous
instantaneous
courteous
spacious
officious
delicious
suspicious
vicious
conscious
tedious
religious
ingenious
various
glorious
notorious
industrious
curious
furious
luxurious
ambitious
obvious
previous
oblivious
noxious
jealous
fabulous
ridiculous
unanimous
enormous
anonymous
synonymous
numerous
prosperous
rigorous
vigorous
ubiquitous
arduous
ambiguous
strenuous
continuous
campus
corpus
virus
census
consensus
versus
apparatus
status
feat
defeat
cheat
neat
retreat
somewhat
flat
diplomat
format
raincoat
float
habitat
react
artifact
enact
compact
interact
subtract
contract
abstract
distract
attract
extract
intact
contact
exact
defect
affect
effect
infect
subject
reject
inject
project
dialect
select
deflect
reflect
neglect
collect
recollect
connect
aspect
respect
inspect
prospect
retrospect
suspect
erect
insect
detect
contradict
addict
predict
conflict
depict
strict
restrict
district
convict
succinct
distinct
instinct
extinct
conduct
byproduct
obstruct
instruct
construct
bet
facet
discreet
greet
budget
target
prophet
diet
bucket
tablet
leaflet
pamphlet
ballet
outlet
plummet
comet
gourmet
magnet
poet
interpret
beset
offset
upset
asset
outset
banquet
craft
draft
theft
gift
shift
lift

drift
thrift
swift
straight
freight
weight
alight
delight
highlight
twilight
plight
spotlight
knight
fortnight
copyright
insight
airtight
drought
bait
trait
inhabit
inhibit
prohibit
exhibit
orbit
elicit
explicit
edit
credit
accredit
audit
albeit
conceit
counterfeit
Fahrenheit
profit
outfit
kit
split
submit
admit

emit
commit
summit
omit
permit
transmit
knit
exploit
inherit
merit
demerit
transit
deposit
quit
recruit
pursuit
wit
halt
melt
silt
tilt
guilt
volt
fault
default
assault
result
insult
consult
vacant
significant
redundant
infant
extravagant
elegant
giant
transplant
dormant
tenant
stagnant
pregnant

contaminant
dominant
predominant
inhabitant
consultant
constant
relevant
irrelevant
buoyant
adjacent
accent
decent
magnificent
innocent
percent
scent
descent
adolescent
precedent
accident
confident
evident
interdependent
respondent
diligent
detergent
urgent
efficient
sufficient
insufficient
ancient
obedient
ingredient
client
lenient
talent
prevalent
equivalent
turbulent
lament
ornament

tournament
placement
announcement
engagement
element
complement
supplement
reimbursement
statement
fragment
judgment
segment
pigment
augment
establishment
sediment
compliment
detriment
installment
comment
disillusionment
environment
garment
ferment
assessment
treatment
commitment
appointment
department
document
monument
instrument
permanent
eminent
prominent
pertinent
component
proponent
opponent
exponent
apparent

transparent
inherent
coherent
current
concurrent
represent
consent
tent
patent
competent
content
potent
consistent
extent
affluent
subsequent
event
invent
faint
mint
joint
pinpoint
appoint
blueprint
confront
haunt
blunt
account
discount
mount
paramount
surmount
stunt
dot
patriot
blot
allot
ballot
plot
knot
spot
pivot
apt
adapt
accept
concept
inept
receipt
script
manuscript
contempt
attempt
exempt
prompt
opt
adopt
bankrupt
interrupt
corrupt
state-of-the-art
chart
depart
counterpart
concert
inert
expert
desert
insert
assert
divert
convert
exert
comfort
transport
export
sort
resort
assort
distort
yoghurt
forecast
beast
steadfast
boast
toast
contrast
vast
modest
manifest
digest
pest
deforest
contest
protest
request
invest
zest
gist
specialist
checklist
moist
resist
insist
consist
persist
linguist
twist
whilst
utmost
boost
signpost
burst
exhaust
robust
gust
disgust
adjust
rust
analyst
catalyst
boycott
astronaut
handout
turnout
sprout
layout
input
output
context
plateau
flu
thaw
flaw
raw
withdraw
jigsaw
review
interview
crew
bow
meadow
shadow
overshadow
widow
endow
anyhow
blow
glow
shallow
swallow
mow
row
narrow
sorrow
burrow
tow
vow
relax
climax
coax
wax
complex
perplex
sex

prefix
suffix
helix
matrix
paradox
orthodox
xerox
influx
decay
gay
clay
delay
display
dismay
spray
portray
X-ray
essay
takeaway
sway
shabby
lobby
thereby
whereby
legacy
pharmacy
democracy
bureaucracy
literacy
conspiracy
accuracy
privacy
policy
vacancy
discrepancy
complacency
tendency
agency
contingency
deficiency
proficiency

currency
frequency
mercy
steady
greedy
tragedy
remedy
comedy
subsidy
tidy
embody
melody
custody
sturdy
obey
kidney
Sydney
attorney
journey
prey
convey
survey
specify
modify
qualify
amplify
exemplify
simplify
magnify
unify
clarify
verify
terrify
diversify
classify
rectify
notify
certify
mortify
testify
justify

strategy
analogy
ecology
archaeology
geology
psychology
physiology
technology
terminology
anthropology
meteorology
allergy
synergy
hierarchy
bibliography
pornography
philosophy
trustworthy
deadly
scarcely
unlikely
namely
timely
rely
ultimately
relatively
literally
tally
bully
monopoly
multiply
comply
apply
supply
particularly
utterly
simultaneously
slightly
shortly
alchemy
yummy

economy
anatomy
accompany
botany
deny
tiny
destiny
penny
balcony
symphony
colony
ceremony
testimony
harmony
irony
deploy
employ
annoy
destroy
therapy
occupy
legendary
secondary
boundary
auxiliary
tertiary
vocabulary
primary
summary
extraordinary
preliminary
veterinary
stationary
itinerary
temporary
contemporary
arbitrary
contrary
anniversary
glossary
military

sanitary
supplementary
commentary
documentary
voluntary
tributary
vary
laundry
surgery
gallery
jewellery
stationery
slippery
nursery
artery
mystery
battery
lottery
query
dairy
enquiry
inquiry
theory
category
compulsory
accessory
mandatory
laboratory
victory
dormitory
territory
inventory
ferry
symmetry
asymmetry
geometry
ministry
mercury
jury
injury
clumsy
controversy
treaty
safety
variety
naughty
capacity
opacity
publicity
elasticity
velocity
commodity
locality
reality
personality
quality
liability
mobility
nobility
facility
utility
calamity
proximity
amenity
dignity
vicinity
community
charity
similarity
popularity
disparity
celebrity
integrity
authority
priority
majority
minority
security
purity
density
diversity
necessity
entity
equity
gravity
productivity
penalty
casualty
novelty
guilty
faculty
warranty
certainty
property
poverty
dynasty
majesty
duty
deputy
levy
envy
galaxy
dizzy
quiz
quartz
buzz

后记：莲花初开见佛时

谨以此文献给在英语学习道路上痛并快乐着的朋友们。

计划

又逢星期五，我的手机响个不停，朋友们纷纷讨论周末出游计划。最后一致决定去Wollongong南天寺礼佛。于是傍晚时分，趁着满天彩霞，我赶紧驾车到加油站加油，超市购物，回家后哼着山歌，拖出水龙头洗车，检查机油，加水，忙得不亦乐乎。

清晨，如往常一样，我被窗外树梢上的两只cockatoo叫醒。cockatoo是澳洲特产的大鹦鹉，比平常鹦鹉大一倍，通体雪白，唯头上顶着浅黄色凤冠，十分美丽。最难得是它们在公园里、小区的草坪树枝上随处可见，且毫不怕人。我身着睡衣懒懒地起身，推开落地窗，步入阳台，沐浴在柔柔晨光中。先向身边枝头上的cockatoo说了声“Good morning”，据朋友说它们是听不懂中文的，再深吸一口花草的清香，抬头看看碧蓝的天空，嗯，今天又是一个好天气。远远传来的一阵汽车声吸引了我的视线，一辆红色老福特从Summer hill小区公园里的parkway上蜿蜒着驶了出来，穿过几片修剪整齐的草坪后，停在我家门前的driveway上。我心中一动，不禁莞尔：英语真是有趣，drive on the parkway, park on the driveway。福特中跳出了五位老友，长期受澳洲日照影响，人人都是活泼开朗阳光型。还没等我出声招呼，他们先嚷成了一片：“J呢，K呢?怎么还没到？”“Harvey，买水果了吗，我要吃瓜子！”“懒猪才起床呀！”“路线搞定了吗？”……我正要一一作答，却听Jenny叫道：“Harvey，睡衣走光啦！”吓得我赶紧鼠窜进屋，扔下身后笑声一片。

出发

等到我们喝完牛奶，啃完面包，J和K才姗姗show up，车队出发。车队成员计有：硕士三人，博士三人，博士后一人，访问学者一人，皆来自China；88年红色老破Ford一辆，来自USA；90年白色老破Toyota一辆，来自Japan。众人中除我外皆是第一次去南天寺，我自然成为了领队。发动引擎，打开音响，一踩油门，载着欢声笑语，冲出了我居住的Summer hill区。不一会儿，手机响起，L博士打来："哥们儿，我的福特老你两岁，你在前面悠着点儿！"

车队首先穿越悉尼市区，我们在一个十字路口被红灯拦下，才发现左边车道并排停着一辆红色Ferrari跑车，右边停一辆黑色敞篷Porsche，各自放着不同的摇滚音乐，车上老外们唧唧喳喳，随着音乐摇头晃脑，看架势也是出游。比我们还幸福兴奋，这可不行！Harvey好胜心强，使个眼色，大家七手八脚摇低了车窗，我猛然把音乐开到最大，于是整个十字路口笼罩在黑豹沙哑的嗓音中："人潮人海中，有你有我……"Ferrari和Porsche上的老外们一愣之后纷纷转头侧目。嘿嘿，知道厉害了吧，车破声音大，这可是我找朋友专门换的一套汽车音响。绿灯亮起，比完音响该比速度了，两旁的车嗖的一声窜了出去。这下我知道了世界顶级跑车提速的厉害，我还在一挡起步时，前面就只剩下了淡蓝色的两缕清烟，真所谓望烟末及（马路上没有灰尘，只偶尔有些汽车尾气清烟）。

出了市区，车队驶上高速公路，不久前方出现一条小径岔路，标志为"Tourist Drive"。Sydney和Wollongong皆是海滨城市，相距两百来公里，除铁路外，两条路径可以通达：高速公路和旅游者线路。高速公路穿梭于崇山峻岭的森林之间，虽然刚出国的朋友对这条公路赞叹不已，认为驾车其上，人生至乐，但对我来说，兴味索然，有时想起还牙痒痒的。一个多小时车程两旁都是莽莽林海，且其间有一段路好像是专门为检验汽车性能而修建的。那是从一个山顶呈30度角笔直的冲下山谷，又笔直的呈30度冲上下一个山顶，总长约七、八公里。我第一次看到此景象时，着实吓了一跳。近处，一辆辆车呼啸俯冲；远处，一辆辆车艰难的上爬。由于地形产生的错觉，满眼都是车，且每一辆从头到尾都看得清清楚楚，煞是壮观。下坡我是没问题，速度快，还超车；可一上坡，人人都超我，我独自享用一条车道，接受其他司机超车时对我的微笑和检阅。今趟我们车队以游山玩水为目的，有的是时间，加之高朋满座，兼有88年高龄Ford，对这条路当然要敬而远之。此时坐在我身边的J为向导员，手捧地图指指点点。我一打转弯灯，毫不迟疑地拐入那条从没走过的Tourist Drive。

森林

按照地图显示，Tourist Drive先从山腰经Royal National Park到达山脚太平洋海岸，然后沿海岸线蜿蜒一百多公里，途经无数沙滩、公园，再穿越几个小镇，最后止于Wollongong市区。Tourist Drive只有往来两条车道，很窄，但一路上十分清净，难得见到其他的汽车，我们乐得放慢车速，进入了National Park。

Royal National Park其实是一大片原始森林，古树参天。车队驶入后，顿感自然之晦明变化。刚开始阳光满路，可见各种生命的欢呼跳动，道旁松鼠，头上鸟雀，万物欣然。而后林雾蒸腾，连忙打开汽车应急灯。再往深处树冠更是遮云蔽日，万籁俱寂，要打开车头大灯。感觉如同时空逆转，我们渐行渐远，回到了远古洪荒。汽车音乐早就关掉，朋友们也缄口不言，大家一起默默体会原始森林的圣洁清幽。忽而道路斗转，景致又变，人人齐声欢呼，一个大湖豁然呈现眼前。湖面如玉，湖水莹然，碧若翡翠。湖畔岚霭阵阵，阳光下如烟如纱。四面群山环绕，头上几片白云飘过，投影波心。至此极景，人人欢喜赞叹。Harvey更是飘飘然，此身非我，我常是苦，十万烦恼丝散落在山水之间。偶有几名老外沿湖边跑步锻炼臭皮囊，我们的车队从他们身旁轻轻掠过，双方都倍感亲切，不住的微笑挥手，衷心祝福。前方见一块路标，开始以为多是提醒有弯道，驶到近处凝神一看，画的却是一只鹅妈妈身后跟三只小鹅，意为：此乃鹅妈妈和小鹅们过街入湖沐浴之地，尔等减速让行，非礼勿视。我不禁松了油们，遵守这个童话世界里的规则。Jenny博士见此牌后却仗着自己是雌性，东张西望大呼小叫，大失体统！

道路渐缓，车队来到山脚。还没驶出原始森林，阵阵温暖的海洋气息已熏得我们心神俱醉。汽车不自觉地加速，峰回路转处，迎面即是壮阔的太平洋。

海滩

远处夏日高照，海天一色，浪卷点点金光，明艳无方。我真倒霉，如此景色却无法细细欣赏！此刻车队正行进在海边悬崖峭壁之上，仍旧是又窄又干净的Tourist Drive，不容丝毫的疏忽。朋友们皆赞此时景色唯有极品飞车游戏中的赛道可比，你有幸驾车兜风，且良朋相伴，此乐何极。我报之以苦笑。大家被阳光一照，太平洋海风一吹，个个胸襟宽广，精神陡长。赏景之余各种稀奇古怪的留学经历、笑话不绝于耳。

驶过了海岸悬崖，来到平坦的海岸沙滩。记不清路过了几个沙滩，只知道大海中有人冲浪游泳，沙滩上人们玩着各种运动，人声喧嚣，欢声笑语一路飘来。中途有L、K胆敢引诱司机Harvey看美女！“看，美女啊，美女！”“看那个beach girl，没穿上衣！”把我恨得咬牙切齿，早忘了色即是空，“好哇，我辛辛苦苦的driving，你们明知我看不了，还敢叫那么大声！”终于忍无可忍，一打方向盘，车队在一片沙滩上小驻。谁知大家下车后怨声载道：为何不来此BBQ；为何不通知带游泳裤，为何不带足球、排球；为何尽是良辰好景虚设云云。我作为领队，难辞其究，只得低头认罪，而后满脸陪笑，下次，下次。

小镇

稍事修整，我们继续上路，穿越过四、五个海滨小镇。小镇中无一栋高楼大厦，均是两层楼的欧式小别墅，色彩轻快明亮。周围绿荫环绕，多是社区公园、高尔夫、足球、网球场。小镇背靠青山，面临海洋，大街上各色酒吧风情迥异，人们三五成群，在阳光下、树荫处把酒言欢。此情此景，无一不可入画。车队穿行其中，人人流连忘返。

礼佛

及至到了Wollongong佛光山南天寺宏伟的山门，众人下车后极目远眺来时路途。Tourist Drive中的森林、海滩、小镇早已让我们忘掉一切的世俗烦恼，个个喜乐无边，着了大欢喜相。表现在外即为人人精神抖擞，才思敏捷，相互挖苦打趣更是暗含禅意，各呈机锋。一干人等嘻嘻哈哈地进了山门，静悄悄地礼佛、抄经、随喜，又嘻嘻哈哈地自由活动。

我独爱山门旁边的一处莲池，莲池周围有一圈草地，上面散布着诸佛石像。前几次来唯见池中茵茵绿叶，今次却正逢两朵莲花新开，不由心生欢喜。我静静地坐在池边，低头数着水中浮云，玩味一年前命途多蹇，一个人上山礼佛时独坐此处的心境。突然听到J的呼唤：“Harvey，用斋啦！”抬头间却望见莲池畔一尊佛像在阳光下奕奕生辉，国外生活的种种欢乐苦难如一道澄澈小溪，缓缓在心中流过，清可见底。心有所思，双手合十，跪了下来。

Harvey